POSSE

DEMONIACAL  ꓕHER

POSSESSION

DEMONIACAL AND OTHER

AMONG PRIMITIVE RACES, IN ANTIQUITY, THE MIDDLE AGES, AND MODERN TIMES

BY

T. K. OESTERREICH

PROFESSOR AT THE UNIVERSITY OF TÜBINGEN

Read &' Co.

Copyright © 2021 Read & Co. Books

This edition is published by Read & Co. Books,
an imprint of Read & Co.

This book is copyright and may not be reproduced or copied in any
way without the express permission of the publisher in writing.

British Library Cataloguing-in-Publication Data
A catalogue record for this book is available
from the British Library.

Read & Co. is part of Read Books Ltd.
For more information visit
www.readandcobooks.co.uk

CONTENTS

viii   CONTENTS

TRANSLATOR'S NOTE

PROFESSOR OESTERREICH, the author of this work, has made a survey of the history of Possession from the most ancient times down to the present day and in all countries of the inhabited globe, together with an analysis of its nature and relationship to other phenomena, such as hysteria and the manifestations of spiritualism.

The subject treated is a very fascinating one, to the general reader as well as to the student of psychology and ethnology. It would be difficult to see the human race in a more fantastic light than that cast by these stories of Possession. The work abounds, moreover, in suggestions for further research.

As regards the text, the authorized French version has been followed in its occasional abbreviations of quotations given in the original work, and M. Sudre's footnotes on spiritualism in France have also been inserted. The German text has, however, been used throughout for purposes of translation. All English quotations have been traced to source except one, which it has not been possible to discover, and classical extracts, many of which the author gives in the original, have either been translated or replaced by corresponding passages from English versions. The passages from the Bible are given in the Rev. Dr. Moffat's well-known version, by the kind consent of Messrs. Hodder and Stoughton, its publishers.

D. I.

FOREWORD

This book is the result of investigations which have been published in the first two issues (simultaneously produced) of the review *Deutsche Psychologie*. The present extensive work is not, however, a mere reprint; it is very much fuller than the original publications. As the subject-matter is gathered from widely scattered literary sources, some of which are difficult of access, so that the reader cannot be expected to examine them, I have not hesitated to quote freely, since first-hand knowledge of the texts cannot be replaced by any secondary account. The attention of classical philologists is especially directed to the passages concerning the oracle of Delphi (pp. 311 *sqq.*) and the cult of Dionysos (pp. 335 *sqq.*). I should think myself well rewarded for my labours if they for their part were induced to approach these two problems, which are of peculiar interest to the philosopher, from a fresh angle.

After the completion of the work I was obliged through considerations of space to renounce the idea of adding a table of relevant literature. Essential works are indicated by the notes.

THE AUTHOR.

Tübingen,
Early March, 1921.

PART I

THE NATURE OF THE STATE OF POSSESSION

INTRODUCTION

THE CONSTANT NATURE OF POSSESSION
THROUGHOUT THE AGES

THE book affording to us inhabitants of the European zone of culture our earliest glimpse of the states called "possession"[1] is the New Testament. Bible stories often give, in fact, an accurate picture of these states, which were extremely frequent in the latter days of the ancient world. To the authors of the New Testament they were evidently very familiar, and their accounts, even should they be recognized as of little or no historical value, bear in themselves the stamp of truth. They are pictures of typical states exactly reproduced.[2]

The following are a few quotations to refresh the reader's memory:

> And as soon as he stepped out of the boat a man from the tombs came to meet him, a man with an unclean spirit who dwelt among the tombs; by this time no one could bind him, not even with a chain, for he had often been bound with fetters and chains and had snapped the chains and broken the fetters — nobody could tame him. All night and day among the tombs and the hills he shrieked and gashed himself with stones. On catching sight of Jesus from afar he ran and knelt before him, shrieking aloud, "Jesus, son of God most High, what business have you with me? By God, I adjure you, do not torture me." (For he had said, "Come out of the man, you unclean spirit.") Jesus asked him, "What is your name?" "Legion," he said, "there is a host of us." And they begged him earnestly not to send them out of the country (Mark v 2-10).

I will pass over the rest of the passage, the alleged entry of the devils into a herd of swine. The same story is to be found in Matthew vii 28-33 and in Luke viii 26-39.

---

[1] In ancient, as also sometimes in later times, it was customary to class as possession other states of enthusiasm or inspiration. I shall at first confine myself here to possession in the accepted sense, and later extend the acceptation gradually in each direction.

[2] Besides the quotations given in the text (Moffat's trans., pub. Hodder and Stoughton), cf. also Mark xii 24 sq., 43 sq., Mark iii 22 sq., Luke xi 14-26.

3

THE NATURE OF THE STATE OF POSSESSION

Some strolling Jewish exorcists also undertook to pronounce the name of the Lord Jesus over those who had evil spirits, saying: "I adjure you to the Jesus whom Paul preaches!" The seven sons of Sceuas, a Jewish high priest, used to do this. But the evil spirit retorted, "Jesus I know and Paul I know, but you—who are you?" And the man in whom the evil spirit resided leapt at them, overpowered them all, and belaboured them, till they rushed out of the house stripped and wounded (Acts xix 18-16).[1]

Now there was a man with an unclean spirit in their synagogue, who at once shrieked out, "Jesus of Nazaret, what business have you with us? Have you come to destroy us? We know who you are, you are God's holy One." But Jesus checked it; "Be quiet," he said, "come out of him." And after convulsing him the unclean spirit did come out of him with a loud cry (Mark i 23-27).

A man from the crowd answered him. "Teacher, I brought my son to you; he has a dumb spirit, and whenever it seizes him it throws him down, and he foams at the mouth and grinds his teeth. He is wasting away with it; so I told your disciples to cast it out, but they could not." He answered them, "O faithless generation, how long must I still be with you? How long have I to bear with you? Bring him to me." So they brought the boy to him, and when the spirit saw Jesus it at once convulsed the boy; he fell on the ground and rolled about foaming at the mouth. Jesus asked his father, "How long has he been like this?" "From childhood," he said; "it has thrown him into fire and water many a time, to destroy him. If you can do anything, do help us, do have pity on us." Jesus said to him, "If you can'! Anything can be done for one who believes." At once the father of the boy cried out, "I do believe; help my unbelief." Now as Jesus saw that a crowd was rapidly gathering, he checked the unclean spirit. "Deaf and dumb spirit," he said, "leave him, I command you, and never enter him again." And it did come out, after shrieking aloud and convulsing him violently. The child turned like a corpse, so that most people said, "he is dead"; but, taking his hands, Jesus raised him and he got up (Mark ix 17-27. Same story in Matthew xvii 14-21, and Luke ix 85-45).

Then a blind and dumb demoniac was brought to him, and he healed him, so that the dumb man spoke and saw (Matt. xii 22).

When he was teaching in one of the synagogues on the Sabbath, there was a woman who for eighteen years had suffered weakness from an evil spirit; indeed she was bent double and quite unable to raise herself. Jesus noticed her and called to her, "Woman, you are released from your weakness." He laid his hands on her, and instantly she became erect and glorified God (Luke xiii 10-18).

Comparing these brief stories with accounts of the phenomena of possession in later times, we find what may be described as the perfect similarity of the facts extremely surprising, while our respect for the historic truth of the Gospels is enhanced to an extraordinary degree. Excluding

---

[1] It is not without importance to the understanding of the New Testament writings and their bearing on the psychology of religion to observe that the term πνεῦμα is not only used in the expression πνεῦμα ἅγιον, but that the devils of the possessed were designated under the name of πνεύματα.

the story of the herd of swine, the narratives are of an entirely realistic and objective character. In particular the succinct accounts of Jesus' relation to these events, his success and failure together with that of his disciples, as well as the particulars of his cures,[1] coincide so exactly with what we know of these states from the point of view of present-day psychology, that it is impossible to avoid the impression that we are dealing with a tradition which is veracious.

In order to show the constant nature of the phenomena of possession throughout the ages and to vindicate the importance of these various quotations, we will place side by side with the extracts from the New Testament several cases from more recent times. It would be easy to count them by dozens and even by hundreds. The lives of the saints of the Catholic Church as related in the *Acta Sanctorum*, are full of stories of possession and its cure. But it is not only in Christian

---

[1] In this connection quotations such as the following, the historical truth of which is incontestable, are extremely characteristic.

> Now when Jesus had finished these parables he set out from there and went to his native place, where he taught the people in the synagogue till they were astounded. They said, " Where did he get this wisdom and these miraculous powers ? Is this not the son of the joiner ? Is not his mother called Mary and his brothers James and Joseph and Simon and Judas ? Are not his sisters settled here among us ? Then where has he got all this ?" So they were repelled by him. But Jesus said to them, " A prophet never goes without honour except in his native place and in his home." *And he did not many mighty works there because of their unbelief*[2] (οὐκ ἐποίησεν ἐκεῖ δυνάμεις παλλὰς διὰ τὴν ἀπιστίαν αὐτῶν) (Matt. xiii 53-58).

A few chapters later Matthew relates how in one instance an exorcism by the disciples of Jesus failed, and he replied to their questions as to the cause of the failure: διὰ τὴν ὀλιγοπιστίαν ὑμῶν, on account of your little faith (Matt. xvii 14-21 ; cf. Mark ix 28 sq.). Both accounts are in full agreement with what psychology would lead us to expect in the attendant circumstances. Moreover, the first report is not even favourable to the miracle-working power of Jesus. It must rest on specially old and reliable tradition which in this passage has not yet been retouched. We should indeed rather expect to read: There he was not able to work many miracles owing to their lack of faith. It is obvious, however, that this mode of expression cannot proceed from a naïf outlook which regarded these cures as miracles. Moreover, Jesus might, in face of the lack of faith opposed to him, have been instinctively withheld from any greater efficaciousness.

---

[2] I have followed the Revised Version in this sentence only, as it is in accordance with the text used by the author. Moffat's version, which I have otherwise used, reads: " There he could not do many miracles owing to their lack of faith " (TRANS.).

literature that such facts are described, it is also in that of non-Christian antiquity.

Let us first take the Greek world. Here, by way of example, is an extract from a dialogue of Lucian (born A.D. 125):

> I should like to ask you, then, what you think of those who deliver demoniacs from their terrors and who publicly conjure phantoms. I need not recall to you the master of this art, the famous Syrian of Palestine, everyone already knows this remarkable man who in the case of people falling down at the sight of the moon, rolling their eyes and foaming at the mouth, calls on them to stand up and sends them back home whole and free from their infirmity, for which he charges a large sum each time. When he is with sick persons he asks them how the devil entered into them; the patient remains silent, but the devil replies, in Greek or a barbarian tongue, and says what he is, whence he comes, and how he has entered into the man's body: this is the moment chosen to conjure him to come forth; if he resist, the Syrian threatens him and finally drives him out.[1]

At the beginning of the third century A.D. the Greek sophist, Flavius Philostratus, in his biography of the ascetic and thaumaturge Apollonius of Tyana, compiled at the request of the wife of Septimius Severus, Julia Domna, a Syrian full of wit and beauty (A. Furtwängler), relates the following:

> . . . These discourses were interrupted by the arrival of the messenger. He brought with him Indians who implored the aid of the Wise Men. He presented to them a poor woman who commended her son to them; he was, she said, sixteen years old, and for two years had been possessed by an evil and lying demon. "On what grounds do you believe this?" asked one of the Sages. "He is," said she, "of particularly pleasing appearance; therefore, the demon loves him; he does not leave him the use of his reason, but prevents him from going to school, from learning to shoot with the bow, and even from remaining in the house; he drags him away into desolate places. The boy no longer even has his own voice; he utters deep and grave sounds like a grown man. The eyes with which he looks forth are not his eyes. All this afflicts me deeply, I rend my bosom and seek to bring back my child, but he does not recognize me. As I was preparing to come here, (and I have thought of it already for a year past), the demon revealed himself to me by the mouth of my child. He declared to me that he is the spirit of a man killed in war who died loving his wife. But his wife having defiled his couch three days after his death by a new marriage, he came to loathe the love of women and has diverted all his passion on to this child. He promised me, if I consented not to denounce him before you, to do much good to my son. These promises tempted me for a little while, but now for a long time past he has been the sole master in my house, where he thinks of nothing but mischief and deceit." The Sage asked her if the child was there. "No," replied the

---

[1] Lucian, *The Lover of Lying* (φιλοψευδής), 16. Complete works, ed. C. Jacobitz, Teubner series.

mother. "I did all that I could to bring him; but the demon threatens to throw him into gulfs, over precipices, in a word to slay him if I accuse him (the demon) before you." "Be at peace," said the Sage; "he will not slay your child when he has read this." And he drew from his bosom a letter which he gave to this woman. The letter was addressed to the demon and contained the most terrible threats towards him.[1]

A Christian author of the following century, Cyril of Jerusalem, gives the following general description of possession:

> ... the unclean devil, when he comes upon the soul of a man ... comes like a wolf upon a sheep, ravening for blood and ready to devour. His presence is most cruel; the sense of it most oppressive; the mind is darkened: his attack is an injustice also, and the usurpation of another's possession. For he tyrannically uses another's body, another's instruments, as his own property; he throws down him who stands upright (for he is akin to him who *fell from heaven*); he perverts the tongue and distorts the lips. Foam comes instead of words; the man is filled with darkness; his eye is open yet his soul sees not through it; and the miserable man quivers convulsively before his death.[2]

Zeno of Verona (died c. 375) writes in precisely the same manner:

> But we, my brethren, who do not give ourselves over to conjectures of the mind, but are taught by God himself . . ., we cannot so much lay claim that the souls of the dead live as rather prove it by manifest facts. For the impure spirits of both sexes which prowl hither and thither, make their way by deceitful flatteries or by violence into the bodies of living men and make their habitation there: they seek refuge there while holding them in a bondage of corruption. But as soon as we enter into the field of the divine combat (exorcism) and begin to drive them forth with the arrow of the holy name of Jesus, then thou mayest take pity on the other—when thou shalt have learnt to know him—for that he is delivered over to such a fight. His face is suddenly deprived of colour, his body rises up of itself, the eyes in madness roll in their sockets and squint horribly, the teeth, covered with a horrible foam, grind between blue-white lips; the limbs twisted in all directions are given over to trembling; he sighs, he weeps; he fears the appointed day of Judgment and complains that he is driven out; he confesses his sex, the time and place he entered into the man, he makes known his name and the date of his death, or shows by manifest signs who he is; so that we generally learn

---

[1] Flavius Philostratus, *Works*, iii, 38, ed. Westermann, Paris, 1849. There is a trans. by E. Berwick, 1809. Apollonius of Tyana was himself a companion of Jesus. Given the romantic character of the whole biography, it is much more proper to regard this narrative as a typical example of cases of possession seen by Flavius Philostratus than as an historical document.

[2] Cyril, *Catechisms*, xvi, No. 15, Engl. Trans., The Catechetical Lectures of St. Cyril, in Library of the Fathers (Oxford, 1839).

that there are many of these who, according to our own memory, persisting in the worship of idols, have recently died a violent death.[1]

The sixth-century French chronicler, Gregory of Tours, is also acquainted with possession and its specific treatment:

> It is not uncommon that on the appointed feast-days those demoniac fall into a state of downright madness in the churches. They break the lamps, to the terror of the assembled parish. But if the oil of the lamps fall upon them the demon leaves them and they regain their right senses.[2]

In the seventh century it is mentioned in the life of St. Gall:

> This young girl, having been held by the cruel persecution of the Old Enemy, was led to the monastery by the care of her parents, who were not of obscure origin. When she entered into the oratory of the blessed Gall the Confessor, she immediately fell to the earth by reason of the assaults of the horrible demon, and rending herself in a lamentable fashion, began to utter loud and terrible cries accompanied by the most filthy words. Then one of the brethren, of the name of Stephen, moved by her distress, recited an exorcism until such time as her torments had ceased. He later told the girl when she had come to herself what penances she should perform, and applied himself to fasting and prayer for her. But as the wretched woman made free use of forbidden meat the demon invaded her forthwith so strongly that she could hardly be held by several persons.[3]

The following cases belong to the beginning of the thirteenth century; they are taken from the oldest biography[4] of St. Francis of Assisi (1182-1226).

> There was a man of the name of Peter in the town of Fulgineus. At that time he was on his way to visit the abode of St. Michael, either in consequence of a vow or else of a penance self-inflicted for his sins, and he drew near to the fountain. While, wearied with travel, he quenched his thirst at this fountain, he thought he saw drinking there demons which had haunted him during three years, and which were horrible to see and to hear. As he went towards the tomb of the Holy Father (St. Francis of Assisi) cruelly torn by the demons in their fury, by a manifest miracle he was marvellously delivered from them as soon as he touched the sepulchre. . . .

---

[1] S. Zenones Episcopi Veronæ Sermones, Ed. Ballerini, 1739, i, 16, c. 3.

[2] Gregory of Tours, Historia Francorum, book x (Migne's Patrology, vol. lxxi).

[3] Vita S. Galli, lib. ii, c. 24 (Pertz, Monumenta Germaniæ historiæ, vol. ii, p. 26).

[4] Brother Thomas of Celano, Vita prima et secunda S. Francisci Assisiensis, Rome, 1880, cap. iii. De demoniacis (Rome edit., 1906, p. 142). There is a translation by A. G. Ferrers Howell, The Lives of St. Francis, London, 1908.

. . . This woman having been brought from the town of Narnius in a great state of madness and wandering of the mind, doing horrible things and uttering incoherent words, there appeared to her in a vision the Blessed Saint Francis, saying: " Make the sign of the Cross." As she replied, " I cannot," the Saint himself made it over her and purged her of madness and demoniac imaginings. . . .

Many men and women, tortured by the divers torments of devils and deceived by their spells, were also delivered by the surpassing merits of the holy and glorious Father. . . .

The following extract relates to a case in the sixteenth century:

The latter (a girl) was possessed by the demon who often threw her to the ground as if she had the falling sickness. Soon the demon began to speak with her mouth and said things inhuman and marvellous which may not be repeated. . . . The girl had always shown herself patient, she had often prayed to God. But when she had called upon the name of Jesus to deliver her, the evil spirit manifested himself anew, he had taken possession of her eyes which he made start out of her head, had twisted her tongue and pulled it more than eight inches out of her mouth, and turned her face towards her back with an expression so pitiful that it would have melted a stone. All the priests of the place and from round about came and spoke to her, but the devil replied to them with a contempt which exceeded all bounds, and when he was questioned about Jesus he made a reply of such derision that it cannot be set down. . . .[1]

Now follows an extract from a narrative of the eighteenth century:

At the unexpected rumour that two possessed women had been brought into the workhouse of that place, I followed the dictates of my pastor's conscience and went to the workhouse on the evening of the 14th of December, 1714. After . . . the paroxysm began in one of the possessed women, and Satan abruptly hurled this invective at me by her mouth: " Silly fool, what are you doing in this workhouse ? You'll get lice here," etc. I made him this answer: " By the blood, the wounds and the martyrdom of Jesus Christ, thou shalt be vanquished and expelled !" Thereupon he foamed with rage and shouted: " If we had the devil's power we would turn earth and heaven upside down, etc. . . . What God doesn't want is ours !"

In the morning, towards 11 o'clock, this possessed woman came at my request, but not willingly, into the church of the place. There, in order that I might inform myself of her most wretched state, I began to sing the canticle: " May God the Father be with us," and after such preparation as I judged necessary I read from the pulpit the two remarkable passages concerning possession in the fifth and ninth chapters of St. Mark, so earnestly and for so long that Satan who was in the possessed cried to me from below the pulpit: " Won't you soon have done ?" After I had replied:

---

[1] J. Kerner, *Geschichten Besessener neuerer Zeit*, Stuttgart, 1834, p. 122.

"When it is enough for God it will be enough for thee, demon !"
Satan broke into complaints against me: "How dost thou oppress,
how dost thou torment me ! If only I had been wise enough
not to enter thy church !" As he cried out impudently: "My
creature must now suffer as an example !" I closed his mouth
with these words: "Demon ! the creature is not thine but God's !
That which is thine is filth and unclean things, hell and damnation
to all eternity !" When at last I addressed to him the most violent
exhortations in the name of Jesus, he cried out: "Oh, I burn, I
burn ! Oh, what torture ! What torture !" or loaded me with
furious invectives: "What ails thee to jabber in this fashion?"
During all these prayers, clamourings, and disputes, Satan
tortured the poor creature horribly, howled through her mouth
in a frightful manner and threw her to the ground so rigid, so insensible that she became as cold as ice and lay as dead, at which
time we could not perceive the slightest breath until at last with
God's help she came to herself. . . .
Although the possessed once more recovered her reason on this
occasion without being able, be it noted, to remember what Satan
had said by her mouth, he did not leave her long in peace after my
departure; he tormented her as before. . . .[1]

Finally, here is another case from the beginning of the
nineteenth century:

The first woman possessed in the Biblical manner with whom
I became acquainted, writes the Swabian poet and physician Justinus
Kerner, I owe to the confidence of Doctor . . . He had sent her
to me for cure, informing me that all treatment by ordinary methods
had been fruitless when applied to this woman.
The patient was a peasant-woman of thirty-four years. . . .
Her past life up to this time had been irreproachable. She kept
her house and showed due regard for religion without being especially devout. Without any definite cause which could be
discovered, she was seized, in August, 1830, by terrible fits of
convulsions, during which a strange voice uttered by her mouth
diabolic discourses. As soon as this voice began to speak (it
professed to be that of an unhappy dead man), her individuality
vanished, to give place to another. So long as this lasted she knew
nothing of her individuality, which only reappeared (in all its
integrity and reason) when she had retired to rest.
This demon shouted, swore, and raged in the most terrible fashion.
He broke out especially into curses against God and everything
sacred.
Bodily measures and medicines did not produce the slightest
change in her state, nor did a pregnancy and the suckling which
followed it. Only continual prayer (to which moreover she was
obliged to apply herself with the greatest perseverance, for the
demon could not endure it) often frustrated the demon for a time.
During five months all the resources of medicine were tried in
vain. . . . On the contrary, two demons now spoke in her; who
often, as it were, played the raging multitude within her, barked
like dogs, mewed like cats, etc. Did she begin to pray, the demons
at once flung her into the air, swore, and made a horrible din through
her mouth.

---

[1] M. Hartmann, *S. M. Andreä Hartmanns Hauspostill*, 1745, quoted
by J. Kerner, *ibid.*, p. 107.

When the demons left her in peace she came to herself, and on hearing the accounts of those present, and seeing the injuries inflicted upon her by blows and falls, she burst into sobs and lamented her condition. By a magico-magnetic (that is to say, hypnotic) treatment . . . one of the demons had been expelled before she was brought to me; but the one who remained only made the more turmoil.

Prayer was also particularly disagreeable to this one. If the woman wished to kneel down to pray, the demon strove to prevent her with all his might, and if she persisted he forced her jaws apart and obliged her to utter a diabolic laugh or whistle. . . .

She was able to eat nothing but a soup of black bread and water. As soon as she took anything better, the demon rose up in her and cried: " Carrion should eat nothing good !" and took away her plate. She often fasted for two or three complete days without taking a crumb of food and without drinking a drop. On those days the demon kept quiet. Through distress, suffering and fasting, she had grown thin and was little more than a skeleton. Her pains were often so great, by night as well as day, as to beggar description, and we like herself were in despair over them.[1]

Narratives such as the foregoing, above all those relating to early Christian times, have long excited the interest of doctors and religious historians, and from time to time formed the subject of monographs. In these circumstances it will be worth while to subject the question to a thorough examination from the psychological point of view, the more so as the most recent descriptions on the medical side are inadequate and have thrown little light. The psychological conception of possession is still so little known that even a man like Harnack thinks it " often defies scientific analysis even in our own times, and leaves us all at liberty to suppose that certain mysterious forces are brought into play. In this domain there are facts which cannot be ignored and yet of which no explanation is forthcoming." Wrede has expressed the same opinion.[2] In reality, there can be no question of particular enigmas in the matter of possession; the province of psychology where they are in fact encountered lies quite elsewhere.

[1] J. Kerner, *Nachricht von dem Vorkommen des Besessenseins*, Stuttgart, 1836, p. 27.

[2] A. Harnack, *Medizinisches aus der ältesten Kirchengeschichte* in *Die Mission und Ausbreitung des Christentums in den ersten drei Jahrhunderten*, 3rd edit., Leipzig, 1915, vol. i, p. 137. W. Wrede, *Das Messiasgeheimnis in den Evangelien*, Göttingen, 1901, p. 25.

CHAPTER I

SOURCES

AFTER these preliminary historical remarks we shall now pass to psychological considerations proper, casting a rapid preliminary glance over the materials on which a psychological study may be based.

Possession has been an extremely common phenomenon, cases of which abound in the history of religion. Only where a high degree of civilization prevails does it disappear or retreat into the shadows. The number of detailed accounts is by no means proportionate to this frequency; in the majority of cases, as in the Δαιμονιζόμενοι of the New Testament, the narratives are so short that no psychological explanation can be founded upon them. Happily we possess a series of sufficiently complete accounts; during the last centuries, in proportion as we approach the present one, their number has become appreciable, and it is not uncommon to light upon matter of this kind when looking through theological and psychiatric literature. Just as states of possession have a general typical resemblance, the same may be said of the relevant documents. The bibliography scattered through this book forms an index to a great number of these, and I shall here confine myself to mentioning those few which constitute sources of the first importance; they are for the use of the reader who desires to consult original documents of a more detailed nature.

The facilities for an analysis of possession are much inferior to those enjoyed by the student of states of ecstasy. For these latter we possess a mass of sources, autobiographical in the widest sense of the word. Autodescriptions of possession are, on the contrary, extremely rare. No one, of course, can say what surprises may await us in the sheaves of manuscripts belonging to the Middle Ages and later centuries now buried in libraries; but judging by what has already been rediscovered we must abandon hope of seeing good accounts brought to light, even in very limited numbers. This poverty of autodescriptive narratives has a profound psychological reason which springs from the very nature of possession. We are to some extent dealing with states involving a more or less complete posterior amnesia, so that the majority of victims of possession are not in a condition to describe it. It is therefore necessary *a priori* to avoid confining ourselves to autodescriptive sources, and to regard this matter as one in which concessions must be made. Not only material coming from observers who have seen in possession purely and simply a morbid psychic state will be regarded as admissible; the most interesting and detailed accounts come precisely from authors who believed in the reality of possession, and when they combine exact observation with good description may very well be used in spite of the writers' outlook.

To the principal sources belong old journals kept by two Swabian doctors of the school of Schelling: Kerner and Eschenmayer, who made therein careful notes of their cases in a manner so admirable as to give a clear picture of the states. Both these authors have a demonological point of view in harmony with the spirit of the last days of romanticism; they believe in the existence of demons, and their invasion of the soul and organism of human beings. Their three works are:

Justinus Kerner, *Geschichten Besessener neuerer Zeit.* Beobachtungen aus dem Gebiete kakodämonisch-magnetischer Erscheinungen, nebst Reflexionen von C. A. Eschenmayer über Besessensein und Zauber. Stuttgart, 1834.

The first part appeared under the title: *Die Geschichte des Mädchens von Orlach,* Stuttgart, 1834. Reprint " with a retrospective historical survey by the author, of some similar cases in antiquity, including those in the Holy Scriptures, a literary-historical supplement by Wilhelm German and two illustrations." Schwäb. Hall, 1898.

Justinus Kerner, *Nachricht von dem Vorkommen des Besessenseins* eines dämonisch-magnetischen Leidens und seiner schon in Altertum bekannten Heilung durch magisch-magnetisches Einwirken, in einem Handschreiben an den Obermedizinalrat Dr. Schelling in Stuttgart. Stuttgart and Augsburg, 1836.

C. A. Eschenmayer, *Konflikt zwischen Himmel und Hölle,* an dem Dämon eines besessenen Mädchens beobachtet. Nebst einem Wort an Dr. Strauss. Tübingen and Leipzig, 1837 (C. St. Case).

Franz von Baader, *Fragment aus der Geschichte einer magnetischen Hellseherin.* Complete works, part i, vol. iv, Leipzig, 1853, pp. 41-60.

Gottlob Müller, *Gründliche Nachricht von einer begeisterten Weibsperson Anna Elisabeth Lohmannin,* aus eigener Erfahrung und Untersuchung mitgeteilt, Wittenberg, 1759 (L. Case).

Of great importance is the case of the mystic Surin (sixteenth century). Details may be found in: Aubin, *Cruels effets de la vengeance du Cardinal Richelieu ou Histoire des diables de Loudun,* Amsterdam, 1716 (cf. particularly pp. 215 sq.)—Delacroix, *Études d'histoire et de psychologie du mysticisme,* Paris, 1908, pp. 328-344—Henry-Marie Boudon, *La vie du R. P. Seurin ou l'homme de Dieu,* Chartres and Paris, 1689.

In addition the *Bibliothèque diabolique,* published at Paris from 1882 onwards by the pupils of the great Parisian clinician Charcot, is of considerable value; it has rendered accessible a mass of old writings, partly printed and partly manuscript. We will cite:

Vols. i and ii : Jean Wier (Johann Wier or Weyer, a physician, the first adversary of belief in witchcraft, 1516-1558), *Histoires, disputes et discours des illusions et impostures des diables, des magiciens infâmes, sorcières et empoisonneurs, des ensorcelez et démoniaques et de la guérison d'iceux,* Paris, 1885 (Orig. edit.: *De præstigiis dæmonum et incantationibus ac veneficiis,* Bâle, 1563).

Vol. iv (Anonymous) : *La possession de Jeanne Féry* (1584), Paris, 1886.

Particularly interesting is book v : *Sœur Jeanne des Anges, supérieure des Ursulines de Loudun* (seventeenth century), Paris, 1886. In this work we have the autobiography of a case of possession which has acquired historic importance.

We must also quote the translation of the work *De magorum Dæmonomania,* of the famous state philosopher Bodinus (Hamburg, 1698), in which several detailed cases will be found.

The following works also contain interesting isolated cases:

F. Sebastian Michaelis, *Histoire admirable de la possession et conversion d'une pénitente*, Paris, 1613.

A. van Gennep, *Un Cas de possession*, "Archives de psychologie," x, 1911, pp. 88-92.

Pfarrer Blumhardt, *Krankheitsgeschichte der G. D. in Möttlingen* (hysteria gravissima); printed in full by Theodor Heinrich Mandel, *Der Sieg von Möttlingen im Lichte des Glaubens und der Wissenschaft*, Leipzig, 1896, pp. 16-87. This is the first complete impression of this remarkable " case-history " (it is untrustworthy as regards a number of points which are for us without importance), only previously known to us by fragments inserted in the biographical notice of Friedr. Zündel (2nd ed. Zürich-Heilbronn, 1881). Thomas Freimann has given, under the title *Die Teufelaustreibung in Möttlingen*, a reproduction which is incomplete and full of inconsistencies (taken, perhaps, from one of the numerous copies in circulation of the Blumhardt original, which was an official deposition).

Anonymous, *Wahre Geschichte der Befreiung eines vom Teufel Besessenen*, translated from the review *Der Missionar*, edited by a learned Catholic society with headquarters at the Palazzo Moroni in Rome (Borgo Vecchio, 165), Aix-la-Chapelle, 1882, 2nd ed. 1887).

Anonymous, *Am Ausgang des neunzehnten Jahrhunderts*. Eine Teufelsaustreibung, geschehen zu Wemding in Bayern, anno 1891, Barmen, 1892. This work contains the story of a modern case of possession, told by the exorcising priests (the M. Case).

The work of Ludwig Staudenmaier (Chemistry master at the Lyzeum of Freising, near Munich): *Die Magie als experimentelle Naturwissenschaft*, Leipzig, 1912, is also of interest as containing a series of personal experiments. There is no doubt that the author, extremely susceptible to the phenomena of psychic control, would some centuries earlier have experienced the most terrible states of possession.

The authors and editors of these cases are almost always silent as to their personal opinions.

In the new French psychiatric, or rather psychological

literature, the following works are of outstanding value and may be recommended for thorough study:

Paul Richer, *Études cliniques sur la grande hystérie ou hystéro-épilepsie*, 2nd edit. revised and considerably enlarged, Paris, 1885.

Pierre Janet, *Un Cas de possession et d'exorcisme moderne*, in *Névroses et idées fixes*, Paris, 1898, vol. i, pp. 375-406.

Aug. Lemaître, *Fritz Algar, histoire et guérison d'un désordre cérébral précoce*, "Archives de psychologie," v, 1906, pp. 78-102.

As regards ancient literature, one of the best works for those who study these problems, although it is not, properly speaking, written from the psychological point of view, is L. F. Calmeil's great book: *De la folie considérée sous le point de vue pathologique, philosophique, historique et judiciaire, depuis la renaissance des sciences en Europe jusqu'au XIXᵉ siècle, description des grandes épidémies de délire simple on compliqué qui ont atteint les populations d'autrefois et regné dans les monastères. Exposé des condamnations auxquelles la folie méconnue a souvent donné lieu.* Paris, 1845, 2 vols. This is a very valuable collection of material. True it does not form a complete survey of the literature of the subject, over-looking as it sometimes does a number of important works. It nevertheless serves as a most useful guide, giving a mass of information direct from original sources. I have borrowed from it more than once.

A great quantity of material has also been utilized by the well-known disciple of Schelling, Joseph von Görres, in: *Die christliche Mystik*, vol. iv, part 1: Die Besessenheit, Regensburg, 1842, but this work, written under orthodox Catholic inspiration as a corollary to the ideas of Schelling, is lacking to an astonishing degree in criticism of any kind.

It is regrettable that the reproduction, even in abbreviated form, of the materials utilized is impossible by reason of their extent. I can only refer the reader desirous of acquiring first-hand knowledge to the original publications.[1] I shall, in addition, make free use of quotations.

---

[1] Here, as generally speaking on every occasion when early sources have to be consulted, the need for the publication of a documentary collection, *Monumenta Psychologica*, makes itself felt.

CHAPTER II

THE EXTERNAL SIGNS OF POSSESSION

REVIEWING the series of cases which have just been cited, their first and most striking characteristic is that the patient's organism appears to be invaded by a new personality; it is governed by a strange soul. This is what has given to these states, from the earliest times when we can observe them up to the most recent, the name of " possession." It is as if another soul had entered into the body and thenceforward subsisted there, in place of or side by side with the normal subject.

This possession is manifested in three ways:

In the first place the possessed takes on a new physiognomy. The features are changed.

> The features which, in their habitual state, express serenity and benevolence, change from the moment when the devil appears in this man, and his individuality vanishes in the most horrible of infernal grimaces. . . .

Of N., who believed herself possessed by the soul of a dead man, it is related:

> As often as the demon took possession of her she assumed the same features which this man had had in his lifetime and which were very well marked, so that it was necessary at every attack to lead N. away from any persons who had known the deceased, because they recognized him at once in the features of the demoniac.[1]

Eschenmayer also gives as characteristics of the C. St. case:

> The appearance of a completely strange individuality with features distorted and quite changed.[2]
> . . . As soon as this demon made himself heard the features of the girl were transformed in a very striking manner, and each time she cast round her really demoniac glances. Some conception of these may be gathered from the picture in Klopstock's Messiah where the devil offers Jesus a stone.[3]

---

[1] Kerner, *Nachricht*, etc., p. 14.
[2] Eschenmayer, *Konflikt*, etc., p. 18.
[3] Kerner, *Geschichten*, etc., p. 105, M. B. case.

17   2

Sometimes possession shows itself in an intermittent form but still with change of personal expression: " Thus persons and faces were metamorphosed with unheard-of rapidity."[1]

The same thing is true of the principal victim of possession in the epidemic of Loudun.   This is what a contemporary eye-witness says:

> . . . that Asmodeus (a demon) was not long in manifesting his supreme rage, shaking the girl backwards and forwards a number of times and making her strike like a hammer with such great rapidity that her teeth rattled and sounds were forced out of her throat. That between these movements her face became completely unrecognizable, her glance furious, her tongue prodigiously large, long, and hanging down out of her mouth, livid and dry to such a point that the lack of humour made it appear quite furred, although it was not at all bitten by the teeth and the breathing was always regular. That Beherit, who is another demon, produced a second face which was laughing and pleasant, which was again variously changed by two other demons, Acaph and Achaos, who came forth one after the other: that Asmodeus having received the command to stay on and the others to retire, the first came back again.[2] Monsieur (brother of Louis XIV who went to Loudun to see the possessed women) having desired to see all the devils which possessed this girl appear, the Exorcist made them come into her face one after another, all making it very hideous but each one causing a different distortion.[3]

This transformation of the physiognomy appears in all descriptions; since the investigations of Flournoy into the case of Hélène Smith there is no longer any reason to cast doubt upon such accounts.   She too showed an alteration of the features, which assumed an immediate resemblance to the portrait of the person whom she professed at the moment to incarnate.

Hélène Smith presented a whole series of personalities, some very diverse. The two most important were the imitations of Marie Antoinette and of the celebrated late eighteenth-century magician Cagliostro, both examples of somnambulistic copies of historical personages. Flournoy thus describes the incarnation of Cagliostro:

> It is only slowly and step by step that Leopold (Cagliostro) succeeds in incarnating himself. Hélène at first feels as if her arms were seized or did not exist; then she complains of disagreeable, formerly painful, sensations in the neck, at the base of the skull, in the head; her eyelids droop, the expression of her face changes and her throat swells into a sort of double chin which gives her a

---

[1] Eschenmayer, *loc. cit.*, p. 47.
[2] *Histoire des diables de Loudun*, Amsterdam, 1716, pp. 226 sq.
[3] *Ibid.*, p. 229.

kind of family resemblance to the well-known picture of Cagliostro. Suddenly she rises, then turning slowly towards the person in the audience to whom Leopold is about to address himself, she draws herself up proudly, even bending slightly backwards, sometimes with her arms pompously folded across her chest, sometimes with one hanging down while the other points solemnly up to heaven, the fingers forming a sort of Masonic sign which is always the same. Soon, after a series of hiccups, sighs, and various sounds showing the difficulty which Leopold experiences in taking possession of the vocal organs, comes speech, grave, slow and powerful, a man's strong bass voice, slightly thick, with a foreign pronunciation and a marked accent which is certainly rather Italian than anything else. Leopold is not always very easy to understand, especially when his thunderous voice swells and rolls at some indiscreet question or the disrespectful remarks of a sceptical onlooker. He stammers, lisps, pronounces all *u* sounds as *ou*, accentuates the final syllables, sprinkles his vocabulary with obsolete words or others unsuited to the occasion. He is pompous, unctuous, grandiloquent, sometimes severe and terrible, but also sentimental. He addresses everyone as " thou " and creates the impression that his listeners are dealing with the grand master of secret societies. . . . When she (Hélène) incarnates her guide, she really takes on a certain facial resemblance to him, and her whole bearing has something theatrical, sometimes really majestic, which is entirely consistent with what may be imagined of the real Cagliostro.[1]

The classic cases of double personality (dédoublement de personnalité) described by Azam[2] and Bourru et Burot[3] also attest a change of countenance.

Physiognomy, closely related to and consistent with which are bearing, gait, etc., is an expression of psychic constitution. As every affective phenomenon has its typical expression, so has the personality regarded as a whole. These phenomena, still imperfectly known and relatively constant, may be designated under the name of " expressive stereotypes " as opposed to expressive movements.[4] They must of necessity participate in the great change which affects the whole personality during possession.

The second characteristic which reveals change of personality is closely related to the first: it is the voice. At the moment when the countenance alters, a more or less changed voice issues from the mouth of the person in the fit. The intonation also corresponds to the character of the new

[1] Flournoy, *Des Indes à la planète Mars*, Genève-Paris, 1900, p. 100.
[2] Azam, *Hypnotisme, double conscience et altérations de la personnalité*, Paris, 1887.
[3] Bourru et Burot, *Variations de la personnalité*, Paris, 1888.
[4] The first attempt, dogmatic but nevertheless very worthy of attention, to explain these expressive stereotypes systematically is due to Lavater.

individuality manifesting itself in the organism and is conditioned by it. In particular the top register of the voice is displaced; the feminine voice is transformed into a bass one, for in all the cases of possession which it has hitherto been my lot to know the new individuality was a man. Thus in Kerner's M. B. case a little girl of eleven years suddenly gave utterance to " a deep bass voice," and later to another, but always with a timbre qualitatively different from the normal. The same thing is true of the maid of Orlach (p. 86). Eschenmayer also observes of his patient C. St.:

> He (the alleged demon) spoke to-day in a voice resembling more than ever a man's bass, and at the same time showed an insolence of look and gesture which beggars all description.[1]

In an old case quoted by Janet, it is said:

> It was a very extraordinary spectacle for us who were there present to see this wicked spirit speak by the mouth of the poor woman and to hear now the sound of a masculine, now that of a feminine voice, but so distinct the one from the other that it was impossible to believe that only the woman was speaking.[2]

In other cases the timbre of the voice is not changed to an extreme degree:

> A voice was heard which might readily have been taken for a strange one, not so much from the timbre as from the expression and articulation.[3]

A good general idea of possession is given by the philosopher Baader's description of a case observed by him in a Bavarian peasant woman of twenty-four years, who side by side with demoniacal possession showed yet another abnormal state, a " sacred " one.

> . . . In truth this satanic reaction grew hourly stronger and the somnambulist, who, in her seizure, spoke like a saint, expressed herself in her ordinary waking state in a somewhat worldly and impious manner (beginning of possession). Her countenance, gestures, and even her manner of speech assumed withal a certain coarse and offensive tone quite foreign to her normal character. Formerly she was willing and submissive; now she showed herself bad-tempered, disobedient, and spiteful. On the evening of the 16th of October the cacodemoniac possession finally broke forth in all its horror with a hideous and yelping laugh. Dr. U. asked her in my presence the meaning of such a laugh, to which she

---

[1] Eschenmayer, loc. cit., p. 59.
[2] Pierre Janet, Névroses et idées fixes, Paris, 1889, vol. i, p. 384.
[3] Blumhardt quoted by Mandel, Der Sieg von Möttlingen, Leipzig, 1896, p. 80.

replied in a hoarse and deep tenor voice, with furious gestures and burning glance, that she was laughing solely because of her prompt conversion which would be as promptly wiped out; and she burst into a torrent of mockery and abuse of everything concerning religion and holy things.

. . . If two states had up to that time been distinguished in her, the ordinary waking state and the magnetic (somnambulistic) waking state, it was now necessary to distinguish three: the ordinary waking state, the good magnetic waking state and the bad magnetic waking state.   The voice, gestures, physiognomy, sentiments, etc., were in the last two states exactly like heaven and hell.   In particular the features changed so rapidly that one could hardly trust one's eyes, nor recognize her in the satanic fit as the same person who was in the good magnetic state.[1]

But the most important particular in which " the invasion of the organism by a strange individuality " is manifested, is the third: the new voice does not speak according to the spirit of the normal personality but that of the new one. Its " ego " is the latter's, and is opposed to the character of the normal individual.   Even if this is described as good and irreproachable, the words uttered by the strange voice generally betray a coarse and filthy attitude, fundamentally opposed to all accepted ethical and religious ideas.   The accounts of these particular cases are full of vile expressions and abuse of all kinds.

The following is reported of the maid of Orlach:

During these fits the spirit of darkness now utters through her mouth words worthy of a mad demon, things which have no place in this true-hearted maid, curses upon the Holy Scriptures, the Redeemer, and all the saints.[2]

The same is true of C. St.:

. . . He straightway began to utter through her mouth mockeries and abuse.   In short, the demon was there.   He flung himself with clenched fists on D. and heaped insults upon him: cheat, scoundrel, etc. . . .[3]

Hardly had he begun to say his prayers when her eyes and whole features were completely changed as on the last occasion. . . . And then these strange sounds were heard: "O ! Ta, Te, Ta!" pronounced with extraordinary rapidity.   All this was accompanied by abuse, clamour, and gesticulation. . . . D. read the prayers again.   When a holy name was pronounced, the demon had an outburst of diabolical fury, and with clenched fists breathed forth threats. . . .   When operations were suspended these outbursts died down also.[4]

[1] F. von Baader, *Sämtlichte Werke*, Leipzig, 1853, vol. iv, pp. 56 sq.
[2] Kerner, *Die Geschichte des Mädchens von Orlach*, p. 36.
[3] Eschenmayer, *Konflikt*, etc., p. 14.
[4] *Ibid.*, p. 19.

Baader cites analogous features in his case:

> In this violent seizure she also spoke of herself in the third person and heaped insults and mockeries on herself with no less fury than on those present.[1]

And Kerner remarks generally:

> . . . that all that these demons say by the mouth of such a man is entirely diabolic in nature and completely opposed to the character of the individual possessed. It consists in mockeries and curses against all that is sacred, against God and our Saviour, and particularly in mockeries and curses directed against the persons whom they possess, whom they outrage by their own mouth and beat with their own fists.[2]

Of case U. the following is reported:

> In this state the eyes were tightly shut, the face grimacing, often excessively and horribly changed, the voice repugnant, full of shrill cries, deep groans, coarse words; the speech expressing the joy of inflicting hurt or cursing God and the universe, addressing terrible threats now to the doctor, now to the patient herself, saying with deliberate and savage obstinacy that he would not abandon the body of this poor woman and that he would torture both her and her near ones more and more. Thus she was one day constrained by the demon to beat her beloved child, when during one of the attacks he knelt down beside his mother to pray for her. The most dreadful thing was the way in which she raged when she had to submit to be touched or rubbed down during the fits; she defended herself with her hands, threatening all those who approached, insulting and abusing them in the vilest terms; her body bent backwards like a bow was flung out of the chair and writhed upon the ground, then lay there stretched out at full length, stiff and cold, assuming the very appearance of death. If in spite of her resistance anyone succeeded in administering something to the patient she at once manifested a violent movement to vomit up again what had been forced upon her. This occurred each time with diabolic howlings and a terrible panting, alternating with satanic bursts of laughter in a piercing falsetto.[3]

These important psychological phenomena are usually accompanied by others, foremost among which are strongly marked motor ones. The affective disorder of the possessed is translated by their movements, which equal in intensity those of veritable raving madmen. It must, however, be added that these movements cannot be entirely resolved into expressions of emotion and their derived manifestations, a great number appearing to come from an autonomous excitement of the motor system. For the movements are partially

---

[1] Baader, *Fragment*, p. 47.   [2] Kerner, *Nachricht*, etc., p. 13.
[3] Kerner, *ibid.*, p. 88.

deprived of sense; they consist in a disordered agitation of the limbs, with contortions and dislocations in the most impossible directions—the body is bent backwards like a bow, etc. The proof that they are not due to simulation or voluntary action is that such contortions cannot, as a rule, be executed voluntarily. Thus in Kerner's case quoted above.

The force with which such movements are executed is, moreover, immensely greater than normal. The writers of case-histories always stress that the united strength of several persons is insufficient to master and hold the patients.

> When Dürr began his magnetic (hypnotic) manipulations, the whole body twisted and reared with such ease and rapidity that one might have believed it under the domination of an external force. Three persons had all they could do to master it, and the friends accompanying me had sometimes to lend a hand. . . . The jerking of the head was intensely violent, so that it had to be constantly held. . . . This fit of rage which lasted a full hour calmed itself when Dürr . . .[1]
>
> All this was accompanied by abuse, uproar, and agitation of the limbs, so that three people had constantly to hold him (Caroline's supposed demon) down. If he was able to seize anyone by the clothing, he held him so firmly that it was difficult to make him let go. . . . He clenched his fist, uttering threats and shook his head with such rapidity that all Caroline's hair was flying loose.[2]
>
> Even if nothing else had shown the existence of an alien and hostile creature, there would have been this diabolic force which he exercised in the weak limbs of a frail girl. Two persons were incapable of mastering her, and one would have been in danger of strangulation. . . .[3]
>
> Quickly he rose (the supposed demon of the patient) with such violence that he sat up on the sofa when it was least expected and could not be forced to lie down again in spite of the aid of the five persons present, mostly strong men.[4]

The greater the religious ceremonial brought to bear in exorcising these states the more violent are the movements. Rather than multiply examples we may quote as typical the account of case M.[5] which is very instructive in its conciseness. It displays all the phenomena dealt with up to the present.

> Since Shrove Tuesday (February 10th) a man called Müller and his wife noted astonishing phenomena in their eldest son M., who was ten years old. He could no longer say a prayer without getting into extraordinary rages, nor suffer near him any object which had been blessed, was guilty of the coarsest offences towards his parents, and showed in his features such a transformation

---

[1] Eschenmayer, *loc. cit.*, p. 15.
[2] *Ibid.*, p. 18.   [3] *Ibid.*, p. 58.   [4] *Ibid.*, p. 91.
[5] *Am Ausgang des neunzehnten Jahrhunderts*, Barmen, 1892.

that they were forced to believe that something extraordinary had taken place. At first the parents sought to obtain from a doctor some remedy for this wretched state of their child, but in vain. . . .

The vicar of the parish was next called upon for help, and sent parents and child to the convent of the Capuchins at Wemding where the care of the patient was at once undertaken according to the prescriptions of the church: . . . On our first visit we found in the child the astonishing manifestations mentioned above. We first pronounced over him the customary benediction. At this he showed such uneasiness, or rather such rage and out-cries, that it was impossible to think of anything except a demoni-acal influence. At the same time he gave proof of a degree of physical strength such as it was impossible to find in a boy of ten years: it was so great that three grown men were hardly able to master him. What the parents had come to seek and what we also so earnestly desired could not be achieved.

As often as the boy had to pass a church, crucifix, or monument raised in honour of the Mother of God or any other saint, he was seized thirty paces away with sudden agitation and fell unconscious to the earth. He had then to be carried away from the pious object, after which he was able to continue his walk. We observed, moreover, that in church he showed terrible uneasiness, quite particularly marked during the holy elevation; he could never turn his eyes, which were always closed, towards the altar. In this wretched state the boy passed almost six months, and as no improvement appeared in spite of prayers, but on the contrary he grew worse each day, the father wrote to his Grace the Bishop of Augsburg begging him to proceed to solemn exorcism.

He obtained the Bishop's permission and the exorcism took place. Father Aurelian, who played the chief part in it, relates in these words what took place:

"With heavy hearts but confident in the help of God, we, Father Remigius and Father Aurelian, proceeded for the first time (in the church) to solemn exorcism. . . . Some time before we began the exorcism the boy boxed his parents' ears in an in-describable manner, and when we had him led to the presbytery a truly frightful scene took place. For when they would have executed our order, the possessed uttered a terrible cry. We seemed no longer to hear a human voice, but that of a savage animal, and so powerful that the howlings—the word is not too strong—were heard at a distance of several hundred metres from the convent chapel, and those who heard them were overcome with fear. It may be imagined what courage we priests needed. And worse was yet to come; when his father tried to bring the boy into the presbytery he became weaker than a child beside him. The weak child flung the strong father to the earth with such violence that our hearts were in our mouths. At length, after a long struggle, he was overcome by his father, the men who were wit-nesses and one lay brother, and led into the presbytery. By way of precaution we had him bound hand and foot with straps, but he moved his limbs as if nothing of the kind had been done. After these preliminaries we disposed ourselves to perform the rite of exorcism, full of confidence in help from on high. We used the grand ritual of Eichstatt. Although this is not mentioned therein, we exposed the fragment of the Holy Cross. When the Sign of the Cross was made with it, the young man uttered an appalling scream. All the time he did not cease to spit forth vile insults against the fragment of the Cross and the two officiants Father Remigius and Father Aurelian. The clamour and spitting lasted without interruption until the recitation of the litanies of the saints. Then took place the exorcism, which we pronounced in Latin. To all our questions the possessed made no reply, but he showed great contempt for us and spat upon us each time. . . .[1]

Paintings and drawings give a clearer idea of possession than any verbal description, and the art of the past includes a whole series of pictures of it. The most important have been published by Charcot and Richer in a special work, others in the iconography of the Salpêtrière, where they may be consulted by the reader.

Charcot and Richer, *Les Démoniaques dans l'art,* Paris, 1887.

Paul Richer, *Études cliniques sur la grande hystérie ou hystéro-épilepsie,* 2nd ed., Paris, 1885.

Gilles de la Tourette, *Sur un tableau perdu de Rubens représentant la guérison de la possédée* (Iconography of the Salpêtrière), v, 1892.

P. Richer and H. Meige, *Documents inédits sur les démoniaques dans l'art, ibid.,* ix, 1896.

Jean Heitz, *Les démoniaques et les malades dans l'art byzantin, ibid.,* xiv, 1901.

H. Meige, *Les tapisseries de Rubens, ibid.,* xiv, 1901.

J. Heitz, *Un possédé de Rubens : la transfiguration du Musée de Nancy, ibid.,* xiv, 1901.

However frequent motor hyper-excitement may be in the possessed—and it is this which has focussed attention on those pathological disturbances—it does not arise in every case; some are entirely without it, and show no tendency to violent activity. In particular it may be absent when the patient believes himself possessed not by a demon but by the soul of a deceased person.

[1] *Loc. cit.,* pp. 5 sq.

CHAPTER III

THE SUBJECTIVE STATE OF THE POSSESSED

1. The Somnambulistic Form of Possession

Now that we know the impression produced by possessed persons on the observer, we shall study the inner aspect of their condition. What is the subjective state of the possessed, what do they feel in their paroxysms of rage, are they in the same condition as raving madmen, or do they present a different reaction ?

A review of the above-mentioned cases at once emphasizes the fact already remarked, that the personality which appears in demoniacal seizures is totally different from that of the normal state. In the old cases it is principally " demons," or " devils," which speak. In some instances there are even several which appear by turns—Jeanne des Anges possessed a whole collection seven in number, which in the manner typical of all these early cases were called Asmodeus, Leviathan, Behemoth, Isacaaron, Balaam, Gresil, and Haman.

Kerner has made similar observations:

> It often happens that we recognize in a single individual not merely one demon but several at once or in succession; there speak in him two, three or more voices and individualities. They say that they have chosen as seat such and such a part of the body, and cause him such and such pains and sufferings. . . .[1]
> There were also in a certain case two men and an old woman, who spoke by the mouth of a possessed woman of thirty-two years of age.[2]

In more recent times, especially in the eighteenth century and still much more in the nineteenth when belief in the devil is diminishing, it is more particularly the souls of the dead " not at peace " who enter into the living. Nevertheless, ancient examples of this are also found. Thus Justin Martyr speaks of men " of whom the souls of the dead had taken

---

[1] Kerner, *Nachricht*, etc., p. 13.   [2] *Ibid.*, p. 40.

possession and who had been cast to the ground and said by all to be possessed of demons."[1] As regards the souls of the dead, the idea that they can enter into man is the more readily admitted in primitive times as certain souls, especially the deeply degraded ones of criminals, are often conceived as wandering. For this reason it is generally bad souls which cause possession, but there are also " good " possessions.[2] Kerner also lays down from personal experience that " it is common to many of these accounts that the demons describe themselves as the outcast spirits of the unhappy dead, just as almost always the good demons (guides) who manifest themselves in agathomagnetism give themselves out as blessed spirits of the dead."[3] Naturally, the mere act of imagining a living person may also lead to possession, but in actual fact this has occurred but rarely; at least, I have only been able to find two cases in literature.

The first is the L. case. The girl in question, aged eighteen years, believed herself to be " bewitched " by a hunter's boy of her acquaintance, and in a part of her fits (in which, however, she retained full consciousness), the latter spoke through her mouth:

> She seemed (writes the exorcist who narrates the case) of a mortal pallor and dragged her limbs languidly; she complained to me of her attack (the fit which was approaching), and that the Evil One in the person of T. (the hunter's boy) had spoken by her mouth, as I had already heard myself in one of her paroxysms.[4]

And he relates of another fit:

> . . . Thereupon she made as if to raise herself from the ground, which she had not the strength to do, and cried out in a masculine voice: " I am a good fellow ! I am . . . " (the name of the young hunter follows in a periphrasis).[5]

The second case is taken from an English author:[6]

> Miss A. B., a young woman of about thirty, experienced a sudden and demonstrative attachment for a man, C. D., living in the same neighbourhood. The affair attracted some unpleasant notoriety,

---

[1] Justin Martyr, *Apologia*, ii, quoted by Kerner, *Geschichten*, etc., p. 7.
[2] Such a case is that related by von Müller, *Gründliche Nachricht*, in which possession by an evil spirit alternates with possession by a good one.
[3] Kerner, *Nachricht*, etc., p. 60.
[4] G. Müller, *Gründliche Nachricht*, p. 22.
[5] *Ibid.*, p. 67.
[6] F. Podmore, *The Newer Spiritualism*, London, 1910, pp. 279 sq.

and the young man, who had apparently acted a rather passive part throughout, abruptly discontinued the acquaintance. Miss A. B. continued, however, to cherish the belief that the man had been influenced by the malice of her enemies, and that he was still profoundly attached to her. A few weeks after the breach she felt one evening a curious feeling in the throat, as of choking—the prelude probably, under ordinary circumstances, to an attack of hysteria. This feeling was succeeded by involuntary movements of the hands and a fit of long-continued and apparently causeless sobbing. Then in presence of a member of her family she became, in her own belief, possessed by the spirit of C. D., personating his words and gestures and speaking in his character. After this date she continually held conversation, as she believed, with C. D.'s spirit; "he" sometimes speaking aloud through her mouth, sometimes conversing with her in the inner voice. Occasionally "he" wrote messages through her hand, and I have the testimony of a member of her family that the writing so produced resembled that of C. D. Occasionally also A. B. had visions, in which she claimed to see C. D. and what he was doing at the moment. At other times she professed to hear him speaking or to understand by some inner sympathy his feelings and thoughts.

Given the mass of fanciful nonsense with which we constantly have to deal in this subject, it is hardly a matter for surprise that no notice has been taken of the difficulty in these two cases of the possessing spirit being at once in his own organism and in a strange one.

Finally, there is " animal possession "; it is no longer a strange human being or a demon who speaks through the possessed, but an animal. But we shall have to return to these primitive phenomena when reviewing possession outside the European sphere of civilization.

The strange individuality which has ostensibly entered into the patient always speaks of himself in the first person; when the mouth of the possessed says " I," this almost always means the intruder and not himself.

This is already abundantly clear in the New Testament cases of possession, but still more so in detailed modern accounts. Here, for example, is Gerber's description of the maid of Orlach:

But the transformation of personality is absolutely marvellous. It is very difficult to give a name to this state; the girl loses consciousness, her ego disappears, or rather withdraws to make way for a fresh one. Another mind has now taken possession of this organism, of these sensory organs, of these nerves and muscles, speaks with this throat, thinks with these cerebral nerves, and that in so powerful a manner that the half of the organism is, as it were, paralyzed. It is exactly as if a stronger man drove the owner from his house and looked out of the window at his ease, making himself at home. For no loss of consciousness intervenes, a conscious ego uninterruptedly inhabits the body. The mind which is now in this girl knows perfectly well, even better than before, what is going on around it; but it is another occupant who dwells in the house.[1]

Before pursuing our explanations further, I shall add two quotations which will serve as examples of the dialogues which are generally carried on between the demon and the spectators. The contents are for the most part very commonplace.

The first dialogue is taken from a seventeenth century narrative concerning a little twelve-year-old servant girl who was possessed:

> . . . David Brendel, who for eleven weeks remained night and day beside the little girl, had amongst others these two remarkable conversations with Satan.
> In the first place he asked the evil spirit if he had also been with the beloved Job and the daughter of the woman of Cana. And the devil replied yes, that he had helped to persecute them finely.
> BRENDEL. Have you also been with the blacksmith's daughter up in the clearing at Meissen ?
> THE DEVIL. Yes, there were a hundred of my companions there; I helped to take the rich man to hell.
> B. Do you also know the traitor Judas ?
> D. He sits beside me in hell.
> B. Did you also know the unrepentant Thief, Pilate, Herod, Dr. Johannes Faustus, Christoph Wagner, and Johannes de Luna ?
> D. Oh, they are my best friends. I have in hell the letter of Faust written with his blood.
> B. Does it not burn ?
> D. Oh no !
> B. Of what use is it to you ?
> D. I must have it so that I may produce it and convict him thereby.
> B. As you know so many things, do you also know how to pray ?
> D. I shall shit down your neck.
> B. What would you do to me, if you had me in your power ?
> D. I should break your neck, and my face would be distorted with rage.
> After that, when Satan had exercised his cruel tyranny to his heart's content and revealed many strange mysteries which must not be spoken of, he began to cry out frightfully by the mouth of the little servant girl, and said: "You are minded to send for the Lord and Master."
> B. You are not far from the mark ! (And he began to read aloud a prayer).
> D. Ha ! ha ! ha ! I learnt to read long before you did !

---

[1] Kerner, *Geschichten*, etc., pp. 48 sq.

B. If you boast of being a conjuror, we men know more than
you, for we can pray and you cannot.
D. No, I shall never be able to do that again.[1]

The following extract dates from the beginning of the
nineteenth century:

. . . While the fit was upon her the possessed woman uttered
the lamentations of the damned in the following terms:
I, to be damned ! I so young ! Oh, how richly I deserve it all !
I will curse to all eternity those who are the cause !
QUES. Who are they ?
ANS. My parents; but it shall be my pleasure to torment them
eternally, them and Calvin.
QUES. Why Calvin ?
ANS. I am the wretched Maury whom he wished to use in order
to produce the belief that he would work miracles. I
deserved it all. She also, his wife. As for her, I will
reproach her eternally with being the cause of my horrible
torments. I should have loved your God so much, and I
am damned so young !
Q. What age were you then ?
A. Twenty-three years. But nevertheless I have deserved it all,
for I was a Catholic. But I denied everything. Do not
do as I did. Do not follow my example: an eternity ! . . .
always to suffer ! . . . endlessly ! and already for so
long . . . and no one thinks of it thus !
Q. You have been suffering for more than three hundred years ?
A. If only after three hundred thousand times as much I had
a minute (of rest) ! . . . But no . . . eternity. . . .
How long the word is ! . . . If a confessor had come (to
see me before my death), perhaps I should have had some
remorse. . . . But no ! Yes, I will curse him eternally. . . .
Do not follow my example. . . . I should have blessed
him through all eternity, your God. . . . I should have
had a reign of glory, instead of which I have a reign of
eternal wretchedness. . . . Calvin bid people to murder
the Catholics who would not change their religion. . . .
If every three hundred thousand (years) I had a minute
(of rest) ! . . . But no ! . . . an eternity ! . . .
Q. How were your parents the cause of your downfall ?
A. They consented to this religion (they were converted) and
let me marry a Protestant. . . . If only I had a minute
(of rest) ! I do not even ask for a minute, only half a minute.
Q. Do the torments of hell grow greater or else do they remain
always the same ?
A. How could they grow greater, since they are infinite ? . .
Oh ! to have seen them once, and never see them again,
these frightful (spectacles ?). . . . I am one with the
demon, I died with the demon, and I shall be with the
demon eternally. . . .[2]

[1] *Historischer Bericht, was sich mit einem bessessenen Mägdlein zu
Lewenberg in Schlesien von Lichtmess bis auf Himmelfarth im Jahre
1605 für überaus schreckliche Dinge zugetragen, beschrieben durch Tobiam
Seilerum*, printed in John Bodinus' *Dæmonomania*.
[2] Van Gennep, *Un cas de possession*, "Archives de psychologie," x,
1911, pp. 91 sq.

The strange individuality even frequently relates a sort of life-history. It is hardly necessary to add that these are a matter of pure imagination or reminiscences (the patient's memories) of the real life of the personality which is supposed to have entered into the organism.

One of these verbal autobiographies of a " possessing spirit " set forth in detail, is found in the " Geschichten " of Kerner. It begins thus:

In my lifetime I was called Caspar B——r (the possessed is a woman of thirty-one years) and I was born in 1783. I went to school, but learnt nothing. Nothing entered into me, and at the time of confirmation I had neither faith nor reason. At home the most important thing, good upbringing of the children, was lacking. My father was sometimes too severe, my mother always too kind; she believed all that I said and I lied continually. I disowned my father and he was perfectly aware of it. When that put him into a rage, I insulted him repeatedly, as well as my mother. Once when I was angry I shook my father and took him by the throat. I learnt milling, but did no good at it; I was inclined to drink and forgot myself with persons of the opposite sex. One of them became pregnant by me. I denied stubbornly that I was the father of the child. I said formerly that I had cleared myself on oath, but that is not true; it is true, however, that I drove the girl to take an oath. When she had sworn she said to me: " This oath will weigh upon your soul." From that minute onwards I had no rest. The devil blinded me and for a long time I nursed the idea of killing the woman, but nothing came of it. I ran after other women, and thought no more of her and the child. Another girl was got with child by me, but I denied it. I urged her also to take an oath, but she did not take it because she had already been with others; as she too was already corrupted, that affair did not trouble me much. Nevertheless, I fell deeper and deeper into evil ways, became addicted to drink, and committed breaches of trust, for which I could always find opportunity. To tell the truth my conscience often awoke, but uneasiness drove me to the ale-houses and I drowned my worries in drink. When I was drunk, I tried to pick a quarrel. Once, at Kirchberg, at Staffel's inn, I knocked down the best of my boon companions. He did not remain dead upon the floor, but died soon afterwards of the blows he had received. This affair had no consequences. As for the comrade's name, I certainly do not know it—I think it was Michel Diller. If my conscience has never been at rest on this new count, I have never repented of what I did. I even went sometimes to communion without acknowledging my sins either before or after nor repenting of them. This only made me sink the deeper in drunkenness. Once I stole a watch from a miller's boy, but it did not occur to anyone that I might have done the trick. I sold it for a song and soon squandered the money. At the mill I constantly cheated the customers, but I also did one good thing: I sometimes gave the stolen flour to the poor. . . .[1]

---

[1] Kerner, *Geschichten*, etc., pp. 92 sq.

All the confessions of " possessing spirits " are analogous; they always consist in admissions of wrong-doing.

We must now examine whether possession entails division of personality.

To theology, which until recently has alone had occasion to concern itself with this question, the reality of an inner division in the state of possession is clearly evident. " The patient's conscience," we read in Harnack, " his will and sphere of activity are duplicated. In all subjective truth—frauds naturally always (?) creep in—he has the impression that there is within him a second being which dominates and governs him. He thinks, feels, and acts now as the one, now as the other, and with the conviction that he is dual. He confirms himself and confirms those around him in this belief by actions which are coolly deliberate, even if inwardly compulsive. Enforced self-delusion, cunning activity, and helpless passivity are here combined in an uncanny fashion. . . ."[1]

If recent detailed accounts are examined from this point of view, we discover with surprise that such a duplication of consciousness is not by any means present in every case. It is lacking in many, even in most; the demon generally controls only the organism, while the subject has completely lost consciousness of his habitual individuality. In those cases which, as we have said, appear to constitute the great majority, things happen in a manner quite different from that laid down by theology. Eschenmayer, from personal observation of eight cases, considers " loss of consciousness " as the essential characteristic of possession. He believes that there is " a sudden loss of consciousness " and a " total ignorance of what has taken place during the fit."[2]

> When the fit occurs, the person immediately loses consciousness, the mind's ascendancy over the body ceases, and it is a completely strange individuality which inhabits the body and may be apprehended through it.[3]

In point of fact, this is true in the majority of cases.

The transition between the two states is, and we must again emphasize this, scarcely ever continuous; the new ego does not grow gradually stronger at the expense of the old

---

[1] Harnack, *Medizinisches aus der ältesten Kirchengeschichte*, p. 105.
[2] Kerner, *Geschichten*, etc., p. 140.   [3] Kerner, *ibid.*, p. 141.

one until the latter has disappeared.   Rather the transition is brusque: there is a loss of consciousness and on re-awakening possession has already taken place.   Inversely, on the cessation of the fit no memory of it remains.   We may give certain examples.

Case of a girl of eighteen years:

> Before either of the demons spoke, the girl closed her eyes, and when she reopened them she did not know what the demons had said by her mouth.[1]

Case of a child of ten observed and related by the professor of Theology, Ch. Kortholtus (1653):

> Throughout the whole duration of the fit, the child knew absolutely nothing of what was happening to or around him; but when he came to himself it seemed to him that he had been asleep all the time. Thus when the fit came on in full daylight and lasted far into the evening (as sometimes happened), the patient, when the evil spirit had gone out of him, could not reconcile himself to the idea that it was already night. When he learnt from anyone after the fit what he had done and said, he could not believe it, and cried when he realized that he had treated someone in a rude or insulting manner. So long as the fit lasted he felt no bodily sensations either, except that the latter became sensible when Satan, on his departure or in bidding good-evening (which he did with filthy words of which chaste ears should remain in ignorance) announced that he was now going to torment him. . . . At the end of the fit he had the whole appearance of someone awakened out of sleep by fright, for his eyes closed a little and immediately afterwards he started up like a person in a sudden access of terror.[2]

The following case also deserves mention:

> Without definite cause she was seized with terrible convulsive fits. They appeared to give rise to a magnetic state in which her own individuality was each time as if abolished. Other persons, dead, so she said, uttered demoniac discourses by her mouth. She awakened from that state to regain her original personality without having the least idea of what had happened to her or what she had said, and was therefore unable to give any information whatever about it. . . .[3]
>
> When the demons left her in peace and she came to herself, heard the stories of those who were present and saw the hurts she had received from blows and falls, she dissolved in tears at being in such a state. . . .[4]

Kerner again relates a case observed by him:

> . . . Suddenly the little girl was tossed convulsively hither and thither in the bed, and this lasted for seven weeks; after which suddenly a quite coarse man's voice spoke diabolically through

---

[1] Kerner, *Nachricht*, etc., p. 42, cf. also the case on p. 19.
[2] Fr. Guden, *Schreckliche Geschichte*, pp. 131 sq.
[3] Kerner, *Geschichten*, etc., p. 74.   [4] Kerner, *Nachricht*, etc., p. 29.

the mouth of this eight-year-old child.   She could not be brought
back to life, for every time the demoniac voice resisted, uttered
maledictions, cursed our Saviour and prayer. . . .   Often she
tried with a diabolical face to beat her father and mother and the
onlookers, or else she insulted them, which was not at all in accordance with her character.   If these things were related to her afterwards, she did not wish to know anything about them, but cried
over what she had done.[1]

Johannes Caspar Westphalus reports[2] the case of a little
girl of ten years, whose fits constantly invaded her normal
psychic life, so that on reawakening the patient seemed to
be in the middle of the conversation and continuing the same
sentence which had been interrupted by the fit in which
she had " lost consciousness " (hysteroepilepsy ?).   Neither
François Bayle nor Henri Grameron,[3] moreover, found any
knowledge or remembrance of the fit in the cases of several
women.

With these cases should be compared the nineteenth-
century one described later, which in the transformation
resulting from the copy of a character shows close kinship
with the case of Hélène Smith turning into Cagliostro.   The
state of possession, before attaining its full maturity, began
by an obvious transformation of the patient's character into
that of a deceased mayor of his locality.

In the autumn of 1835 I was taken to the house of a well-to-do
farmer of F., a man called G. of thirty-seven years of age.   Until
his thirtieth year this man had been, by common account, a worthy
fellow, quiet and reasonable.   In his vicinity there was a mayor
who was greatly addicted to drink, extremely proud and quarrelsome.   He had never been on good terms with F.   He died when
the latter reached the age of thirty.
A year later F. was seized with frequent pains, with distensions
of the abdomen, and distorsions of the facial muscles.   But the
most astonishing thing was that his character and mode of life
were at the same time completely transformed.   F. who had
previously been very sober, began to drink enormously; from
peaceable he became quarrelsome, and from modest extremely
proud and arrogant, trying to give orders to everyone in the village,
which drew down upon him heated quarrels and rebukes.
All this caused his wife to fall into the most extreme poverty,
especially when F., formerly such a hard worker, would no longer
attend to his crops.   Nevertheless this new state of affairs was not
continuous; it often lasted for weeks and months, and in the
intervals the old F., sober, modest and peaceable, reappeared until
the bad character took the stage again.

[1] Kerner, *Nachricht*, etc., p. 29.
[2] *Pathologica dæmoniaca*, etc., Lipsiæ, 1707, pp. 9 sq. and 17 sq.
[3] *Relation de l'état de quelques personnes prétendues possédées*, Toulouse,
1682, pp. 10 sq. and 67.

. . . This singular state grew more continuous and more marked during five years, and spelt destruction to the happiness of the household.

In the sixth year F. one day without apparent reason spat in his wife's face and suddenly spoke with a completely strange voice. " And do you know who did that ?"   " Unhappy wretch !" she replied, upon which the voice shouted: " Sow ! don't you know then that I have been in this ass for six years ?   I am the mayor S., and I will drive all you oxen in pairs !" Thereupon he was thrown to the ground by the most violent convulsions. From that day onwards the demoniac voice of the late mayor spoke by the man's mouth, and it was recognized that the complete individuality of the former had for a long time past got the upper hand of his own.

When the demon was at peace in him . . . the old F., amiable and gentle, reappeared and was greatly upset at having recently spoken and acted in so different a fashion. But while he was lamenting thus his eyes were often forcibly closed (the shutting of the eyes indicated the presence of the demon) and the other personality appeared with its curses on God, prayer and F. himself. This individuality came forward with particular rapidity when F. wished to engage in prayer, and rolled him upon the ground in convulsions.[1]

These cases, which it would be easy to multiply, will perhaps be sufficient to prove that the possessed do not always or even generally preserve a clear consciousness of their fits. It is the " demon " alone which expresses itself by their mouth during the fits and the normal individuality has totally disappeared. This is in no way contradicted by the particularly remarkable fact already indicated, that the " possessing spirit " (we retain this terminology for the sake of brevity) is not without intellectual knowledge of that normal individuality. The new personality possesses — whether always in totality the documents do not allow us to judge conclusively, but it seems to be so—an " objective knowledge " of it, but in the way in which we know other people; its relationship is that of a quite distinct individual.

Thus Gerber, who seems to have been a keen observer, relates of the fits of possession of the maid of Orlach:

And in all this the girl herself is not forgotten: he (the possessing spirit) speaks of her, he knows quite well that she is alive, but he pretends *that she is not there, that it is he who is there*,[2] and he pours out abuse and calumnies against the girl herself, whom he never calls anything except " the sow."[3]

---

[1] Kerner, *Nachricht*, etc., pp. 44-46.   [2] Kerner, *ibid.*, p.
[3] *Ibid.*, p. 31.

Another observer says the same thing of the patient U.:

> In the demoniac state or at the onset of possession, the patient always speaks of herself in the third person and it is not then permissible to speak to her; anyone wishing to be understood must rather speak to the demon himself.[1]

This purely logical consciousness which the possessed have of their normal individuality should not be in any way confused with personal consciousness.

Are we confronted in these cases with two new subjects, two " egos " ? If this hypothesis is accepted there are two possible interpretations: we must either believe in the physiologically or metaphysically conditioned appearance of a new subject bearing no relation to the first, the normal one, except that both certainly sprang from the same original physiologico-metaphysical source, or else in a real division of the first subject. In this hypothesis the fact that the subject of the division observed nothing would show no contradiction; it should rather be said that in the nature of things it *cannot* observe anything. The subject only registers the processes which properly belong to it, the states, the forms of activity and affectivity which are its own. If a state is no longer its own but belongs to a second subject, the first immediately ceases to observe it. If there is division of the subject we have therefore two series of psychic processes: the one belongs to the one subject and the other to the other. Neither of the two possesses an immediate knowledge of the other, nor does the subject observe anything of the processes of division. It is also true to say in this connection that only what it in some way perceives belongs to it. There is no immediate communication from subject to subject, but only and always imitation, imagination, intuition.

By the unaided use of intelligence, by the understanding alone, we can conceive no idea of the manner in which such a division is accomplished. This is because with us the unity of the subject is an ultimate one beyond and behind which we cannot penetrate. Our imagination is limited to subjects which exist continuously; we cannot form the remotest idea of how the division of a subject is effected, except by transferring to it, although it is psychic, the general concept of division borrowed from objects in space. All resources fail

---

[1] Kerner, *ibid.*, p. 85.

us here; we cannot observe this process, nor can we from other experimentally acquired ideas concerning the realm of psychic phenomena deduce any kind of conclusion on the subject of the experience, any more than we possess *a priori* any categories, any primordial forms of thought which would permit of it. In whatever way we try to approach the subject, we find ourselves bounded by our horizon which knows in the first place one subject before the process of division, and two subjects afterwards. The phenomenon of splitting-off of the second from the first is inscrutable to us. It would even in reality be doubly incomprehensible, in the first place because it entirely escapes our knowledge, and in the second, because so far as we know the first subject would have nothing to do with it. Psychologically-empirically regarded, this is never the case: the subject always remains what it is. And even if a change took place in its states and affections it would always remain this same subject which can never be mistaken, whereas in the division of a corporate cell the mother-cell after the division generally no longer exists as such: it has become divided. We here touch deliberately upon a point where the hypothesis of division comes into contradiction with logic.

If the subject is something absolute, not only from the point of view of functions or composition, but as constituting a unity in itself and for itself, its division is in every way impossible, particularly if it must be effected without change.

It would be possible to refuse an absolute value to this line of argument because it derives arbitrarily from unities of a functional or compositional nature. These are not in fact susceptible of division unless the first is divided and therefore fundamentally eliminated. But is the same thing true of the division of real unities ?

It seems to me that this objection cannot be accepted. It is inherent in the very idea of division that the thing which divides thereby suffers prejudice. Its unity does not brook disturbance; otherwise its very being ceases to exist; it does not remain to the full extent what it was before.

Whatever attitude we may adopt concerning the possibility of division in the subject, it must nevertheless be asseverated that in the present state of our knowledge it is completely undemonstrable, and personally I cannot see the general lines on which demonstration could be tackled.

If the metaphysical division of the ego or the appearance of a new subject in the organism is admitted, we come back, this time, moreover, with our eyes open, to the old theory of possession which postulated the existence of two different egos in the organism; always, however, with this difference, that the old theory talked of " spirits " which enter into the body, while the new believes either in a metaphysical division of the primary subject or in the " endogenous " appearance of a new subject. In other words, it supposes that there is an absolutely new subject, having until that moment no existence in the world, but which nevertheless does not " incarnate itself," in the old sense of the word, in the body.

We must, moreover, bear in mind that the new subject would bring with it a quantity of " innate " ideas: not everything that it says will be founded upon its own experience; it would know innumerable things without having experienced them, and would be master of speech and a number of other complex capacities without any apprenticeship.

As regards psychology without a subject[1] and its interpretation of disturbances of personality, I shall not criticize it again here, but refer the reader to the thorough examination to which I have subjected it in my *Phänomenologie des Ich*.

After what has been said the only adequate explanation of possession is that postulating a simple alteration in the functions of the ordinary subject. The subject presents no division, nor does any new ego appear in the organism: these hypotheses are entirely superfluous and are beset with the gravest difficulties. It is one single and identical subject which finds itself now in the normal, now in the abnormal state. The individuality, the personality, is only a state of the subject, it is a system of determined functional and affective dispositions.[2] They may change in certain pathological conditions and thus constitute a " second " personality, but apart from this the subject remains the same; nothing is

[1] There is no single phrase in English which gives the exact connotation of "subjektlose Psychologie," which I have literally translated " psychology without a subject." It may, however, be taken to refer to the school of psychology, which, denying the existence of a single continuing " ego," analyzes the personality in terms of a series of separate though correlated psychological states (TRANS.).

[2] Cf. my *Phänomenologie des Ich*, Leipzig, 1910, book i, pp. 315 sq.

changed except its states, the manner in which its functions are operating, and its dispositions.   If the subject no longer considers himself the same, if he believes, especially from the numerical point of view, that he is another subject and not that he is in another state, this is false and should be considered as a passing delusion.

The truth of this assertion becomes fully evident if we consider cases where no radical transformation of the personality takes place in a single operation, but the alteration in the psychic system unfolds slowly and as it were before our eyes.

A state such as those which have been described, in which the normal individuality is temporarily replaced by another and which leaves no memory on return to the normal, must be called, according to present terminology, one of *somnambulism*.   Typical possession is nevertheless distinguished from ordinary somnambulistic states by its intense motor and emotional excitement, so much so that we might hesitate to take it for a form of somnambulism but for the fact that possession is so nearly related to the ordinary form of these states that it is impossible to avoid classing them together.   There are other reasons in support of this, to which we shall return later.   Whatever the reader may think on this question of terminology, the most important thing is to see clearly that we are dealing with a state in which the subject possesses a single personality and a defined character, even if this is not the erstwhile one.   The subject retains the memory of these past states, but he can no longer be conscious that this other personality has normally been his. He considers himself as the new person, the " demon," and envisages his former being as quite strange, as if it were another's: in this respect there is complete analogy with the ordinary somnambulistic variations in personality.   As applied to this form of possession, which seems to have been very frequent, in fact, more so than any other, the statement that possession is a state in which side by side with the first personality a second has made its way into the consciousness is also very inaccurate.   Much more simply, it is the first personality which has been replaced by a second.

The accepted term for this state is " somnambuliform possession," or more simply " demoniacal somnambulism."

2. THE LUCID FORM OF POSSESSION

Side by side with the somnambulistic form of possession there exists another yet more interesting. It is distinguished by the fact that the patient does not lose consciousness of his usual personality, but retains it. In the midst of the terrible spectacle which he presents in the fit, he remains fully conscious of what is happening; he is the passive spectator of what takes place within him.

Careful observers have noted this fact for a long time past. Thus the distinction between the somnambulistic and non-somnambulistic forms of possession is clearly indicated—not, of course, under those names, but in a manner corresponding to the fact—in the early Christian writer John Cassian (c. 350-c. 435). In his *Collationes patrum*, one of the two personages of the dialogue expresses himself thus:

> What you say happens to the possessed when they are in the grip of the unclean spirit, namely, saying or doing what they would not or being constrained to do such things as they know not, is not contrary to our aforementioned teaching. For it is very sure that they do not all bear this invasion by spirits in the same way. Some are so excited that they take no account of what they do or say; but others know it and remember it afterwards.[1]

The following is related of the epidemic of possession at Kintorp (sixteenth century):

> A little before their fits and during the same, they breathed from their mouths a stinking breath which sometimes continued for several hours. In their malady none ceased to have a sane understanding, to hear and recognize those around them, although by reason of the convulsion of the tongue and the parts used for breathing they could not speak during the attack.[2]

Kerner also was not unaware that there were cases of this kind. He writes:

> Some of these patients, when the demon manifests himself and begins to speak in them, close their eyes and lose consciousness as in magnetic sleep; the demon then often speaks through their mouths without them knowing it. With others the eyes remain open and the consciousness lucid, but the patient cannot resist, even with his full strength of mind, the voice which speaks in him; he hears it express itself like a quite other and strange individuality lodged within him and outside his control.[3]

---

[1] *Collationes patrum*, vii, 12. Petschenig (Vienna, 1886-88), trans. Gibson in *Nicene and Post-Nicene Fathers* (Oxford and New York, 1894), xi.

[2] Calmeil, *De la Folie*, i, 269; quoted from S. Goulard, *Histoires admirables et mémorables*, Paris, 1600, vol. i.

[3] Kerner, *Nachricht*, etc., pp. 13 sq.

As it is of great importance to know the manner in which these possessed persons feel their state, I shall, in view of the rarity of precise accounts, quote freely.

The first case is that of a Spanish abbess who was involved in an epidemic of possession at Madrid (1628-31).

The request of Doña Teresa breathed candour and humility. Having related the misfortunes which had befallen three of her companions, she added:

When I began to find myself in this state I felt within me movements so extraordinary that I judged the cause could not be natural. I recited several orisons asking God to deliver me from such terrible pain. Seeing that my state did not change, I several times begged the prior to exorcise me; as he was not willing to do so and sought to turn me from it, telling me that all I related was only the outcome of my imagination, I did all that in me lay to believe it, but the pain drove me to feel the contrary. At length on the day of Our Lady the prior took a stole, and after having offered up several prayers, asked God to reveal to me whether the demon was in my body by unmasking him, or else to take away these sufferings and this pain which I felt inwardly. Long after he had begun the exorcisms and while I was feeling happy to find myself free, for I no longer felt anything, I suddenly fell into a sort of swooning and delirium, doing and saying things of which the idea had never occurred to me in my life. I began to feel this state when I had placed on my head the wood, which seemed as heavy as a tower. This continued in the same way during three months and I rarely felt myself in my normal and natural state. Nature had given me so tranquil a character that even in childhood I was quite unlike my age and loved neither the games, liveliness nor movement habitual to it. Accordingly it could not but be regarded as a supernatural thing that having reached the age of twenty-six years and become a nun and even an abbess, I committed follies of which I had never before been capable. . . . It sometimes happened that the demon Peregrino (that is, the sister possessed by this devil, who played the part of superior to the devils) was in the second-floor dormitory when I was in the parlour, and he would say: " Is Doña Teresa with the visitors ? I will soon make her come. . . ." I did not hear these words, but felt inwardly an inexpressible uneasiness, and rapidly took leave of the persons who had come to see me, doing this without previous deliberation. I then felt the presence of the demon who was in my body; I began without thinking to run, muttering, " Lord Peregrino calls me "; so I came where the demon was, and before arriving there was already speaking of whatever thing they had under discussion and of which I had had no previous knowledge. . . . Some people said that we feigned to be in that state through vanity, and I especially to gain the affection of my nuns and other serious persons; but in order to be convinced that it was not this sentiment which actuated us it suffices to know that out of our full number of thirty nuns there were twenty-five who were in this state, and that of the five others three were my best friends. As for outside persons, we were in a state more likely to inspire them with fear than to make us beloved and sought after.[1]

---

[1] Calmeil, *De la Folie*, ii, pp. 3 sq.

In very severe cases of possession the consciousness may also remain perfectly clear, as is shown by the following instances:

> . . . Finally it often threw him (speaking of an old man) to the ground with all its strength, even while he was praying. These fits often decreased for a period of six months, and then again grew worse. In the years which followed . . ., the convulsions often flung him out of bed at night. The strangest thing was that he was then constrained to insult and abuse wife and children; without being able to give any reason he could no longer endure these latter.
>
> The death of his wife, whom moreover he dearly loved, brought no change to this state any more than did a second marriage which he contracted in spite of these fits. He was advised, although a Lutheran, to apply to the Catholic priests. In presence of such of these as were able to work on him his head turned convulsively and he uttered involuntary roarings, but without articulate words. With others, however, the malady did not make itself felt, but when he went away from them it raged anew with all the more violence. . . .
>
> He had grown much thinner, and when he spoke of his state his head and body were convulsed at frequent intervals and shrank together visibly. He was also suddenly and without being able to resist, obliged to cry out like an animal.
>
> In his natural state he seemed a very gentle and reasonable man and spoke accordingly, but in the midst of a conversation the expression, attitude, and tone of voice would change brusquely and he would begin to walk precipitately and make movements as if he were full of anger: notwithstanding which he was always fully conscious.[1]

One of Kerner's women patients thus describes her own state:

> When the magnetism (the hypnosis) had been applied during three weeks I was obliged immediately after the magnetization to pronounce, in part mentally and in part by soundless movements of the lips, beautiful religious sentences from which I drew great hope of a cure, and the fits became less frequent. But after three weeks had elapsed the Evil One who was hidden within me began to rage again. I was obliged almost without ceasing to utter cries, weep, sing, dance, and roll upon the ground where I went into horrible contortions; I was forced to jerk my head and feet in all directions, howl like a bear and also utter the cries of other animals, things which had, moreover, all happened before on previous occasions.[2]
>
> I strove vigorously (on the doctor's instigation) to repress the fits, but only succeeded at the end of fourteen days and solely by the help and prayers of a dear and very pious woman.
>
> I am never absent, I always know what I am doing and saying, but I cannot always express what I wish; there is something within me which prevents it. In the most furious fits I dare not offer the slightest resistance, for I should only make myself more

---

[1] Kerner, *Nachricht*, etc., pp. 50 sq.   [2] *Ibid.*, pp. 62 sq.

unhappy, and force is, moreover, of no avail; it is therefore voluntarily that I give myself up to the power of the Evil One and let
him rage, for it is only so that I can once more get a little rest.[1]

Eschenmayer relates of the C. St. case observed by him:

> . . . The strange and demoniac individuality which formerly
> contented itself with shouting and uttering animal cries by her
> mouth, began to speak diabolical words. The girl retained con-
> sciousness when the voice spoke, but she could not prevent it
> even by trying with all her might; she heard it resound externally
> like that of a strange individual lodged within her, without being
> able to control or do anything with it.[2]
>
> His (the possessing spirit's) rage was always directed against
> Dürr; when he could do nothing to him with hands and feet (C. St.
> was held down) he spat upon him. Between whiles C. was often
> heard sighing, " Oh, my God !   Oh, my God !"[3]
>
> . . . She had heard and seen everything which happened.
> *For she never lost consciousness*, but in spite of her efforts she could
> not resist the demon when he took possession of her body. We
> asked her whether the tears which the demon shed must not have
> been inspired by her, but she denied it positively.[4]

In the same way Janet relates of his patients:

> . . . He murmured blasphemies in a deep and solemn voice:
> " Cursed be God," said he, " cursed the Trinity, cursed the Virgin
> . . ." then in a higher voice and with eyes full of tears: " It is not
> my fault if my mouth says these horrible things, it is not I . . .
> it is not I. . . .   I press my lips together so that the words may
> not come through, may not break forth, but it is useless; the devil
> then says these words inside me, I feel plainly that he says them
> and forces my tongue to speak in spite of me."
>
> . . . The demon twisted his arms and legs and made him endure
> cruel sufferings which wrung horrible cries from the wretched
> man.[5]

The derangements caused by possession in the victim's
actions are particularly striking:

> . . . Finally the conversation had to be broken off because the
> impression which it made upon him put him completely out of
> temper. He became very weak and was hardly able to utter
> another word. The hands fell inert. We begged him to make
> Caroline wake up in order to revive her a little; at first he would
> not, and it was only by begging that he induced him to do it. But
> then a strange scene began. Someone stood before C. with the
> coffee which the demon did not like. As often as she wished to
> put it to her lips, he came back and she took nothing. If the bowl
> was taken from her, C. came back and wished to drink. Thus
> personalities and faces alternated with a hitherto unheard-of
> rapidity.[6]

---

[1] *Ibid.*, pp. 64 sq.   [2] Eschenmayer, *Konflikt*, etc., p. 4.
[3] *Ibid.*, p. 15.   [4] *Ibid.*, p. 28.
[5] P. Janet, *Névroses et idées fixes*, i, pp. 384 and 383.
[6] Eschenmayer, *Konflikt*, etc., pp. 46 sq., cf. p. 123.

But hardly had D. and R. accompanied her to the staircase
when they dragged her in again to the door, for the demon would
not let her go further. . . . When she had lain down on the sofa
he at once began his diabolical grimaces, shook his fist at us, and
as on the first occasion had a fit of violence during which he shook
Caroline's head so terribly that all her hair flew out around her—
a torture from which she expected the worst, for it always rendered
her unconscious. We then applied ourselves four to one to hold
her head and arms and master him, but he rose up again with
great violence.[1]

. . . The demon had grown yet more hardened, and Caroline
complained that he prevented her from praying either by obsceni-
ties, abuse, or suffering.[2]

During the most violent compulsive motor manifestations
the consciousness sometimes remains perfectly clear. The
following is a case in point:

. . . On the 3rd of January he was taken with a fit so violent
that he believed that if it were repeated he would die. This
fit was of the following nature: the devil threw him into the air
and when he had fallen raised his feet one after the other with
terrible rapidity, making them fall and strike the earth at the same
rapid rate and with a noise that was heard from a long distance,
and which two storeys away resounded like a horse's gallop. Soon
he began to move his arms in circles with the same furious speed,
and to fling himself hither and thither in the bed. We laid him on
two sacks of straw, which were lying upon the floor, so that he
might not do himself an injury. Night and day these unspeakable
torments continued.[3]

Little by little the devil manifested himself more and more by
day. Until now he had only uttered a shrill whistling by the
mouth of the tormented man; in the last days he passed to other
sounds which were like the cries of divers animals. Soon he crowed
like a cock, hissed like a serpent, mewed like a cat, called like
a cuckoo, and finally neighed like a horse.

Then came the most dangerous period. The state of the brother
grew considerably worse and his will, which had until then remained free to resist the devil, often became as if paralyzed. From
time to time the devil twisted his face in order to make a mock of
our worthy father—but the latter said to those around him: "You
should not laugh at these dreadful things but should most earnestly
execrate this demon from hell!" This continued until the expulsion, which took place the other day.[4]

In the afternoon of Thursday the 10th of February, the entry
of the evil spirits really took place. It was pointed out to me
that he had whirled round in a circle three times in a strange
manner, and when I caused the brother who had observed him to
imitate it, that so modest a brother would not indulge in such
buffooneries of his own accord. He came into my room to dance to

---

[1] Eschenmayer, *Konflikt*, pp. 56 sq.
[2] *Ibid.*, p. 92.
[3] Anonymous, *Wahre Geschichte der Befreiung eines vom Teufel
Besessenen* (translated from the review *Der Missionar*, 2nd ed., Aix-
la-Chapelle, 1887, pp. 6 sq.
[4] *Ibid.*, pp. 8 sq.

a light tune. Nevertheless he once more took a staunch resolution to vanquish the infernal influence and began to sing the canticle " All to the honour of my God." The dances which he executed, now and also later, were very finished ones in which he showed much grace and elegance, accompanied by bows, etc. It should be noted that the possessed man had never in his life put one foot before the other to dance, which showed that it was certainly the devil who was the real dancer. Suddenly he cried: " Who wants to come to hell ?" He screamed and clawed with both hands. The devil was therefore present once more.[1]

The possessed was in my room: he danced incessantly. It caused the poor brother atrocious sufferings, as he was obliged to abandon his body to these compulsory and endless dances. When the diabolic voice cried through his mouth: " We will dance him to death !" the exorcism was hurried on.[2]

It is clear that these cases present phenomena entirely similar to those appearing in a number of modern cases of divided personality, such as I have described at length in the first book of my *Phänomenologie des Ich*.

A mild form of these phenomena is by no means rare. They include all cases in which an individual feels that another person thinks within him and criticizes him.

" I feel," said a woman patient of Sollier, " that another person is drawn out of me, as if my limbs were stretched to form new ones. The last time that this happened to me the sensation was so strong that I joked about it, saying, ' I am in the same case as father Adam when his wife was taken out of his side.' The person is absolutely similar to myself. . . . She speaks just as I do, but is always of a contrary opinion. . . . I feel her especially in my head, preventing me from speaking so that she may say the opposite of what I think. This lasts for whole days and exasperates me when I am obliged to hold a conversation. It leaves me with a head like a block of wood for a long time."[3]

If we imagine such secondary processes growing stronger and stronger, not stopping short at mere compulsive ideas, but reaching the stage when a strange vital sentiment is also imposed on the individual, together with, as it were, the whole character of another person, it will be seen that we are getting perceptibly nearer to true possession. Possession with conservation of the original consciousness is a strict extension of the state of a patient of Janet-Raymond who experienced a strong impulse to imitate the bearing of shop-girls and often succumbed to it when he was alone.

A young man of twenty-nine years, Ch., has been subject for the last eighteen months to the kind of fits which are somewhat

[1] *Ibid.*, pp. 16 sq.   [2] *Ibid.*, p. 18.
[3] P. Sollier, *Les Phénomènes d'autoscopie*, Paris, 1903, pp. 19 sq.

gratuitously described as somnambulism. The patient's mother, who has sometimes, but rarely, been present when the fits took place, has described them; but above all—and this is worthy of note—the patient himself has done so; it is he who relates in his own way what he experiences and what takes place. Almost every day, preferably in the morning, he may be surprised alone in his room in strange attitudes. He stands before a mirror and seems to smirk and simper at himself. He smiles, half closes his eyes, throws sidelong looks, bends down and gives little shakes of the head or makes beckoning gestures with his hand. Then he walks about the room, but it is not at all his ordinary gait: he advances with mincing steps, his body swaying to and fro with brusque sideway movements. He balances his hips as if to swing a dress from side to side, and in fact runs his hands over an imaginary skirt, always accompanying this performance with grimaces and little shakes of the head. From time to time he comes to a standstill and changes his style: he now assumes a grave and majestic mien; his eyes are half closed in an expression of modesty and dignity, but he maintains his womanly deportment with its undulating skirts and chatters under his breath, bending right and left. This performance is prolonged with many variants in the grimaces and attitudes for several hours.

If we now question the patient and ask him what those ridiculous scenes mean, he is quite ready to give an account of them and explain them himself, for he remembers them perfectly and will describe in great detail the strange sentiments which animate him while he is indulging in his little comedies. . . .

" If I make these grimaces it is not my fault," he repeats, " it is one of those girls who has eclipsed me again. You cannot imagine the mischief they do me. They are little girls whom I have met every day for two years past in this wretched quarter where I am obliged to live. I feel driven to take up my stand along the road by which they go to the workroom and in this way they eclipse me. When I am alone there are moments in the day when I am no longer my own man: the picture of one of these girls appears to me so vividly that I see her talking, gesticulating . . . It is so clear and precise that I follow the movements of her head and copy them without realizing it. Then it is useless for me to seek myself, it seems to me that I disappear, I lose my ego, my real existence; it is as if I no longer existed, as if they had taken my place. My body takes on the manners of one of them, her funny little ways, the little bird's head moving all the time. When another invades me she produces a different impression, carrying the head high and proudly; others give me erotic ideas or oblige me to chatter like themselves; in fact, each of them transforms me . . . . I feel such self-disgust that I even beat myself; I have put up genuine struggles against this other ego, but it is all in vain. I spend hours seeking for myself in the midst of the impressions left upon me by these girls, and against my will I disappear more and more."[1]

To-day we no longer have the same conviction. A more exact analysis shows that the states of mind apparently

[1] F. Raymond and Pierre Janet, *Dépersonnalisation et possession chez un psychasthénique.* " Journal de psych. norm. et pathol.," 1904, vol. i, pp. 28 sq.

belonging to a second ego are really a part of the original individual.

In early psychological theory such cases are naturally regarded as showing two souls one within the other. The demon has not only entered into the strange organism but into the human soul. " A spirit may dwell within a spirit " declares Kerner.[1]

In the case of the Janet-Raymond patient there is an obsessive state of intuition and imitation. The sense of life which animates the girls takes possession of him and fills him to such a point as to produce compulsive imitation of their bodily movements.

In principle the state of possession is of exactly the same nature. The documents reproduced show how the possessed are filled against their will with psychic activity and, as it were, a complete personality, a demon. But everything is incomparably stronger and more violent than in the case of Janet's psychasthenic, and the scope of these phenomena is also much wider. His case showed bodily attitudes and movements of moderate amplitude. Here, on the contrary, speech also proceeds from the patients, who think and feel with far more acute intensity, and also manifest affective and motor phenomena of such force that several adults are incapable of mastering a frail girl. Finally, there are a number of passive derangements of attitude against which the patient's will is equally powerless. His head is twisted, his tongue hangs far out of his mouth, his body is bent backwards like the arc of a circle, so that the feet almost touch the head, etc.

The compulsive actions are particularly impressive in the case of Jeanne Féry:

> The devils constrained her to cry out in such a way that the clamour never on any occasion lasted less than two or three hours. Often, moreover, seizing her by night, they threw her from her bed . . . several times they prevented her from eating and drinking for the space of three days.
>
> . . . What is more, these same devils feeling their strength little by little to grow less by the power of God in his Church, did their utmost to take away her life. Thus one day amongst other things they led her so swiftly to the river which runs hard by behind the cloister and plunged her therein so cleverly that

---

[1] Kerner, *Nachricht*, etc.

her guard had no succour but to shout for help. Nevertheless, whatever efforts they made to submerge her they were in no way able to do her harm; but she was, by divine grace, and by the good aid of the nuns her fellows, dragged out and brought back safe and sound to the chamber. But they did not for all that desist from following their cruel enterprise: for one day they threw her out of the windows of her chamber into the courtyard of the monastery. And three separate times did they take her up to the highest storeys of the house in order to throw her down, but their efforts were frustrated by divine protection.[1]

In the following case the state was confined in the beginning to compulsive movements which did not at first appear to imply any division of personality, then finally this latter supervened under the influence of the medical " treatment ":

A young gentleman used from time to time to fall into a certain convulsion, having now the left arm alone, now a single finger, now one thigh, now both, now the backbone and the whole body so suddenly shaken and tormented by this convulsion that only with great difficulty could four menservants hold him down in bed. Now it is a fact that his intellect was in no way disturbed nor tormented: his speech was untrammelled, his mind not at all confused, and he was in full possession of all his senses, even at the height of this convulsion. He was racked at least twice a day by the said convulsion, on coming out of which he was quite well except that he felt prostrate with fatigue by reason of the torments which he had suffered. Any skilled doctor might have judged that it was a true epilepsy if the senses or the mind had been deranged withal. All the best doctors being called in, judged that it was a convulsion approaching very nearly to epilepsy which was excited by a malignant vapour enclosed in the backbone, from whence the said vapour spread only to those nerves which have their origin in the backbone, without in any way attacking the brain. This judgment having been formed as to the cause of the sickness, nothing of what the art prescribes was left undone to relieve this poor sick man; but in vain we put forth all our efforts, being more than a hundred leagues from the cause of the maladg.

For in the third month they discovered that it was a devil who was the author of this ill, who declared himself of his own accord, speaking freely by the mouth of the sick man in Latin and Greek, although this latter had no knowledge of Greek. He discovered the secrets of those who were there present, and principally of the doctors, mocking at them because with useless medicines they had almost caused the death of the sufferer. Any and every time that his father came to see him, as soon as he saw him from afar he cried out: " Make him go away, do not let him come in, or else take from him the chain round his neck," for being a knight he wore, according to the custom of the French knights, the collar of the Order from which hung the image of St. Michael. When aught from the Holy Scriptures was read in his presence he became much more irritated, indignant, and agitated than before. When

---

[1] *La possession de Jeanne Féry* (1584) " Bibliothèque diabolique," vol. iv, pp. 8 sq.

the paroxysm had passed the poor tormented man remembered all that he had done or said, repenting thereof and saying that against his will he had done or said those things.[1]

We have very full information concerning the possession of Jeanne des Anges, who has left us an autobiography. This is not the best personal evidence available; as coming from a highly hysterical person of somewhat weak moral nature, it must be accepted with great reserve; but in any case it is interesting enough and not least so as constituting an authoritative source of information concerning a personality of this psychic type.   In the study of possession it has *inter alia* some importance as showing how the excitement of anti-religious sentiments resulting from the influence of the idea of possession, is partially accepted by an hysterical young nun not particularly well suited to the life of devotion, but who, on the other hand, does not rise above the religious ideas of her environment but conforms to them outwardly from force of habit and upbringing.   This partial acceptance takes place when the ideas are, moreover, so potent that the girl is impelled to suffer their ascendancy which is stronger than her own will.   Like many other cases of possession the state is further complicated by hallucinatory phenomena which, however, I shall have no occasion to discuss.

At the commencement of my possession I was almost three months in a continual disturbance of mind, so that I do not remember anything of what passed during that time. The demons acted with abounding force and the Church fought them day and night with exorcisms.[2]

My mind was often filled with blasphemies and sometimes I uttered them without being able to take any thought to stop myself.   I felt for God a continual aversion and nothing inspired me with greater hatred than the spectacle of his goodness and the readiness with which he pardons repentant sinners. My thoughts were often bent on devising ways to displease him and to make others trespass against him.   It is true that by the mercy of God I was not free in these sentiments, although at that time I did not know it, for the demon beclouded me in such a way that I hardly distinguished his desires from mine; he gave me, moreover, a strong aversion for my religious calling, so that sometimes when he was in my head I tore all my veils and such of my sisters' as I could lay hands on; I trampled them under-

---

[1] A case of Ambroise Paré, quoted by Calmeil, *De la Folie*, etc., vol. i, pp. 176 sq. *Œuvres complètes d'Ambroise Paré*, Paris, 1841, vol. iii, pp. 68 sq.
[2] *Sœur Jeanne des Anges*, " Bibliothèque diabolique," p. 65.

foot, I chewed them, cursing the hour when I took the vows. All this was done with great violence, I think that I was not free.[1]

. . . As I went up for Communion the devil took possession of my hand, and when I had received the Sacred Host and had half moistened it the devil flung it into the priest's face. I know full well that I did not do this action freely, but I am fully assured to my deep confusion that I gave the devil occasion to do it. I think he would not have had this power if I had not been in league with him. I have on several other occasions had similar experiences for when I resisted them stoutly I found that all these furies and rages dispersed as they had come, but alas, it too often happened that I did not strongly constrain myself to resist, especially in matters where I saw no grievous sin. But this is where I deluded myself, for because I did not restrain myself in little things my mind was afterwards taken unawares in great ones. . . .[2]

At this reply the evil spirit got into such a fury that I thought he would kill me; he beat me with great violence so that my face was quite disfigured and my body all bruised with his blows. It often happened that he treated me in this way.[3]

As for outward things, I was much troubled by almost continual rages and fits of madness. I found myself almost incapable of doing any good thing, seeing that I had not an hour of the liberty to think of my conscience and prepare myself for a general confession although God caused me to be moved towards it and I was so minded.[4]

By far the best account that we possess of these states comes from the French mystic Surin, who, already much exhausted by a long and rigorous life of asceticism, himself fell a victim in the course of his exorcisms to the great seventeenth-century epidemic of possession at Loudun.

His narrative is so interesting that it should be reproduced in all its details so far as these have hitherto been given to the public. One important manuscript is still unpublished, and unfortunately the war precluded me from consulting this document, which the authorities of the Bibliothèque Nationale had, with a kindness deserving of thanks, expressed readiness to communicate to me,[5] and which may be presumed to contain many further matters of interest. It is so easy to divest Surin's writings of the theological form in which he describes his condition that this necessitates no explanations. He holds his state to be possession in the true sense of the word, and construes it as a result of his sins.

---

[1] *Sœur Jeanne des Anges*, p. 71.   [2] *Ibid.*, p. 79.
[3] *Ibid.*, p. 85.   [4] *Ibid.*, p. 108.
[5] In this connection I must point out that the statement of H. Diels (*Internationale Monatschrift*, book ix (1915), pp. 133 sq.), according to which the French Bibliothèque Nationale, at the Government's suggestion, categorically refused an exchange service with Germany, is inaccurate.

Surin's chief testimony is a letter to a spiritual friend written on May 3rd, 1635, and which seems in the first place to have been printed separately. It is generally quoted from the extracts of Calmeil[1] and Ideler,[2] but their versions are not very complete and Ideler's translation is slightly inaccurate in places. I shall therefore go back to the presumably complete version found in the work: *Cruels effets de la vengeance du Cardinal Richelieu ou Histoire des Diables de Loudun.* This book appeared anonymously, and is by a writer called Aubin.

There are scarce any persons to whom I take pleasure in recounting my adventures, save your Reverence, who listens to them willingly and derives from them reflections which would not readily occur to others who do not know me as does your Reverence. Since the last letter which I wrote you I have fallen into a state very different from anything I had anticipated, but in full conformity with the Providence of God concerning my soul. I am no longer at Marennes, but at Loudun, where I received your letter recently. I am in perpetual conversation with the devils, in the course of which I have been subject to happenings which would be too lengthy to relate to you and which have given me more reason than I ever had to know and to admire the goodness of God. I wish to tell you something of them, and would tell you more if you were more private. I have engaged in combat with four of the most potent and malicious devils in hell. I, I say, whose infirmities you know. God has permitted the struggles to be so fierce and the onslaughts so frequent that exorcism was the least of the battlefields, for the enemies declared themselves in private both by night and day in a thousand different ways. You may imagine what pleasure there is in finding oneself at the sole mercy of God. I will tell you no more, it suffices that knowing my state you should take occasion to pray for me. At all events, for the last three and a half months I have never been without a devil at work upon me.

Things have gone so far that God has permitted, I think for my sins, what has perhaps never been seen in the Church, that in the exercise of my ministry the devil passes out of the body of the possessed woman and entering into mine assaults and confounds me, agitates and troubles me visibly, possessing me for several hours like a demoniac. I cannot explain to you what happens within me during that time and how this spirit unites with mine without depriving me either of consciousness or liberty of soul, nevertheless making himself like another me and as if I had two souls, one of which is dispossessed of its body and the use of its organs and stands aside watching the actions of the other which has entered into them. The two spirits fight in one and the same field which is the body, and the soul is as if divided. According to one of its parts it is subject to diabolic impressions and according to the other to those motions which are proper to it or granted by God. At the same time I feel a great peace under

---

[1] Calmeil, *De la Folie*, vol. ii, pp. 59 sq.
[2] *Versuch einer Theorie des religiösen Wahnsinns*, vol. i, pp. 394 sq. (Halle, 1848).

God's good pleasure and, without knowing how it arises, an extreme rage and aversion for him, giving rise to violent impulses to cut myself off from him which astonish the beholders; at the same time a great joy and sweetness, and on the other hand a wretchedness which manifests itself by cries and lamentations like those of the demons; I feel the state of damnation and apprehend it, and feel myself as if transpierced by the arrows of despair in that stranger soul which seems to be mine, while the other soul which is full of confidence laughs at such feelings and is at full liberty to curse him who is the cause; I even feel that the same cries which issue from my mouth come equally from the two souls, and am at a loss to discern whether they be caused by joy or by the extreme fury with which I am filled. The tremblings with which I am seized when the Holy Sacrament is administered to me arise equally, so far as I can judge, from horror of its presence which is insufferable to me and from a sincere and meek reverence, without it being possible for me to attribute them to the one rather than the other or to check them. When I desire by the motion of one of these two souls to make the sign of the cross on my mouth, the other averts my hand with great swiftness and grips my finger in its teeth to bite me with rage. I scarcely ever find orisons easier or more tranquil than in these agitations; while the body rolls upon the ground and the ministers of the Church speak to me as to a devil, loading me with maledictions, I cannot tell you the joy that I feel, having become a devil not by rebellion against God but by the calamity which shows me plainly the state to which sin has reduced me and how that taking to myself all the curses which are heaped upon me my soul has reason to sink in its own nothingness. When the other possessed persons see me in this state it is a pleasure to see how they triumph and how the devils mock at me saying: " Physician, heal thyself; go now and climb into the pulpit; it will be a fine sight to see him preach after he has rolled upon the ground." *Tentaverunt, subsannaverunt me subsannatione, frenduerunt super me dentibus suis.*

What a cause for thankfulness that I should thus see myself the sport of the (evil) spirits, and that the justice of God on earth should take vengeance on my sins ! What a privilege to experience the state from which Jesus Christ has delivered me, and to feel how great is the redemption, no longer by hearsay but by the impress of that same state; and how good it is to have at once the capacity to fathom that misery and to thank the goodness which has delivered us from it with so many labours ! This is what I am now reduced to almost every day. It is the subject of great disputes, and *factus sum magna quæstio,* whether there is possession or not, and if it may be that such untoward accidents befall the ministers of the Gospel. Some say that it is a chastisement of God upon me to punish an error; others say some other thing, and I am content and would not change my fortune with another, having the firm persuasion that there is nothing better than to be reduced to great extremities. That in which I am is such that I can do few things freely: when I wish to speak my speech is cut off; at Mass I am brought up short; at table I cannot carry the morsel to my mouth; at confession I suddenly forget my sins; and I feel the devil come and go within me as if he were at home. As soon as I wake he is there; at orisons he distracts my thoughts when he pleases; when my heart begins to swell with the presence of God he fills it with rage; he makes me sleep when I would wake; and, publicly, by the mouth of the possessed woman, he boasts of being

my master; the which I can in no way contradict. Enduring
the reproach of my conscience, and upon my head the sentence
pronounced against sinners, I must suffer it and revere the order
of Divine Providence to which every creature must bow. It is
not a single demon who torments me; there are usually two; the
one is Leviathan, the adversary of the Holy Spirit, for according
to what they have said here, they have in hell a trinity whom the
magicians worship: Lucifer, Beelzebub, and Leviathan, who is
third in hell, as some authors have already observed and written.
Now the works of this false Paraclete are quite contrary to those
of the true, and impart a desolation which cannot be adequately
described. He is the chief of all our band of demons and has
command of this whole affair which is perhaps one of the strangest
ever seen. In this same place we see Paradise and Hell, nuns
who taken in one way are like Ursula and in the other worse than
the most abandoned in all sorts of disorders, filth, blasphemy, and
rages. If it please your Reverence, I do not at all desire that you
should make my letter public. You are the only one to whom,
except for my confessor and my superiors, I have been willing to
say so much. It is but to maintain between us such communication as may assist us to glorify God in whom I am your very humble
servant.
                                       JEAN-JOSEPH SURIN.

   And by way of post-scriptum, I beg you to have prayers said
for me of which I have need, for during whole weeks I am so stupid
towards heavenly things that I should be glad if someone would
make me say my prayers like a child and explain the *Pater Noster*
to me simply. The devil has said to me: I will deprive thee of
everything and thou shalt have need to keep thy faith for I will
make thee besotted. He has made a pact with a witch to prevent
me from speaking of God and so that he may have strength to keep
my spirit broken, and I am constrained, in order to have some
understanding, to hold the Holy Sacrament often against my head,
using David's key to unlock my memory. . . .
   I am content to die since Our Lord has done me this grace to
have retrieved three consecrated Hosts which three witches had
delivered into the hands of the devil, who brought them back to
me publicly from Paris where they were under the mattress of a
bed and left the Church in possession of this honour, to have given
back in some measure to her Redeemer what she had received of
Him, having ransomed it from the devil's clutches. I do not know
if Our Lord will soon take my life, for being hard put to it in this
affair I gave it to Him and promised to part with it for the price
of these three Hosts. It seems that the devil, by the bodily ills
which he inflicts on me, desires to exercise his right and gradually
wear me out.

   This narrative is a document of the utmost value, which
offers striking confirmation of all that we have hitherto said
as to the nature of possession. At the same moment Surin
feels himself full of profound peace and furious rage. His
soul is " as if divided," he is filled simultaneously with
different sentiments;[1] one of these is normal, it is that of

   [1] On sentiments of a dual nature, further details will be found in my
Phänomenologie des Ich, vol. i, chap. xiv.

Surin in the narrowest sense; the other is of a compulsive and coercive nature, and is regarded by Surin as belonging to the demon. It is very evident from his account how false is the conception which supposes that there are really two egos in the consciousness, as has hitherto been maintained by the majority of authors treating of possession, (an error which I also shared until I made a closer study of the problems of the ego.) He says as clearly as possible that both groups of sentiments belong to him in person; he is filled at the same time with serene joy and foaming rage. And if he does not accept the rage it nevertheless appears to him that the strange soul is " like to his own." In reality it is his also, only these states have a character of compulsion. If he is of opinion, like all analogous cases, that his state is dual, it is an illusion which tries to impose itself upon him, but to which he never completely surrenders; it always remains clear to him that the second sentiments are states which belong to him equally. This is particularly well demonstrated by his remark that he seems to himself to have become Satan: in fact, this individuality is a new and extremely complex state of himself, as is his original individuality. Up to this point he has a certain right to say that he has assumed a Satanic personality.

The conception that there are really two different subjects and not merely two different states of one and the same subject presents insurmountable difficulties of interpretation. How, indeed, would it be possible for Surin to say of himself that he feels the rage and anger of the demon, that he finds himself in a dual affective state and that the second soul is also similar to his own ? How could he feel sentiments immediately if they were not his own sentiments ? How is it possible to imagine one ego entering into another with subsequent direct apprehension thereby ?

Whichever way we turn, it is impossible to avoid the conviction that the impressions of others are only experienced indirectly (*nacherlebt*) and not immediately like our own. This " after experience " has not necessarily an active character; it may also be purely passive or compulsive.

There is really a separate problem, as we are beginning to perceive, in the fact that the interpenetration of mind by mind is not possible, and that no one ever experiences anything but his own emotional states. This is evidently not a purely empirical statement, for then the contrary state of things might also formerly have been realized. We shall have to establish a necessity in the realm of empirical knowledge, exactly as we affirm in all certitude that the movement of a body can take place only in the present and the future, but no longer in the past. As a matter of fact, the position of such judgments from the point of view of the theory of knowledge is not yet explained, however obvious they may be.

The quotations which we have made from Surin are supplemented by the still unpublished manuscript of the Bibliothèque Nationale of Paris. Delacroix has given extracts from it in his excellent work, *Etudes d'histoire et de psychologie du mysticisme.*[1] I have borrowed from him the following:

> Surin's turbulent state of possession, to which the quotation given above relates, ceased after he had succeeded in his exorcisms at Loudun and brought about the recovery of the principal case of possession in the convent, Jeanne des Anges. It was, however, not given to Surin to regain his first state; he traversed a peculiar state of depression which did not show the same excitement as the first, but which visibly belongs to the group of phenomena of possession. He came out, as he himself relates, " of the manifest obsession which rendered the presence of the Evil One in his person sensible to him, and passed into an inner travail of the most extreme nature."
>
> These torments lasted no less than approximately twenty-five years.
>
> . . . He came to lose all power of movement and even of speech, and towards the autumn of that year he left Loudun. He became so overwhelmed that he lost all ability to preach or to take part in conversation. . . . His suffering rose to a pitch of violence where he even lost the power of speech and was dumb for seven months without being able to say Mass, read or write, even to dress and undress himself, or, in short, make any movement. He fell into a sickness unknown to all the doctors, whose remedies were of no avail. Thus he passed the whole winter.

Surin describes his state as a " constriction " (*resserrement*). It was a case of motor inhibitions due to autosuggestion, but other phenomena also supervened.

> One morning he found himself troubled in his natural mind by fits of rage which rendered him altogether contemptible in his own eyes; that is to say, there appeared in him compulsive sentiments for which he imputed blame to himself.
>
> He had temptations to suicide and even made a serious attempt. He had an " extreme and vehement impulse to kill himself." Even when he was conscious of doing some good action he thought he was disobeying God by leaving the ranks of the damned to which he had been relegated. He also had fits of hatred against

---

[1] Paris, 1908, chapter on *Peines mystiques.*

Jesus Christ. . . .   He had heretical ideas, notably that of Calvin on the Eucharist, and very violent temptations against chastity.

He reached a condition in which he could neither walk nor stand upright, nor attempt to dress and undress himself. . . . He was driven to outrageous things contrary to human intelligence.   He kept reason and awareness.   But " this horrible power which governed me made me do what I would not and I accomplished it to the letter. . . ."

In spite of all this his soul did not cease from looking towards God.   " Often in the midst of these infernal pains came impulses to unite myself to Jesus Christ in unions with Him which were very sweet and the memory of which greatly touches me now, but which were completely lost and forgotten when the despair returned. . . .   It is yet another marvel that during all this time of my greatest sufferings and despair I composed all the canticles on divine love which being gathered together have made a whole book . . . and gave myself great strength by composing them . . . ."   In his trials he felt at once despair of acting in conformity with the will of God and desire to do so.

This state of Surin is essentially of the same nature as the case of possession at Loudun already cited.   It is nevertheless distinguished therefrom by the lack of compulsive acts of violence and in addition, at least as it seems from Delacroix' publication, by something very important to us: the absence of the idea of possession.   It seems that Surin simply regarded himself as a sick man.   " They are in no wise madnesses, but extreme sufferings of the mind," said he. Those around him were incapable of reading his mind and regarded him as mad during the twenty years which his illness lasted, by reason of the great number of senseless compulsive actions which he committed and his inability to make others understand him—his voluntary actions were always thwarted by inhibitions or compulsions—and he was inscribed upon the registers of his Order as sick in mind. This was justifiable inasmuch as from the psychic point of view he was really seriously ill, but unjustifiable inasmuch as it is only customary to class as insane those whose understanding deserts them in their fits.

The total duration of the illness of Surin, who was already a neurotic exhausted by ascetic practices when he came to Loudun, amounted to more than twenty years; he was delivered from it in the last years of his life, but then fell into another abnormal state which cannot be studied here.[1]

Surin's autoanalysis should be read in conjunction with

[1] Particulars of this will be found in vol. ii of my *Phänomenologie des Ich.*   Cf. also Delacroix, *op. cit.*

the statements of Ludwig Staudenmaier.[1] Following on experiments in the writing known as automatic, a number of obsessive personalities developed which he thereafter cultivated more or less voluntarily, but which subsequently acquired a high degree of autonomy and finally produced in him a strong resemblance to the possessed, particularly of the non-somnambulistic type of Surin.   Only the element of violent agitation remained absent.   Although Staudenmaier also fails to interpret the case aright—he leans towards the synthetic conception of the ego which prevails in Franco-English psychology—his analyses nevertheless show with great clarity that the compulsive functions of his own ego are concerned throughout.   These functions developed to an extraordinarily high degree, so that he came to feel them as highly obsessive.   Staudenmaier seems never to have fallen into the somnambulistic state properly so called, but like Surin to have retained full and uninterrupted consciousness of his state.   (In addition to these phenomena and others purely psychological, particularly hallucinations, he developed other abnormal psycho-physical manifestations, the reality of which is beginning to be generally recognized, but whose nature is still unexplained, for which reason I shall not discuss them.)

From the beginning of his experiments in automatic writing Staudenmaier preserved the full or almost full consciousness of what he wrote under compulsion in the passive state.   There was therefore no complete unconsciousness of the writing as has been claimed, at least with reference to other cases.   But the character of the writing was without doubt purely passive.   He wrote compulsively with his sensory consciousness, but not voluntarily.   Acoustic sensations were soon added: he heard immediately before what he had to write, and this phenomenon rapidly took precedence, so that Staudenmaier finally gave up the writing completely and contented himself with listening to the voices with which he was able to converse while fully conscious.   Some of these voices were evil in character, as we have seen in other cases.   In spite of a proper realization that they were not incarnated spirits, Staudenmaier treated

[1] Staudenmaier, *Die Magie als experimentelle Naturwissenschaft*, Leipzig, 1912.

them as autonomous beings, as did the early cases of possession, spoke to them, reproached them, etc., which evidently favoured the development of these secondary phenomena.

I will confine myself to reproducing a few particularly interesting extracts from his description:

> In the end the inner voice . . . made itself heard too often and without sufficient reason, and also against my will; a number of times it was bad, subtly mocking, vexatious, and irritable. For whole days at a time this insufferable struggle continued entirely against my will.
>
> Often the statements of these so-called beings proved to be fabrications. Opposite the house where I lived a strange tenant was just moving in. By way of test I asked my spirits his name. Without hesitation I received the reply: *Hauptmann von Müller.* It later proved that the information was completely false. When in such a case I afterwards reproached them gently, I often elicited this sincere reply: " It is because we cannot do otherwise, we are obliged to lie, we are evil spirits, you must not take it amiss !" If I then became rude they followed suit.
>
> " Go to blazes, you fool ! You are always worrying us! You ought not to have summoned us ! Now we are always obliged to stay near you !" When I used stronger language it was exactly as if I had hurled insults at a wall or a forest: the more one utters the more the echo sends back. For a time the slightest unguarded thought that passed through my mind produced an outburst from the inner voices.[1]

Particularly precious is Staudenmaier's admission that little by little the nexus of personal sentiments corresponding to the different voices manifested themselves in him.

> Later there were manifested in a similar manner personifica-tions of princely or ruling individuals, such as the German Emperor, and furthermore of deceased persons such as Napoleon the First. At the same time a characteristic feeling of loftiness took possession of me; I became the lord and master of a great people, my chest swelled and broadened almost without any action on my part, my attitude became extremely energetic and military, a proof that the said personification was then exercising an important influence. For example, I heard the inner voice say to me majestic-ally: " I am the German Emperor." After some time I grew tired, other conceptions made themselves strongly felt and my attitude once more relaxed. Thanks to the number of personalities of high rank who made their appearance in me, the idea of grandeur and nobility gradually developed. My highness is possessed by a great desire to be a distinguished personality, even a princely or governing personality, or at least—this is how I explain after the event—to see and imitate these personalities. My highness takes great interest in military spectacles, fashionable life, dis-tinguished bearing, good living with abundant choice beverages, order and elegance within the house, fine clothing, an upright military carriage, gymnastics, hunting and other sports, and seeks

---

[1] *Ibid.*, pp. 20 sq.

accordingly to influence my mode of life by advice, exhortations, orders, and threats.   On the other hand, my highness is averse to children, common things, jesting and gaiety, evidently because he knows princely persons almost exclusively by their ceremonial attitude in public or by illustrations.   He particularly detests illustrated journals of satirical caricatures, total abstainers, etc. I am, moreover, somewhat too small for him.[1]

In other words, Staudenmaier is moved by personal sentiments which are not identical with his own and which he does not fully accept.   But these states of feeling are also and naturally states of his own ego and not those of another. He excludes them *a priori* from his character or else gives himself up to them for a time and imagines that he has passed into another psychic state.   For example, in the following case which concerns a feeling that he is a child:

> Another important rôle is played by the " child " personifica-tion: " I am a child.   You are the father.   You must play with me."   Then childish verses are hummed, " The little wheel goes thud, thud, thud," " Comes a little flying bird."   Wonderfully tender childishness, and artless ways such as no real child would show in so marked and touching a manner.   In moments of good humour I am called Putzi, or else he says simply " My dear Zi." When walking in town I must stop at the toy-shop windows, make a detailed inspection, buy myself toys, watch the children playing, romp on the ground, and dance in a ring as children do, thus consistently behaving with an entire absence of loftiness.   If on the request of " the child " or " the children " (at times there occurred a division into several kindred personalities), I happen to pause in a shop and look over the toy counter, this personification bubbles over with joy and in a childish voice cries out ecstatically: " Oh, how lovely !   It's really heavenly !"[2]
> Since the " child " personification has acquired a greater in-fluence over me, not only has my interest in childish ways, toys, and even shops increased, but also my search for childish satisfactions and the innocent joys of the heart, a fact which acts upon the organism, rejuvenating and refreshing it, and driving away many of the cares of the grown man, accustomed more and more to use his intelligence.   In the same way a number of other personifica-tions also have a beneficial effect upon me.   For example, my interest in art and understanding of artistic things have increased considerably.   Particularly remarkable and characteristic of the profound division which takes place in me is the following fact: that whereas my interest in art was formerly very slight, especially as regards that of antiquity and the Middle Ages, certain of my personifications are passionately interested in these latter and have continually impelled me to devote attention to them.[3]

It will not be surprising to find that with Staudenmaier the sentiments of strange personalities also have an influence on the physiognomy.

[1] *Ibid.*, pp. 29 sq.   [2] *Ibid.*, p. 30.   [3] *Ibid.*, p. 70.

The facial expression often had a character of its own, and I no longer displayed my known and habitual features, a fact which did not escape the persons who knew me well.[1]
. . . It also often happened that my features changed visibly. When the notions of grandeur were particularly active in me I found on glancing into the mirror that the whole expression of my face was becoming that of Napoleon. I could often recognize merely by a glance what cerebral centres were playing the leading part, for they visibly imprinted on me the lineaments of the persons, real and fictitious, whom they were imagining most vividly.[2]

The phenomena of obsessive personality alone are remarkable, but the fantastic nature of the psychic image grows still more marked in a number of cases: at times there arises a very remarkable inter-relationship between the possessed and the personality imposing itself upon him. It is not merely impulses and inhibitions which traverse the normal life of the individual and may, as in the case of Staudenmaier, disturb it so little that those around him have no knowledge of them, the possessed retaining a sane judgment of his state and not being, therefore, deranged in the strict sense; but the phenomena of obsession take forms which at first sight disconcert even the modern psychologist and oblige him to bethink himself in order that the sequence of the psychical processes may become quite clear to him. The possessed, already filled with the idea that a strange spirit has entered into him, behaves towards his abnormal state in a manner consistent with this belief. Like Staudenmaier he addresses the demon in his soul, talks to him, petitions him, etc.; in short, treats him as an ordinary living person. And now comes the most remarkable fact: the " second " personality behaves as if it really were such a being. It gives replies, makes promises, feels repentance, just like a real person.

Things may reach the point of an audible conversation between the possessed and his state of psychic compulsion. In such cases we are confronted by a marked aggravation of this state which also appears in modern nervous affections, where it takes the form of a colloquy with pseudo-hallucinations.

In possession, therefore, everything is accentuated. It is not in imagination that the possessed hears someone answer him, his own organs of speech enter into movement which is not voluntary but automatic and compulsive.

[1] *Ibid.*, p. 28.   [2] *Ibid.*, p. 101.

Thus there occurs the singular spectacle of two persons appearing to express themselves through the same body. It is said in one case that the phenomenon was of such a nature " that one seemed to hear two persons engaged in a sharp dispute and loading one another with abuse."[1]

In certain cases we have exact information as to the gist of these " conversations with oneself," and even possess fragments of them. They are in the same naïf form which the " possessing spirit " uses sometimes in furnishing autobiographic details.

The " obsessing personality " in lucid possession behaves both towards the outside observer and the exorcising priest as if it were a real person, a statement equally true of somnambulistic possession. The documents quoted have already contained some examples; reports show that the possessing spirit talks with the exorcist, grows angry with him, insults him, attacks him, replies to questions—in short, behaves as if a demon had entered into the body of the possessed.

The accounts of possession are full of these things. In lucid cases the " demon " also converses with the person who " speaks to " him. It is as if actors interpolated here and there in their parts replies improvised on the spur of the moment. There is only this essential difference, that they would act voluntarily whereas the possessed replies on compulsion. I will quote examples taken from original texts:

> Caroline related that the night before when she was reciting a long canticle he had intervened several times in a great rage; but that, when reminded of his promise, he had remained quiet from one o'clock onwards.[2]
> Caroline told us several times that the demon, in consequence of the scurvy tricks of his comrades in hell, was always made to waver in well-doing, which she felt deeply, and was only able to keep him in the right way by remonstrances and incessant prayers. But she perceived that she could not master him unaided and keep him from backsliding.[3]
> . . . On the other hand, Caroline received this morning at seven o'clock from the higher angels the order to make another serious effort alone with him. She obeyed. She began by prayers and supplications. She exhorted him in so lively a manner that the demon was moved thereby and prayed. He repeated three canticles after her. In the beginning it was to all appearance with earnestness. She went through each passage of the verses as if she were teaching him the catechism, aptly and well, so that he

---

[1] Quoted by Janet, *Névroses et idées fixes*, Paris, 1898, i, p. 884.
[2] Eschenmayer, *Konflikt*, etc., p. 30.   [3] *Ibid.*, p. 67.

might apply everything to his inner state. We marvelled at the cleverness with which she said: " Look, my dear child, it is thus that you should understand it." In this way she brought him to speak of confession, but this already was only by forcing him. In the end he was, at her express injunction, to say the Lord's Prayer three times. The first time he got through it, but we observed that his seriousness was vanishing. The second time when he was in the middle of the prayer he began to laugh. To our reprimand he replied arrogantly: " I won't pray any more !" Caroline tried to force him, but in vain; the angel told her that she must give it up. This attempt had lasted from seven to eleven o'clock in the morning.[1]

When he was asked whether he also went to church, he replied that he liked to go, not to hear the sermon but to see beautiful and well-dressed ladies. . . . As for the Gospel, he had never troubled about it but had believed that he would go to heaven. When we asked him whether after death he had not at least been permitted to go and see it, he replied: " What do you suppose ! I wasn't allowed to have a taste of it, for the Old Man (it was thus that he referred to Satan) came and growled: " Off with you to hell !" His departure thither was hastened with a kick, then the Old Man got out the register of sins, read him all his own, and with an ironic smile said to him: " Look, W., I tempted you, then seduced you; why did you always listen to me ? Now you are mine!" No man knows the half of his sins, but they are all recorded there in writing as fine as a hair.

He gave with a shudder of fear particulars of the place in hell where he had been. " Everything which is here esteemed beautiful, lovable, and agreeable, becomes down there hateful, nauseating, and shapeless. The devil forces one to continual copulation with the women with whom one has had one's way on earth. There is a stench, filth, and loathsomeness which can hardly be borne," etc., etc.[2]

In many other cases there are also " attempts at conversion " of the demon. The exorcist speaks as if he had before him a sinner to convert. Thus conversations of the following type occur:

> . . . Although all the manifestations appeared unfavourable
> I wanted . . . to make an attempt to know whether there was in
> him any response to good. I asked gravely: " Can you repeat
> ' God be merciful to me a poor sinner and receive me with pity
> in the name of our Lord Jesus Christ ?' " He refused and told us
> contemptuously to mind our own business, saying: " I shall not
> do it, and even if I did, what good would it do me ? For me all
> pity is lost !" Nevertheless, we did not leave him but comforted
> him with suitable passages from the Gospels. In the end he began
> to stammer like a child: " Go-Go-God !" Here he stopped and
> said: " Ah, if you knew how much that costs a damned soul you
> would not insist !" . . .[3] Soon he lent ear to our remonstrances
> and we took up again the thread of yesterday's conversation. He
> now had the choice of preparing for initiation by becoming pro-
> gressively better or else being expelled by violence. Again we

---

[1] *Ibid.*, p. 113.   [2] *Ibid.*, p. 16.   [3] *Ibid.*, pp. 22 sq.

commanded him to repeat after us: "God be merciful . . ." which he did with less effort. As for our desire to make him say Our Father, he at first refused obstinately, asking how he could say "Father" when he was damned and lost. Earlier, earlier, it might have been possible. . . .[1]

Already during the repetition (of a canticle) it was observed that he was profoundly agitated. But soon he was seized with a lively repentance of his sins and, breaking into poignant lamentations, wrung his hands, imploring the pity of his heavenly Father. "Yes, yes," cried he, "compassionate and pitiful!" All his features were animated by an emotion hitherto unknown to his heart. From his eyes flowed the tears of repentance, he was overwhelmed with indescribable grief.[2]

It will be noted that all these cases relate to conversations with the "demon" during which the possessed kept their full consciousness. Eschenmayer expressly emphasizes this:

> She had heard and seen all that occurred. For she never lost consciousness, but in spite of her utmost efforts she could not resist the demon when he took possession of her body. We asked her then if the tears which the demon shed must not have been inspired by her, but she denied it positively.[3]

In the narrative of Ambroise Paré we read:

> This demon, constrained by the ceremonies and exorcisms, said that he was a spirit and was not damned for any crime. Being questioned as to who he was, or by what means and by whose power he tormented this gentleman thus, he replied that he had many dwellings where he hid and that at the time when he left the sick man at rest he went to torment others. For the rest, that he had been projected into the body of this gentleman by a certain person who should be nameless, that he had entered by the feet, creeping up to the brain, and that he would go forth by the feet when the day covenanted between them should have come. He discoursed of many other things according to the custom of demoniacs. I assure you that I do not bring this forward as a new thing, but so that it may be known that sometimes devils enter into our bodies and torture them with unheard-of torments. Sometimes also they do not enter in, but trouble the good humours of the body or else send the bad ones to the principal parts.[4]

Although these conversations may be very remarkable, our distrust of the whole state is greatly enhanced by the fact that the demon only replies very cautiously to ticklish questions. Thus the demon of Caroline St. did not like to be questioned as to his earthly past.

> This was the opportunity for recalling to him old, earthly relationships, a matter on which he replied with great reluctance. In the end the conversation had to be broken off, because the impression

---

[1] *Ibid.*, p. 24.   [2] *Ibid.*, p. 25.   [3] *Ibid.*, p. 28.
[4] Quoted by Calmeil, *De la Folie*, i, 178, Œuvres Complètes d'A. Paré, Paris, 1841, iii, 64.

which it made on him was completely distasteful. He became very weak and was hardly able to utter another word. The hands fell inert.[1]

When questions by means of which we desired to explore more deeply the secrets of healing and grace were asked, we were generally rebuffed with the reply: " You are going too far; that also I ought not to tell; it is left to each man's faith."[2]

Nevertheless, as a more complete study of pathological cases shows, it would be quite false to conclude that this generally results from cheating, that C. St. was deliberately playing a part. Such a conception of fraud on the part of the possessed must be regarded as an absurd hypothesis when the cases are considered as a whole and it is observed how the patients suffer from their state. It is certain that these dialogues are most intimately bound up with the terrible motor excitement of the fits. No one will ever pretend, however, that this latter is simulated, for the bodily strength displayed by the possessed during the fits is so great that they are revealed as pathological at the first glance.

And now, how are all the cases to be explained ? Is there a second apperception so that the obsessing personality is in reality entirely autonomous, existing side by side with the normal one and understanding what the exorcist says to it ? And also, when the possessed reprimands the spirit who is within him, does the latter hear, does it understand, and does it according to circumstances accept the rebuke or not ? The " psychology without a subject " which we have rejected is inclined in the first case to answer in the affirmative, since it regards the demon merely as a secondary psychic complex which is in essence of a nature entirely similar to that of the individual himself, and consequently hears and understands as he does. In the second case, where we are dealing with the relations between the possessed and his demon, psychology without a subject has not yet pronounced itself. Manifestly it ought also to admit between the two complexes reciprocal relations, in part purely intellectual, since the demon reacts to thoughts not expressed aloud.

Together with psychology without a subject, into which we do not wish to enter more deeply, we also reject its explanation of the reciprocal relations between the possessed and his demon.

[1] Eschenmayer, *Konflikt*, pp. 46 sq.
[2] *Ibid.*, p. 125.

The true state of things is essentially the same as when I converse mentally with someone and in imagination hear him reply, by which means a conversation may be enacted. In these circumstances the arguments of the other person may also have a character of compulsion.

In the case of possession there is nothing more than an extraordinary accentuation of this phenomenon. Instead of the discussion being purely and simply a figment of the imagination, there is simultaneous compulsive excitement of the vocal organs and eventually yet other actions of a compulsive nature. But there is no essentially new phenomenon; we are dealing throughout and always with parasitic psychic obsessions. There develops in the psyche a sort of secondary system of personality which directs the person's life against his will. The subject loses control over a considerable number of his states, and it is this part of his personality which plays the obsessive rôle of a demon. The fact that the latter, questioned on delicate matters, hesitates and refuses to reply, should be thus interpreted—the imaginary person conducts himself exactly like a real one. Compulsions are not in themselves entirely heterogeneous in the psychic life, but in their character of intellectual processes are of exactly the same nature as all others of their kind. They are distinguished by the single fact that they are not of a voluntary or simply passive nature, but are accomplished against the will of the subject.

If we bear very clearly in mind that the processes in question as intellectual functions resemble in principle all others of the same category, we shall be less surprised that they are not entitled by their content to a place entirely apart. They may be characterized by comparing them to the performance of a more or less eminent actor who plays his part in more or less close accordance with the author's text.

Particularly remarkable and noteworthy is the impression gleaned from a survey of accounts of the demon's general conduct: we feel that it is " incoherent " and " incalculable." This is a fact which strikes every careful reader with a knowledge of psychology. It is nevertheless, at least in one respect, a complete delusion. For if by way of experiment we adopt the point of view that a strange " spirit " has lodged in the soul of the possessed, this impression disappears and

5

his conduct does not seem to be less the result of determination and motive than that of a real living person.

Considered from another standpoint, however, this highly deceptive appearance is not really so deceitful after all. For in effect the conduct of the ordinary man also defies calculation; we know none of the psychic laws which would enable us to forecast it. Only intuitive sympathy enables us to experience after the event and consequently to " understand " why a man acts now in this fashion, now in that.

If this intuition ceases, as is the case at least in the first moment when we realize that we are dealing not with a possessing spirit but with compulsive phenomena, we at once lose the feeling of an intimate connection between the mere verbal declarations and the other " demoniac " reactions. We now realize very plainly how unpredictable the reactions of a personality really are, not because the conduct of the demon is much more haphazard and irregular than that of real persons, but rather because the reactions of the latter are just as fortuitous and incalculable as those of the demon.

But if we now consider that in the compulsive functions there is also an " inner coherence " analogous to the expression of a real personality, and that they proceed from a personal consciousness, even though it be only secondary and obsessive, we once more have the feeling[1] when intuition of this state resumes its sway, of an inner coherence in these compulsions; with nevertheless this difference: we now know that there is merely a deceptive appearance and not an entirely genuine second person. Not an entirely genuine person, I say, for such a person appears only when the subject becomes identified with this second personality, as in true demoniacal somnambulism. So long as we are not dealing with such a case the second person remains unreal and apparent; it is no more than a body of compulsive functions.

The casual observer of possessed persons always has the impression that there are two wills in the same individual. This is particularly clear in the already quoted narrative of Eginhard:

> It was a very extraordinary spectacle for those of us who were present to see this wicked spirit express himself through the mouth

---

[1] The word is not used in the sense of an emotional phenomenon, but, in default of a better expression, in the sense attributed to it in common parlance.

of the poor woman and to hear now the sound of a masculine voice, now that of a feminine one, but so distinct the one from the other that we could not believe that the woman alone spoke but thought we heard two people in a lively quarrel loading one another with abuse.   And in effect there were two persons, there were two different wills—on one side the demon who wished to break the body of which he was in possession, and on the other the woman who wished to be delivered from the enemy who obsessed her.[1]

Does this description correspond exactly to the facts ?

Such is far from being the case, for the possessed do not speak with a dual will properly so called, they speak from processes which impose themselves upon them, but they do not say that their will is exercised alike in both directions. They only exercise it on one side, while on the other they suffer and rebel.   This is a fact of the greatest importance, for it shows that the very core of our personal being is in the will.   Our states may be what they please, and in fact they may be exceedingly strange and contradictory; they are " ours " in the proper and strict sense of the word because we voluntarily range ourselves on their side.   Until that moment they do not reach the heart of our being.

There are naturally other states and functions which we repudiate but which nevertheless make good their claim as belonging to us; for if not they would have to be those of another subject and in that case we should not be able to experience them, in the proper sense of the word, as original states, but only to imagine them.   We should then be once more confronted with the same psychological situation of sentiments due to obsessive imagination which the subject rejects by the action of the will.

Something happens here to which we habitually pay no attention—namely, that all entirely normal states and functions, before becoming such, have to pass through another stage, that of *acceptance*.   In the normal subject there are as a rule only a relatively small number of processes which do not pass this test, and they generally vanish very quickly after repudiation.   In pathological cases these processes may on the contrary be extremely numerous, arise with great intensity, and be uncoercible.   But they are nevertheless states of the subject, and in exactly the same measure as

---

[1] Quoted by A. Maury, *La Magie et l'astrologie*, 3rd edit., Paris, 1864, p. 327 and P. Janet, *Névroses et idées fixes*, Paris, 1898, vol. i, p. 384.

those which have attained to acceptance, with this sole difference, that the first are obsessive processes to which the subject feels himself compelled, while in the second case he appropriates them to himself by the action of the will. *Only the will*, in the narrowest sense of the word, has no need to pass through this stage of acceptance.

The existence of such a threshold of acceptance is not contradicted by the fact that sometimes a process is refused at a certain moment to arrive at acceptance later. In these cases it is the judgement of the subject which has been modified, a change usually of a passive nature and which as a rule defies real explanation. But it also remains a fact that every process has to undergo a more or less careful examination before being completely accepted. The result in the case of analogous processes is not, however, always the same, this being dependent on whether it has or has not been preceded by changes in the censor.

In order to complete the survey of this subject attention should be drawn to the fact that a conversation may seem to be exchanged between compulsions. Cases have occurred in which the individual did not appear to be possessed by a single spirit but by several, which spoke through him in succession and even held discussions amongst themselves. Thus in the case published by van Gennep[1] the individual was possessed by the " spirit of a dead man." This latter was questioned as to relations in the Beyond and made all sorts of replies until a demon intervened and reproached him with unveiling transcendental secrets.

(At first it is the spirit of the dead man incarnated in the possessed which speaks to the narrator.)

> . . . Do not pray for the damned, for prayer is a torture in hell . . . it is a redoubling of pains. . . . I am speaking to you as a damned soul, do you hear ? Do you understand ?
>
> Here the damned discoursed for an hour with a gloomy, terrifying and melancholy eloquence, and that with such rapidity that it was impossible to write down what he said. Then after this monologue he continued:
>
> Do not follow my example. . . . If only after five million million centuries I had a minute's rest. . . . But no ! it is always eternity. . . .
>
> Are your parents damned too ? the narrator asks the spirit.
>
> . . . My parents are here, happily, for I can make them suffer.

---

[1] *Archives de psychologie*, x, 1911, p. 92.

Here there is a change of scene: *it is a demon who takes the place of the damned and threatens to double his torments because he has unveiled the mysteries of hell.*

In these cases of dual possession also there is merely an exaggeration of the state in which every dramatist or novelist finds himself when he hears various persons holding conversations.

The relations between the demon and the possessed in various circumstances call much more urgently for comment and explanation. The former expresses himself on this subject, in cases of somnambulistic possession as well as others, exactly as if he had introduced himself into the latter. The researches of the nineteenth century have enabled us to throw light on somnambulistic and hypnotic states, and the facts as observed are so astonishing that the obstinate persistence of belief in the demon is not in any way surprising; it must even be said that it disappeared from the scene before a complete psychological explanation of possession was possible. For a long time people contented themselves on the most difficult points with the conviction that pathological manifestations were involved.

Observations by the demon about the possessed may be found, for example, in the case of Caroline St., who was sometimes in a somnambulistic state and sometimes in one of possession.

The demon said of Caroline. . . . Prayer is generally too irksome for him, as well it may be, for Caroline prays much and says: " The blood of Jesus Christ cleanse me from all my sins "; and adds every time the prayer that it may also cleanse W. (the demon), so that she prays for him also—the silly thing ![1]

He related himself how Caroline had prayed and had spoken to him on the previous night. The protecting spirit (a vision which Caroline has in addition to her phenomena of possession) had not guarded him sufficiently; the evil spirits had come back, had mocked him and striven to turn him aside once more. On the apostrophe of Caroline who was weeping bitterly he had again seen things differently, had decided to remain good and had left her in peace.[2]

. . . Then he touched upon his relations with Caroline. He said: Since he had been converted (in the lucid state she had sought to convert him) and felt the same as herself, he could no longer clearly distinguish herself from him. The two of them were so united in their prayers, in their canticles, and generally in all that they did and refrained from doing, that she asked him constantly: " Is it you, W., or I ?" for as he not only speaks with her voice

---

[1] Eschenmayer, *Konflikt*, etc., p. 24.   [2] *Ibid.*, p. 31.

but also thinks with her mind, his being is completely confounded in hers, he has exactly her voice except only when he is excited and provoked to fight; then he resumes his manly voice with a heavy strain on her vocal organs.[1]

The apparent confusion of the two minds is particularly evident in Lemaître's case observed in our own times.

The case is one of somnambulistic possession and concerns a schoolboy of fourteen, Fritz. The spirit which is in him is called Algar and professes to be an Armenian. A few quotations will show the relations between Algar and the possessed boy.

> . . . Then Fritz rose and spoke in a deep guttural voice with a strong exotic accent which obliged me to make him repeat several words which were badly enunciated. My own questions will be found in parentheses.
> (Has Fritz seen or read any Armenian?) "Picture postcards."
> (When and how did Algar appear?) "Fritz was twelve years old. It was one day when he was very tired with having studied his geography. . . . (Discretion obliges me to leave out several passages which I replace by dots). As a punishment he had been told to work . . . in the garden. Fritz refused and was given a box on the ears. (Will Algar remain long with Fritz?) It is necessary for another two months, or perhaps less, until the cure, but M. Lemaître must help by making Fritz come more often than every Wednesday. (What relations are there between the Algar family and Fritz?) The family has done much to comfort Fritz when he was scolded, especially the daughter. . . . Algar was the first name of the son, aged about twenty. . . ."

During lesson-time Fritz had, in a short fit of somnambulism, recited some Latin verses.

> (Who composed the Latin verse which Fritz said to me in the course of a lesson?) "I know Latin and Fritz can write it when I am there. It is, however, better that he should not tire himself with the study of this language which is too difficult for him."[2]
> (How comes it . . . that Fritz quoted to me a verse which I finally discovered in Horace?) "I did not know," replied Algar, "that that verse was from Horace, but if I re-discover it this is because Fritz must have heard or read it some time at school, even although he never learnt Latin there."
> It is true that Algar has only dwelt in Fritz for three years, but that does not prevent him from bringing up from the depths of his consciousness accidentally and without any desire to do so, poetry casually heard many years before. Thus . . . Algar expresses himself in the following terms about some verses: "I wrote this

---

[1] *Ibid.*, pp. 83 sq.
[2] A. Lemaître, *Fritz Algar*, "Archives de psychologie," v, 1906, pp. 85 sq.

poem which Fritz had probably heard recited by a servant when he was four or five years old."

. . . On the subject of Fritz' total amnesias Algar adds: " All that Fritz loses (in his somnambulism and fits of abstraction) it is I who get hold of it."[1]

How are these strange declarations to be explained ? Is it true that in the principal person there is yet another who understands everything for the second time and retains the memory of it ?

The position is essentially simpler and will be easier of approach if we remember what we have learned elsewhere about somnambulism. In typical somnambulism memory extends over the whole life, including normal periods as well as previous periods of somnambulism. The contrary is true of the normal state in which memory of the somnambulistic state is almost always impossible. The admirable researches of Janet,[2] as also of others, have shown, moreover, that when the waking state A and the somnambulistic state B of an individual X show very wide general differences from the psychic and characterological point of view, the person in the somnambulistic state **B** is not always willing to identify himself with the normal individual, but sometimes speaks of him in the third person, although he sees before him a l the past life of the individual X, and A as well as B are no other than particular states of X. An error of judgement has arisen: instead of recognizing that the general psychic state of X has changed, the subject falls into the mistake of no longer regarding states so foreign to himself as his own, but seeing them as a separate person.

Something else also escapes Fritz-Algar. In the Algar state he embraces all his past life, the normal periods as well as the (short) somnambulistic ones; he has even a certain hypermnesia: he remembers events which were not present to the memory in the normal state. But instead of realizing his own identity in the various successive periods he makes the mistake of believing that the normal state of Fritz is quite another person. As, however, he sees before him in memory the whole of Fritz' life he interprets the positions by thinking he is always present in Fritz and has full control of his memory. On exceptional occasions Algar has an

[1] *Ibid.*, p. 88.
[2] P. Janet, *L'Automatisme psychologique*, Paris, 1889, pp. 131 sq.

intuition that he only represents a part of the psychic existence of Fritz:

> (Where did you get this name of Algar?) "I am Algar and do not know who gave me this name, but I may have got it out of Fritz."
> (Then you are in some sort Fritz' consciousness?) "Exactly."[1]

Thus the problem resolves itself very simply,[2] and the solution throws light on the last remaining riddle.

Algar also predicts some of Fritz' future actions, which the latter will carry out while himself half-unconscious. One day, for example, he declared to Lemaître: "Fritz will be taken home again to-day without knowing it, he will write a poem which he will bring to-morrow and perhaps also a Latin sentence."

On the following day Fritz did in fact bring both: on one sheet of paper the poem which, without knowing how, he had written on the previous evening before dinner, and on the other sheet a Latin verse of which he did not know the meaning and which he must have written after dinner[3] (manifestly under an inner compulsion).

Algar had boasted—he is a true Armenian—of possessing a special language and script. Lemaître therefore begged him to write in that language.

> After a few seconds he replied in the affirmative, and that Fritz when awake would remember nothing about it. "In the night I am going to tell Fritz to write in my handwriting. He will not know that it is my doing, but I will make him get up and go back to bed again afterwards, and then on the next day he will see these childish scribblings and say: ' Isn't it funny, I found this on my table !' "[4]

The psychological state of things is here as follows: during somnambulism Fritz (Algar) proposes to write a poem on his return home. Then he executes this intention and in doing so falls back into an abnormal state (he had meanwhile returned to his normal one). The intention to carry out an action is realized in exactly the same way as many hypnotic suggestions, compulsively and mechanically, even if not, as a rule, unconsciously. The resolution taken by

---

[1] A Lemaître, *loc. cit.*, p. 90.
[2] It is amusing that Fritz' aversion for Latin manifests itself in the somnambulistic state also.
[3] *Ibid.*, p. 86.   [4] *Ibid.*, p. 88.

Fritz in the somnambulistic state remains alive under the threshold of consciousness, even after he has returned to normal, and fulfils itself as soon as the prescribed moment arrives. Everything occurs as if Fritz had received a corresponding suggestion from a hypnotist, the only difference being that in the present case it is not a hypnotist but actually Fritz who introduces into himself the " determining tendency " (autosuggestion) which will later release the action.[1] The error concerning the non-identity of Fritz and Algar therefore leads Fritz the somnambulist into a remarkably inept mode of speech. He ought to say, " I propose to do this and that, this intention is realized in such a way that I observe nothing of it and am afterwards astonished to see the writing in question on the paper " (we may suppose that Fritz the somnambulist knows that things must happen thus, because he remembers previous cases where in the same way he proposed acts when in a state of somnambulism, and remembers, perhaps by a sort of hypermnesia[2] how such somnambulistic resolutions were carried out later in the waking state, mechanically, without full consciousness). Instead of that he says, " I (Algar) will do this and that and Fritz will be very much surprised afterwards to find a letter written."

Here are two other examples of realization of a tendency created during somnambulism.

Lemaître agreed with Fritz the somnambulist that the latter should add to a piece of homework a sheet with a poem on it. When Fritz in the waking state gave in his exercise book on the following day, Lemaître duly found the agreed paper inside without the normal Fritz having the least idea that there was an extra sheet in the book.[3]

---

[1] Naturally the question at once arises of studying more closely this parallelism between external hypnotic suggestion and voluntary somnambulistic determination; it is an extremely interesting problem of experimental psychology, our knowledge of suggested actions being, generally speaking, inadequate. There are, moreover, plenty of other problems. Thus it seems that Algar was able to disappear at will, that is to say, that Fritz was able voluntarily to end his somnambulism and recover his normal state, while the converse was manifestly not within his power.

[2] The generally hypermnesic character of Fritz' somnambulism is also demonstrated by the creation and use of a personal alphabet which would have taken some time to learn in the normal waking state.

[3] *Loc. cit.*, pp. 92 sq.

Another time Lemaître agreed with Algar that the latter should write him a letter and gave him an addressed envelope for the purpose. This was executed in the following manner:

> He explained to me that he had written his letter in one or two minutes during the previous night at one a.m., and that he at once slipped it into the envelope which I had given him. For this purpose Algar had made Fritz get up for a few minutes. Fritz had this envelope containing the letter in his pocket all day Friday without knowing it, then in the evening Algar, taking advantage of an errand which Fritz had to do at the shoemaker's, took possession of his person and dropped the letter into the box.[1]

In the circumstances it will not be surprising to find that Algar, that is to say, Fritz in the somnambulistic state, remembers all sorts of previous states having the character of possession and over which Fritz had no control, which he was not able to " assimilate."

> (Did Algar know the two personalities who were in Fritz a few weeks ago ?) "Yes, for I was already in him, but I should not have been able to merge them single-handed." (When did this double personality begin ?) "At school, and it would not have developed but for Fritz' troubles. Between us (Algar and myself) we have made it disappear and when Fritz is well again he will never have known me. Then I shall go away, you will be able to explain everything to him and he will have difficulty in believing it.
> (Why did Fritz' second personality always play the part of an important personage ?) It was so that he should not be too harshly treated, because, for example, as a general one is better used than as a private, and because while commanding he liked to go away. People had made his illness much worse, they laughed at him when he put on a new tie or new shoes, and gave him nicknames . . . and this was his form of revenge.[2]

There is no contradiction in the fact that Algar remembers these states of Fritz although at that time he was not " in Fritz." Algar is no other than Fritz in the somnambulistic state. But somnambulism implies a hypermnesia relating to the subject's whole life, so that Algar remembers facts in Fritz' life which occurred at a time when Algar was not yet there, that is to say, before Fritz showed these somnambulistic troubles and modifications in the general psychic structure of the personality which are distinguished by the name of Algar. The very contradiction that Algar remembers states of Fritz dating from a period when he, Algar, was not

[1] *Ibid.*, pp. 94 sq.
[2] *Ibid.*, pp. 89 sq. Fritz suffered from obsessive day-dreams in which he always saw himself playing the part of a great personage.

there, shows with the utmost possible clarity that Algar is not a spirit which has introduced itself into Fritz from without but Fritz himself in the somnambulistic state. The fact that Lemaître did not refrain from reproducing all Algar's declarations, however disconcerting and strange they might appear, gives to his publication a unique value as bearing upon the theory of the ego.

It is not fully clear how Fritz-Algar comes to predict so accurately that he will vanish at the time of Fritz' cure and that the latter will not remember him. Is this due to hypermnesia of things perhaps heard by Fritz at some time and relating to the course and cure of his possession or else to autonomous conjectures founded on his own experiences and the knowledge acquired from them that Fritz in the waking state does not remember the somnambulistic periods ?

Finally we will draw attention to another interesting analogous case. In early Christian literature there exists a passage where the possessing spirit also makes statements as to the state of mind of the possessed at the moment of possession. It does not much matter that in this case possession is not by a demon but by the Holy Spirit conceived entirely as a person. The quotation relates to Montan, the founder of " Montanism." Several utterances of the Holy Spirit are enunciated by his mouth, in one of which the Holy Spirit describes as follows Montan's state when inspired:

> Behold, man is like a lyre—And I come flying unto him like a plectrum—The man sleeps—And I am waking—Behold it is the Lord—Who draws men's hearts out of their breasts—And who gives to man a heart.[1]

This passage is remarkable because in the whole of literature I have not found another in which the second person of the possessed says something about the *occasionally recurring* condition of the first.

Even the somnambulists of Janet[2] are silent on this point; true, however, they were not questioned about it.

By reason of this lack of documents it is difficult to say anything more on the psychic mechanism which Montan's words really attest. It seems as if there had been as it were

---

[1] St. Epiphanius (Hær.), 48, 4, ii, p. 430), ed. Dind, quoted by Bonwetsch, *Geschichte des Montanismus*, Erlangen, 1881, pp. 19 sq.

[2] *L'Automatisme psychologique*, Paris, 1888.

a residue of the first " person " in the total field of consciousness: this is what would be indicated by the word " sleeps."
It is with the new person in the man as if the first slept.
The passage also shows that man possesses in this second
state as well as the first a sense of the ego, for otherwise the
following utterance would have no meaning: " That God
takes men's hearts out of their bosoms and gives them a
heart " (another heart evidently). This second heart is
that of the Paraclete.

We must consider once more the other saying from the
mouth of Montan: I, the Lord, God, the Almighty, *descending
into man, ἐγώ κύριος ὁ θεός ὁ παντοκράτων καταγιγνόμενος ἐν
ἀνθρώπῳ.*[1]

It shows at least that, in this case also, the new person is
so placed as to be only *per nefas* in the man in question.[2]

[1] Epiphanius (Hær.), 48, ii.
[2] This interpretation of the words of Montan is found also in their
translator Weinel (*Die Wirkungen der Geister im nachapostolischen
Zeitalter bis auf Irenäus*, Freiburg, 1899); but Weinel forgets that the
normal personal consciousness has disappeared, and therefore falls
into a completely false interpretation; he pays no attention to the fact
that the personality gifted with apperception who thus remarks that
the ordinary person sleeps is not at all this latter but the new and divine
one.

Weinel himself offers (*loc. cit.*, pp. 92 sq.) these observations: " Montan has perfectly described the prophet's personal experience, or rather
not Montan but the ' Lord ' who speaks. (Here follows the sentence
quoted above uttered by the mouth of Montan.) In this state the man
is as if he slept or as if his heart, the seat of consciousness according to
the ancients, were drawn out of his bosom and a strange power had
given him another for such time as it should speak by his mouth. It
is with him as often with us in dreams: as if he were only the spectator
or auditor of what the strange force which has ' taken possession of him '
says and does. As in a dream he hears only a distant and strange
voice which uses his vocal organs like a plectrum striking the strings.
And this state had seized him as if some strange thing had ' flown ' into
him, like a puff of wind or a heady perfume. All this is not depicted
by the man but by God who is within him. We may wonder whether
the man in his waking state remembers it.

" . . . He who carries the spirit within him shows to a marked degree
the need to elucidate his state, to explain this strange thing which has
come suddenly into his life and imposed itself upon him. This is what
gives rise to these naïf theories formulated from time to time, partly
in the waking state and partly in ecstasy. We will allude here only
to the Clairvoyante of Prevorst who has reflected at length upon her
state and who in the half-waking condition wrote rhymes similar (at
least in certain cases) to the words of Maximilla.

" ' Play of thought—Thou dost bear me away from the goal—My
prescience is subtle—So works in me the other's thought—Among the
intruding thoughts—Of the earthly tumult—Remains long flickering—
The sense of spiritual things.' "

In striking agreement with what we have already said about the character of possession according as the possessed do or do not offer a strong resistance to the anti-religious compulsions, is what has been handed down concerning the frequency and distribution of the incidence of possession and obsession.

Before proceeding further, I must interpolate a remark on the terms *possession* and *obsession*. Under the name of obsessions modern French psychology includes in a general way all the states of compulsion.[1] Under the name of possession are designated two particular groups of states, demoniacal somnambulism as well as the state of inner division in which the individual imagines he feels the demon as a second self within him.

It should be clearly stated that the theological psychology of the present time, like that of the Middle Ages, classes these phenomena of division as obsessions and only reckons as possession well-developed demoniacal somnambulism. This is the definition of Poulain, one of the most eminent specialists in the new theology:

> We shall call a person possessed by the demon in the strict sense of the word when at certain moments the latter makes him lose consciousness and then seems to play in his body the part of the soul: he uses, at least to all appearance, his eyes to see with, his ears to listen with, his mouth to speak with, whether it be to those present or to his companions. It is he who suffers as if from a burn if his skin is touched with an object which has been blessed. In a word, he seems incarnated.
>
> We shall call a person obsessed when the demon never makes him lose consciousness but nevertheless torments him in such a manner that his action is manifest: for example, by beating him.[2]

But it must be said that this terminology has not always been strictly observed. The more nearly the state of obsession approximates, at least apparently, to possession, the more readily is this designation applied. Thus the case of Surin has always from the beginning been called possession, whereas it should have been called obsession by reason of the retention of intelligence.

In the case of the Clairvoyante of Prevorst, however, it is she herself in her character of clairvoyante who gives an account of her state, while in the case quoted above it is the Paraclete.

[1] *E.g.*, Pierre Janet in *Les Obsessions et la psychasthénie*, Paris, 1903.

[2] A. Poulain, *Des Grâces d'oraison. Traité de théologie mystique,* 5th edit., Paris, 1906, p. 423.

It is, moreover, extremely important to remember that although we call such a state of division *obsession*,[1] it is far from true that all obsessions are consequently states of division.

Modern psychopathic literature on the subject contains descriptions of an extraordinary number of compulsive phenomena which have not, however, been felt as " possession " by the persons concerned. The richest collection of cases is found in the great work of Pierre Janet, a French psychologist—originally psychology master in a secondary school at le Hâvre, but now for years past director of the Psychological Institute of the Paris Psychiatric Clinic of the Salpêtrière—*Les Obsessions et la Psychasthénie*.[2] It includes hundreds of the most diverse examples.

Hardly less rich are the materials which Löwenfeld has accumulated in his book: *Die psychologischen Zwangserscheinungen*.[3]

The forms of obsession are innumerable. Some patients are haunted by the idea that they have committed a crime or an offence of some sort against religion; others by the idea that they are suffering from an illness. Yet others are prone to ask themselves mentally all sorts of questions on any and every occasion. Some have a mania for counting their steps or the paving-stones in the streets. Others are haunted by the dread of being contaminated by the objects which they touch. Yet others cannot resist the impulse to wash their hands at every moment. There is no idea, no tendency, no torturing conception which may not be capable of assuming compulsive possession of the mind[4] without the patient thereby losing consciousness of the morbid character of the process taking place within him.

I have had, writes H. Oppenheim, to treat several lawyers, jurists, and doctors who were worried to death by the obsessive

---

[1] Thus the expression *obsessio* was used arbitrarily in the sense of possession in a *Responsum* of the theological faculty of Rostock, as early as the year 1691 (cf. Magikon, *Archiv. für Beob. a. d. Gebiete d. Geisterkunde*, 1853, see vol. v, p. 227.
[2] Two vols., Paris, 1903. Vol. ii., which gives a detailed analysis of these cases, was written in collaboration with the neurologist of the Salpêtrière, F. Raymond.
[3] Wiesbaden, 1904.
[4] The psychological structure of these states, which is insufficiently explained by psychiatric literature, has been closely analyzed by me in the first vol. of my *Phanomenologie des Ich* (chap. xiii).

idea of having made a mistake, of having forgotten something in their prescriptions. It is not rare in obsessions to have committed a morally reprehensible action. Thus an intelligent lawyer had had his windows furnished with shutters when the idea occurred to him that this was an act of cowardice. He was unceasingly tormented by this display of moral inferiority and consulted not only doctors but also philosophers, ecclesiastics, etc. When he came to ask my advice the trouble had lasted, with intermissions, for twenty-five years.[1]

Sometimes it is the idea of being destined to attempt the life of another, amongst the patient's near ones, which makes its way into the mind and becomes obsessive. One of my patients could not go into the street because he was distracted by the idea of wounding someone with his walking-stick or umbrella.[2]

Obsession is a peculiar torture when almost every idea takes the form of an interrogation, when on every sensory impression, every action, irresistably arouses the question: What does that mean? Why am I doing that? Why do I do such a thing and not such another? Why is this object in this place? etc. It may even be completely absurd conceptions bearing no relation to the normal mentality of the individual which assume obsessive domination. For example, one of my patients was obsessed by the idea that he carried the head of his dead father under his arm, that his skin was that of a mouse, etc. There are other cases in which the patient must exhaust himself in the search for certain names. Thus I treated a woman who strove to find a name for every object and who had no rest until she had written it down; she had sacks full of pieces of paper inscribed with names. With other women it is a sort of mania for orientation and analysis. They must keep an exact account of what they have thought during a certain time, of what they have done, of the objects which they have seen in going through a room, of the order in which these were arranged when they passed them, etc.[3]

These compulsive ideas may also have a religious content, the most frequent taking the form of blasphemy.

To speak evil of divine things, to think of the devil while saying prayers and to insult God instead of praying to him . . . to be able to utter nothing but coarse and malevolent expressions of hatred against God, to rebel against him and curse him, to utter blasphemies as soon as the thought of religion occurs. . . . Swine of a God, etc., such are the words which a number of these patients repeat.[4]

Such states are not identical with possession. They may facilitate its appearance, but in themselves fall short of it.

It also behoves us to be circumspect about sources. Authors often say that the devil has entered into a soul even if according to our terminology there is nothing beyond the

[1] H. Oppenheim, *Lehrbuch der Nervenkrankheiten*, 6th edit., Berlin 1913, ii, pp. 1525 sq.
[2] *Ibid.*, p. 1526.   [3] *Ibid.*, p. 1525.
[4] P. Janet, *loc. cit.*, i, p. 12.

ordinary compulsive phenomena without the sentiment of a second personality being imposed. It is only when the person feels himself divided that we speak of true possession.

It is evident. that such possession must arise much less often to-day than formerly when belief in the devil prevailed. All compulsions, even when very mild, were immediately personified, but this did not mean that every obsessive idea resulted in an immediate division of personality.

As regards the growth of compulsions in the psyche, certain prominent systematic theologians are of opinion that possession never attacks, except in very rare and transitory cases, persons who strive earnestly after moral and religious perfection.[1]

They really find this a matter of experience. Meynard also thinks " that it is excessively rare that possession should appear in souls called to the contemplation of God and to an intimate union with him; it is rather a punishment than a purifying trial."[2]

This, however, can only be affirmed of the most extreme forms of possession, for authors worthy of credence report that almost all exorcising priests themselves fell victim to possession.

On the other hand, obsessions are very often encountered in persons of deep religious life: all the biographies of saints and mystics are full of such cases. There is nothing surprising in this, for in order to become a mystic it is necessary to have an inner leaning towards persistent processes.

Thus Suso speaks of " the imaginings of the evil spirits," of the " insinuations of the evil spirit," which he heard from time to time. He characterizes them as " hateful thoughts which the evil spirit puts into me against my will."[3]

> Amongst his sufferings there were three intimate ones which were very painful to him. One of them consisted in false ideas concerning the faith. Thus it occurred to him to wonder how God had been able to become man and other similar things. The more resistance he offered the more he went astray. God left him for

---

[1] Poulain, op. cit., p. 424. Scaramelli, Direttorio Mistico, v, 41. Schram, Institutiones theologiæ mysticæ, Augsburg, 1777, no. 208 (ed. of 1848, no. 217).
[2] Meynard, Traité de la vie intérieure, vol. ii, no. 139.
[3] Heinrich Suso, Deutsche Schriften in neuhochdeutscher Schriftsprache, ed. by H. Denifle, Munich, 1880, book i, pp. 488 sq.

almost nine years in these tribulations with sorrowful heart and weeping eyes which implored the aid of God and all the saints. . . .

Another intimate suffering was a vague sadness. Without inter mission his heart was heavy; it was as if a mountain weighed upon it. . . .

But the third intimate suffering was that he was assailed by distressful thoughts, that his soul would never find healing and would be damned eternally whatever good he might do and what- ever application he might show, that the fact of his being one of the Just was of no avail, and all was lost in advance. And thus he afflicted his soul day and night. When he had to go to the choir or do some other good action his miseries returned and he lamented " Of what use is it to you to serve God ? To you it is only a curse, there will never be any healing. Give over betimes; you are lost even as you set about it. . . ."

As these terrible torments had lasted for about ten years. . . .[1]

Even in sermons Suso comes round to the subject, and we learn in this way that for some time he was haunted by obses- sive impulses towards suicide.

Now there are four different sufferings which are the direst of all that the human heart is called upon to bear, so dire that no one could conceive such suffering hearts to exist had he not experienced them himself or unless it were given him from God; if their suffer- ings leave them not (and their sufferings would be lightened if they only turned to God) then will they endure the most painful of all tribulations. The depth of these sufferings should be measured not by the harm which they do to the soul but by the active torment which they inflict. The four sufferings are as follows: doubt in matters of faith, doubt of the mercy of God, thoughts of revolt against God and his saints, and temptations to take one's own life.[2]

This whole description is eloquent of the fact that Suso suffered from states of psychic compulsion. The word temptation (*Anfechtung*) is not really proper to these states, for it is generally used when it is desired to express that the moral attitude of the individual endangers something or another. Thus Luther occasionally speaks of a purely physical malady as an " Anfechtung." But where the word is used for psychic phenomena it implies that the individual experienced these within himself against his will. Suso resists all the sufferings enumerated by him: doubt in matters of faith, doubt of the mercy of God, anti-religious ideas and ideas of suicide. But this means that all these were states of spiritual obsession (consequent on a nervous system broken down by incredible practices of asceticism lasting over a long period of years).

[1] *Ibid.*, pp. 90 sq.
[2] H. Suso, *Deutsche Schriften* (in der Originalsprache), ed. by K. Bihl- meyer, Stuttgart, 1907, p. 498.

The case of Ste. Jeanne de Chantal who had " violent temptations and torments of soul " is the same.   Her seven or eight last years were passed in a continual moral anguish of death which only disappeared in the last months of her life.   " Dryness " (that is to say, drying-up of the sentiments of religious exaltation), doubts as to the mysteries, inclination to blaspheme God, the feeling that God hated her, evil thoughts about those near her and scruples of conscience, all these torments assailed her.[1]

Maria von der Menschwerdung suffered like Suso from suicidal tendencies.

> One day when I found myself near a window I had a horrible temptation to throw myself down, for my understanding was completely darkened.[2]
> . . . And at this very moment a terrible inner force impelled me to throw myself down from hatred of God.   Particularly once during the crossing; this temptation to suicide was so sharp and strong that had there not chanced to be a balustrade near by my soul to which I clung I should have thrown myself into the sea.[3]
> It is shown by experience that God always sends trials to souls which strive after perfection; and sometimes throughout their whole lives.   All the biographies of the saints give proof of it, and the masters of spiritual knowledge establish it by common consent.   This general rule applies more particularly to souls greatly given to prayer, especially if they are favoured with mystic gifts of grace. . . .   " If ever," says Scaramelli, " my book falls into the hands of a person who aspires through vain motives to infused contemplation, I beg him to reflect on the cruel pincers that must rend his flesh, and the wine-press of many sufferings beneath which he must groan before attaining to it.   Perchance then all frivolous desire for these favours will vanish from his heart."[4]

The complete disappearance in possessed persons of consciousness of the original personality seems therefore to depend to a considerable extent on the voluntary resistance offered by the patient to these phenomena of psychic compulsion.   If resistance is weak, the compulsions end by suppressing the primary personality.   This is fully consistent with the fact that children scarcely ever retain consciousness in their compulsive state, but are immediately dominated by the phenomenon.   Their individuality is not yet sufficiently strong and capable of resistance.

As regards the distinction which Poulain draws between

---

[1] Quoted by Poulain, *La Plénitude des grâces*, vol. ii.
[2] *Ibid.*, vol. ii.   [3] *Ibid.*, vol. ii.
[4] A. Poulain, *Grâces d'oraison*, 5th edit., Paris, 1906, p. 895.   Scaramelli, *Direttorio Mistico*, v, 41.

possession and obsession, this is a matter of well-established tradition. Ribet also distinguishes in the same way:

> Possession is the invasion by the demon of the body of a living man, whose organs he exercises in his own name and at will, as if the body had become his.[1]
> In possession the spirit acts from within and seems to be substituted in the body for the soul which animates and moves it.[2]

Obsession, on the other hand, is thus defined:

> An extrinsic compulsion which, while leaving to the mind the consciousness of its vital and motor action upon the organs, nevertheless imposes itself with such violence that the man feels within him two beings and two principles in mutual conflict: the one external and despotic which seeks to invade and dominate, the other internal, that is to say the soul itself which suffers and struggles against this foreign domination.[3]

It is naturally false to designate possession as " external " while obsession is called " internal," the first representing a domination of the body, the second a domination of the mind. Possession does not denote a lesser but rather a deeper disturbance of the mind than does obsession.

It should be observed that in addition to internal obsession Ribet admits an external kind which consists in visions of a demoniacal nature. The temptation of St. Anthony by visions of women is a case in point. In this kind of obsession the devil manifests himself as it were outside the individual and not within him.

We have defined possession as a state of compulsion. This may be transformed in several ways. The first consists in the subject gradually weakening in his resistance to the compulsive processes which constitute the essence of the " demon "; they begin to be accepted. Even this proceeding is obviously not altogether subject to the control of the will —the general opinion that it is so is fallacious. On the contrary the subject may realize very clearly the way in which resistance is slowly worn down within him. When the struggle is relinquished the patient ceases simultaneously as a rule to harbour compulsive ideas and to imagine the consciousness of the second personality. In the last analysis it was only a travesty, a personification of the compulsions.

---

[1] M. J. Ribet, *La mystique divine*, Paris, 1883, vol. iii, pp. 191 sq.
[2] *Ibid.*, p. 179.
[3] *Ibid.*, pp. 179 sq.

C. St. offers good examples of this:

> The worst thing is that she should no longer be able to dis-
> tinguish whether the evil thoughts and intentions come from her
> or from the demon. The angel said: "It is sad; take care lest
> thy soul suffer harm." In the night she nevertheless appeared to
> recover strength and from four to five o'clock she prayed very
> heartily, which I heard from below.[1]
> In the afternoon towards two o'clock she engaged in a violent
> conflict which lasted until six o'clock and in which faith and doubt,
> perseverance and irresolution alternated constantly. She now
> began continually to parry his thrusts and used the same spiritual
> weapons against the demon as the latter had formerly used against
> Satan.[2] At first we paid no attention, taking it for a pure mimicry,
> and often said: "Let the Evil One talk away and take no notice."
> But she replied: "You don't understand. If I do not repulse
> each one of the attacks which he makes against my soul, he enters
> more deeply into me and I am lost."
> The angel knew this better than we did and often cried: "He is
> cast down; press forward in faith or thy soul will suffer for it."
> The spiritual infection seemed to become greater and greater, and
> to deprive her of all her good thoughts and intentions, so that she
> cried out as if in despair that to him who would take her life she
> would give a great reward; what she suffered inwardly was in-
> describable; everything was now contradiction. If she said with
> all her strength of will: "The Evil One must give way !" the voice
> replied from the depths of her heart: "No, he will remain !" If
> she said in faith: "The Lord will come and will deliver me,"
> "No !" said the inner voice, "the Lord will not come and will
> not deliver thee !" We therefore had to judge for ourselves
> whether it was possible that this martyrdom should last any
> longer. True, the angels who were always at her side did not fail
> to speak words of consolation to her, but the struggle was not
> mitigated thereby.[3]

The case of C. St. shows very clearly and more than once,
as has already been seen,[4] this fear of becoming powerless
against the compulsions. Here is another quotation:

> We already saw that the demon and Caroline were completely
> united in the period of conversion, so that in utterances of various
> kinds, prayers, recitation of canticles and psalms, C. often asked:
> "It is you, W., or I ?" In particular during the struggle with
> Satan, being afraid that he might give way while her organs and
> speech were in action, she often used to ask: "Are you there ?"
> to which he generally replied: "Never fear, I am here !"[5]

After passing through this psychological condition development may occur along one of two lines. The first leads to
demoniacal somnambulism. The original personality vanishes
and in its place comes the second, which was hitherto a mere
compulsive state. This seems to be the rule with young people,

[1] Eschenmayer, *Konflikt*, etc., p. 149.
[2] I have not examined further the phenomena thus alluded to.
[3] *Ibid.*, pp. 132 sq.   [4] *Ibid.*, p. 93.
[5] *Ibid.*, p. 13. An explanatory theory of Eschenmayer follows.

as with them the original personality is not yet so strong as in adults. Or else there occurs little by little, in proportion as the compulsive functions are accepted, a fusion of the two personal consciousnesses; the individual remains conscious of who he is, but his character suffers a complete change for the worse. This second phenomenon seems often to occur in the modern " demoniacal fits " of highly hysterical persons. So far as the relevant literature, with its lack of precision, allows us to judge, the subject now seems far from struggling against demoniacal states as he did formerly under the influence of the religious periods. Then there existed compulsive states of the most violent character, whereas it appears that to-day the element of compulsion is lacking. The patients give way much more easily to the impulses and suffer no division of consciousness; they abandon themselves heart and soul to the fits of frenzy.[1]

Generally speaking, all states of emotional compulsion have a strong tendency to become the true nature of the individual. Thus a patient whom I have been able to examine closely remarked one day: " An obsessive state of feeling will be experienced as belonging to the subject far more readily than an obsessive idea, in spite of any criticisim which it may incur."[2]

The strength and duration of resistance to the compulsive processes generally depends on the force of character of the individual. The more sharply his character is in opposition to the compulsive feelings the more energetically does he combat them. Conversely, the more affinity these sentiments have to his own being, the more readily are they accepted.

It will therefore not be surprising to find that in the case of devout persons having attained a high degree of holiness possession seems confined to the early stages of their career, before they have advanced to the higher degrees of ecstasy.

---

[1] It is urgently desirable that the detailed psycho-pathological analysis of hysteria should at length be extended to the acute states of hysterical excitement. The accounts and descriptions, some of them classic, of the investigators of that malady: Charcot, Richer, Gilles de la Tourette, Pitres, Janet, Sollier, Binswanger, Hartenberg, etc., are insufficient for the needs of psychology.

[2] *Journal für Psychologie und Neurologie*, viii, p. 62.

Poulain, who has studied Catholic mysticism for forty years, ventures the statement:

> From the lives of the saints it appears evident that a strong diabolic domination manifests itself to the highest degree before the stage of ecstasy or revelations or really divine visions is reached. Sometimes it is for a time, when the divine revelations are interrupted, but sometimes also it comes in the midst of these very evidences of grace.[1]

The autobiography of Jeanne des Anges permits us conversely to realize how much less clearly marked is the division of mind in a characterless and morally inferior person than in others.[2]

At the beginning, indeed, she was not subject to compulsions, as is clearly shown by a series of quotations from her biography:

> They generally acted in conformity with the inclinations which I harboured within me, which they did so subtly that I myself did not think to have demons. I took as an insult that I should be told to distrust myself, and when anyone spoke to me of possession by them I felt greatly moved to anger against those persons who spoke to me thereof, being unable to refrain from showing my resentment. Little by little I took a great loathing for the things of God, in such wise that I left off all kinds of prayer, audible as well as silent. When I was at any observance of the community I suffered very great uneasiness; it is true that I did not do myself the violence necessary to resist my inclinations. Through this laxity I fell into such great hardness of heart that none of the things of God any longer touched me more than as if I had been of bronze.[3]

It is the same with sexual feelings. She conceived a passion for a priest and abandoned herself to it in imagination without any effort of will.

> They (the demons) inspired me with desires to see and talk to him. . . .[4] It is true that I have been faithless to combat the impure thoughts and impulses which I felt . . . If I had heartily studied to mortify my passions, never would the demons have wrought such havoc in me.[5]
> . . . His operation in me was to oppose himself to all the actions which concerned the worship of God in my soul. I must admit with truth that my cowardice had given to this wretched spirit a great hold over my heart. For the space of two years or more he kept me in a continual state of spiritual deadness, with inconceivable hardness of heart; I used to go for a week without performing any act of adoration. If I was constrained to go to Mass

---

[1] *La Plénitude des grâces*, ii, 198.
[2] *Bibliothèque diabolique*, vol. v, Paris, 1866, p. 13, cf. particularly the introduction by the editors Légué and G. de la Tourette, pp. 1-51.
[3] *Ibid.*, p. 66.   [4] *Ibid.*, p. 67.   [5] *Ibid.*, p. 69.

or to some other regular exercises, it was without paying any attention; my mind was occupied in finding means to prevent others from serving God.

This accursed spirit insinuated himself into me so subtly that I in no way realized his workings. I took no trouble to get out of this miserable state; I did not fail to recognize the great peril I was in as regards my salvation; I resolved in despair to be damned, and my salvation became a matter of indifference to me.[1]

We see that up to this point Jeanne des Anges, quite unlike the majority of similar patients, gave way without any effort of will to the anti-religious tendencies which arose in her. For this reason she long retained an undivided personality and did not at once present the phenomena of compulsion.

But we must not be misled: the Jeanne des Anges case belongs to the same category as all the other cases of possession. She too shows the development of an emotional state different in character from her ordinary emotional excitements. But it does not appear in her obviously and at once; for just as the feeble-minded show no compulsive ideas, such phenomena being transformed into delusions through the critical inferiority of the subjects, so with persons of more or less weak moral resistance the abnormal sentiments which would change in normal individuals into feelings of compulsion, immediately become genuine and fully accepted owing to the lack of character of their hosts.

Nevertheless we are dealing with phenomena *sui generis* which very manifestly follow other psycho-physical laws from those governing the true primary feelings, even as experienced by these individuals so little capable of resistance, and which above all have a different, although not yet determinable, origin. For the development of this abnormal state of feeling in Jeanne des Anges is inexorable. It reaches the point of blasphemy. Of herself the patient offers no energetic resistance, but nevertheless the words are already uttered in a manner which is automatic and compulsive rather than personal and voluntary. Thus at this period Jeanne des Anges realizes that these are not normal affective states to which she is now subject; their character of compulsion becomes manifest and at certain moments, when resistance is stronger, there is a distinct division of consciousness. Subsequently we reach a stage characterized by acts of violence.

[1] *Ibid.*, pp. 70 sq.

My mind was often filled with blasphemies, and sometimes I uttered them without being able to take any thought to stop myself. I felt for God a continual aversion, and nothing inspired me with greater hatred than the spectacle of his goodness and the readiness with which he pardons repentant sinners. My thoughts were often bent on devising ways to displease him and make others offend against him. It is true that by the mercy of God I was not free in these sentiments, although at that time I did not know it, for the demon beclouded me in such a way that I hardly distinguished his desires from mine; he gave me moreover a strong aversion for my religious calling, so that sometimes when he was in my head I used to tear all my veils and such of my sisters' as I might lay hands on; I trampled them underfoot, I chewed them, cursing the hour when I took the vows. All this was done with great violence; I think that I was not free.

The spirit of these wretches (the demons) and mine came to be one and the same thing, so that, through their influence, I adopted all their sentiments and expressed all their interests as if they had been mine; I was indeed very desirous of doing otherwise, but could not compass it; it is true that I did not work to that end with sufficient efforts and perseverance. The difficulties which I found in this combat often made me give up, for in truth it needs little to give great power to the demon when he is in possession of a body.[1]

The following declarations show, moreover, how Jeanne des Anges recognizes lucidly the abnormal and compulsive character of the phenomena, how nevertheless she sometimes accepts them willingly and even induces them, so that it is impossible for the division of consciousness to become permanent in her.

I lamented continually at the bottom of my heart and asked God to send me some person who should penetrate to the depths of my soul and recognize the disorders which these accursed spirits created with my unruly passions. . . . I felt that I had scarcely any further strength to resist the horrible temptations which I suffered.

The devil often tricked me by a lurking satisfaction I had in the agitations and other extraordinary things which he wrought in my heart. I took an extreme pleasure in hearing them discussed and was very well content to appear more tormented than the others, which gave great strength to these accursed spirits for they are well pleased to be able to beguile us into watching their operations, and by that means they insinuate themselves little by little into our souls and acquire great ascendancy over them; for they contrive so that we feel no dread of their malice. On the contrary they make themselves familiar to the human spirit and win from it by these little satisfactions a tacit consent to operate in the mind of the creature whom they possess which is very harmful to them (the possessed), for by this means they impress upon them whatever they please and make them believe what they desire, the more readily in proportion as they are the less regarded as the enemies of salvation; and if they are not very faithful to God and attentive to their conscience they are in danger of committing great sins and

---

[1] *Ibid.*, pp. 71 sq.

falling into grave errors. For after these accursed spirits have thus insinuated themselves into the will they partly persuade the soul of what they desire. . . .

This is the way in which they often treated me; whence it came about that I was almost always in remorse of conscience, and with good reason, for more often than not I saw quite well that I was the prime cause of my troubles and that the demon acted only according to the openings which I gave him.[1]

It is not that I think myself guilty of the blasphemies and other disorders into which the demons have often thrown me, but that having let myself be carried away by their suggestion in the beginning, they took possession of all my inner and outer faculties to use them according to their will and afterwards threw me into these great disorders.[2]

As I presented myself at Communion, the devil took possession of my head, and after I had received the blessed host and half moistened it the devil threw it in the priest's face. I know well that I did not do this thing, but I am fully assured to my great confusion that he would not have had this power if I had not been in league with him. I have experienced similar things on several other occasions, for when I resisted them strongly I found that all these furies and rages melted away as they had come; but alas, it too often happened that I did not make very violent efforts to resist, chiefly in things where I saw no grave sin; but in this I deceived myself, for as I did not restrain myself in the little things my spirit was afterwards surprised into great ones and the demons who possessed me had the subtlety not to confront me with evil suddenly but little by little.[3]

. . . My malady was as much within me as without.[4]

. . . For a long time I had no freedom except at night, and thus I could not make known the state of my soul.[5]

. . . I cannot express the violent torments of mind which I suffered during that time. I say with truth, I do not think that there has ever been anyone who resisted God so much as I or who was so hotly pursued.[6]

. . . They gave me very evil desires and feelings of quite licentious affection for the persons who might have helped my soul, so as to lead me to further withdrawal from communication with them.[7]

One night, when I had arisen to say orisons, I felt myself much tormented by unseemly thoughts.[8]

One day he (a demon) would have prevented me from communicating in order to make me interrupt my novena. To this end Behemoth (another demon) and he laid hold of my head as soon as it was morning and agitated me in such a way that although I recognized my disorder I had no force in me to prevent it. All that I could do was to submit myself to the command of God and accept my disorder as a punishment for my infidelities.[9]

. . . I felt forming within me in a very intelligible manner a voice which told me that. . . .[10]

. . . Three days during which my mind was exercised by divers thoughts on all these things, together with fear of speaking out about them.[11]

---

[1] Ibid., pp. 76 sq.   [2] Ibid., p. 78.   [3] Ibid., pp. 79 sq.
[4] Ibid., pp. 86 sq.   [5] Ibid., p. 100.   [6] Ibid., p. 103.
[7] Ibid., pp. 103 sq.   [8] Ibid., p. 135.   [9] Ibid., p. 168.
[10] Ibid., p. 173.   [11] Ibid., pp. 174 sq.

Given the whole character of Jeanne des Anges it is not surprising that the sexual feelings hitherto suppressed by her religious calling should have broken violently loose during possession. This is what happened moreover to her companions, who took her as model for their derangements. The acts of exorcism which have come down to us contain on this subject a mass of disgusting details. This is what Légué and G. de la Tourette say:

> Each day they were exorcised in the various churches of the town. Jeanne des Anges attracted particular attention by the violence of her fits, the obscenity of her language, and her cynical postures. . . . The inventions of the most licentious imagination would find it difficult to come anywhere near the facts. The pen refuses to set down here the cynical actions which were customary with Jeanne de Anges and her companions, and the obscene remarks to which they incessantly gave utterance.[1]

The case of Jeanne des Anges is finally remarkable from another point of view. It shows that in certain circumstances movements, even of great violence, may occur in possession without a concomitant affective state.

> Although I was outwardly in a state of great agitation, I felt within a calm and brightness which were the effect of what the Father said to the demon, for although I understand Latin not at all and the demon did what he could to distract my attention, I could not but make many reflections upon the wickedness of souls which are unfaithful to God and upon the happiness of those who are faithful to him.[2]
>
> I had a furious contortion which bent me backwards; my face became frightful. . . . I should say that, when the demon wrought this contortion of which I have spoken, he impressed upon my spirit a lively sense of the destruction which he brings, and thus it seemed to me that I was a damned soul.[3]

The compulsions often thwart and disturb the purely interior actions of the subject. This is demonstrated with particular clarity by the fact that Jeanne des Anges makes it a matter for remark when these derangements are lacking in her.

> For the period of a month I found much liberty in all my religious exercises; it seemed that my enemies had lost their accustomed power to hinder me by their disturbances from performing them.[4]
>
> . . . He (an exorcist) could not give me back my outward liberty; I sometimes had it inwardly.[5]
>
> I sometimes had my liberty when I was not at all with Father Surin.[6]

---

[1] *Ibid.*, pp. 22 sq.   [2] *Ibid.*, pp. 111 sq.   [3] *Ibid.*, p. 205.
[4] *Ibid.*, pp. 114 sq.   [5] *Ibid.*, p. 122.   [6] *Ibid.*, p. 175.

CHAPTER IV

THE GENESIS AND EXTINCTION OF POSSESSION. EXORCISM

How does possession originate ?

In the majority of cases no differently from any of the other simultaneous duplications of personality. There may be *a priori* two emotional states, parallel and separate, which co-exist and create at first sight the impression of an inner division of the mind. Or else there are simply compulsions which form the centre of crystallization of possession. As soon as their special psychological character is recognized, the general view of possession current at the time or in the patient's circle immediately causes these compulsions to be interpreted as arising from a second individuality. According to the disposition of the person affected this may easily and automatically lead to imaginative identification with the second personality; the autosuggestion resulting from distress of mind must favour this. Nevertheless, in looking through the accounts of possession, one hesitates to regard all cases as alike in this respect and to believe that the imposed consciousness of a second personality was always the first cause of possession.

Much more probably it was often rather the conviction of being possessed which brought about a real division of the mind, whereas in the divisions observed to-day the relation is reversed: first there arises a genuine division of the inner life, and then the individual declares himself dual.

The difference is due to the fact that in the times and social circles to which the majority of cases of possession belong, there was a general belief in possession, whereas in our modern civilization this is entirely on the decline. The reign of superstition was responsible for the fact, as the abundance of documents at our disposal show at every step, that the mildest compulsions were immediately taken for demoniacal possession. Modern pathology establishes that these processes do not in themselves represent any real inner division, and we are therefore driven to the inevitable conclusion that by no means all those described as possessed experienced genuine division of personality, for this is not so easily produced by autosuggestion.

Thus it is by no means true that all the numerous saints and ascetics affected by obsessions had dual personalities; apparently 'scarcely any of them have shown more than the most commonplace compulsions. If our theory is right there has always been either—and we shall regard this as being the rule—unreasoned and muddled acceptance of a prevalent superstition, or, even where it is lucid, purely intellectual and autosuggested conviction of an entirely unreal inner division. Where, however, division does arise, it is entirely primary, " spontaneous," and does not result from the autosuggestive action of previous intellectual conviction.

Another very frequent cause of possession is the sight and company of possessed persons. This at once furnishes the explanation of epidemics of this nature.[1] Exorcising priests were particularly exposed to this " infection," and scarcely one of them escaped it completely. *L'Histoire des diables de Loudun*[2] quotes an old writer of the seventeenth century who reports that " the Exorcists almost all participate, more or less, in the effects of the Demons by vexations which they suffer from them, and few persons have undertaken to drive them forth who have not been exercised by them."[3]

It is hardly necessary to remark that the true source of this infection is not the mere sight of the possessed but the concomitant lively belief in the demoniacal character of their state and its contagious nature.

A case of such infection has already been met with in the exorcist Surin.

But in the epidemic of Loudun several other exorcists were also affected: Fathers Lactance, Tranquille and Lucas. Detailed accounts of their cases have come down to us.[4]

---

[1] By way of curiosity we will mention this note on the epidemic of Kintorp: . . . Now, some were more tormented than others, and some less. But this was common to them, that as soon as one was tormented, at the mere sound the others shut away in various rooms were tormented also. (Calmeil, *De la Folie*, i, pp. 269 sq., quoted from Goulard, *Histoires admirables*, i, Paris, 1600).

[2] Amsterdam, 1716.   [3] *Ibid.*, p. 207.

[4] Calmeil, abstract of *Histoire des diables de Loudun*, ii, pp. 54-69.

We shall meet that of Father Tranquille later. *L'Histoire des diables de Loudun* reproduces a contemporary narrative concerning Lucas who was stricken immediately after Tranquille:

> For when the Extreme Unction was administered to him (Father Tranquille) the demons, feeling the efficacy of this sacrament, were obliged to raise the siege; but it was not in order to go far away, inasmuch as they entered into the body of a good Father, a very excellent Friar who was there present, and have always possessed him since; whom they vexed at first with contortions and agitations very strange and violent, puttings-out of the tongue and most frightful howlings; redoubling their rage again with every unction given to the sick man, and increasing it afresh at the sight of the Most Holy Sacrament which was fetched; because the real presence of this Man and God in one forced them to let die in peace him for whom in this last journey they would have desired to lay some snare. Thus at the moment of his death, in their fury and rage which they had because they could lay no further claim to him, they cried out horribly: "He is dead!" as if to say: "It is all over, we have no further hope of this Soul." Thereafter, falling more fiercely than ever upon the other poor friar, they agitated him so strangely and terribly that although the Brethren who held him were quite numerous they could not prevent him from aiming kicks at the dead man until he had been carried out of the room; and he remained thus violently and cruelly agitated day and night until after the burial, so that it was always necessary to leave Brethren to assist him.[1]

Father Lactance (who had expelled three demons from the prioress of Loudun):

> "While he was about this work . . . was much harassed by these evil spirits, and lost in turn sight, memory, and consciousness; suffering from sickness, obsessions of the mind and various other distresses."

Later he became still worse: "he was always raving and furious during his malady," until at length he died.[2]

Calmeil claims, although I do not know on what grounds, that the excitement of the corybantes was of the same infectious character.

> Almost always the ancient corybantes, leaping in cadence to the sound of their cymbals, with violent movements of the head, imparted their enthusiasm to those who watched them too closely.[3]

As in other psychic states, a psychic infection of possession is naturally produced amongst those who live together.[4]

---

[1] *Histoire des diables de Loudun*, pp. 354 sq.   [2] *Ibid.*, pp. 206 sq.
[3] Calmeil, *loc. cit.*, ii, 161.
[4] Two cases in Kerner, *Geschichte Besessener neuerer Zeit*, pp. 104-112.

But there are yet other ways in which possession may arise. One of these begins with a hallucination: the new person is at first corporeally represented as some little distance away. Then it draws near to the individual and suddenly seizes upon him in order to "incarnate" itself in him. The crudest possible conceptions evidently underlie this kind of possession; it is not only a strange soul which enters into man, it is even a strange body !

To this group belongs the case of the maid of Orlach who was obviously a creature of very limited intelligence.[1]

> From the 25th of August onwards the black spirit subjected her to more and more violent temptations; he no longer remained under disguises outside of her, but made himself master, as soon as he appeared, of her whole interior. He entered into her and henceforward uttered by her mouth demoniac discourses. . . .
>
> From the 24th of August the black monk always appears to her in the same way. In the midst of her work she sees him in human form (a masculine shape in a frock, as if issuing from a dark cloud; she can never clearly describe his face) coming towards her. Then she hears as if he spoke a few brief words to her, for example generally: "Won't you yet give me an answer ? Take care, I shall torment you !" and other similar things. As she stubbornly refuses to answer him, (naturally remaining quite mute), he always continues: "Well, I shall now enter into you in your despite !" Then she sees him approach, always from the left side, feels as it were a cold hand which seizes the back of her neck, and in this way he enters into her. She then loses the sense of her individuality properly so called. She is now no longer present in her body; on the contrary a deep bass voice makes itself heard, not in her person but in that of the monk, with the movement of her lips and with her features, but diabolically distorted.[2]
>
> Hardly had she arrived there when the black spirit appeared to Magdalene. He now had something white on his head, like a tuft, which stood out in contrast to his dead black colour. He said: "So I'm here again, eh ? You are going to cry because this is the last time ! You see that there is something white on me." When he had pronounced these words he went towards her, seized her with a cold hand by the back of the neck, she lost consciousness and he was once more within her.[3]

In the same primitive way arose the possession of C. St. in Eschenmayer's case:

> Four years ago C. was one day going home from her work when she met in the street the apparition of a woman which spoke to her. Suddenly something like a cold wind blew down her neck as she was speaking, and she at once became as if dumb. Later her voice returned, but very hoarse and shrill.[4]

---

[1] As Kerner remarks: "It was very difficult to get book learning into her head, although she was good for work of other kinds; thus later on she never spent her time in reading books" (*Ges. Bes.*, p. 20).

[2] *Ibid.*, pp. 35 sq.   [3] *Ibid.*, p. 42.

[4] Eschenmayer, *Konflikt*, etc., pp. 1 sq.

From the course of the malady it is clear that the girl, without much education, immediately believed that a spirit had entered into her.

These cases generally illustrate the most primitive way in which states of possession are generated. The strange soul is conceived as a material breath, ψυχή, and at its entry into the body it enters also into the mind, as yet incapable of distinguishing itself clearly therefrom.

At so primitive a level of culture and with patients of such enhanced autosuggestibility, it is not surprising that a state of possession should readily arise. The individual at once feels the strange spirit in his mind which is not yet sharply differentiated from his body.

In other instances the autosuggestion of possession breaks out quite unexpectedly, as in the following case observed in Japan and reported by Bälz. The person in question was suffering from exhaustion following typhus and was also nervous from birth. The form of possession is here " animal," that is to say the victim believes herself possessed not by a human being but by the spirit of an animal.

> A girl of seventeen years, irritable and capricious from child-hood, was recovering from a very bad attack of typhus. Around her bed sat, or rather squatted in Japanese fashion, female relations chattering and smoking. Everyone was telling how in the dusk there had been seen near the house a form resembling a northern fox. It was suspicious. Hearing this, the sick girl felt a trembling in the body and was possessed. The fox had entered into her and spoke by her mouth several times a day. Soon he assumed a domineering tone, rebuking and tyrannizing over the poor girl.[1]

Consciousness of guilt may also produce the illusion of possession by means of autosuggestion. The Catholic priest, B. Heyne, relates the following " from the reports of the missionary fathers ":

> A Chinese catechumen wished to take part in a heathen marriage where sacrificial meat is customarily eaten. She had been ex-pressly warned against it a short time before. She transgressed the interdiction and after the meal believed herself to be possessed.[2]

With this should be compared the case of Achille reported below by Janet.

Finally we shall emphasize as vital, because it furnishes a further explanation of the great frequency of possession

---

[1] Bälz, *Wiener klinische Wochenschrift*, 1907, p. 1041.
[2] B. Heyne. *Ueber Besessenheitswahn*, Paderborn, 1904, p. 62.

under the influence of belief in the devil, the fact that possession has often been cultivated by the doctor from the most insignificant beginnings.

The cause of this strange fact is that all possible ailments were laid to the account of the demon. " The number of demoniaco-magnetic affections," says Kerner again, " is really very great."[1]   For years possession might only be able to manifest itself by pains, cramp, etc.   In this respect Swabian romanticism descended very nearly to the level of the primitive races who believe that all maladies and misfortunes are caused by demons.   It was a revival of German mediæval Christianity, which in some circumstances considered animals and houses too as possessed and subjected them to exorcism.[2]

According to Kerner the doctor's task in suspected cases was to bring the demon to light, that is, where as yet no extreme psychic disturbance existed, to produce it.   Kerner says expressly that before the cure the demon must be made to speak, which the exorcist commanded him to do " in steadfast faith and in the name of Jesus."[3]

He says very naïvely:

> Only novices or wicked persons can be so mistaken as to think that magico-magnetic treatment begins by putting into the minds of these patients the idea of a malign second personality.[4]

In order fully to elucidate this doctrine we must be allowed to amplify with a sample case of the " hidden demon " type such as may also be found in Kerner's works.   A patient writes of himself:

> Already in my first youth I had had heartburn from the stomach with which there came to me against my will all sorts of strange and tormenting ideas causing inward struggles and melancholy. But these sufferings were often of short duration, for I was able to put an end to them by fervent prayer.   They were often completely interrupted for several years at a time until I was in my thirtieth year, but this condition then set in again with increased violence and frequency.
>
> I had recourse to all sorts of medical treatment, but in vain, for the malady rose year by year and finally reached the head.   I was tortured with twitchings, prickings, and dizziness in the head which often made it seem as if I were being struck on the back of the neck

---

[1] Kerner, *Nachricht*, etc., p. 60.
[2] Bodinus, *Dæmonomania*, Hamburg, 1698, p. 156.   Calmeil, *De la Folie*, i, p. 183.
[3] Kerner, *Nachricht*, etc., p. 10.   [4] *Ibid.*, p. 11.

with the fist and my body dragged upwards as if someone wished to throw me to the ground with murderous violence. It often seems to me that I have on my head a weight of several quintals which must break down my legs. This attack comes on almost every day and I feel that under this heavy burden my feet leave prints on the ground. From day to day these terrible pains increase, together with diabolic thoughts of blasphemies against God which are a most anguishing inner torment. This agitation in my body and these painful eructations are often most violent during prayer and I then have horrible feelings of suffocation.

For a long time past I have used quantities of every conceivable medicine to cure these pains, but always without result.

PHILIPP NEGELE,
Forester.

BUBENORBIS,
12th Jan., 1836.

Kerner adds:

The forester Negele is a very intelligent and truthful man. There is no doubt that his malady is of a demoniaco-magnetic character, although no demon speaks by his mouth. A magico-magnetic treatment would probably induce the demon to speak. It will be very difficult for him to be cured by any other treatment.[1]

Jeanne des Anges also became possessed in good earnest thanks to exorcism.[2]

In particular cases the compulsive idea is developed into a complete obsessive personality, a " demon " because by suggestion practised upon this latter a cure succeeds more easily. Thus in his case Janet from the first spoke directly to the demon; it is true that he did not subsequently proceed in the manner of the old exorcists.[3]

In the following case the practice of exorcism resulted in a strange voice suddenly beginning to speak in a man who for years past had suffered from fairly severe compulsive phenomena without nevertheless reaching a complete inner division:

A man of seventy-one years, an old magnetic demoniac, wished also . . . to ask for help. In his thirty-sixth year this man had had, according to his own account, a swelling in the region of the stomach accompanied by sharp pains. In spite of this he was able to eat all kinds of food, and even found himself obliged, contrary to his former habits, to eat heavily. As his pains continued to make themselves felt day and night, without leaving him any

---

[1] Kerner, *Nachricht*, etc., pp. 57 sq. There is in Kerner (*Geschichten*, etc., pp. 110 sq.) another case in which possession was produced, or at least enormously intensified, by exorcism.

[2] *Bibliothèque diabolique*, vol. v, Sœur Jeanne des Anges, Paris, 1886, p. 17.

[3] P. Janet, *Un cas de possession et d'exorcisme moderne*, in " Névroses et ideés fixes," i, Paris, 1898.

7

rest although the swelling of the stomach had subsided, he used for two years a great many medicines, but without result. He nevertheless noticed that during prayer there was always something which seemed to rise up from his belly. Finally it often threw him to the ground with great violence even while he was praying. These attacks often ceased for six months, then came on again with increased strength. . . . The strangest result was that he found himself constrained to insult and abuse his wife and children; in particular, and without being able to give any reason, he could no longer endure these latter.

The death of his wife, whom he dearly loved, brought no change in his state, nor did a second marriage which he contracted in spite of his attacks. He was advised, although a Lutheran, to go to the Catholic priests. In the presence of those who were able to work on him his head turned convulsively backward and he uttered involuntary roarings, but without articulate words; with the others his malady gave no sign, but as soon as he left them it raged anew with added violence. . . .

In spite of these disorders he was, at least from time to time, able to work. According to his wife it was only a few years since he had himself carried the stones to a great building which he had undertaken.

He had grown very thin, and when he spoke of his state his head or body was suddenly bent and visibly drawn inwards. Without being able to prevent it he would suddenly be obliged to cry out like an animal. . . .

In his natural state he looked a quiet and gentle person and spoke accordingly. But in the middle of the conversation the facial expression, bodily posture, and tone of voice often changed suddenly, he became irascible, walked gesticulating as if filled with anger, but nevertheless always retained the full use of his senses. He is a peaceable and God-fearing man, but not bigoted, and his wife is like him. . . .

The magico-magnetic treatment had the result of obliging the demon who had hidden in him for thirty-six years to speak forthwith. A strange demoniac voice then made itself heard by his mouth, which had never happened before.[1]

These singular " methods of treatment " are of great interest from the psychological point of view, for they show that by artificial means and in appropriate suggestive and autosuggestive conditions it is possible to induce division of the psychic life. Naturally this method might still be applied with success to many ignorant persons, and we should then be in an ideal position, theoretically speaking, to explore the psychology of possession in a truly experimental manner. But from the practical point of view the student could hardly bring himself to provoke these disturbances voluntarily, for, as the literature of the subject shows they are far easier to cause than to cure. It would be difficult to make them disappear by hypnotic suggestion, because persons affected

[1] Kerner, *Nachricht*, etc., pp. 49 sq.

by compulsive phenomena are only slightly, if at all, susceptible to hypnosis. For this reason we should, at least before trying to induce possession, impart in the state of hypnosis the suggestions which would later serve to make it disappear. In any case attempts of this nature would entail such a responsibility that they are to be deprecated.

Finally yet another case may be cited in which timely psychiatric treatment intervened before the demoniac visions resulting from a priest's suggestion of the idea of possession had produced derangements of the personality.

> The fits of sleep generally succeeded convulsive attacks; V. was not forewarned of their advent. Their duration varied from one to four days, and they ended in tears and depression. " Everything seemed odd to me, I did not recognize myself at all." The greater the efforts to calm and console her, the more her tears redoubled. In addition she was prostrate with fatigue.
>
> At Lariboisière (a hospital) the almoner came to see her after her attacks; he told her that it was the devil who made her ill. Presently under the influence of this idea her malady redoubled in intensity and in the delirious period of the convulsive fits she saw the devil. " He was tall, with scales and legs ending in claws; he stretched out his arms as if to seize me; he had red eyes and his body ended in a great tail like a lion's, with hair at the end; he grimaced, laughed, and seemed to say: " I shall have her !""
>
> The nun and the almoner had persuaded her that she was possessed by the devil because she did not pray enough, and that she would not recover. She had masses said for which she paid a franc or one franc fifty; she confessed and took communion; the almoner sprinkled her with holy water and made signs over her.
>
> Sometimes V. saw the devil between her fits. If she was in bed she hid her face under the bedclothes to escape from the apparition; but she saw it nevertheless. The more she was talked to about the devil the more she saw him and the more violent and frequent became her attacks.
>
> In the first months of her admission to the Saltpêtrière she still had diabolic visions.   As she went to church less and no one talked to her any more about the devil, she gradually regained her tranquillity and finally got rid of the idea " that she belonged to the devil."[1]

The fact that possession springs from belief in the devil joined to auto- and hetero-suggestion accounts for the fact that it has always been most extensive in the least educated classes of society.

> Hardly any example is known of possession in a really cultured individual. This affliction generally befalls persons of inferior station, which explains the coarse and vulgar tone of the alleged demons.[2]

---

[1] *Iconographie de la Saltpêtrière*, iii, pp. 106 sq.
[2] Perty, *Mystische Erscheinungen*, p. 344, quoted by Kiesewetter, *Geschichte des Okkultismus*, vol. ii, p. 669.

Finally, as regards the artificial extinction of possession, it has always been suggestive in character and has even resulted from " exorcism," that is to say, the emphatic ordering of the so-called demon to leave the possessed person. The stories of the Gospels are in this respect typical of the procedure of exorcism at all times. It has never varied, either in the time of Jesus or during the millenaries before and since. The exorcist always speaks to the demon and tries to induce him, by contingent threats and in the name of a deity (Jesus, etc.), to leave the possessed. The most frequent procedure has been one of threats and commands.

Exorcism presents the exact counterpart of the genesis of possession. In the same way that the latter springs from a man's belief that he is possessed, conversely it disappears, when the exorcism is successful, through his belief that it will no longer continue. The inner nature of this effect of conviction on psychic phenomena is not known and cannot be elucidated. The theory of suggestion can do no more than recognize it. Just as we can say little about the physiological effects of suggestion and autosuggestion, the production of vesications and bleeding stigmata, so do their deep-seated psychic effects escape our closer knowledge. We cannot avoid the difficulty by merely affirming the connection between faith and the changes which it brings to pass. What should, however, be possible is a more exact analysis of the psychic state during enhanced suggestibility.[1]

Of specimens of exorcism there is no lack. We possess some dating from the first days of the Christian era, and also from earlier times. Recent finds of papyri have been particularly rich in them, but it should be noted that as sickness and possession have often been identified, the great abundance of exorcisms does not correspond to an equal number of true cases of possession, but to pathological states of every kind. Exorcisms of possession properly so called are in the minority.

As example of these latter we shall give the grand formula taken from the magic papyrus of Paris and published by Wesseley. It certainly served against possession, since the demon was summoned to give an account of himself. Accord-

---

[1] Th. Lipps, *Zeitschrift für Hypnotismus*, vol. vi, and O. Vogt, *ibid.*, vol. v, have given excellent analyses of suggestion.

ing to Deissmann it is an exorcism of Jewish origin into which a pagan has introduced the name of Jesus.

> Against demoniacal possession. The tried formula of Pibechis (a celebrated magician). Take of the juice of green fruits, together with the plant Mastigia (?) and lotus-pith, and heat it with marjoram (the colourless kind); then pronounce the following words: " Joel, Ossarthiomi, Emori, Theochipsoith, Sithemeoch, Sothe, Joe, Mimipsothiooph, Phersothi. Αεεῑογō, Joe, Eochariphtha; get thee out of N.N." (and other formulæ). But write the protecting charm on a tablet of tin: " Jæo, Abraothioch, Phtha, Mesentiniao, Pheoch, Jæo, Charsok," and hang it upon the sick person. To every demon it is a thing of fear which he dreads. Place thyself in front of the patient and conjure him. The formula of exorcism is the following: " I conjure thee by the God of the Hebrews, Jesus (later interpolation from a non-Jewish source), Jaba, Jæ, Abraoth, Aia, Thoth, Ele, Elo, Æo, Eu, Jiibæch, Abarmas, Jabarau, Abelbel, Lona, Abra, Maroia, Arm, appearing in fire, thou, Tannetis, in the midst of plains, and snow, and mists; let thine inexorable angel descend and put into safe keeping the wandering demon of this creature whom God has created in his holy Paradise. For I pray to the Holy God, putting my reliance in Ammonipsentancho." Say: " I conjure thee with a flood of bold words: Jakuth, Ablanathanalba, Akramm." Say: " Aoth, Jathabathra, Chach-thabratha, Chamynchel, Abrooth. Thou art Abrasiloth, Allelu, Jelosai, Jœl: I conjure thee by him who manifested himself to Osræl by night in a pillar of fire and in a cloud by day and who has saved his people from the hard tasks of Pharaoh and brought down on Pharaoh the Ten Plagues because he would not harken. I conjure thee, demoniac spirit, to say who thou art. For I conjure thee by the seal Solomon placed upon the tongue of Jeremiah that he might speak. Say therefore who thou art, a celestial being or spirit of the airs.[1]

A detailed history of Christian exorcism is to be found in the seventh book, second part, of A. J. Binterim's work: *Die vorzüglichsten Denkwürdigkeiten der christ-katholischen Kirche*.[2] In the third essay entitled " Of Energumens and their Treatment in the Primitive Church," the information furnished by the early Christian writers about the possessed is collected and dealt with.

Like so many other things in the Catholic Church, the growth of exorcism came to an end at the time of the Counter-Reformation. This was due to the publication in 1614, consequent on the repeated request of Paul V, of the *Rituale Romanum*. The rite of exorcism formulated therein has remained the accepted one up to the present time.

---

[1] A. Deissmann, *Licht vom Osten*, 3rd edit., Tübingen, 1909, pp. 192 sq.
[2] Mainz, 1838.

Amongst other works the *Manuale Exorcismorum*[1] gives a complete insight into the procedure of exorcism. It contains instructions as to how exorcisms should be carried out and gives a great number of ritual formulæ. These latter are in some instances voluminous, the most important occupying close on forty pages.

Exorcism never draws its strength from the exorcist, but is always carried out in the name of God, of Jesus, etc. The Manual warns the exorcist that he is dealing with an ancient and astute adversary, strong and exceedingly evil: *antiquo et asturo hoste, forti et nequissimo.* The first arm and the most important is therefore a lively faith, an absolute confidence in God and Jesus. The exorcist must be convinced that *nihil se posse absque ejus singulari assistentia et auxilio.*

By way of subjective preparation for exorcism he must compose himself inwardly. *Revocabit mentem et spiritum a curis et negotiis sæcularibus eamque pacatam et tranquillam reddere studebit meditationibus piis et precibus.* Preliminary fasting and prayer are also recommended: *Nunquam ad exorcisandum accedet nisi prævio ieiunio vel aliis pœnitentiæ et satisfactoriis operibus nisi præsens necessitas aliud videatur exigere. Incessanter orabit etiam privatim aliosque ad prædicta bona opera et pietatis exercitia invitabit eleemosynasque elargiri curabit.*[2]

The scene of the exorcism should in general be the church or some other place consecrated to God. Only in cases of urgency may it take place in a private house. Women and children should be excluded, as well as the vulgar curious. But the exorcist should not operate without witnesses. He should provide *ut adsint viri graves et pii, præsertim clerici, Sacerdotes vel Religiosi, si haberi possint, qui non solum erunt testes sacrarum actionum, sed etiam ipsum iuvabunt orationibus et piis desideriis.*[3] It is left to the discretionary power of the exorcist to decide whether the exorcism shall take place in public or not.

---

[1] *Manuale Exorcismorum,* continens Instructiones et Exorcismos ad eiiciendos e corporibus spiritus malignos et ad quævis maleficia depellenda et ad quascumque infestationes dæmonum reprimendas: R. D. Maximiliani ab Eynatten S.T.L. Canonici et Scholastici Antverpiensis industria collectum. Antverpiæ, 1626.

[2] *Ibid.,* p. 3   [3] *Ibid.,* p. 20.

At Loudun there must have been at times as many as 7,000 spectators.

The exorcisms of Nicole de Vervins (1566) were also great spectacles. All the Catholics and Protestants came in crowds from the surrounding district to the cathedral of Laon, the civil authorities were also present, and the Huguenots claimed reserved seats;[1] nothing was lacking except the collection of an entrance fee. It almost came to a serious fight between the armed Catholic priests with their following and the retainers of a Protestant landowner of the district.

The principal exorcism of the *Rituale Romanum* published by order of Paul V is enclosed between long prayers at the beginning and end and in the middle is inserted another prayer, so that the whole is divided into five parts: prayer, exorcism, prayer, exorcism, prayer, again interrupted in many places by readings from the Scriptures. From the psychological point of view this construction is by no means inept. While the exorcism seeks to work upon the " demon " by threats and commands, the prayers are designed to help the possessed person, reinforcing his desire to be delivered from the demon, and increasing his confidence in the divine power which is invoked. Nevertheless cures by a single application of exorcism appear to have been rare; exorcisms last as a rule for days, weeks, months and even years. The impression made upon the possessed by the conjuration is further enhanced by signs of the cross (✠) and the winding of the priest's stole round his neck together with layings-on of hands; sacraments, holy water and other sacred objects are also used. The exorcist must speak as is formally pre-scribed, *constanter et magna cum fide.*

Two passages from the exorcism may be given as example:

Exorciso te, immundissime spiritus, omnis incursio adversarii, omne phantasma, omnis legio, in nomine Domini nostri Jesu Christi; ✠ eradicare et effugare ab hoc plasmate Dei. ✠ Ipse tibi imperat, qui te de supernis cœlorum in inferiora terræ demergi præcepit. Ipse tibi imperat, qui mari, ventis et tempestatibus imperavit. Audi ergo et time satana, inimice fidei, hostis generis humani, mortis adductor, vitæ raptor, iustitiæ declinator, malorum radix, fomes vitiorum, seductor hominum, proditor gentium, in-citator invidiæ, origo avaritiæ, causa discordiæ, excitator dolorum. Quid stas et resistis cum scias Christum Dominum vires tuas

---

[1] Louis Langlet, *Etude médicale d'une possession,* thesis, Paris, 1910, p 45.

perdere ? Illum metue, qui in Isaac immolatus est, in Joseph venumdatus, in agno occisus, in homine crucifixus, deinde inferni. Triumphator fuit (*Sequentes, Cruces fiant in fronte obsessis*). Recede ergo in nomine Patris ✠ et Filii ✠ et Spiritus ✠ sancti, da locum Spiritui sancto, per hoc signum ✠ Crucis Jesu Christi Domini nostri. Qui cum Patre et eodem Spiritu sancto vivit et regnat Deus per omnia sæcula sæculorum.[1]

Adiuro te serpens antique, per Judicem vivorum et mortuorum, per factorem tuum, per factorem mundi, per eum qui habet potestatem mittendi te in gehennam, ut ab hoc famulo Dei N., qui ad Ecclesiæ sinum recurrit, cum metu et exercitu furoris tui festinus discedas. Adiuro te iterum ✠ (*in fronte*) non mea infirmitate, sed virtute Spiritus sancti, ut exeas ab hoc famulo Dei N. quem omnipotens Deus ad imaginem suam fecit. Cede igitur, cede non mihi, sed ministro Christi. Illius enim te urget potestas, qui te Cruci suæ subiugavit. Illius bracchium contremisce, qui devictis gemitibus inferni, animas ad lucem perduxit. Sit tibi terror corpus hominis ✠ (*in pectore*), sit tibi imago formido Dei ✠ (*in fronte*). Non resistas, nec moreris discedere ab homine isto, quoniam complacuit Christo in homine habitare. Et ne contemnendum putes, dum me peccatorem nimis esse cognoscis. Imperat tibi Deus ✠ Imperat tibi maiestas Christi ✠. Imperat tibi Deus Pater ✠, imperat tibi Deus Filius ✠, imperat tibi Deus Spiritus ✠ sanctus. Imperat tibi sacramentum Crucis ✠. Imperat tibi fides Sanctorum Apostolorum Petri et Pauli, et ceterorum Sanctorum ✠. Imperat tibi Martyrum sanguis ✠. Imperat tibi continentia Confessorum ✠. Imperat tibi pia Sanctorum et Sanctarum omnium intercessio ✠. Imperat tibi Christianæ fidei mysteriorum virtus ✠. Exi ergo transgressor, exi seductor, plene omni dolo et fallacia, virtutis inimice, innocentium persecutor. Da locum dirissime; da locum impiissime: da locum Christo, inquo nihil invenisti de operibus tuis, qui te spoliavit, qui regnum tuum destruxit, qui te victum legavit. . . .

Adiuro ergo te, draco nequissime, in nomine Agni ✠ immaculati, qui ambulavit super aspidem et basiliscum, qui conculcavit leonem et draconem, ut discedas ab hoc homine ✠ (*fiat in fronte*), discedas ab Ecclesia Dei ✠ (*fiat signum super circumstantes*), contremisce et effuge. . . .[2]

In later times the curative action of Christian exorcism derived mainly from the solemn nature of the ritual. The Latin tongue ceased to be generally understood by the uncultured victims of possession.

In place of command and menace, other methods of healing may also be used. In the C. St. case of Eschenmayer, for example, efforts were formally made to convert the demon.

The feature common to all methods is that the exorcist always addresses himself to the possessing spirit, never to the possessed. In clear cases of somnambulism it would moreover be inherently impossible to speak to the possessed because he does not generally react when called by his ordinary name. It is different in cases where the normal personality

---

[1] *Manuale* . . ., pp. 44 sq.   [2] *Ibid.*, pp. 46 sq.

is preserved, and where it would be perfectly conceivable for the exorcist, in our day the doctor, to try to convince the patient that the demon will leave him at a given time. But even to-day, in the only case of this kind known to me, the doctor, that is to say, the psychologist, addressed himself to the demon,[1] for the undoubted reason that the patient is more accessible to strong suggestion in the somnambulistic than in the waking state.

It is worth emphasizing that as a rule success depends on the authority and power of suggestion of the exorcist. It is even important, particularly in a religious period, that he should himself be religious and convinced of the reality of possession if by that means his faith in the success of exorcism is increased. Secondary expedients of a suggestive nature are also brought to bear.

In this connection Kerner formulates in his dogmatic way that:

> The cure is produced magically by prayer and conjurations, and chiefly by the name of Jesus pronounced with an assured faith.[2]
>
> But this magic influence (conjuration) must be given forth with the firmest will and faith, as if addressed to a real demon and not a malady, and the conversation with the articulate demon must be carried on in the same way. . . .
>
> If the prayer and conjuration are not carried out with the most complete faith that there is a real demon incarnate (and not poison from a scratch, etc.) no cure follows.[3]
>
> In the same way that a firm faith is required of him who conjures the demon, the patient should for his part and so far as in him lies take care not to weaken, and everything which might distract him must be kept from him. Persons able to perform conjuration with much faith are found rather amongst shepherds than amongst the educated.[4]

Harnack similarly remarks:

> The message of Christian preaching does not alone suffice to cure the malady. Behind it there must be firm faith and a person sustained by that faith. It is not prayer which heals but he who prays; not the letter, but the spirit; not the exorcism, but the exorcist.[5]

It might better be expressed: *It is the faith of the possessed himself* in the joyful message which comes to his aid; his shortcomings are, however, helped by an adequate personality in the messenger.

---

[1] This is Lemaître's case.   [2] *Nachricht*, etc., p. 17.
[3] *Ibid.*, p. 18.   [4] *Ibid.*, p. 19.
[5] Harnack, *Medizinisches aus der ältesten Kirchengeschichte.* In *Texte und Untersuchungen zur Gesch. der altchrist. Literatur*, viii, pp. 105-59.

There is no doubt that in present-day Christian missions there still survives something of that joyful assurance, that faith in the domination of the world, which animated primitive Christianity, and that their strong influence where they have penetrated rests essentially on the same factors which led early Christianity to success: the preaching of the Redeemer with an ardour free from all egotism, ready for sacrifice, even death, and combined with a standard of personal conduct corresponding to the faith.

This great power which the exorcists alone have exerted has been described by St Jerome (348-420) in the episode of Hilarion the anchorite which is contained in the highly apocryphal biography of the latter. The facts are, however, not beyond the bounds of possibility.

> Nor must we omit to tell that Orion, a leading man and wealthy citizen of Aira, on the coast of the Red Sea, being possessed by a legion of demons was brought to him. Hands, neck, sides, feet, were laden with iron, and his glaring eyes portended an access of raging madness. As the saint was walking with the brethren and expounding some passage of scripture the man broke from the hands of his keepers, clasped him from behind and raised him aloft. There was a shout from all, for they feared lest he might crush his limbs, wasted as they were with fasting. The saint smiled and said: " Be quiet and let me have my rival in the wrestling match to myself." Then he bent back his hand over his shoulder till he touched the man's head, seized his hair and drew him round so as to be foot to foot with him; he then stretched both his hands in a straight line, and trod on his two feet with both his own, while he touched the man's head, seized his hair and drew him round so as to be foot to foot with him; he then stretched both his hands in a straight line, and trod on his two feet with both his own, while he cried out again and again. " To torment with you ! Ye crowd of demons, to torment !" The sufferer shouted aloud and bent back his neck till his head touched the ground, while the saint said, " Lord Jesus, release this wretched man, release this captive. Thine it is to conquer many, no less than one." What I now relate is unparalleled: from one man's lips were heard different voices and as it were the confused shouts of a multitude. Well, he too was cured, and not long after came with his wife and children to the monastery bringing many gifts expressive of his gratitude. . . .[1]

In more than one case the demon lays down conditions on which he will depart. Bälz has observed some of these cases in Japan. Here is one:

> At the end of some weeks a renowned exorcist of the sect of the Nuhiren was summoned and proceeded to solemn exorcism. Neither excommunication nor censing nor any other endeavour

---

[1] Jerome, *Life of St Hilarion*, 18. Library of Nicene and Post-Nicene Fathers, second series, vol vi, St Jerome, pp. 306-307.

succeeded, the fox saying ironically that he was too clever to be taken in by such manœuvres. Nevertheless he consented to come out freely from the starved body of the sick person if a plentiful feast was offered to him. " How was it to be arranged ?" On a certain day at four o'clock there were to be placed in a temple sacred to foxes and situated twelve kilometres away two vessels of rice prepared in a particular way, of cheese cooked with beans, together with a great quantity of roast mice and raw vegetables, all favourite dishes of magic foxes: then he would leave the body of the girl exactly at the prescribed time. And so it happened. Punctually at four o'clock when the food was placed in the distant temple the girl sighed profoundly and cried: " He has gone !" The possession was cured.[1]

Exorcism is not, however, efficacious in all cases, but generally speaking we have as yet no precise evidence as to why suggestion is used with effect in one case and not in another.

A case in which all the forms of suggestion, even hypnotic, failed, was observed by Bälz at Tokio. We shall have occasion to quote it again later.

—My efforts to produce a cure by verbal suggestion or otherwise— —by hypnosis, electrical manipulations, etc.—did not succeed. The patient had passed without success through the hands of so many professional suggestionists, priests, and exorcists of all sorts that I could do nothing more in that direction. Her malady had taken the form of a regularly periodic obsession and she tried to make terms with it. Between the fits she had the full use of her reason, except that she was easily frightened. Her memory had not suffered essentially, nor was there any sign of degeneration. I do not know what became of her.[2]

The following is a cure of a somewhat violent nature also reported by Bälz:

Many cases of cure by the threat of sharp weapons are known. In Japan a despairing father tied his youngest daughter, who was possessed by a fox, to a pillar and rushing upon her with drawn sword cried: " Wicked spirit, if thou dost not forthwith leave this child I will kill you both !" The girl was cured.[3]

The phenomena of exorcism correspond to those of the genesis of possession. Like the intruding spirit the spirit to be expelled is in most cases conceived as something subtly material which must be driven from the body and which leaves it by a specific place.

For this reason it sometimes happens that the spectators

---

[1] *Wiener klinische Wochenschrift*, 1907, p. 1041.
[2] *Ibid.*, pp. 984 sq.   [3] *Ibid.*, p. 1092.

are subject to delusions or even hallucinations. For example, an account of a case of possession dating from 1559 relates:

> . . . and the evil spirit was at length driven out of the girl and made its way through the window like a swarm of flies.[1]

We will quote by way of curiosity a modern case observed by d'Allonnes, in which every method of treatment, religious exorcism and medical hypnotism alike, was fruitless until the cure was operated by the sole and unaided virtue of— methylene blue.

> . . . At length she even had recourse to doctors. It must be admitted that they are the only persons who obtained any result. They prescribed pills containing methylene blue, the sole effect of which is to colour the urine. This coloration produced a great effect on Alexandra and her devil; he no longer dared approach that part of the body which he believed to be poisoned.[2]

But there are also cures by simple autosuggestion, the most remarkable of which is that of the maid of Orlach. Its starting-point was a hallucination occurring at a time when there was as yet no possession.

> . . . That same day at half-past seven the girl perceived at the back of the cowshed, against the wall, the grey shape of a woman whose head and body were enveloped in something like a black band. This apparition beckoned to the girl with its hand.
> An hour later when she was giving forage to the stock the same form appeared to her again and began to speak to her. It said: " Flee from the house ! Flee from the house ! If it is not pulled down before the 5th of March of the coming year a misfortune will happen to you. . . . Promise me that you will do it !"
> The girl then gave the promise. Her father and brother were present and heard her speaking, but saw and heard nothing else.[3]
> On the 23rd of August there was a new hallucination, the apparition of a white spirit which again recalled the promise to pull down the house on the given date. From this moment onwards the girl's father made arrangements to demolish his house and build a new one, so marvellous did this appear to many people.[4]

After more than five months the possessed was brought to Kerner. As he records, he encouraged the parents' belief—

> . . . "in the demoniacal possession of their child, and this was mainly for the girl's sake and in order to be able to subject her to a more searching observation. I explained her state solely as a malady against which all the usual medicaments would be

[1] Kerner, *Geschichten*, etc., p. 123.
[2] Dupray, *Psychologie d'un démon familier*, " Journal de psychol.," vol. iii (1906), p. 532.
[3] Kerner, *Geschichten*, etc., pp. 22 sq.   [4] *Ibid.*, p. 85.

useless so that they had up to that time rightly refused for their daughter the aid of all the chemists' bottles, boxes of pills, and pots of ointment. To the girl also I recommended no remedy except prayer and low diet. As for the action of magnetic passes which I only tried upon her two or three times, the demon tried to neutralize them immediately by counter-passes made with the girl's hands. This remedy also failed as did, generally speaking, all others without this causing me any anxiety, because I had in any case recognized the girl's state as demoniaco-magnetic and had confidence in the divination of the better spirit, that which had promised her cure before the 5th of March. I left her in this belief without anxiety."[1]

See below the account of the real healing.

Yet more remarkable is the following self-cure, on the occasion of which an exorcist had an hallucination and spoke automatically by the mouth of the possessed, so that another possession supervened side by side with the demoniacal one. (I shall not study this phenomenon.)

On January 26th at eleven o'clock in the morning, the very hour that the girl in a waking state (told, as she said, by an angel), had announced as the hour of her deliverance, the cessation of these incidents (fits) took place. The last that was heard was a voice issuing from the girl's mouth and crying: " Impure spirit, come out of this child ! Knowest thou not that this child is my best-beloved !" Then she recovered consciousness.

On January 31st the same state returned with all its symptoms. . . . On February 9th, which had similarly been indicated by the girl on January 31st as the day of deliverance, her torments came to an end in the same way as the first time. On February 9th at noon, after the same voice had several times announced his departure, these words were heard to come from the girl's mouth: " Hence, impure spirit ! This is a sign of the last time !" The girl awoke and has remained in good health up to the present day.[2]

Finally in many cases where, as in the epidemics of possession, the fits had generally no deep-seated foundation in an hysterical affection but were more or less voluntarily induced, it was sufficient simply to isolate the patients in order to restore their peace of mind. This was the case with Jeanne des Anges and her companions: with isolation all the phenomena ceased at once.[3] (Owing to fresh exorcisms they were subsequently called forth again.)

Janet undertook a psychological exorcism of a refined nature upon one of his patients who had already been ill for four months before coming into his hands. He first assured himself that the psychological cause of the phenomena of

---

[1] *Ibid.*, p. 40.
[2] *Ibid.*, pp. 105 sq.
[3] *Bibliothèque diabolique* (1886), v, p. 19.

compulsion was remorse of conscience for a conjugal fault. The procedure employed by Janet to end the possession consisted simply in putting the patient into a state of somnambulistic suggestion and then sorting out and gradually effacing all the memories which tormented him. The apogee and crux of this treatment was to suggest the presence of the patient's wife who appeared before his hallucinated eyes and solemnly forgave him.

This scene of pardon was only an hallucination, but although its elements were therefore false they constituted for the patient's conscience a living reality so strong in its effect that the oppressive memory and remorse disappeared in him, together with all the phenomena of possession.

By reason of its interest, I will quote the principal passages of Janet's account.

> The patient is a man of thirty-three years who was brought to the Salpêtrière four years ago in Charcot's time. I was able closely to examine this person confided to my care, and was fortunate enough to restore his reason completely in a few months. The cure has been maintained for more than three years and the patient has been followed up for a sufficient length of time to render it possible now to study his delirium, examining the means which effected the cure and which may be called modern exorcism, and finally to extract from this observation the maximum of information possible. There is, moreover, no objection to my relating the misadventures of this unfortunate man; I will give him a false name and change that of his native place together with his social position; the psychological and medical facts alone will be accurate. . . .
>
> Achille, as we will call him, belonged to a family of peasants in a small way in the south of France; he was brought up amongst simple people, evidently without much education. This confirms Esquirol's remark that the delirium of possession is to-day practically confined to the lower classes. His parents and the villagers were superstitiously inclined and strange legends were current about his family. His father was accused of having at some previous time given himself to the devil and of going every Saturday to an old tree-trunk to converse with Satan who handed him a bag of money. . . .
>
> . . . Achille was hereditarily predisposed to insanity . . .; he was a degenerate in the classic sense of the word.
>
> Achille had a normal childhood; he was educated in a little grammar school and showed himself studious and diligent although of only average intelligence; he had in particular a very good memory and read voraciously without much selection. He was sensitive to impressions, took everything seriously " as if it had really happened," as he said, and remained upset for a long time after a fright, a punishment, or the slightest incident. He did not share the superstitions of his village and even had very few religious beliefs. He might have been declared almost normal had he not frequently had sick headaches and had certain small

facts which seem to me to have their significance not been observed. Although very sensitive and affectionate he did not succeed in making friends, but was always alone and rather an object of ridicule to his schoolfellows. . . .

Achille, having left school early . . . engaged in a small business. . . . A very fortunate thing for him was that he married early, towards the age of twenty-two years, a kindly and devoted woman who corrected several imaginative aberrations and made him sensible and happy for several years. He had one child, a little girl who grew up absolutely normal, and everything went well with him for about ten years. Achille was thirty-three years old when he experienced a series of accidents which brought him in the course of a few months to the Saltpêtrière. . . .

Towards the end of the winter of 1890 Achille had to make a short journey necessitated by his business, and returned home at the end of a few weeks. Although he said he was quite well and made efforts to appear in good spirits, his wife found him changed. He was gloomy, preoccupied, he scarcely ever kissed his wife and child and spoke very little. At the end of several days this taciturnity increased and the poor man had difficulty in muttering a few words during the course of a day. But his silence assumed a quite peculiar aspect: it ceased to be voluntary as at first; Achille was no longer silent because he did not wish to speak, but because he was not able to speak. He made fruitless efforts to utter a sound and could no longer manage it ; he had become dumb. The doctor consulted shook his head and found the case very grave; he tested the heart, examined the urine, and concluded that it was general debility, a modification in the humours, dyscrasia, perhaps diabetes, etc., etc. The fear of all these drove Achille distracted—he rapidly recovered his speech in order to complain of all sorts of pains. . . .

As at the end of a full month there was no perceptible improvement, Achille went to consult another doctor (who diagnosed angina pectoris).

The unfortunate man took to his bed and was overcome by the blackest depression. He no longer did anything and moreover no longer understood a word of what he read, often seeming unable even to grasp the remarks addressed to him. To all the questions of his despairing wife, he replied that he did not know what depressed him in this way, that he still kept a stout heart, but that in spite of himself he felt the most gloomy presentiments. He slept from time to time, but even in sleep his lips moved and murmured incomprehensible words while tears streamed from his eyes. At length his presentiments appeared to be realized. One day when he was more depressed than usual he called his wife and child, embraced them despairingly, then stretched himself upon his bed and made no further movement. He remained thus motionless during two days while those who watched beside him expected at every moment to see him breathe his last.

Suddenly, one morning, after two days of apparent death, Achille arose, sat up with both eyes wide open, and broke into a frightful laugh. It was a convulsive laugh which shook his whole body, a laugh of unnatural violence which twisted his mouth, a lugubrious laugh which lasted for more than two hours and was truly satanic.

From that moment everything was changed. Achille leapt out of bed and refused all attention. To every question he replied: " Do nothing, it is useless, let us drink champagne, it is the end of the world." Then he uttered horrible cries, " They are burning me, they are cutting me to pieces." These cries and wild movements lasted until the evening, then the unhappy man fell into a troubled sleep.

The reawakening was no better; Achille related to his assembled family a thousand dreadful things. The demon, said he, was in the room, surrounded by a crowd of little horned and grimacing imps; still worse, the devil was within him and forced him to utter horrible blasphemies. In fact Achille's mouth, for he declared that he had nothing to do with it, abused God and the saints and repeated a confused mass of the most filthy insults to religion. Yet graver and more cruel was the fact that the demon twisted his legs and arms and caused him the most hideous sufferings which wrung horrible cries from the poor wretch. This was thought to be a state of high fever with transitory delirium, but the condition was lasting. Achille but rarely had calmer moments when he embraced his daughter, weeping and deploring his sad fate which had made him the prey of demons. He never expressed the least doubt as to his possession by the devil, of which he was absolutely convinced. " I have not believed sufficiently in our holy religion nor in the devil," he often said ; " he has taken a terrible revenge, he has me, he is within me and will never leave me."

When he was not watched, Achille escaped from the house, ran across the fields, hid in the woods where he was found the next day completely terrified. He tried especially to get into the cemetery, and several times was found lying asleep upon a grave. He seemed to long for death for he took poisons; he swallowed laudanum and part of a little bottle of Fowler's drops; he even tied his feet together and thus bound threw himself into a pond. He nevertheless managed to get out, and when found on the edge said sadly : " You can see well enough that I am possessed by the devil, since I cannot die. I have made the test demanded by religion, thrown myself into the water with my feet tied together, and I floated. Ah, the devil is certainly in me !" It was necessary to shut him up in his room and watch him closely; after three months of this raving, which terrified his poor family, they had to make up their minds, somewhat tardily and on the advice of a wise doctor, to take him to the Saltpêtrière as the most propitious place to-day for the exorcism of the possessed and the expulsion of demons.

When Charcot and my friend Mr. Dutil, who was the head of his clinic, handed over this interesting case to me, I at once remarked in him all the recognized signs of possession as described in the mediæval epidemics. . . . He (Achille) muttered blasphemies in a muffled and solemn voice: " Cursed be God," said he, " cursed the Trinity, cursed the Virgin !" . . . then in a shrill voice and with eyes full of tears: " It is not my fault if my mouth says these horrible things, it is not I. . . . I press my lips together so that the words may not escape, may not break out, but it's no use, I can feel plainly that he says them and makes my tongue speak in spite of me. . . . It is the devil who drives me to do all these other things," said Achille again. " I do not want to die, and he drives me against my will to make away with myself. . . . For instance, he is speaking to me at this moment . . ." and he resumes in his deep voice: " Priests are a worthless lot !" then in his high voice: " No, I won't believe it !" and there he was talking with the devil and arguing with him. It often happened that he disputed in this way with his demon who had the bad habit of criticizing him incessantly. " You lie," said the devil to him. " No, I am not lying," replied the poor man. . . .

The possessed did not merely feel the action of the devil within themselves, they saw and heard him.   Achille did the same. . . .

These signs (the stigmata) and especially the last (insensibility) also existed in the case of the unfortunate Achille.   True, his insensibility was not continuous, but when he twisted his arms in convulsive movements, they could be pricked and pinched without his observing it. . . .   When I tried to comfort the poor man and calm him a little I was extremely ill received: all my efforts were useless.   I vainly sought to gain an ascendancy over Achille, to force him to obey me; as a last resource I tried whether it was not possible to send him to sleep in order to have more power over him in a hypnotic state; all in vain, I was unable by any means to suggest or hypnotize him; he answered me with insults and blasphemies, and the devil, speaking by his mouth, mocked my impotence. . . .

At my special request the almoner of the Saltpêtrière was good enough to see the patient, and also tried to console him and teach him to distinguish true religion from these diabolic superstitions; he had no success and told me that the poor man was mad and rather needed the help of medicine than of religion.   I had to try again.

I then observed that the patient made many movements unconsciously and that, absorbed in his hallucinations and ravings, he was extremely absent-minded.   It was easy to take advantage of his absence of mind to produce in his limbs movements which he executed unwittingly.   We all know those absent-minded people who look everywhere for the umbrella which they are meanwhile holding without knowing it.   I was able to slip a pencil into the fingers of his right hand and Achille gripped and held it without noticing anything.   I gently directed the hand which held the pencil and made him write a few strokes, a few letters, and the hand, carried away by a movement which the patient, absorbed in his ravings, did not realize, continued to repeat these letters and even to sign Achille's Christian name without him noticing it.   It is generally known that such movements, accomplished in this manner without the knowledge of the person who seems to produce them, may be designated as automatic, and they were extremely numerous and varied in the case of this patient.

Having noted this point I tried to produce these movements by mere command.   Instead of speaking direct to the patient, who, as I well knew, would have replied with insults, I let him rave and rant as he pleased, while standing behind him I quietly ordered him to make certain movements.   These were not executed, but to my great surprise the hand which held the pencil began to write rapidly on the paper in front of it and I read this little sentence which the patient had written without his knowledge, just as a few moments before he had unconsciously signed his name.   The hand had written: " I won't."   That seemed a reply to my order. I must evidently go on.   " And why won't you ?" said I quietly to him in the same tone; the hand replied immediately by writing: " Because I am stronger than you."   " Who are you then ?" " I am the devil."   " Ah, very good, very good !   Now we can talk !"

It is not everyone who has had the chance of talking to a devil; I had to make the most of it.   To force the devil to obey me I attacked him through the sentiment which has always been the darling sin of devils—vanity.   " I don't believe in your power," said I, " nor shall I do so unless you give me a proof."   " What

8

proof ?" replied the devil, using as always to reply to me the hand of Achille who suspected nothing. " Raise this poor man's left arm without him knowing it." Immediately Achille's left arm was raised.

I then turned towards Achille, shook him to attract his attention, and pointed out to him that his left arm was raised. He was greatly surprised and had some difficulty in lowering it. " The demon has played me another trick," said he. That was true, but this time he had played the prank on my instructions. By the same procedure I made the devil execute a host of different actions, and he always obeyed implicitly. He made Achille dance, put out his tongue, kiss a piece of paper, etc. I even told the devil, while Achille's mind was elsewhere, to show his victim some roses and prick his finger, whereupon Achille exclaimed because he saw before him a beautiful bunch of roses and cried out because he had had his fingers pricked. . . .

Thanks to the foregoing method I was able to go further and do what the exorcists never thought of doing. I asked the demon as a final proof of his power to have the goodness to send Achille to sleep in an armchair, and that completely, so that he should be unable to resist. I had already tried, but in vain, to hypnotize this patient by addressing him directly, and all efforts had been useless; but this time taking advantage of his absence of mind and speaking to the devil, I succeeded very easily. Achille tried in vain to struggle against the sleep which overcame him, he fell heavily backwards and sank into a deep sleep.

The devil did not know into what a trap I had lured him: poor Achille, whom he had sent to sleep for me, was now in my power. Very gently I induced him to answer me without waking, and I thus learnt a whole series of events unknown to everyone else, which Achille when awake in no way realized, and which threw an entirely new light on his malady. . . .

In spite of the sleep in which Achille was apparently plunged he heard our questions and was able to reply: it was a somnambulistic state. This somnambulism, which had come on during our conversation with the devil and in consequence of a suggestion made to this latter, is not at all surprising. During the course of his malady Achille had several times shown analogous conditions; by night and even by day he fell into strange states during which he seemed raving, and woke later retaining not the slightest memory of what he had done during these periods.

. . . Achille . . . once put to sleep, was able to tell us a mass of details which previously he had not known or had known without understanding. In this state of somnambulism he related his illness to us in a manner completely different from heretofore. What he told us is very simple and can be summed up in a word: for the last six months he had had in his mind a long train of imaginings which unfolded more or less unconsciously by day as well as by night. After the manner of absent-minded people he used to tell himself a story, a long and lamentable story. But this reverie had assumed quite special characteristics in his weak mind and had had terrible consequences. In a word, his whole sickness was nothing but a dream.

The beginning of the malady had been a grave misdeed which he had committed in the spring during his little journey. For a short time he had been too forgetful of his home and wife. . . . The memory of his wrong-doing had tormented him on his return and produced the depression and absence of mind which I have described. He was above all things anxious to hide his misadventure from his wife and this thought drove him to watch his lightest word. He believed at the end of a few days that he had forgotten his uneasiness, but it still persisted and it was this which hampered him when he wished to talk. There are weak-minded people who can do nothing by halves and constantly fall into curious exaggerations. I once knew a young woman who, wishing similarly to hide a fault, began to dissemble her thoughts and actions. But instead of dissembling on the one matter she was carried away to the point of hiding and garbling everything, and began to lie continually from morning until night, even about the most insignificant things. In a sort of fit she let slip the confession of her fault, obtained pardon for it and completely ceased to lie. In the case of Achille it was the same thought of something to hide which produced this time not lying but complete mutism. It is already evident that the first stages of the malady are explained by the persistence of remorse and the phantasy which it occasioned.

Already the anxieties, the day and night dreams, were growing more complicated. Achille overwhelmed himself with reproaches and expected to fall victim to all sorts of sufferings which would be no more than legitimate punishments. He dreamed of every possible physical disorder and all the most alarming sicknesses. It is these dreams of sickness which, half-ignored, produced the fatigue, thirst, breathlessness and other sufferings which the doctors and the patient had taken successively for diabetes and heart trouble. . . .

Achille was always dreaming. Who has not had similar dreams and wept over his sad fate while watching his own funeral ? These dreams are frequent with hysterical people who are often heard softly to murmur poetic lamentations such as: " Here are flowers . . . white flowers, they are going to make wreaths to lay on my little coffin," etc. Achille, sick and suggestible, went further; in spite of himself he realized the dreams and acted them. Thus we see him say farewell to his wife and child and lie down motionless. This more or less complete lethargy which lasted for two days was only an episode, a chapter in the long dream.

When a man has dreamed that he is dead, what more can he dream ? What will be the end of the story which Achille has told himself for the last six months ? The end is very simple, it will be hell. While he was motionless and as if dead, Achille, whom nothing now came to disturb, dreamed more than ever. He dreamt that, his death being an accomplished fact, the devil rose out of the pit and came to take him. The patient, who during somnambulism related his dreams to us, remembered perfectly the precise moment during which this deplorable event took place. It was towards eleven o'clock in the morning, a dog was barking in the courtyard at the time, disturbed no doubt by the stench of hell; flames filled the room, innumerable imps struck the poor wretch with whips and amused themselves by driving nails into his eyes, while through the lacerations in his body Satan took possession of his head and heart.

It was too much for this weak mind; the normal personality with its memories, organization and character which had until then subsisted somehow, side by side with the invading dream, went under completely. The dream, until then subconscious, found no further resistance, grew and filled the whole mind. It developed sufficiently to form complete hallucinations and manifest itself by words and actions. Achille had a demoniacal laugh, uttered blasphemies, heard and saw devils, and was in a complete state of delirium.

It is interesting to see how this delirium was constituted and how all the symptoms which it presents may be explained as consequences of the dream, as manifestations of psychological automatism and division of personality. The delirium is not solely the expression of the dream, which would constitute simple somnambulism with strictly consistent actions manifesting no disorder; it is formed by the mingling of the dream and the thought of the previous day, by the action and reaction of the one upon the other. Achille's mouth utters blasphemies, that is the dream itself; but Achille hears them, is indignant, attributes them to a devil lodged within him, this is the action of the normal consciousness and its interpretation. The devil then speaks to Achille and overwhelms him with threats, the patient's interpretation has enhanced the dream and sharpened its outlines.

If we wished to cure our unhappy Achille, it was completely useless to talk to him of hell, demons and death. Although he spoke of them incessantly, they were secondary things, psychologically accessory. Although the patient appeared possessed, his malady was not possession but the emotion of remorse. This was true of many possessed persons, the devil being for them merely the incarnation of their regrets, remorse, terrors and vices. It was Achille's remorse and the very memory of his wrong-doing which we had to make him forget. This is far from being an easy matter—forgetting is more difficult than is generally supposed.

In my work on the history of a fixed idea I have shown how this result might be approximately obtained by the process of " dissociation of ideas," and that of " substitution." An idea or memory may be considered as a system of images which can be destroyed by separating its constituents, altering them individually and substituting in the whole certain partial images for those previously existent. I cannot here repeat the examination of these processes, I merely recall that they were applied afresh to the fixed idea of this interesting patient. The memory of his transgression was transformed in all sorts of ways thanks to suggested hallucinations. Finally Achille's wife, evoked by a hallucination at the proper moment, came to grant complete pardon to her spouse, who was deserving rather of pity than of blame.

These modifications only took place during somnambulism, but they had a very remarkable reaction on the man's consciousness after awakening. He felt relieved, delivered from that inner power which deprived him of the full control of his sensations and ideas. The sensibility of the whole body was restored, he recovered the full use of his memory, and far more important, began to take an objective view of his ravings. At the end of only a few days he had made sufficient progress to laugh at his devil and himself explained his madness by saying that he had read too many story-books. At this period a curious fact must be noted: the delirium still persisted during the night. When asleep, Achille groaned and dreamt of the torments of hell: the devils made him climb a ladder which mounted indefinitely and at the top of which was placed a glass of water, or else still amused themselves by driving nails into his eyes. The delirium also existed in the subconscious writing where the devil boasted that he would soon reclaim his victim. These facts still show us therefore the last traces of the delirium which might persist without our knowledge. This should be carefully noted, for a patient abandoned at this point would before long fall back into the same divagations.

Thanks to analogous measures the last dreams were transformed and soon disappeared completely. . . . The patient no longer had the same complete forgetfulness after somnambulism nor was he now so deeply anæsthetic during the subconscious writing. In a word, after the disappearance of the fixed idea the unity of the mind was being reconstituted.

Achille was soon completely cured. . . . It is pleasant to add that since his return to his little village the patient has often sent me news of himself and that for the last three years he has preserved the most perfect physical and moral health. . . .

This case shows how useful it may be to analyze the ideas of possession and to throw a patient suffering from compulsions into complete somnambulism because of the enhanced suggestibility of this state. In addition the case shows what importance emotional excitement may have in giving rise to possession; in some people it enhances susceptibility to auto-suggestion to an extraordinary degree. But to cite a preceding affective experience is not, in spite of the view maintained by many psychoanalysts, to give an " explanation " of possession.

Truth to tell, exorcism has not always been successful. " In such desperate cases," says Kerner,[1] " we vainly wish ourselves as mighty as the disciples of Jesus." It seems that exorcism failed conspicuously to help when possession had developed not in an hysterical temperament but on neurasthenic and psychasthenic ground such as results from ascetic mortifications. Thus the possession of Surin resisted all exorcism. It disappeared gradually in consequence of a spontaneous transformation of the psychic state, but not as a result of suggestion or autosuggestion.

Whereas in spite of all his torments Surin escaped with his life, two other exorcists concerned in the struggle with the epidemic of Loudun, Lactance and Tranquille, succumbed to possession. This death is one of the most frightful which can be imagined, the patient being sick in mind while fully conscious, and a prey to excitement so violent that finally the organism breaks down under it. I know only this one case, of which we possess a detailed account.

In the following year, 1638, the famous Father Tranquille died. He was a Capuchin preacher, the most illustrious of all the exorcists then remaining. In his last hours he uttered frightful

---

[1] Kerner, *Geschichten* . . ., p. 25.

cries which were heard by all the neighbours of the Capuchin convent, and the report soon spreading to the report soon spreading to the convent there were a great number of people who made their way towards the convent and the adjacent streets in order to hear these cries and see for themselves if the rumours were true. No one went there but was convinced, and still to-day there should be no one who is not convinced of the truth of this thing, seeing the circumstantial account of the death which has been given to the public by a Capuchin and of which the following is an extract:

Father Tranquille was a native of Saint Rémi in Anjou. He was the most famous preacher of his time. Obedience summoned him to the exorcisms of Loudun. The devils, fearing this enemy, came forth to meet him in order to frighten him if it were possible, and caused him to feel on the road such debility in the legs that he thought to have stopped and remained where he was. For four years he was employed as an exorcist, during which time God purified him by tribulation like gold in the furnace. He thought at first that he would expel the demons promptly, trusting in the authority which the Church has received from Our Lord. But having learned his mistake by experience he resolved to have patience and await the will of God. Fearing that his talents were a snare and would be an occasion for pride to him, he desired to abstain from preaching and gave himself entirely to exorcism. The devils, seeing his humility, were so enraged thereby that they resolved to take up their abode in his body. All Hell assembled for this purpose and nevertheless was unable to achieve it, either by obsession or full possession, God not having permitted it. It is true that the demons made sport in his inner and outer senses; they threw him to the ground, cried out and swore by his mouth; they made him put out his tongue, hissing like a serpent; they bound his head about, constricted his heart and made him endure a thousand other ills; but in the midst of all these ills his spirit escaped and was at one with God, and with the help of his companion he always promptly routed the demon who tormented him and who in turn cried out by his mouth: " Ah, how I suffer ! " The other monks and exorcists pitied Father Tranquille in his sufferings, but he rejoiced in them marvellously. . . .

The devils having resolved to bring about his death . . . they attacked him more fiercely than ever on the day of Pentecost when he was to preach, and the time for the sermon having come he was not disposed for it. His confessor commanded the devil to leave him alone and the Father to go into the pulpit from obedience, which he did and preached with more satisfaction to his hearers than if he had passed weeks in preparation. . . . After this sermon the devils besieged him yet more than before. He said mass on three or four days, at the end of which he was constrained to remain in bed until the Monday when he died. He vomited filthy stuff which was thought each time to be a token of the expulsion and from which those around contrived to gather some hope of relief, but the surgeon judged him to be in a very serious condition and said that unless God soon arrested the course of this diabolic work it was impossible that he should survive, for as soon as he had taken any food, although with appetite, the demons made him spew it out with such violent palpitations of the heart that the strongest would have died of them. They gave him headaches and nausea of a kind not mentioned either in Galen or Hippocrates and in order to explain the nature of which one must have suffered them like the good Father. They cried out and raged through his mouth and nevertheless his mind was always clear. All these torments were joined to a continuous fever and various other unexpected complications which cannot be understood by those who have not seen them and who have no experience of the ways in which devils act upon the body. . . . Thus he died in the forty-third year of his age. . . .[1]

The caution which should be exercised when the equivocal word " possession " is used in bald accounts is also necessary in dealing with the formulæ of exorcism.   No one of them may be considered as evidence of the presence of true possession. Such charms were applied to ordinary physical maladies when these were mistaken for demoniacal possession.   •

The idea of possession, in all its original scope, still persists in our own time.   At bottom the ecclesiastical benediction of a church is an echo, for it signifies putting the building into a state of resistance to anti-divine forces.   The blessing of livestock and their fodder has this same meaning and is often carried out by simple people even to-day.   Corresponding inversely to this blessing is the exorcism of one who is already given over to the powers of darkness.   These two, benediction and exorcism, need not, moreover, be very sharply discriminated from the practical point of view.   The blessing is often the expulsion of supposititious demoniac intruders who may possibly be present.   The " Manual " already quoted above gives numerous examples of exorcism of this kind.   Here is one:

Exorcismus pro maleficato in proprio corpore.
Alia formula exorcisandi maleficiatos quoscumque.
Remedia contra febres, pestem et alias infirmitates naturales.
Remedia spiritualia contra philtra amatoria.
Remedia spiritualia pro impeditis per maleficia, ope dæmonum, in matrimonio.
Modus exorcisandi circa quævis animalia per maleficia et veneficia afflicta.
Exorcismus contra maleficia lacticiniorum (foods composed of eggs and milk) et aliorum comestibilium, frugum, etc.
Exorcismus pro lacte.
Exorcismus pro butyro (butter).

Here is an example of exorcism for milk:

Ecce Crucem ✠ Domini, fugite partes adversæ, vicit leo de tribu Juda, radix David.   Exorciso te, creatura lactis in nomine Dei patris omnipotentis ✠, et in nomine Jesu Christi ✠ filii eius Domini nostri, et in virtute Spiritus ✠ sancti, ut fias exorcisatum in salutem fidelium, et sis omnibus ex te sumentibus sanitas animæ

---

[1] *Histoire des diables de Loudun*, pp. 347 sq.

et corporis, et effugiat atque discedat a te nequitia omnis ac versutia diabolicæ fraudis, omnisque nocendi facultas in te omnis modo per ministros satanicos introducta.[1]

The following is an example of ancient exorcism against children's maladies. It comes from Egypt; sickness itself was there considered as a demoniacal being.

> Go hence, thou who comest in darkness, whose nose is turned backwards, whose face is upside down and who knowest not why thou hast come (repeat). Hast thou come to kiss this child? I will not let thee kiss him. Hast thou come to send him to sleep? I will not let thee do him harm. Hast thou come to take him with thee? I will not let thee carry him away. I have secured his protection against thee with afa root, onions and honey, sweet to men but evil to the dead.[2]

In the *Bibliothèque universelle suisse*[3] Henri A. Junod has depicted under the title: *Galagala, Tableau de mœurs de la tribu des Rongas* (Delagoa coast) and in the delightful form of a novel, a personal experience of primitive exorcism in the case of a man suffering from pulmonary inflammation. In spite of the witch-doctor's formal diagnosis of possession and his violent exorcism by noise, the patient showed not the slightest symptom of possession.

Yet more interesting is the account given by a traveller in Guiana of a primitive cure for headache. In that case also there is no question of exorcism proper since the fever was not taken for possession, but nevertheless treatment by primitive exorcism is so nearly allied that the case should be cited. It is the only one where, to my knowledge, the traveller himself underwent the cure. It is in Bastian's work: *Ueber psychische Beobachtungen bei Naturvölkern.*[4] It gives a very clear impression of the terrible nature of primitive medical treatment which temporarily plunges the patients into an entirely abnormal state of mind. Such being the case with a European ethnologist it may be imagined to what degree the native, far more suggestible, must be thrown off his psychic balance.

This closes our survey of the typical states of possession. Their nature has always consisted in phenomena of pyschic

---

[1] *Manuale exorcismorum*, p. 245.
[2] H. Schneider, *Kultur und Denken der alten Ægypter*, 2nd ed., Leipzig, 1909, pp. 364 sq.
[3] One hundred and first year, vol. ii, 1896, pp. 512-551.
[4] Publications of the Gesellschaft für Experimental-Psychologie zu Berlin, vol. ii, Leipzig, 1890, pp. 6-9.

compulsion, the aggravation of which not infrequently renders the victims somnambulistic. Motor hyperexcitement, however frequent it may be, is not necessarily a constituent part of possession.

The appearance of possession, particularly in its gravest forms, is always in point of fact associated with belief in the devil. It is this belief which by means of autosuggestion nourishes possession and maintains it.

So far as age is concerned, the first appearance of possession is not connected with any given time of life. But as regards sex, the predominance in women is extraordinarily marked. Out of thirteen cases related by Kerner and in part observed by him, there are only two men, aged 37 and 71; all the other cases concern girls and women, aged, so far as particulars are available, 8, 10, 11, 20, 31, 32, 34, 36 and 70 years. Thus the climacteric periods are almost solely involved. These numbers are in essential agreement with those derived from other sources, except that perhaps the male sex is slightly, but not much, better represented. The epidemics of possession have almost always smitten convents of nuns or similar establishments, men being only occasionally affected. For the rest, the possessed almost all belong to the uneducated lower classes.

In addition to the states which we have studied there are others, rarer, it is true, in which the persons concerned affirm in the same way that they are possessed, that there is a spirit within which torments them, but where the general condition is nevertheless different in that it attests no phenomena of compulsion. These are cases of mere delusion or even of real hallucinatory ideas which may have a very different origin. The mildest cases concern uneducated people who, in order to explain maladies, particularly of a psychic nature, adopt the vulgar notion of possession. The more serious ones concern paranoiacs, paralytics and other persons suffering from diseases of the mind which produce hallucinatory ideas and in whom the delusion of possession arises. Such affections defy exorcism, or if not, a new illusory idea will immediately take the place of a former one. It must be admitted that such a purely intellectual form of possession exists, but it is undoubtedly very much more rare indeed than the true states of possession; so rare, in fact, that

I cannot quote one indubitable case in all the documents known to me. I shall therefore give up all idea of dealing with it further.

It is impossible to concur in the description of " true cases of possession " which Pelletier and Marie apply to patients who harbour the delusion of having parasites in the body.[1] Such a terminology must lead to the most mischievous confusion. Possession should only be spoken of in cases where derangements exist of the nature of those analyzed in this book. Naturally they may be associated with these ideas of parasites, but the latter alone do not authorize us to speak of possession.

A further development of these ideas of parasites into states of possession seems to Séglas to be frankly a modern form of possession:

> This assimilation of the delirium of possession by small animals to the early demoniacal delirium may be demonstrated by the evidence of mixed cases. I have observed several very clear ones, amongst others that of a woman who professed to be possessed by the devil who had entered her body in the form of microbes which she designated by a strange name and which played all sorts of malicious tricks on her. This case shows the association of the two ideas, demoniacal possession united with the modern conception of the microbe, the form which the devil was supposed to have taken.
>
> This woman had, moreover, very severe cœnesthesic troubles, a particular form of delirium and a very clearly marked duplication of personality; she also had ideas of negation, such as that of having no stomach, no intestines, no tongue.
>
> I have made similar observations concerning another woman patient who was possessed by a tænia (tapeworm).[2]

Furthermore it must be emphasized that in French psychological literature another state is included under the name of " possession." In this state, at least according to the Franco — Anglo-Saxon school of psychology headed by P. Janet, the psychic processes attributed to the " possessing spirit " are no longer in the consciousness, lucid or somnambulistic,[3] of the individual, but remain completely unconscious.

---

[1] *L'Origine cénesthésique des idées hypocondriaques microzoomaniaques* in *Bullet. de l'Institut. gén. psych.*, vol. vi (1906), pp. 64 sq.

[2] *Ibid.*, p. 64.

[3] No objection need be taken to this expression which is here used for the sake of brevity.

The patient observes that his arms and legs execute without his knowledge and in his despite complicated movements, he hears his own mouth command or mock him; he resists, discusses, fights against an individual who has sprung up within him. How can he interpret his state, what is he to think of himself? Is he not reasonable when he pronounces himself possessed by a spirit, persecuted by a demon which dwells within him? How can he be in doubt when this second personality, taking its name from the most well-known superstitions, declares itself as Ashtaroth, Leviathan or Beelzebub? The belief in possession is only the popular rendering of a psychological truth.[1]

This psychological truth consists precisely, according to Janet, in the fact that beside the conscious psychic phenomena belonging to the normal individual, yet others unfold in the organism which do not belong to this first individual but are bound up into a second ego. (Janet and almost the whole of the new Franco—Anglo-Saxon psychology hold the view that the ego is merely a synthesis of psychic processes.) Such states would naturally be quite different from those which we have hitherto studied. If they existed, the expression " possession " would be much less metaphorical when applied to them than to other cases, for there would really exist in the individual a second mind, entirely autonomous, side by side with the first and disputing with it for the control of the organism.

Whatever bearing it may have upon our subject, we cannot here go into the question of ascertaining whether such cases exist. But it is indissolubly connected with the problem of the unconscious, that is to say, whether there exist psychic processes which are completely " unconscious," as Janet understands the word, and what is their extent. The above-mentioned state of possession would then represent the maximum development of the unconscious. I will reserve the elucidation of this question for a general study of the unconscious, as it can only be resolved along such broad lines.

As we have already observed, it is of great importance to the criticism of sources[2] to know that in an early stage of

---

[1] P. Janet, *L'Automatisme psychologique*, Paris, 1888, pp. 440 sq.

[2] There may, moreover, be found amongst these sources narratives completely grotesque in character. For example: " Those who are possessed by demons speak with their tongue hanging out, through the belly, through the natural parts; they speak divers unknown languages, cause earthquakes, thunder, lightning, wind, uproot and overthrow trees, cause a mountain to move from one place to another, raise a castle in the air and put it back in its place, fascinate the eyes and dazzle them. . . ." (A. Paré, *Œuvres*, 9th edit., Lyon, 1633, quoted by

civilization no psychic disturbance is counted amongst the distinguishing symptoms of possession, whereas simple bodily derangements are regarded as sufficient proof of its existence. According to the belief of primitive peoples, not only every spiritual affection but also every physiological one is the consequence of an intruding spirit within the sufferer. This idea has persisted far into the higher realms of civilization; that of the Euphrates and Tigris region was completely permeated by it as well as that of Egypt.

In other words, by no means all the states designated as " possession " in the raw materials of history are such within the meaning of the present work, and, moreover, by no means every exorcism transmitted to us envisages these latter states, many examples relating only to physiological disturbances and their conjuration.

This identification of all sorts of maladies with possession is of great importance as a suggestive factor in the genesis of true, *i.e.*, psychological possession, because such a belief by its universal prevalence creates an atmosphere particularly favourable to autosuggestion; conversely the present-day conception that, generally speaking, nothing of the nature of possession exists, is a powerful obstacle to the development of the states which we have analyzed.

Naturally the present time does not show a complete absence of states akin to possession. Possession has appeared to us as a particularly extensive complex of compulsive phenomena, which naturally exist in great numbers to-day, every marked nervous state habitually bringing them in its train. But these processes do not now develop with the same ease as formerly when the autosuggestion of possession supervened.

Literature contains innumerable examples of such compulsive functions. I have given some particularly characteristic ones in connection with the psychological analysis of psychic compulsions in my *Phänomenologie des Ich* (vol. i, chap. xiii).

Yet more interesting is another state which is apt to

Calmeil, *De la Folie*, vol. i, p. 176.) Belief in the possession of animals also exists, moreover. It is related of Hilarion that he once cured a possessed camel. Cf. J. Burckhardt, *Die Zeit Constantins des Grossen*, Leipzig, 1880, p. 389. Also in the New Testament the devil once passed into a herd of swine.

produce in the persons concerned the idea that they are guided by an extraneous power and which still to-day produces the idea of possession although generally in a transitory form. It is the state of affective and voluntary inhibition which so strikingly dominates the clinical picture of acute psychasthenia.

In such states of psychasthenic inhibition the individual loses all consciousness of his activity yet nevertheless sees himself act. The " determining tendencies " create action but are only feebly felt, so that the person considers his own actions as an enigma. This state readily produces the idea that the actions have originated in an extraneous power, another individual. The fact remains, however, that educated patients of to-day do not, on the mere suggestion, really accept this idea.

> When I was small, says Rp., I used to feel a mysterious power which compelled me and took away my liberty; I believed then that it was the Holy Virgin; to-day I feel the same thing, and wonder whether I am not under a malign spell.
>
> " I am exasperated," says Nadia, " always to feel something mysterious which holds me back and prevents me from succeeding in my ambitions . . . it seems to me that the fates are against me and always will be so long as I live . . . it is as if there were a fatal destiny hovering over my head which never leaves me . . . it is my fate which will bring about what I am most afraid of and make me grow fat, so that I may be still more worried . . . there is a force which drives me to take ridiculous oaths, it is the devil who drives me."
>
> " I have incessantly," says Gisèle, " the feeling of a stronger power which holds me, the feeling that I struggle against something greater; it is this power which I have called God and which I am also tempted to call the devil . . . ;" and Lise always speaks in the same way: " It seems to me that I profane something sacred by struggling against this greater power; that is what constantly makes me think of the devil."[1]

In the same way a case of acute psychasthenia handed over to me by O. Vogt for thorough psychological enquiry had in the beginning shown a certain idea of possession. Under the influence of the doctor's explanations this had at once disappeared, so little resemblance do these psychasthenic ideas bear as a rule to obsessive ideas.

Certain of the graver forms of hysteria, at which we shall now glance, show a much greater likeness to the classic cases

---

[1] P. Janet, *Les Obsessions et la psychasthénie*, Paris, 1903, i, pp. 275 sq.

of possession than do these psychasthenic states, so quiet in their demeanour.

It was Charcot and his school who recognized that such a relationship existed to some extent. Charcot has spoken definitely of a " demoniacal attack," and it is described in detail, with numerous suggestive documents, in the admirable work of Richer.[1] If the descriptions there given of certain hysterical states—to which I can only here refer the reader—are compared with accounts of possession, we are driven to the conclusion that the phenomena involved are essentially the same. The contortions and violence of excitement are alike in both, and it seems agreed that in both certain patients retain full consciousness and memory of their states.

> During this kind of attack the loss of consciousness is not complete. Some patients even remain fully conscious of their state, and at the end of the fit assert that during its course they were unable, for all their efforts, to master their agitation. When they succeeded in doing so for a few moments they only ended by bringing on a more violent fit soon afterwards.[2]
>
> Marc . . . and Ler . . . (two of Richer's patients) themselves distinguish quite clearly the attacks which they call their " twistings " (*tortillements*) from the others which are the severe attacks. They can even foretell from the intensity of the phenomena of the aura what kind of attack is coming on. They greatly prefer the severe attacks to the twistings: in the first they completely lose consciousness, whilst in the second they say that they lose consciousness for only a few minutes at a time (during the epileptoid period) and complain of suffering the most frightful tortures imaginable.[3]

The affective states are also the same as in possession. This may be seen in the following case where the patient really lost consciousness during the fits. It is reproduced as an example of modern hysterical " demoniacal attacks."

> . . . Suddenly terrible cries and howlings were heard; the body, hitherto agitated by contortions or rigid as if in the grip of tetanus, executed strange movements: the lower extremities crossed and uncrossed, the arms were turned backwards and as if twisted, the wrists bent, some of the fingers extended and some flexed, the body was bent backwards and forwards like a bow or crumpled up and twisted, the head jerked from side to side or thrown far back above a swollen and bulging throat; the face depicted now fright, now anger, and sometimes madness; it was turgescent and purple; the eyes widely open, remained fixed or rolled in their sockets, generally showing only the white of the sclerotic; the lips

---

[1] P. Richer, *Études cliniques sur la grande hystérie*, Paris, 1885, pp. 808 sq.
[2] *Ibid.*, p. 202.   [3] *Ibid.*, p. 200.

parted and were drawn in opposite directions showing a protruding and tumefied tongue.

If fright predominated the head was slightly inclined towards the neck and thorax, the two clenched hands clutched the eyes and forehead tightly giving from time to time glimpses of a drawn face and haggard eyes; the body was as it were huddled up, the legs and thighs close to the trunk; the patient either lay on one side twisted upon herself, or on her face with legs doubled up on the abdomen and both hands hiding her face.

If anger was in the ascendant she flung herself upon the obstacle, tried to seize, clasp and bite it; often she was her own victim, tore her hair, scratched her face and bosom, rent her clothing, and during this melancholy spectacle aggravated the frightful nature of the scene by an accompaniment of cries of pain and rage.

The patient had completely lost consciousness.[1]

The relationship between these fits and possession is sufficiently obvious.

But are the states completely identical, as Richer and almost all French psychologists assert ?

A closer study shows that such is not the case and it is very regrettable that this should not hitherto have been adequately recognized, for it would otherwise have been considered essential to enquire more deeply than heretofore into the psychic state during hysteria of the interesting cases which the Saltpêtrière has had the opportunity of studying.

The great difference between modern hysterical attacks and the old states of possession is psychic. Viewed from the outside, as regards contortions and motor excitement the states are similar; but from the psychological point of view, in so far as the study of modern cases permits us to formulate a judgement, they are, owing to the attitude adopted by the patients towards their fits, totally different. To-day they consider them as natural phenomena, pathological manifestations, even although they sometimes try to resist them. They never doubt for a single instant that they and they alone experience these states which even now seem often to show a compulsive character (a consequence of their persistence, even when an individual struggles against them). Formerly, on the contrary, the idea of possession supervened and occasioned an automatic development of the compulsion in the direction of a secondary personality. Judging by the reports, no manifest second personality ever speaks by the mouth of modern patients, a fact showing between hysteria and possession a difference so radical that, at least from the psycho-

[1] *Ibid.*, pp. 441 sq.

logical point of view, it is impossible to speak of the states as in any way identical.

So profound is the influence of general outlook on psychic processes that it imprints on even the most acute manifestations of hysteria widely varying physiognomies. It would be interesting, if such an attempt were possible, to analyze closely in the documents of psychiatric literature this transformation of hysterical attacks under the influence of progress.

It would be a chapter from the history of psychic pathology —a history hardly as yet seriously broached by the method of psychology—and in particular from the history of hysteria, for hysteria really has a history. And if it is not alone in this —psychasthenia is also not without its history, and the hallucination-systems of psychoses, particularly paranoia, often bear a certain " stamp of the times "—its history is, owing to the acute suggestibility which characterizes this state, quite particularly voluminous. An historical survey of psychic pathology would only be possible on a very wide basis and after a thorough and fairly exhaustive study of general historical sources bearing on the story of the mind and of civilization. It would raise the question of the diverse psychic constitution of races and nationalities with an acuteness proportionate to the light thrown on that great psychological problem, the psychic decadence of whole epochs. All these are problems far exceeding in scope its particular domain of psychology.[1]

[1] Henri Cresbron (? Cesbron) has given an interesting preface to a history of hysteria in his thesis for the doctorate of medicine: *Histoire critique de l'hystérie* (Paris, 1909). This work is at once a history of hysterical phenomena in European civilization, of research, and of the various theories of hysteria. The first subject is somewhat less well treated than the second; the author has, moreover, confined himself in the main to the French literature of hysteria.

PART II

THE DISTRIBUTION OF POSSESSION AND ITS IMPORTANCE FROM THE STANDPOINT OF RELIGIOUS PSYCHOLOGY

CHAPTER V

SPONTANEOUS POSSESSION PROPERLY SO CALLED AMONGST PRIMITIVE RACES

HAVING in the previous chapters made a detailed study of the psychological nature of possession, we shall now proceed to examine its importance from the standpoint of religious and racial psychology.

In order to investigate this question we must distinguish two forms; possession as we know it represents only one, in addition to which there is another, very similar and at the same time very different. Whilst the states of possession hitherto considered are, taken as a whole, absolutely involuntary, so that the patient desires ardently to be rid of them, there is another form of possession voluntarily provoked by the possessed and the advent of which he seeks by every possible means. We shall have to deal with this second voluntary and desired form of possession later. For the moment we shall still confine ourselves to the first and consider the *extent of its distribution.*

This may be said to be universal, for there is no quarter of the globe where such phenomena have not occurred. The great majority of the cases designated by the name of possession have, in fact, been no more than physical maladies, considered, as we have seen, by primitive peoples as due to the entry of a demon into the human body.

As regards the wide dissemination of the first-named or involuntary type of possession throughout the Christian era, I have already given at the beginning of this work a series of testimonies demonstrating the constant nature of its manifestations from century to century and thereby justifying the fact that I have based my analysis on documents belonging to widely different periods.

To the foregoing evidence I shall now add further material in order to show that possession essentially similar in nature has occurred outside the bounds of Christian civilization.

The documents cited have no pretension to be exhaustive. In perusing the accounts of ethnological travel I have constantly found new cases, but this increase in documentation brings nothing fundamentally new. Fresh matter can only be expected from a detailed study of particular cases, which is not possible except to an investigator living for a long period of time on the spot or to a missionary. Further systematic research into all existing documents, including those still undiscovered or widely dispersed, would have only an ethno-geographical significance inasmuch as it would give, with all possible plenitude, a general view of the distribution of these phenomena amongst the various branches of the human species, a task falling outside the scope of our subject. A detailed discussion of cases quoted will generally be superfluous, as everything necessary to their understanding is to be found in explanations already furnished.

I shall begin with primitive civilization, as regards which the data concerning spontaneous possession are still exceedingly scanty. The majority of the relevant documents which I can produce relate to Africa, where happily the main regions furnish their contribution so well that we may consider possession as a frequent phenomenon widely disseminated throughout this giant continent.

Here are first some cases observed amongst the Kabyles by Mayor, a missionary at Moknea, and later communicated to Flournoy by H. Besson.[1]

> First case: I was called one day to go to a woman who used often to come to the station. I knew her as a sensible person, affectionate towards everyone, intelligent, quiet, natural, healthy in body and mind. I found her sitting in front of the house surrounded by numerous people. A priest, holding a lighted wick in front of the sick woman's mouth, was commanding the " spirit " to depart. Hearing the sound of my steps on the gravel, Fatma cried out in a completely changed voice: " I do not want him who comes with his iron-shod boots, I will not see him, I do not want the Gospel." I had not finished speaking to her before she became natural again and at once declared that she had distinctly felt herself under the influence of the devil. Two years later she had another fit.
>
> Second case: M. and Mme. Mayor had gone to a Kabyle village to hold a service. They found a woman named Teitem struggling in the grip of several persons who held her fast; she wanted at all costs to run away. The missionary was told that " the demon had

[1] H. Besson, *Notes sur quelques " possessions " en Kabylie*, "Archives de psychologie," vol. vi (1907), pp. 387 sq.

smitten this woman," the expression used by the natives to denote
these cases. The priest was exorcising her and commanding the
demon in the name of all the saints in the Arab calendar to depart.
A strange voice issuing from the woman's mouth refused energetically. M. and Mme. Mayor were both seized with the feeling
that they were in presence of a demoniac influence. They began
to pray. During the prayer the voice cried: " Go away !" Then
the woman returned to her right senses. Later she was again
taken with similar fits.

Third case: A man was known locally as being " sick of the
demon." When in his right senses he obtained shelter in the
mosques and monasteries. He often came to the station, where
M. Mayor used to give him food and talk to him; his demeanour
was that of a quiet beggar. When the fits took him, however, he
used to flee into forests and caves, and wound himself with stones
and pieces of wood. He one day came to the station in the course
of an attack; he did not recognize M. Mayor and fled with wild
gestures as soon as he was approached.

When he came to himself he declared positively that during
his fits he was possessed " by an evil spirit."

M. Mayor observed (Besson adds) several other cases of the
same kind, but the three quoted are the most characteristic.
Here are the general observations which up to the present he has
been able to make on these unfortunate people: the fits come on
suddenly and go off in the same way, leaving the body in a certain
lassitude. The voice is changed; the glance is fixed and haggard,
but the eyes are in a normal position; the pulse beats regularly.
The patient recognizes neither relatives nor children; he refuses
to eat or drink; a force drives him to run away. His moral being
seems changed, and it is as if there were a substitution of personalities. The presence of the missionary excites him to the highest
degree or else frightens him, whereas, restored to his right mind,
he shows affection and confidence towards " the man of the Book."
Some cases have a fit every month, others every six months.
Some only have two or three, or even a single one, in their lifetime.
The proportion of women affected by this malady is greater than
that of men.[1]

The distinguished ethnologist Frobenius has collected
documents relating to possession in Central Africa.[2] We
shall take cognizance of them later in so far as they deal with
voluntary possession. But they also contain accounts of
spontaneous possession which by their data as to its genesis
furnish an ideal complement to other reports, the great
majority of which give hardly a glimpse of how possession
arises amongst primitive people. It emerges from Frobenius'
accounts that the phenomenon is the same as we have already
seen amongst the quite uncultured representatives of central
European civilization.

[1] *Ibid.*, p. 388.
[2] Leo Frobenius, *Und Afrika sprach.* . . . Wissenschaftlich er-
weitete Ausgabe des Berichts über den Verlauf der dritten Reiseperiode
der deutschen innerafrikanischen Forschungsexpedition aus den
Jahren 1910 bis 1912, vol. ii, Berlin, 1912, chap. xi.

Frobenius' work, based on the stories of the natives whose confidence he had won, describes an exorcism in detail. It conveys the impression that primitive man is much more suggestible than his civilized brother. The latter may perhaps be frightened in the darkness of the night, and when he is very much afraid it may seem to him as if from somewhere a shape emerged. Primitive man at once suffers hallucination and may through terror when confronted by the ghost fall into a lethargic condition with transitory psychic disturbance; at least, Frobenius' narrative can hardly be otherwise construed.

> To a man who goes out by night it may befall to be met by a *babaku* (a black spirit) who gives him a sickness. The *alledjenu* (another name for the spirit) may then go his way, but the man has been deprived of his intelligence, he is sick.[1]

A little later Frobenius feels able to explain more exactly these statements of the natives.

> At the moment when the babaku makes the man ill, the latter utters cries and falls in convulsions. His face is distorted and he makes convulsive movements. He later falls into a condition of lethargy. It must obviously be understood from this that the babaku throws him to the ground and goes on his way. If he lies there apathetically they say that the babaku has gone on his way. . . .[2]
> His family, to which he returns in this state, awake (this certainly means from the lethargy) but ill, can do nothing aright with him. As soon as the cause of the affair is known to be an alledjenu the family goes to seek the *gusulfa*, that is to say the " old woman " who has the functions of *magadja* (priestess) in the Bori (an African religious animism). The latter receives the sick man and summons her partner, the *adjingi* (priest). Neither can do anything without the other. There is between the two a remarkable relationship which is in strict agreement with the fact that according to the legend the Djengere and Magadja are bound together, so that neither can accomplish anything without the other. . . .
> Thus our patient is taken by his family to the gusulfa and the latter calls in the adjingi. She asks the family for a red cock. . . . She prepares the ceremony of the fire and smoke while the adjingi goes into the bush and gathers all the roots and ingredients necessary for the cure.
> A certain broth is then prepared for the sick man. He must also inhale a certain smoke.
> But the most important thing is when the sick man is wrought upon through the sense of hearing.
> . . . A goye-player, a violinist (otherwise a guitar-player) is summoned. When he plays before the patient he must reproduce in music the names of the various alledjenus. According to the ancient rite each alledjenu had, indeed, his tones, concords, harmony,

---

[1] *Ibid.*, p. 252.   [2] *Ibid.*, p. 254.

and melody. It was a musical language, just as there still exists to-day a flute-language and a drum-language.

Thus the goye-player expresses in notes the name of the alledjenu. And when the name of the one who has brought the sick man to such an evil pass is pronounced, he returns and fills the man from head to foot.[1]

Or as Frobenius has described it again and more exactly later:

> . . . When the music, be it of the violin or guitar, speaks the name of the alledjenu again, the sick man once more cries out, falls into convulsions and manifests great excitement, but relapses once more into a state of the most complete indifference. And all this seems to mean that the babaku has again filled him from head to foot and then left him.[2]
>
> After it has been recognized which alledjenu is concerned, the adjingi rubs the patient with medicine and the sitting continues day and night for seven days to the sound of the violin and the beating of the calabash.
>
> Three days later the patient is carried into the bush and washed. Then the babaku who possessed that man or woman departs.[3]

That we are dealing here, as Frobenius thinks, with " a sort of epileptic state," does not appeal to me as probable, and these fits from the way in which they come on and disappear rather produce the impression of depending on external suggestive conditions. This is in perfect agreement with what Frobenius relates of the solemn sacrifice which takes place three days after the expulsion of the babaku; on this occasion sundry onlookers fall into similar states which, however, seem to disappear promptly of their own accord.

> Three days later comes the sacrifice of a white ram. . . . It is killed, cooked and eaten, and after this repast there occur great dances and protracted rejoicings, during the course of which the second essential part of the cult is accomplished, when very often one of the farifarus suddenly inspires one after another of the onlookers. They start to execute violent leaps, pirouette in the air, and suddenly drop to the ground on their back. It is this part of the ceremony which is sometimes turned into an amusement by the Bori people; the sacred dances degenerate into triviality. . . . As a matter of fact, this dance is all that the people show to strangers. But the essential part of inspiration by the farifarus (white spirits), greatly desired by the people of Bori, resides in the prophetic spirit which takes possession of the dancers.[4]

A fact showing yet more clearly the autosuggestive character of these states is that they occur when the people of Bori indulge in the forbidden use of beer.

[1] *Ibid.*, pp. 252-254.
[3] *Ibid.*, pp. 254 sq.
[2] *Ibid.*, p. 254.
[4] *Ibid.*, p. 255.

The people of Bori and Asama drink no beer. When a follower of Bori takes beer, the alledjenu swoops down upon him like the wind. His eyes are filled with darkness. Then the alledjenu has seized him; the man falls as if dead.[1]

For his restoration to health a ceremony similar to that described is carried out. The possibility that some of these states may be of a true epileptic character is naturally not excluded; it is to be presumed that epileptic fits originally served as a model for the autosuggestive states and that the latter are an imitation of them. However that may be, it is untrue to say that nothing except epileptic fits occurs.

Entirely analogous to the C. St. case of Eschenmayer already cited are the declarations that " each spirit is like a wind, is itself a wind," and that " when someone is overthrown by a spirit of Bori in a storm of wind, he at first lies as if dead."[2] This means that a gust of wind, supposedly animated, may determine the fit in a predisposed person, in the same way that Eschenmayer's patient believed her possession to have been occasioned by a gust blowing over her.

Here is a case slightly more detailed. It comes from Abyssinia and is reported by Waldmeier of the Bâle Missionary Society, who writes:

It often happens in Abyssinia that people seem possessed by an evil Spirit. The Abyssinians call it Boudah. I witnessed these wonderful and dark occurrences many times, but will relate one only—and even in this case I must not describe the most horrible and disgusting details. One evening when I was in my house at Gaffat, a woman began to cry out fearfully and run up and down the road on her hands and feet like a wild beast, quite unconscious of what she was doing. The people said to me: " This is the Boudah ; and if it is not driven out of her, she will die." A large number of people gathered round her, and many means were tried, but all in vain. She was always howling and roaring in an unnatural and most powerful voice. At length a man was called, a blacksmith by profession, of whom it was said that he was in secret connection with the evil spirit. He called the woman, who obeyed him at once. He took her hand in his and dropped the juice of the white onion or garlic into her nose, and said to her—or rather to the evil spirit which possessed her:

" Why didst thou possess this poor woman ?"   " Because I was allowed to do so."   " What is thy name ?"   " My name is Gebroo."   " Where is thy country ?"   " My country is Godjam."   " How many people didst thou take possession of ?"   " I took possession of forty people, men and women."   " Now I command thee to leave this woman."   " I will leave her on one condition."   " What is that condition ?"   " I want to eat the flesh of a donkey."   " Very well," said the man, " thou mayst have that."

---

[1] *Ibid.*, p. 256.   [2] *Ibid.*, p. 257.

So a donkey was brought which had a wounded back from carrying heavy loads, and its back was quite sore and full of matter. The woman then ran upon the donkey and bit the flesh out of the poor creature's back; and though the donkey kicked and ran off, she did not fall down, but clung to it just as if she was nailed on the animal's back. The man called the woman back to him, and said to the evil spirit: "Now art thou satisfied?" "Not yet," was the reply, and a disgusting mixture was asked for, which was prepared for the woman and put down in a secret place which she could not see; but when the man said to her, "Go and look for your drink," she ran on all fours like an animal to that very place and drank the whole potful to the very last drop. Then she came back to the man, who said again: "Now take up this stone." It was a very large stone which she would not have been able to move in her natural condition, but she took it up with ease upon her head, and turned round like a wheel until the stone flew off on one side and she on the other on the ground. The man then said: "Take her now away to bed, for the Boudah has left her." The poor woman slept for about ten hours, and awoke and went to her work, and did not know anything of that which had passed over her, nor what she did and said.[1]

From East Africa Dannholz reports the following:

Deceitful spirits give the *mpepo* sickness, which seems to be a sort of possession. This malady particularly affects women, and is considered as a noble and distinguished affliction. Hysteria perhaps plays some part in it, although various phenomena are not capable of explanation by hysteria. Many persons affected speak in a strange voice, the women in a deep bass or in a foreign tongue, Swaheli or English, although they neither understand nor speak it. After the arrival of the " spirit " who operates in the sick person, the people speak of *mpepo ya mzuka*, possession by the vampire, *ya-ijeni*, by a kind of spirit related to the *mzuka*, *ya Msuaheli*, by the male of the Swaheli, *ya Mringa*, by the Masai, *ya Mkamba*, by the male of the Kamba, *ya Mzungu*, by the Europeans, and also *ya nkoma*, generally by the spirit of a dead person. Abnormal eagerness for food, pepper, and other strong condiments as well as for bright, gaily-coloured clothing and other showy things characterizes possession. On request the " spirit " sometimes relates the story of his life, boasts of his crimes, indulges in the most filthy language, and suddenly the possessed is seized by a fit of rage punctuated by convulsions. To the rhythm of the mpepo drum she dances in a wild and terrifying manner until completely exhausted, after which she feels a temporary relief. The malady breaks out in epidemic form, descends upon whole regions, and even spreads from the coast into the interior. It was not known in former times, but seems to have made a recent appearance in East Africa. It has been observed that Christian natives are not subject to it, and in Mbaga various persons sick of the mpepo have been cured by the words of our Christians, by prayer and a sober train of life. The heathen never offer victims to the deceitful spirits, but rather drive them out of the sick by exorcism, although the use of sacrifice is beginning to be rumoured.[2]

---

[1] *The Autobiography of Theophilus Waldmeier*, London, 1886, p. 64.
[2] J. J. Dannholz, *In Banne des Geisterglaubens*, Züge des animistischen Heidentums bei den Wasu, in der deutschen Ost Afrika. Leipzig, 1916, p. 23.

Part of this description might well have been taken from the account of no matter what case of possession in Central Europe, so completely do the states correspond. The remark that possession in East Africa comes on in epidemic form is interesting. Given the great suggestibility of primitive peoples, spiritual epidemics must generally be frequent amongst them, but unfortunately we possess up to the present very few accounts.

Here is, however, a note on the suggestive effect of possession in Madagascar:

> In Madagascar the *saccare* were evil demons by whom men and women were possessed. Flacourt reports: "They appear in the form of a fiery dragon and torment men for ten to fifteen days. When that occurs a sword is put into their hand and they take to dancing and leaping with strange and unrestrained movements. The men and women of the village surround the possessed man or woman and dance with him, making the same movements in order, so they say, to relieve the sick person. Often there are in the crowd possessed persons who are seized by the diabolic spirit, and this sometimes happens to a great number."[1]

It may be assumed without further ado that these " possessed " were not so previously but became so while accompanying the sick person.

We are particularly well informed as to the states of possession observable amongst the Ba-Ronga (near Delagoa Bay) in South-East Africa, who are amongst the most carefully studied of the African tribes. We are indebted to the missionary Henri A. Junod[2] for a thorough general investigation of their manners and customs.

Amongst the Ba-Ronga possessing spirits are never those of the tribal ancestors, but of those of the Zulus or the Ba-Ndjao.

> It seems that states of possession first appeared amongst the Zulus; perhaps they coincided with the always sensational departure of the young men who went to work in the diamond mines

---

[1] A. Bastian, *Der Mensch in der Geschichte*, vol. ii, p. 559. Flacourt's work, *Histoire de la grande île de Madagascar*, has not been accessible to me.

[2] Junod first published the result of his enquiries in book x (1898) of the *Bulletin de la Société Neuchâteloise de Géographie*, then in a book published in 1898 at Neufchâtel under the title: *Les Ba-Ronga, étude ethnographique sur les indigènes de la baie de Delagoa*. An augmented edition of this work appeared in English: *The Life of a South African Tribe*, 2 vols., Neufchâtel, 1913. To this we must add the memoir on a case of possession of great importance to us, *Galagala*, which appeared in the Swiss periodical *Bibliothèque universelle*, in June, 1896.

of Kimberley or the gold mines of Johannesburg or Natal, and who travelled through the regions inhabited by the Zulus.[1]

It seems that these Ba-Ronga travellers were quite often possessed by Zulu spirits.[2]

Possession by the Ndjao seems to be more malignant than by the Zulus. The possessed may be recognized by a string of beads which they wear on the head or around it.[3]

This disease has spread enormously amongst the Thonga (the group of peoples in South-East Africa to which the Ba-Ronga belong) in the last thirty years. It is said to have been very rare, even unknown, previously; since then it has become quite an epidemic, although it is actually rather on the decrease. Possession is more frequent amongst the Ba-Ronga than in the Northern clans.[4]

Junod describes possession as falling like a bolt from the blue on to the victims:

> I have carefully studied the history of many cases of possession amongst the Ba-Ronga (see *Bulletin de la Société Neuchâteloise de Géographie*, tome x, p. 388). Most of them have begun by a distinct crisis, in which the patient was unconscious, but which does not seem to have been brought about by any previous nervous trouble.[5]
>
> I will now give full details of the case of Mboza, who was himself possessed at one time, and later on became a regular exorcist. After having worked in Kimberley for some time, he returned home in good health. But soon afterwards, he was lame for six months. He attributed his difficulty in walking to rheumatism (shifambo). There was some improvement in his condition, but he began to feel other symptoms: he lost his appetite and almost completely ceased to eat. Here is his testimony: " One day, having gone with another young man to gather juncus, in order to manufacture a mat, the psikwembu started at once in me " (ndji sunguleka hi psikwembu psikuñwe). I came back home, trembling in all my limbs. I entered the hut; but suddenly I arose to my feet and began to attack the people of the village; then I ran away, followed by my friends, who seized me and at once the spirits were scattered (hangalaka). When conscious again, I was told I had hurt a Khehla (a man with the wax crown, i, p. 129), and had struck other people on the back: " He !" said they, " he has the gods " (or he is sick from the gods, a ni psikwembu).[6]

The decision as to whether possession really exists in so doubtful a case depends in the last resort not at all upon the symptoms presented by the suspected person but upon a kind of game of dice. Suspicious symptoms are specially persistent pain in the side and particularly loud and irrepressible hiccupings. The diagnosis is almost sure as soon as an apparently groundless aversion is manifested. But when the various bones which are thrown into the air as dice

[1] Junod, *Les Ba-Ronga*, p. 440.   [2] *Ibid.*, p. 440.
[3] *Ibid.*, p. 441.   [4] Junod, *The Life* . . ., vol. ii, p. 436.
[5] *Ibid.*, pp. 437 sq.   [6] *Ibid.*, p. 438.

arrange themselves in a certain way, the suspicions are considered as verified or else as unfounded. In the first case the name of the exorcist is chosen from those available (they are called *gobela*) by means of the dice. These are even used to fix the order of the exorcist's operations and the remedy to be applied.[1]

" In former times, the only remedy was waving a large palmleaf (milala) in front of the patient. This was deemed sufficient to ' scatter the spirits.' Now the treatment is much more complicated."[2] In the first place a medicine, the composition of which does not here concern us, is administered to the patient. After he has taken it, he must spit to the four quarters of the wind, pronouncing the sacred syllable *tson*, which has the power of moving spirits and begging life from them. Then a prayer is addressed to the gods.

To this very peaceful first part of the exorcism is added a veritable witches' sabbath with tambourines, conducted according to the results of a new casting of the dice.

In the hut, right in the centre, sits the patient. Melancholy, with downcast eyes and fixed glance; he is waiting. . . . Everyone in the district knows that to-day, this evening, when the new moon appears, the strange and terrible conjuration will take place. All who have ever been possessed are present. The master of the proceedings, the " gobela," whom the bones have designated, holds in his hands his tambourine, the skin of one of the great monitor lizards common among the hills, stretched on a circular wooden framework. In the beautifully calm evening air and as if to contrast hideously with the sun sinking in purple glory, the first tap resounds. It radiates, stretches on every side, travels through the thickets to the surrounding villages, and then there is sensation, an outburst of joy, made up of curiosity, malice, I know not what unconscious satisfaction. Everyone hastens up at this well-known sound, all hurry towards the hut of the possessed, and all desire to take part in this struggle, this struggle against the invisible world. Several persons are gathered there, some with their tambourines, some with great zinc drums picked up in the vicinity of the town . . . others with calabashes filled with small objects which are shaken and make a noise like rattles . . . and now, crowding round the patient, they begin to beat, brandish, and shake as violently as possible these various instruments of torture. Some graze the head and ears of the unhappy man. There is a frightful din which lasts through the night, with short interruptions, and until the performers in this fantastic concert are overcome by fatigue.

But this is only the orchestra, the accompaniment to which must be added, and it is of the greatest importance, *singing*, the

---

[1] Junod, *Les Ba-Ronga*, pp. 441 sq.
[2] Junod, *The Life*, etc., vol. ii, p. 439.

human voice, the chorus of exorcists, a short refrain following a yet shorter solo, but which is repeated a hundred, nay a thousand times, always to the same end for which all work seriously and doggedly: that of forcing this spiritual being, this mysterious spirit which is present, to reveal himself, to make known his name . . . after which his evil influence will be exorcised. These chants are at once naïf and poetic. They are addressed to the spirit, extolling him, seeking to flatter him, to win him over, in order to gain from him the signal favour of giving himself up. Here is the first of those which I heard . . . one day when I was travelling and when, hearing a tremendous din behind the bushes, I jumped out of my waggon and fell into the very midst of a scene of exorcism:

> Chibendjana ! u vukela bantu !
> (Rhinoceros, thou attackest men !)

vociferated the singers around a poor woman who seemed lost in I know not what unconscious dream. My arrival hardly abated this infernal racket, notwithstanding the fact that the appearance of a white is generally an event in the villages of this district.

When hours pass by without any visible effect being produced on the patient, the refrain is changed. The night is perhaps far spent, the dawn is approaching.

> Come forth, spirit, or weep for thyself until the dawning.
> Why then are we evilly intreated ?

Or else by way of further emphasis, they go so far as to threaten the spirit that they will go away for good if he does not deign to accede to the objurgations of these delirious drummers:

> Let us go away, bird of the chiefs ! Let us go away.
> (Since you frown upon us).

The melodies of these exorcists' incantations are of a particularly urgent, incisive, and penetrating character.

This insistence is rewarded, the patient begins to give signs of assent. This means that the " Chikouembo " is preparing to " come out." The onlookers encourage him:

> Greeting, spirit ! Come forth gently by very straight ways. . . .

That is to say: do not hurt the possessed, spare him ! Overcome at length by this noisy concert the possessed is worked up into a state of nervous tension. As a result of this prolonged suggestion, a fit, the hypnotic character of which is very evident, commences. He rises, and begins to dance frantically in the hut. The din redoubles. The spirit is begged to consent at last to speak his name. He cries a name, a Zulu name, that of a dead former chief such as Manoukoei or Mozila, the ancestors of Goungounyane; sometimes, strangely enough, he utters the name of Goungounyane himself, although he is still alive . . no doubt because the great Zulu chief is regarded as invested with divine power. A woman formerly possessed told me that she enunciated the word *Pitlikeza*, and it transpires that this Pitlikeza was a sort of Zulu bard who had wandered about the Delagoa country when she was still a girl. She was convinced that the soul of this individual had embodied itself in her, several decades after his passage through the district.[1]

In the case of Mboza the patient was covered with a large piece of calico during all the drum performance. A first medicinal

---

[1] Junod, *Les Ba-Ronga*, pp. 443-447.

pellet was burnt under the calico, in a broken pot full of embers, a male pellet (made with the fat of an ox or a he-goat); no result having been obtained, a second pellet, a female one made from fat of a she-goat, was introduced. Nwatshulu prayed the gods. . . .
When the second pellet was nearly all burnt, Mboza began to tremble; the women sang with louder voices. The *gobela* shouted amidst the uproar: "Come out, Ngoni!" Then he ordered the singers to keep quiet, entered under the veil and said: "You who dance there, who are you? A Zulu? A Ndjao? Are you a hyena?" The patient nodded his head and answered: "No!" "Then you are a Zulu?" "Yes, I am. . . ." And, during a pause, he said: "I am Mboza." Mboza was a Ronga who died in Kimberley many years ago. The uproar was resumed and the third pellet was introduced. This is the "pellet *par excellence*," neither male nor female, the one which is expected to have the strongest effect. Mboza suddenly rose, threw himself on the assistants, beat them on the head, scattered them all right and left, and ran out of the hut feeling as if the spirits were beating him! "Everyone saw that day that I had terrible spirits in me." In the crisis of madness the patient sometimes throws himself into the fire and feels no hurt, or falls in catalepsy (a womile, lit., becomes dry), and strikes his head against wood, or the ground, without feeling pain.[1]
But let us finish the description of the possessed man's fit. He dances, leaps wildly. Sometimes he flings himself into the fire and feels nothing, or else ends by falling rigid as if in catalepsy . . . his head striking against a block of wood or the earth, but he appears to feel no pain.
The concerted drumming may last for four days, a week, two weeks. I know a woman (who has now become a Christian under the name of Monika) who had to endure it for seven days. Everything depends on the nervous condition of the patient and the exhaustion produced in him by fast and suffering.
When the spirit has declared his name and title he is henceforth known and they may begin to question him. Spoon, the diviner, whose wife has been twice possessed, by the Zulus and the Ba-Ndjao, told me about one of these confabulations. He was in a neighbouring village when suddenly messengers came to fetch him urgently saying: "Your wife, who was present at a witch-dance in such a place has been seized with the madness of the gods." He went to the place in all haste and saw that she was in fact out of her senses and was dancing like one possessed. He had never previously had any idea that she was possessed by a spirit. This spirit began to speak when she grew a little calmer, and replied to questions put to him: "I have entered into this *ligodo*, that is this body, this vessel, in such and such a way."
"The husband had gone to work in the gold mines. I attached myself to him in a certain place when he was seated on a stone, and when he had returned to the house I forsook him to enter into his wife." "Are you alone, spirit?" is often asked. "No, I am there with my son and grandson," he will perhaps reply, or else if it is suspected that there are indeed several spirits with him those present continue to beat the drum to drive out the whole host. Sometimes the possessed pronounces as many as ten names.
During this confabulation the spirit, speaking by the mouth of the

[1] Junod, *The Life of a South African Tribe*, vol. ii, p. 443.

sick man but remaining perfectly distinct from him, sometimes demands presents and there is one in particular which must be offered in order to satisfy and dismiss him. . . . Blood, blood in abundance is in fact necessary to effect the cure of the sick man and induce the noxious indweller to cease from harm.

Generally a she-goat is fetched if the sick person is a man, a he-goat if it is a woman. The exorcist who has presided over the whole cure returns and causes the onlookers to repeat the song which brought on the first fit. The possessed begins to grow excited and present the symptoms of raving madness which we have already described. Then the animal is stabbed in the side and he flings himself upon the wound, sucks, greedily swallows the flowing blood, and frantically fills his stomach with it. When he has drunk his fill the beast must be taken away by force. He must be given certain medicines (amongst others one called *ntchatche* which seems to be an emetic) and goes away behind the hut to vomit up all the blood which he has drunk. By this means, no doubt, the spirit or spirits have been satisfied and duly expelled.[1]

The patient is then smeared with ochre. The animal's biliary duct is fastened into his hair, and he is bedecked with thongs made from the skin of the goat which has been cut up. These various ceremonies must symbolize the happiness and good fortune which the bloody sacrifice has secured for the sick man. All the drum-beaters, who are persons formerly possessed, arm themselves with these thongs also, crossing them over the chest in the ordinary way.[2]

Does this mean that everything is now over? So violent a nervous attack, so complicated a series of disturbing ceremonies leave behind them a state of commotion and shock from which the possessed does not immediately recover. It appears that from time to time, in the evening, the *bangoma*, those who have passed through this initiation, are again seized with the characteristic madness and even sometimes strike their neighbours with the little axe which the Ba-Ronga use in their dances. By day they are in their right senses. This is not all; the fact that they have been in a special relationship with the spirits, the gods, confers upon them prestige and particular duties. They have themselves become *gobela* and may henceforth take part in the exorcism of the sick. They will perhaps earn money with their famous drums: this is why these ceremonies are in some sort an initiation; this is also why certain individuals are not sorry to be possessed and readily submit to the torture of the witches' sabbath. . .[3]

This narrative is confirmed in an interesting manner by the communications of the missionary A. Le Roy. This distinguished investigator has given an excellent general account of the religions of the Bantu races which people the greater part of South Africa, the Kameroons, the Congo, and from Lake Victoria Nyanza to the Cape. Le Roy is led by his subject to mention the important part played by possession, although he resigns himself to admitting in conclusion that a thorough study has not yet been possible and will be no more

[1] Junod, *Les Ba-Ronga*, pp. 446 sq.
[2] *Ibid.*, p. 448.   [3] *Ibid.*, p. 448.

so in the future.   What he is able to report agrees fully with the observations of Junod.

> Another very frequent manifestation of the spirit world is possession.   Sometimes the possessing spirit is of human origin, but more often is one of those perverse and malign beings whose origin is little known and who feel for man nothing but jealousy, rancour and rage.   The first thing to do in such a case is to call in a specialist who will make the spirit speak and will know what exorcist should be asked to deliver the sick man.   The expert arrives, he in turn asks the spirit who he is, why he has entered there, what he wants, etc., then after these preliminaries have been accomplished, steps are taken to satisfy him.   Sometimes he will say nothing, and the wizard must make up for this dumbness; but more often he speaks and is obeyed.   Finally after tom-toms, ritual dances and very long and complicated ceremonies—they may last several days and nights—a sacrifice, whatever one is desired, is offered, the possessed drinks the blood of the victim, the onlookers take part in the " Communion " and the spirit departs . . . sometimes.   If he remains, everything must begin again, but then another wizard is called in.
> What are we to think of these possessions ?
> A number of them are easily explicable: they are cases which can be cured by ordinary medicines, and the best of exorcisms, also the least costly, is then a strong purge. . . .
> But there are others where the most sceptical mind must admit to being puzzled—when, for example, the possessed woman—for they are very often women—disappears by night from the dwelling and is found on the following morning at the top of a high tree, tied to a branch by fine lianas.   After a sacrifice has been offered and the lianas which held her have become loosened she glides like a snake down the trunk, hangs for several moments suspended above the ground; when she speaks fluently a language of which she previously knew not a single word, etc.
> And the natives report many other marvels, which they profess to have witnessed.
> It would be very interesting to verify, with all possible strictness, these facts and many others; unhappily all this is hidden with the greatest care from the eyes of the European and even if the latter can penetrate to a ceremony of this kind the natives will either tear him in pieces rather than allow him to look on or will break it off and disperse.[1]

Animal possession also exists in Africa.   Bastian relates, quoting D. and Ch. Livingstone, that in South Africa it is believed that many men can transform themselves temporarily into lions.   These men from time to time leave their homes and wander about filled with the delusion that they are changed into lions.[2]

---

[1] A. Le Roy, *La Religion des primitifs*, 2nd ed., Paris, 1911, p. 347.
[2] Otto Stoll, *Suggestion und Hypnotismus in der Volkerpsychologie*, 2nd ed., Leipzig, 1904, p. 282 sq.

A. Werner also cites a case of animal possession from Central Africa:

> A number of murders had taken place near Chiromo in 1891 or 1892, and were ultimately traced to an old man who had been in the habit of lurking in the long grass beside the path to the river, till some person passed by alone, when he would leap out and stab him, afterwards mutilating the body. He admitted these crimes himself.
>
> He could not help it (he said), as he had a strong feeling at times that he was changed into a lion and was impelled as a lion to kill and to mutilate. As according to our view of the law he was not a sane person, he was sentenced to be detained " during the chief's pleasure," and this " were-lion " has been most usefully employed for years in perfect contentment keeping the roads of Chiromo in good repair.[1]

Such are the most important documents that I can furnish at present on possession in Africa.

As regards the continent of Asia, the majority of the available accounts relate to India, China and Japan. They will be found below in the section relating to possession in the higher civilizations. Nevertheless we shall also refer to them here, for the psychic state of the lower strata of the population amongst which possession generally manifests itself is not essentially higher than that of the primitive world and scarcely higher than that of the most backward European peoples in the Middle Ages.

From the primitive zone proper we have information from the Malay Archipelago in particular, especially concerning the Bataks. In these islands transitory states of possession are an everyday phenomenon from which the Christian Bataks are not immune.

The missionary Metzler reports from Silindung, at a time when Christianity had already triumphed:

> The heathen were celebrating a sacrifice on behalf of a young man sick of a spirit. A Christian came forward as a medium and confessed later to the missionary. He had prayed with his wife that God might protect him from the evil spirit; nevertheless he had come into this village against his will and without his knowledge, he had been possessed and was filled with the deepest shame when he later came to himself. A Christian woman confessed that the spirit had entered into her and she had not known what was happening. The elder of the village and several notables were watching her when the music began in a neighbouring village. The elder said to her: " You are a Christian, the evil spirit no longer has anything to do with you." When he had prayed the woman became

---

[1] A. Werner, *British Central Africa*, London, 1906, pp. 87 and 171.

10

quiet, but after a while she fell back into the same state. Although the men held her with all their might they could not in the end resist her; she escaped from them and dashed towards the heathen village.   Later she came to see the missionary, confessed her sins with tears and was ashamed to be seen in public.   " How could I have abandoned my little children all alone in the middle of the night if I had been in my senses ?   I have also two brothers who died a fortnight ago; I should not therefore have gone to such a place if I had known in the least what I was doing."   Another woman declared in the same circumstances that she did not know how she had come into the village and that she was terribly ashamed afterwards.   The two women are, moreover, zealous in the practice of religion.[1]

A recipient of baptism at Si Morangkir (Silindung) had previously been a medium and the spirits wished to reclaim her.   During a sickness she sprang suddenly from her couch, began to dance in the house like one possessed, and said to her relations that they must bring him (that is, the spirit) yet another victim formerly promised, failing which she would give them no peace.   When she had come to herself she asserted and strenuously maintained that she did not know what had occurred.[2]

Owing to the facility with which possession occurs amongst the Bataks they show still less clear difference between spontaneous and provoked states than is seen amongst other primitive peoples.   In the narratives which we owe to baptized natives the fact is so obvious that they would have to be completely dismembered by anyone desiring to separate the two kinds of origin.   For this reason I prefer to return to these documents again later.

[1] Proceedings of the *Rheinische Mission*, 1886, pp. 80 sq.
[2] *Ibid.*, p. 73.

CHAPTER VI

SPONTANEOUS POSSESSION IN THE HIGHER CIVILIZATIONS

(i.) In the Past

FROM primitive peoples we shall now pass to civilized ones in order to make a rapid survey of the extent to which possession is prevalent amongst them.

In the civilizations of antiquity, the country best known for faith in spirits and demons is the region of the Euphrates and Tigris. Delitzsch even asserts that " the Catholic doctrines founded on the New Testament belief in demons and devils, *concerning bewitched, obsessed and possessed persons* whom the priest alone can cure because he has the devil in his power (whence so many ecclesiastical customs, such as the nailing of written exorcisms over the doors and windows of houses, etc.), have their complete parallel in Babylonian magic."[1]

To the Babylonians and Assyrians alike the real world appeared filled with demons. Anyone reading or even merely glancing through the thick volumes published up to the present containing texts of conjurations of all sorts which have come down to us, written for the most part in cuneiform characters on clay tablets, gathers a depressing and even terrible impression of the world in which according to their own belief these peoples lived. At every corner evil spirits were on the watch, and in addition to this menace there was danger from the spells of numerous witches, in whom everyone believed implicitly. To these men the world must have appeared gloomy, full of calamities, as strange as the reconstructions of their curious buildings appear to us. The exorcisms are so numerous that they constitute the major part of cuneiform religious inscriptions; and they must certainly date back

---

[1]. Delitzsch, *Mehr Licht*, Leipzig, 1907, p. 61, note 23.

beyond the purely Babylonian tradition to the Sumerians. At the time of the Babylonian captivity these demonological beliefs passed into Judaism and thence to Christianity, where they had a fresh and terrible blossoming in the European Middle Ages.

Delitzsch is therefore not wide of the mark in describing Mesopotamia as the cradle of the sinister belief in demons. It is true in so far as European belief is concerned and may be considered as demonstrated by literary remains and written documents, the same holding good of the Christian belief in angels. It must be recognized that already before the introduction of Christianity demonological ideas existed in Europe, but their formidable development in the Middle Ages is due to the influence of the primitive East.[1]

In Mesopotamia as in primitive societies, all forms of sickness including psychic ones were considered as the work of evil spirits, a sort of possession. To combat them innumerable formulæ of conjuration were used and have come down to us. Unfortunately to the best of my knowledge no texts containing information as to possession in Babylon have yet come to light. Up to the present they have all been concerned with the exorcism of sickness and not of possession in our sense of the word.

It therefore seems to me that Delitzsch, in the italicized words of the above quotation, goes a little too far. In the sources which he kindly indicated to me on a personal request, I have been unable to discover documents adequate to support him.[2] The collected works of Jastrow and Jeremias on Babylonian religion and civilization[3] contain just as little. At the utmost it may be possible to read as a state of possession the following passage, which

---

[1] *Ibid.*, p. 40.

[2] R. Campbell Thompson, *The Devils and Evil Spirits of Babylonia*, 2 vols., London, 1903-1904 (Luzac's Semitic Text and Translation, series xiv and xv). H. Zimmern, *Beiträge zur Kentniss der babylonischen Religion*, Leipzig, 1901 (Assyriologische Bibliothek, edited by F. Delitzsch and P. Haupt, xii). Knut L. Tallqvist, *Die assyrische Beschwörungsserie Maqlû*, from the originals in the British Museum. In *Acta Societatis Scientiarum Fennicæ*, xx, Helsingfors, 1895.

[3] Morris Jastrow, *Die Religion Babyloniens und Assyriens*, 4 vols., Giessen, 1905-12. Alfred Jeremias, *Handbuch der orientalischen Geisteskultur*, Leipzig, 1913.

is Thompson's English version of a Babylonian cuneiform inscription:

> . . . in the desert . . . they spare not,
> . . . the ghoul after the man hath sprinkled
> Spreading heart disease, heartache,
> Sickness (and) disease over the city of the man
> Scorching the wanderer like the day,
> And filling him with bitterness;
> Like a flood they are gathered together
> (Until) this man revolteth against himself
> No food can he eat, no water can he drink,
> But with woe each day is he sated.[1]

The interpretation of this picture as a state analogous to possession is evidently very hazardous; and it would certainly be no more than analogous. For the present, therefore, I can give no document of any value on possession in the region of the Euphrates and Tigris. On the other hand an Egyptian inscription gives us indirect proof, at least so far as Syria is concerned, that possession existed there.

In a temple at Thebes in Egypt has been found an inscription in the form of a short story in which a Syrian princess is represented as possessed by an evil soul.[2] It runs thus:

His Majesty (the King of Egypt) was in Mesopotamia engaged in receiving the year's tributes; the princes of the whole earth came to prostrate themselves in his presence and implore his favour. The people began to present their tributes: their backs were loaded with gold, silver, lapis-lazuli, copper, *tanater* wood. Each in turn (offered his dues). When the chief of Bachtan caused his presents to be brought he placed his eldest daughter in the forefront so as to implore His Majesty and beg from him the favour (of life?). This woman was beautiful, she pleased the King above all things; he gave her, as first royal wife, the name of Neferou Ra (beauty of the sun), and on his return to Egypt he caused her to accomplish all the rites of the queens.

In the year 15, on the 22nd day of the month of Epiphi, while His Majesty was in the building of Tama, the queen of temples, engaged in chanting the praises of his father Ammon-Ra, master of the thrones of the earth, in his noonday panegyris of the Ab, the seat of his heart, it happened that for the first time they came to tell the King that a messenger from the prince of Bachtan was bringing rich presents to the royal spouse.

Led into the King's presence with his offerings he said, invoking His Majesty: "Glory to thee, sun of all peoples! Grant us life in thy presence." Having thus pronounced his adoration before His Majesty he went on to speak thus: "I have come to thee, supreme King, oh my lord, for Bint-Reschid, the young sister of

---

[1] Thompson, *loc. cit.*, vol. i, p. 117.
[2] E. de Rougé, *Étude d'une stèle égyptienne* in "Journal asiatique," 5th series, vol. xii, 1858, pp. 253 sq.; and also *Œuvres*, tome xxiii, of the *Bibliothèque égyptologique*, Paris, 1910, p. 282.

the queen Neferou-Ra; an evil has entered into her substance; let Thy Majesty be pleased to send a man learned in science to examine her."

The King then said: "Let the college of Hierogrammatists be brought hither, the doctors of mysteries (of the interior of our palace ?)." When they had come instantly, His Majesty said to them: "I have had you summoned to hear what is asked of me, choose me amongst you a man of wise heart (a master with nimble fingers ?)." The basilicogrammatist Thothem-Hesi having presented himself before the King received the order to set out for Bachtan with the prince's emissary.

When the man knowing all things had arrived in the land of Bachtan he found Bint-Reschid obsessed by a spirit; but he recognized himself (powerless to drive it out ?).

The prince of Bachtan sent a second time to the King to say to him: "Supreme sovereign, oh my lord! If Thy Majesty would order that a god should be brought (to the country of Bachtan to combat this spirit ?)."

This new request came to the King in the year 26, in the first of the month of Pachons, during the panegyris of Ammon; His Majesty was then in the Thebaid. The King came back into the presence of Chons, the god tranquil in his perfection, to say to him: "My good lord, I return to implore thee on behalf of the daughter of the prince of Bachtan." Then he caused Chons, the god tranquil in his perfection, to be taken towards Chons, the counsellor of Thebes, a great god driving out rebels.

His Majesty said to Chons, the god tranquil in his perfection: "My good lord, if thou would'st turn thy face towards Chons, the counsellor of Thebes, the great god driving out rebels, and send him to the country of Bachtan by a signal favour."

Then His Majesty said: "Give him thy divine virtue, I will then send this god that he may cure the daughter of the prince of Bachtan."

By his most signal favour, Chons of Thebaid, the god tranquil in his perfection, gave four times his divine virtue to Chons, counsellor of Thebes. The King commanded that Chons, counsellor of Thebes, should be sent in his great *naos* with five little *baris* and a small chariot; numerous horsemen walked on his left and on his right.

The god arrived in the country of Bachtan after a journey of a year and five months. The prince of Bachtan came with his soldiers and his chiefs to meet Chons the counsellor; having prostrated himself with his face to the ground, he said to him: "Thou comest then to us, thou descendest amongst us by the orders of the King of Egypt, the sun, the lord of justice, approved by the god Ra."

Then came the god to the abode of Bint-Reschid; having communicated his virtue to her, she was instantly relieved. The spirit which dwelt within her said in the presence of Chons, the counsellor of Thebes: "Be thou welcome, great god who drivest out rebels; the town of Bachtan is thine, the peoples are thy slaves, I myself am thy slave. I will return to the gods from whence I came to content thy heart on the matter of thy journey. Let Thy Majesty be pleased to order that a feast be celebrated in my honour by the prince of Bachtan."

The god deigned to say to his prophet: "The prince of Bachtan must bring a rich offering to this spirit."

While these things were taking place and while Chons the coun-

sellor of Thebes was conversing with the spirit, the prince of Bachtan remained with his army, seized with deep fear. He caused
rich presents to be offered to Chons, counsellor of Thebes, and also
to the spirit, and celebrated a feast in their honour; after which the
spirit departed peacefully where he would, at the order of Chous,
the counsellor of Thebes.

The prince was transported with joy, as were all the people of
Bachtan.

Then follows the description of the return of Chons to
Egypt.

The contents of this inscription show that possession
was a phenomenon well known in Syria as well as in Egypt.
Erman attributes the inscription to the fourth century B.C.
The legend itself is older.[1]

According to Harnack the priests of Egypt were, moreover, " celebrated exorcists from very remote times."[2]

It is possible that several Egyptian papyri in which κάτοχοι
are mentioned also offer proof of the existence of states
analogous to possession. The hypothesis formulated by
K. Sethe[3] that the word κάτοχοι should not be taken to mean
" possessed " but that it was used purely and simply to denote
men who had not the right to leave the sanctuary of Serapis,
has been rejected by the other investigators. It even appears
to be demonstrated that the expressions κάτοχος, ἐν κάτοχῇ
εἶναι, etc., denote a subjection to the temple and not a state
absolutely identical with possession in the usual sense of the
word. But on the other hand it does not indicate imprison-
ment properly so-called. This theory of Sethe is in conflict
with the sayings of the κάτοχοι themselves, from which it
emerges that they were not kept in the sanctuary by any
external constraint. They might leave it at any moment;

[1] Cf. also Ad. Erman, *Die Betreschstele*, in Zschft. für ägyptische
Sprache und Altertumskunde, xxi (1883), pp. 54-60.

[2] A. v. Harnack, *Die Mission und Ausbreitung des Christentums
in den ersten drei Jahrhunderten*, 3rd ed., Leipzig, 1915, vol. i, p. 138.

[3] Kurt Sethe, *Sarapis und die sogenannten κάτοχοι des Sarapis* :
Zwei Probleme der griechisch-ägyptischen Religionsgeschichte, in
Abhandlungen der Kgl. Gesellschaft der Wissenschaften zu Göttingen,
Phil.-histor. Klasse, Neue Folge, vol. xiv, 1913, No. 5. Sethe's work
has been answered by Wilcken in " Archiv für Papyrusforschung,"
vol. vi (1920), pp. 184-212; *Zu den κάτοχοι des Serapeums* (cf. partic.,
pp. 186 and 197). Sethe in turn has replied under the title: *Wilcken,
Zu den κάτοχοι des Serapeums* in the " Göttingische gelehrte Anzei-
gen," 176th year (1914). Diels has upheld Wilcken: *Zu Philodemos,
Ueber die Götter*, vol. i, Abhandlungen der Kgl. Preuss. Akad. der Wiss.,
1915, Phil.-hist. Kl., No. 7, p. 78, note 1.

what held them there was solely *an inner compulsion from the god* who had taken possession of them.   A psychic affection due to the god must have arisen.[1]   Unfortunately the evidence as yet available does not permit a thorough study of its exact nature.   It has been thought that the κάτοχοι were distinguished only by special dreams like those desired and obtained by persons frequenting certain secret and consecrated parts of the temple.   Wilcken had already advanced this explanation at an earlier date.

> Abandoning the idea of imprisonment of the κάτοχοι, I see in the κατοχή an entirely inner relationship of a mystic kind between Serapis and his worshipper.   The god holds him, takes possession of him (κατέχει) so that he is a possessed of god.   We cannot, however, conceive of a lasting ecstasy, for the state often continued for several years, but of a lasting subjection during which he was in close communion with the divinity, receiving his commands, etc.   Only the god could liberate him (λύειν) after which he generally returned to his own country, whereas formerly in the state of subjection he had had no right to leave the precincts of the temple.   The means by which the god enters into communion with the κάτοχος, particularly in the act of taking possession (κατοχή), and that of liberation (λύσις) is manifested in a dream.[2]

If this interpretation is correct, we find here a new conception of possession: he who received dreams from a divinity would be possessed.   It nevertheless appears to me that the cause of the compulsion which is implied in κάτοχος has not as yet been considered.   The above theory would entail the supposition that the god had given in these dreams the command to remain in the sanctuary.

There is also in Sethe a piece of evidence which may be considered as a proof that states analogous to possession existed in Egypt.   He declares that certain constellations give rise to disturbances in hearing and speech amongst men born under their sign and that these men become possessed in the temple, so that they prophesy and fall sick in mind.[3]

In view of the passage from Vettius Valens, also quoted by Kroll,[4] it may be admitted as certain that with the κάτοχοι

---

[1] This is, as I have lately observed, the opinion of W. Schubarth: *Ein Jahrtausend am Nil.   Briefe aus dem Altertum verdeutscht und erklärt*, Berlin, 1912, p. 21.

[2] L. Mitteis and Wilcken, *Grundzüge und Chrestomathie der Papyruskunde*, Leipzig, 1912, vol. i, 2, p. 180 sq.   Cf. Erwin Preuschen, *Mönchtum und Sarapiskult*, 2nd edit., Giessen, 1903.

[3] Sethe, *loc. cit.*, xiv (1913), pp. 69 sq.

[4] *Catalogus codicum astrologorum græcorum*, Brussels, 1904, vol. v, 2, p. 146.

there was question not merely of dreams, but seemingly of possession in the true sense of the present work: ἐν ἱεροῖς κάτοχοι γίγνονται ἀποφθεγγόμενοι ἢ καὶ τῇ διανοίᾳ παραπίπτοντες.[1]
But what leads the κάτοχοι to the sanctuary ? On this point Kroll gives a reply once more taken from Vettius Valens: ἐγκάτοχοι ἐν ἱεροῖς γίγνονται παθών ἢ ἡουνῶν ἕνεκα.[2] Misfortune also brought men to the sanctuary (ἡδονῶν does not give the exact sense. Kroll proposes σινῶν instead. Might not the correct reading perhaps be ὀδυνῶν ?).

As regards the further question of how the spiritual subjection to the temple was effected, no sufficient explanation has yet been offered. Nothing can be gathered from the accounts of eye-witnesses except that the κάτοχοι felt themselves bound to the sanctuary until liberated by the god. Concerning the nature of the bond and the way in which liberation followed we are for the present reduced to conjecture.

That psychic κατέχεσθαι were often desired emerges from a fragment of Philodemos to which Diels has drawn attention in his edition of the remains of that author's writings on the gods. It is there stated in an Epicurean-rationalistic style:

> Everything is full to weariness of people who try to fall into a god-inspired " temple sleep," to receive the ecstasy of the holy spirit, to dedicate their thankofferings to the nude statues, and to hold tambourines raised on high in their hands while visiting all the available gods.[3]

This passage also shows that the κάτοχοι were not put under restraint against their will. But on the other hand a contradiction appears in the fact that they—at least, some of them—longed for deliverance after having become κάτοχοι. It must often enough have happened that they attained the psychic state of κατοχή more easily than the subsequent deliverance therefrom. The thing obtained was a " deep sleep " (κάρος) as well as a true state of possession.

Sudhoff interprets the documents in question thus:

> To be possessed by the god, that is the κατοχή. When he experiences this feeling of possession the κάτοχος goes to the temple to be delivered from his malady or from some other affliction.

---

[1] Vettius Valens, *Anthologiarum libri*, ed. G. Kroll, Berlin, 1908, lib. ii, cap. xvi, p. 73 and also pp. 24 sq.
[2] *Ibid.*, lib. ii, cap. vii, pp. 63 and 29 sq. *Catalogus*, v, 2, p. 146.
[3] H. Diels, *Zu Philodemos . . ., loc. cit.*, p. 78. The Greek as restored by Diels is doubtful in places.

He sleeps in the temple and either is directly delivered from the demon of sickness or else receives in sleep the indication of what he must do in order to be cured.[1]

Thus according to Sudhoff the κατοχή already existed before entry into the temple and was not produced afterwards.

It is to be hoped that future discoveries of papyri will shed that clear light which is still wanting, as much through lack of documents as through the ambiguity of the word κατέχεσθαι which is discussed by Sethe. He also gives a number of documents which may allude to similar κάτοχοι in other temples.

A deeper insight into the psychological states of many of these "temple-dreamers" is moreover given by the ἱεροὶ λόγοι of Ælius Aristides.[2] Nothing is to be found on the word κάτοχος—there is, moreover, an interval of three centuries between them and this author; the papyri in question belong to the middle of the second century B.C., while Aristides lived in the second century A.D.

The theologian Semler has already collected from classical antiquity a very large number of testimonies concerning possession, for the purpose of showing its diffusion amongst Christians and non-Christians.[3] More recently Julius Tamborino has again collected systematically the documents of Christian and non-Christian antiquity.[4] His collection is in many ways much wider in scope than that of Semler, but nevertheless fails to contain all the passages which the latter has gathered together.

[1] Mitteis and Wilcken, loc. cit., p. 222.
[2] It is regrettable that this author has not yet been translated into German (nor English—TRANS.), as he is considered the most difficult of the Greek writers. In the ἱεροὶ λόγοι his language is sometimes so difficult that it would remain incomprehensible in places except to philologists, were it not for the existence of an old Latin translation by G. Cantor. It appeared at Bâle in 1566 without the Greek text and has been re-edited with the Greek by Jebb at Oxford in 1722-30. The whole of this author's writings are of such importance to the history of religion in his time that a translation should be made with all speed. For Aristides, cf. F. G. Welcker, Kleine Schriften, 3rd part, Bonn, 1850, pp. 89-156; G. Misch, Geschichte der Autobiographie, vol. i, Leipzig, 1907, pp. 302 sq. Herm. Baumgart, Aelius Aristides, Leipzig, 1874.
[3] Commentatio de dæmoniacis quorum in novo testamento fit mentio, editio quarto multo iam auctior, Halæ, 1777. This is supplemented by his: Umstandliche Untersuchung der damonischen Leute oder sogenannten Besessenen, nebst Beantwortung einiger Angriffe, Halle, 1762, pp. 41 sq.
[4] De antiquorum dæmonismo, Giessen, 1909, Religionsgeschichtliche Versuche und Vorarbeiten, vol. vii, 3.

The contrast between the pre-Christian and Christian eras is striking enough, according to the documents adduced by Tamborino. Judging by the number of pages, the difference is not great; the whole bulk of documents relating to the non-Christian epoch occupies twenty-four pages, while those of the Christian period occupy twenty-eight. But on closer inspection it appears that for the first part all the possible quotations relating in a general way to states of enthusiasm have been collected, even the briefest references in detached phrases, while the second admits only real states of possession and veritable descriptions. In addition the Christian testimonies are not even complete, as may be convincingly shown by a simple comparison with the index-volume of the *Bibliothek der Kirchenväter*, and in order to make the second part correspond to the first its scope would have to be extended, and all evidence relating to states considered as inspired by the Holy Ghost included. The space occupied by the testimonies of the Christian era would then be infinitely the greater. This contrast between the two groups of evidence can scarcely be explained, except by admitting that possession has played a much more important part during the Christian era than in earlier times.

As regards Greek civilization, the Homeric period as well as the classical period proper are strikingly empty of these demoniacal manifestations. This is in keeping with their conception of life, so lacking in mists and half-lights that even now in moments of depression we go to the Homeric poems for brightness and joy of living.

Neither the possessed person nor the idea of possession plays any part in Homer. Nevertheless, Finsler thinks he sees a glimmering of this idea in many places:

> The true sense of the word (δαίμων) has persisted unchanged in the adjective δαιμόνιος. It designates someone of whom a demon has taken possession, a possessed person. This meaning is everywhere evident, whether Zeus, in his terrible speech, calls Hera " mad-woman " or whether Hector consoling the weeping Andromache calls her " little fool."[1]

Even granted that this be so, the belief in possession rings no truer than when we say that someone is " possessed by

[1] Georg Finsler, *Homer*, 1st part: *Der Dichter und seine Welt*, 2nd edit., Leipzig, 1914, p. 270. The passages referred to are from the *Iliad*, iv, 31 and vi, 486.

the gambling fiend." Under Homer's sun the daylight is too splendidly bright for a serious belief of this nature.

In the same way the seers of Homer, whether men or women, are not possessed; they know the future, they have visions, they may fall into great agitation of mind, but their ego always remains human; no divine person speaks by their mouth. The oracle of Delphi is only mentioned once. The idea of possession is really demonstrable in the poet himself: it is not he who sings, but the muse within him: Μῆνιν ἄειδε, θεά—᾽Ανδρα μοι ἔννεπε, μοῦσα. Frankly speaking, this idea seems more conventional than real.

In later times a great change appears to have taken place in the Greek conception of the world. The historically obscure centuries between the Homeric and classical periods seem to have been filled to an extraordinary degree with belief in the invasion of the real, and even of the human soul, by the transcendental. But then, no more than later, did it tend to weigh heavily on life. Belief in the immanence of the divine occupied a far more prominent place than the corresponding belief in the diabolic. In the mysteries, oracles, and also the Dionysiac cult it was everywhere the divine, and not the diabolic which broke through the outer husk of this world and streamed into the soul of man. Any attempt to characterize the religious spirit of Hellenism must needs represent this divine inspiration as one of its lofty and specific aspects.

Those centuries, so poor in tradition, which lie between the Homeric period and the sixth century B.C. witnessed the first blossoming of divine enthusiasm.[1] Presumably the phenomena of possession in the sense in which we use the words here were not infrequent during this period, but no evidence appears to have been handed down, so that we are reduced to draw psychological inferences by analogy.

In the fifth century B.C. the intensification of man's inner life in relation to divine passions seems to have been reduced

[1] " The appearance of prophets inspired by the Divinity (Sibyls, Bacchids, etc.) in sundry regions of Greek Asia Minor and ancient Hellas is one of the phenomena characteristic of the religious life of a well-defined period, that fateful time which immediately preceded the philosophic age of the Greeks " (Erwin Rohde, *Psyche*, 2nd edit., vol. ii, p. 65).

to normal proportions.[1] (Moreover, divine inspiration when it is complete exceeds the bounds of the " purely human.") In this respect Plato's attitude towards ecstasy is characteristic: he knows it, even recognizes it, but has never himself been in that state. The ἐνθουσιασμός which he experienced and which is imparted and preached in his writings never exceeds reasonable limits. This is consistent with the fact that Plato was in perfect health,[2] while Plotinus, the true ecstatic, had a completely pathological temperament.[3]

As states of divine possession are generally of a voluntary nature, or at least desired, we shall deal with them first.

The nearer antiquity draws to its close the more the picture alters. A completely different conception of life replaces the classical one. The spiritual element, still conceived as acting in the world externally to man, loses its divine character more and more, or else this latter ceases to remain predominant. In the Hellenic period spirits begin to come forth from every corner and the clearness of the sky is darkened by their swarming. The air is filled with a horde of demons; they besiege man and take possession of his inner life. Anguish, fear and horror now lay hold on the soul which was formerly drunk with the divine Eros; it was as if the Olympians forsook the earth for the second time. For the educated of early Christian times to fall gradually and increasingly under the power of these dark ideas they must already have been widely spread among the lower classes. Nevertheless faith in divine possession did not disappear, as we shall see later; but belief in a world swarming with evil spirits stands out in strong relief as the chief characteristic of the period. It finally made its way into philosophy, even although on this pinnacle of life the conception of the reality of the gods and the possibility of their filling the human soul kept its predominance until the end.

[1] A detailed account of divine passions will be found in vol. ii of my *Phänomenologie des Ich.*
[2] Moreover, the Plato of the last years shows in some respects, such as his moral rigorism, tendencies closely related to those of Kant and which overstep the classical domain.
[3] Cf. in the first place Porphyry's *Life of Plotinus.* A meagre collection of documents on Plotinus by François da Costa Guimarais: *Contribution à la pathologie des mystiques, anamnèse de quatre cas,* Paris, 1908, pp. 7-13.

Harnack[1] characterizes as follows the situation in the second century A.D.:

> The distinguishing trait of belief in demons in the second century consists first of all in the fact that it spreads from the obscure and lower strata of society to the upper ones, and even finds its way into literature, becoming far more important than before; secondly in that it no longer has beside it a strong, simple, and open religion to keep it under; furthermore in that the power of the demon, hitherto considered as morally indifferent, is now conceived as evil; finally in the individual application of the new religion which at that time numbered the mental affections also among its consequences. If all these causes are taken into consideration, the extraordinary spread of belief in demons and the numerous outbursts of demoniacal affections must be attributed to the combined effects of the well-known facts that in imperial times faith in the ancient religions was disappearing, the individual began to feel himself free and independent, and to realise his own essential being and responsibility. Being no longer held and bound by any tradition, he wandered amongst the heaped-up ruins of the traditions, now reduced to lifeless fragments, of a fast disappearing world, seeking out first one, then another, only in many cases to end, driven by fear and hope, in finding a deceitful support in the most ridiculous of them or else falling ill over it.

May we not also see in the close contact established from the time of Alexander the Great onwards with the civilization of the Euphrates and Tigris, the very home of demonology, another essential cause of the spread of belief in demons ?

Jacob Burckhardt expresses himself thus on the subject of further development in the third and fourth centuries, during which belief in demons gradually and completely destroyed the monotheism built up by the influence of philosophy:

> It is a humiliating testimony to the slavishness of the human spirit where the great forces of history are concerned that the philosophy of the period, professed in part by persons of real worth and armed with all the learning of the old world, here (as regards monotheism) wandered into the most obscure byways. Although it marks an advance in the moral domain we have no choice, so far as the early fourth century is concerned, but to rank it among the superstitions.[2]

> There were still, of course, pure hearts and clear intellects who held fast to the unity of God in the spirit of earlier, better times; but in most cases this conviction was beclouded by demoniacal elements.[3]

---

[1] *Medizinisches aus der ältesten Kirchengeschichte* in: Texte und Untersuchungen zur Geschichte der altchristlichen Literatur, vol. viii, p. 108.

[2] J. Burckhardt, *Die Zeit Konstantins des Grossen*, 2nd edit., Leipzig, 1880, p. 215.

[3] *Ibid.*, p. 230.

Pagans, Jews, and Christians were alike convinced that spirits and the dead could be conjured. We are not dealing, moreover, with a forcibly imposed belief like that in the existence of witches in the last centuries, but with a hundred unequivocal declarations, spontaneous and consequently very various, made by writers, some of whom are circumspect and generally of high moral tone.[1]

Two particularly good descriptions of possessed persons taken from pagan Greek literature (Lucian and Philostratus) have already been reproduced above (p. 6).

A very interesting light is thrown on the theoretical consequences of possession by a passage from the Christian author Clement of Alexandria. Referring to Plato he writes (erroneously) that the latter deduced from the observation of cases of possession certain theories as to the language of the gods which seems to be spoken by the mouths of the possessed:

> Plato attributes a dialect also to the gods, forming this conjecture mainly from dreams and oracles, and especially from demoniacs, who do not speak their own language or dialect but that of the demons who have taken possession of them. He thinks also that the irrational creatures have dialects, which those that belong to the same genus understand. . . . But the first and generic barbarous dialects have terms by nature, since also men confess that prayers uttered in a barbarian tongue are more powerful.[2]

Nevertheless, pagan antiquity is not the main source to which we owe our knowledge of possession in the ancient world, It is rather derived from Christian literature, the New Testament and Patristic writings, from which it appears that possession has been of very frequent occurrence in the Mediterranean basin since the time of Christ.

It would be entirely false to believe that possession was confined to the Jews; it was common throughout the world of late antiquity, and the cure of demoniacal affections was a distinguishing characteristic of all the religious and magic-working prophets of the time. If the most important information comes from Christian literature, this is certainly because it has survived in relatively much greater quantities than non-Christian writings. How few fragments of the copious Hellenic literature have come down to us! With what difficulty do we reconstruct the richly developed religious life of Hellas! and how often we have nothing but the in-

---

[1] *Ibid.*, p. 243.
[2] Clement of Alexandria, *Stromata*, i, 21, 142 (Ante-Nicene Christian Library, vol. i, p. 443. Edinburgh, 1867).

formation involuntarily preserved in the polemical works of the Christians to serve as basis for conclusions *a posteriori* on lost writings! The invasion of the barbarians who conquered the Roman Empire has destroyed infinitely less than did the Christian hatred and persecution of the heathen. Never in the world's history has so vast a literature been so radically given over to destruction. Nor is its historical value the only thing involved: the influence of antiquity on the present would have been still greater had more of the literature of its later times been preserved.

From whence comes the greatly increased importance which belief in demons assumed at that time amongst the Greeks and Romans? " This has not yet been explained," says Harnack.[1] But at least he feels safe in saying that there is " a strong presumption that very widespread ideas may have represented the course and events of the world as subject to the influence of demons who ruled the air. Astrology also came into play." It cannot be admitted that Jewish and Christian influences were solely responsible for the spread of belief in demons, as it had permeated the whole Empire before the second century; but these two, like other eastern religions, especially that of Egypt, may have contributed to it.

The extent to which possession must have spread is attested by the fact that there was a whole body of exorcists, as to-day " bone-setters " practise side by side with learned physicians.[2] Possession existed not only in the provinces, but, according to the evidence of Justin Martyr, in the Roman metropolis also. That the number of energumens became very great is evidenced by the frequency with which possession is mentioned by the Fathers of the Church, but above all by the existence of general rules for its treatment. We find, for instance, in Dionysius the Areopagite that possessed persons should be excluded from the holy sacraments and ordinations, but admitted to interments.[3]

The description of Sulpicius Severus also shows (assuming

---

[1] Harnack, *Die Mission und Ausbreitung des Christentums in den ersten drei Jahrhunderten*, 3rd ed., revised and augmented, Leipzig, 1915, vol. i, p. 138.
[2] *Ibid.*
[3] Justin Martyr, *Apol.*, ii, 6. It would be interesting to know whether possession also existed in Athens, the centre of learning, and if so in what circles and from what date.

it not to be exaggerated) that the number of possessed persons had become very considerable. Of a monk particularly successful in exorcism he says:

> He, therefore, was to a wonderful degree visited by people who came to him from every part of the world. I say nothing about those of humbler rank; but prefects, courtiers and judges of various ranks often lay at his doors. Most holy bishops also, laying aside their priestly dignity, and humbly imploring him to touch and bless them, believed with good reason that they were sanctified, and illumined with a divine gift, as often as they touched his hand and garment.[1]

This last sentence, however, throws doubt on whether the persons referred to were always possessed in the true sense of the word.

No information concerning epidemics of possession appears to be available.

The identity of the states of that period with better-known modern ones is evident, not merely from the general description of single cases, but also from numerous details.

Thus we already find related by Gregory the Great a multiple possession of one and the same individual:

> . . . And forasmuch as she was by the enemy continually and cruelly tormented, her kinsfolk that carnally loved her, and with their love did persecute her, caused her to be carried for help to certain witches; so utterly to cast away her soul, whose body they went about by sorcery to relieve. Coming into their hands she was by them brought to a river and there washed in the water, the sorcerers labouring a long time by their enchantments to cast out the devil that had possessed her body: but by the wonderful judgment of Almighty God, it fell out that while one by unlawful act was expelled, suddenly a whole legion did enter in. And from that time forward she began to be tossed with so many varieties of motions, to shriek out in so many sundry tunes, as there were devils in her body. Then her parents, consulting together, and confessing their own wickedness, carried her to the venerable Bishop Fortunatus, and with him they left her: who, having taken her to his charge, fell to his prayers many days and nights, and he prayed so much the more earnestly, because he had against him, in one body, an whole army of devils; and many days passed not, before he made her so safe and sound, as though the devil had never had any power or interest in her body.[2]

---

[1] Sulpicius Severus, *Dialogues*, i, 20. ("A Select Library of Nicene and Post-Nicene Fathers of the Christian Church," second series, Oxford, 1894, vol. xi, p. 33.)

[2] Gregory the Great, *Dialogues*, i, c. 10. ("The Dialogues of Saint Gregory, surnamed the Great . . . translated into our English tongue," Paris, MDCVIII, re-edited E. G. Gardner, London, 1911, p. 39.)

Apparent possession by animal demons seems also to have occurred. Jerome reports in his biography of St. Paula that she met in the neighbourhood of Samaria possessed persons whose behaviour was in some respects that of animals:

> She heard how men howled like wolves, barked like dogs, roared like lions, hissed like serpents, bellowed like bulls.[1]

An example of the infection of a priest by a demoniac is found in Gregory the Great:

> And behold, straight upon the bringing of the relics of St. Sebastian the martyr into the oratory, a wicked spirit possessed the aforesaid matron's daughter-in-law, and pitifully tormented her before all the people. The priest of the oratory, beholding her so terribly vexed and lifted up, took a white linen cloth and cast upon her; and forthwith the devil also entered into him, and because he presumed above his strength, enforced also he was by his own vexation, to know what himself was.[2]

The autosuggestive genesis of possession is also very evident in certain cases. Thus the extreme fear of demons led to the onset of possession as a consequence of past sins. Amongst numerous examples we will again quote a case related by Gregory the Great:

> . . . To relate only a small part of what the abbot and prior of this convent told me. One day two brethren were sent to buy something for the needs of the convent. One was younger and seemed cleverer; the other was older and should have supervised the first. As they went on their way he who should have looked after the younger man committed a larceny, unwittingly, with the money which had been given to them. As soon as they had returned to the convent and on the very threshold of the house of piety, he who had committed the theft fell to the earth, seized by the evil spirit, and suffered great torments. When the evil spirit had left him he was questioned by all the monks who had hastened to the spot; he was asked if he had not misappropriated the money received. He denied it and was tormented a second time. When the evil spirit had again left him he was again questioned but again denied and was once more given over to torment. He denied eight times and eight times was tormented. At the eighth falsehood he confessed the sum of money which he had stolen. He did penance, prostrated himself, admitted his sin and the evil spirit returned no more as soon as he had accomplished the expiation.[3]

[1] Saint Jerome, *Epistula*, c. viii, 13, ed. Migne, i, p. 889. Jacob Burckhardt, *loc. cit.*, p. 447.
[2] Gregory the Great, *loc. cit.*, i, c. 10. *Dialogues*, etc., pp. 38-39.
[3] Gregory the Great, *To Rusticiana, Patrician* (Epistles, book xi, no. xliv).

Another case is handed down by Sulpicius Severus. A monk renowned as an exorcist became himself possessed.

> But in the meantime, just as honour accrued to the holy man from his excellence, so vanity began to steal upon him from the honour which was paid him. When first he perceived that this evil was growing upon him, he struggled long and earnestly to shake it off, but it could not be thoroughly got rid of by all his efforts. . . . Betaking himself, therefore, with fervent supplication to God, he is said to have prayed that, power being given to the devil over him for five months, he might become like to those whom he himself had cured. . . . That most powerful man—he, renowned for his miracles and virtues through all the East, he, to whose threshold multitudes had gathered, and at whose door the highest dignitaries of that age had prostrated themselves - laid hold of by a demon, was kept fast in chains. It was only after having suffered all these things which the possessed are wont to endure, that at length in the fifth month he was delivered, not only from the demon, but (what was to him more useful and desirable) from the vanity which had dwelt within him.[1]

Early Christian testimonies must, as always, be accepted with a certain reserve. It certainly does not appear that all maladies were considered as forms of demoniacal possession, but the conception of possession was nevertheless much wider than our own.

Whereas Plato considered sin to be a sickness of the soul, Christianity regarded it as possession and of a nature even graver than the usual form, inasmuch as in the latter the possessed realizes his state, while in sin the contrary obtains. Cassian remarks:

> Although it is a fact that those men are more grievously and severely troubled, who, while they seem to be very little affected by them in the body, are yet possessed in spirit in a far worse way, as they are entangled in their sins and lusts. For as the Apostle says: " Of whom a man is overcome, of him he is also the servant." Only that in this respect they are more dangerously ill, because though they are their slaves, yet they do not know that they are assaulted by them, and under their dominion.[2]

There is an irreconcilable contradiction in Cassian's express and emphatic statement that the possessed may be neither execrated nor despised,[3] when he cannot be said to adopt this point of view as regards the immoral, although

---

[1] Sulpicius Severus, *loc. cit.*, i, c. 20 (p. 84).

[2] *Cassian's Conferences*, vii, ch. xxv. ("A Select Library of Nicene and Post-Nicene Fathers of the Christian Church," second series, Oxford, 1894, vol. xi, p. 371.)

[3] *Ibid.*, p. 500.

he conceives that they should be given credit for the fact that they are unaware of their possession.

As for the moral judgement to be passed on the possessed, there seems to have been no unanimity whatever. A Father of the Church, the Syrian Rabbulas, writes that "priests should not give the Host to possessed persons lest the Most Holy Thing be profaned by contact with demons."[1] Cassian, on the contrary, was of the opinion that they should receive communion every day if possible as a spiritual remedy.[2] It would be unjust to withhold it from them on the strength of the saying that pearls should not be cast before swine, that the communion should not become the devil's food. There does not appear to have been any general relationship between the morality of the individual and the genesis of possession; it came on as an autosuggestive consequence of sin, but occurred also amongst the saints. Cassian says:

> But we know that even saintly men have been given over in the flesh to Satan and to great afflictions for some very slight faults, since the divine mercy will not suffer the very least spot or stain to be found in them on the day of judgment, and purges away in this world every spot of their filth, as the prophet, or rather God himself says, in order that he may commit them to eternity as gold or silver refined and needing no final purification.[3]

Christianity had the greatest share in the use of exorcism as a means of cure:

> The Christians made their appearance throughout the whole world as exorcists of demons, and exorcism was a very powerful missionary and propagandist weapon. They were concerned not merely with exorcising the demons which inhabit man, but also with purging them from the atmosphere and the whole of public life. For the century (the second) was under the dominion of the spirit of darkness and his legions. . . . The whole world and the atmosphere surrounding it was peopled with devils; all the formalities of life—not only the worship of idols—were governed by them. They sat upon thrones and surrounded the infant's cradle. The earth, God's creation though it is now and for ever, became in very truth a hell.[4]

It is very interesting that Christianity, engaged in combat with possession, should have professed to have a greater power of overcoming it than exorcists of any other persuasion.

[1] *Rabbulæ Edesseni Canones*, Migne, P.G., vol. lxxvii.
[2] Cassian, *loc. cit.*, v, ch. xxv. ("A Select Library," etc.)
[3] Cassian, *ibid.*, p. 496.
[4] Harnack, *Die Mission*, vol. i, p. 141. Cf. also H. Achelis, *Das Christentum in den ersten drei Jahrhunderten*, Leipzig, 1912, vol. i, pp. 132-147.

> For numberless demoniacs throughout the whole world, and in your city (Rome) many of our Christian men exorcising them in the name of Jesus Christ, who was crucified under Pontius Pilate, have healed and do heal, rendering helpless and driving the possessing devils out of the men, though they could not be cured by all the other exorcists and those who used incantations and drugs.[1]

It seems, indeed, that this was not a matter of mere personal conviction, but was really the case; the Christian exorcists were able to record the greatest successes, because they answered best to those requirements which we have learnt to recognize as necessary to the success of exorcism. The Christians possessed absolute certainty of victory, founded on their faith in Christ. To this was added the high moral value of their doctrine, which opened to them the hearts of the sick and the oppressed. That deliverance from all the burdens of the soul which the modern man experiences when he enters a circle of true believers in Jesus must have occurred in a far higher degree amongst the Christians of the two first generations to whom the memory of Christ was still a living thing. Men were alive who had known Him, or their sayings had been heard by the ears of those present, and to this must be added the belief in His imminent second coming. It is difficult for us to conceive any idea of the conviction and exaltation of these early Christians. How strong their influence must have been, when their religion was still young, their faith still fresh and vivid, not yet overlaid with the grey dust of two hundred years of dogmatics! The great success of the Christian exorcists is therefore readily understood, and its reality is attested by the fact that other exorcists who were not true Christians, and even certain Jews, likewise uttered conjurations in the name of Jesus[2] (as already happened in Palestine in Jesus' lifetime: Mark ix 88).

Origen declares that the Christian exorcists were generally uneducated people.[3] Were the possessed also ?

Whereas in Justin's day (100–150) there was no distinct body of exorcists, one already existed in the time of Origen (182–252). Exorcisms took place free of charge, and nothing was used except prayer and " forms of conjuration so simple

---

[1] Justin, *Apol.*, ii, 6. (Ante-Nicene Christian Library, vol. ii. Justin Martyr, pp. 76-77, Edinburgh, 1868.)

[2] For further details, cf. Harnack, *loc. cit.*, p. 142.

[3] Quoted by Harnack, *loc. cit.*, p. 153.

that the simplest man was able to apply them " (Origen).
The demon was also threatened with punishments.[1] It
therefore appears that exorcisms were conducted in a manner
essentially the same as was later prescribed in the *Rituale
Romanum*, only the formulæ were obviously much simpler
and very flexible; no rigid schematization had as yet taken
place, nor must it be forgotten that the exorcists were simple
and uncultured people. The beginning was devoted to the
recitation of the liturgy, then followed prayers, and the
exorcism proper came last. It was accompanied by the
laying on of hands, the breath of the Spirit was breathed on
the possessed, and signs of the cross made. There were also
written formularies of exorcism. Probst even declares that
in the *Rituale Romanum* one such has been preserved to us
as the essential basis.[2]

Cures from a distance are also found, although exceptionally. Sulpicius Severus relates of a monk: " He not only cured
the possessed when he was present or by his word, but also
when he was absent by the fringes of his hair-shirt or by
letter."[3]

Exorcism seems in many cases to have been accompanied
by certain requirements as to the conduct of the possessed.
A true belief in God is indicated by Origen as the surest remedy
against demons; then followed fasting and prayer—all stipulations which increased the sick man's faith in the termination
of his sufferings.

According to Origen, it was a rule never to question the
demons nor to speak to them, for God did not desire that
Christians should become the listeners and disciples of
demons.[4] The claims of certain Christians (*e.g.*, Justin
Martyr) to command unconditional success in their exorcisms
and their categorical denial of it to other persons are naturally
quite false and in contradiction to evidence from other
sources. Tertullian even goes so far as this monstrous
exaggeration: " The wicked spirit, bidden speak by a follower
of Christ, will as readily make the truthful confession that he

[1] Some details concerning these exorcisms have been collected
by Fred. Probst; *Sakramente und Sakramentalien in den drei ersten
christlichen Jahrhunderten*, Tübingen, 1872, pp. 46 sq.
[2] *Ibid.*, pp. 52 sq.
[3] Sulpicius Severus, *loc. cit.*, p. 115.
[4] Origen, *In num. hom.* 16 n. i, p. 418, quoted by Probst, *loc. cit.*,
p. 44.

is a demon, as elsewhere he has falsely asserted that he is a god."[1]

Not all had the same success, and this depended on their possession or lack of the χάρισμα. Unfailing success would be contrary to the theory. "The force of the exorcism," says Origen expressly, "lies in the name of Jesus which is spoken and in which his Gospels are proclaimed." There is involved, moreover, a very primitive magic spell, the "name-spell." All the attempts of Christian theologians to endow Christianity with a sublimity beyond the accumulated primitive beliefs of the period are useless. Let us listen to Origen explaining the magic charm of the name of Jesus:

> Then we say that the name Sabaoth, and Adonai and the other names treated with so much reverence among the Hebrews, are not applicable to any ordinary created thing, but belong to a secret theology which refers to the Framer of all things. These names accordingly when pronounced with that attendant train of circumstances which is appropriate to their nature, are possessed of great power; and other names, again, current in the Egyptian tongue, are efficacious against certain demons who can only do certain things; and other names in the Persian language have corresponding power over certain spirits; and so on in every individual nation, for different purposes. And thus it will be found that, if the various demons upon the earth, to whom different localities have been assigned, each one bears a name appropriate to the several dialects of place and country. He, therefore, who has a nobler idea, however small, of these matters, will be careful not to apply differing names to different things. . . .[2]
>
> And I do not dwell on this, that when the name of Zeus is uttered there is heard at the same time that of the son of Kronos and Rhea, and the husband of Hera and brother of Poseidon, and father of Athene and Artemis. . . . And when one is able to philosophize about the mystery of names, he will find much to say respecting the titles of the angels of God, of whom one is called Michael and another Gabriel, and another Raphael, appropriately to the duties which they discharge in the world, according to the will of the God of all things. And a similar philosophy of names applies also to our Jesus, whose name has already been seen, in an unmistakable manner, to have expelled myriads of evil spirits from the souls and bodies (of men), so great was the power which it exerted upon those from whom the spirits were driven out. And while still upon the subject of names, we have to mention that those who are skilled in the use of incantations, relate that the utterance of the same incantation in its proper language can accomplish what the spell professes to do; but when translated into any other tongue it is observed to become inefficacious and feeble.

---

[1] Tertullian, *Apol.*, c. 23. *The Writings of Tertullian* (Ante-Nicene Christian Library, vol. xi, Edinburgh, 1869).

[2] Origen, *Against Celsus*, i, 24. (Ante-Nicene Christian Library, vol. x, Writings of Origen, pp. 421-22, Edinburgh, 1869.)

And thus it is not the things signified, but the qualities and peculiarities of words, which possess a certain power for this or that purpose. And so on such grounds as these we defend the conduct of the Christians, when they struggle even to death to avoid calling God by the name of Zeus, or to give him a name from any other language.[1]

According to the belief of these first Christians the efficaciousness of the exorcism pronounced in the name of Jesus had nothing to do with Jesus himself; it was from the five letters J-E-S-U-S arranged in that particular order that the curative action proceeded! The reproaches levelled by Harnack against Reitzenstein and modern classical philology in general, of having represented Christianity in its early days as too near to primitive conceptions and misconstrued figurative expressions literally, proves unfounded on this point. Naturally this does not in any way detract from the lofty character of Christianity's world-wide message.

The most detailed exposition of possession and its treatment in the Church of the past centuries, as well as of exorcism, is to be found in the *Memoirs* of Anton Josef Binterim,[2] which also contain an unequalled collection of descriptions from that period.

As regards the diffusion of possession in ancient Jewry, only one case is to be found in the Old Testament: it is the history of the evil spirit which at times descended upon Saul.

Now the spirit of the Eternal departed from Saul, and an evil spirit from the Eternal scared him. So Saul's courtiers said to him: " Here is an evil spirit from God scaring you! Let your servants now before you offer a suggestion: let them discover some skilful player on the lyre; then whenever the evil spirit overpowers you, he shall play music, and you will get better." Saul answered his courtiers: " Look me out a man who plays well, and bring him to me."

(David was then brought). And whenever the evil spirit from God overpowered Saul, David would take the lyre and play music, till Saul breathed freely; then all would be well and the evil spirit would depart from him.[3]

. . . Next day an evil spirit from God overpowered Saul, and he raved within his house. David was playing music for him as usual, and Saul had a spear in his hand; he raised the spear, saying

---

[1] Origen, *Against Celsus*, i, 25. *Ibid.*, pp. 421-23.
[2] A. J. Binterim, *Die vorzüglichsten Denkwürdigkeiten der christ-katholischen Kirche aus den ersten, mittleren und letzten Zeiten*, vol. viii, part i, chap. 5, Mainz, 1831.
[3] 1 Sam. xvi, 14 sq. (Moffat's edit.).

to himself: " I will pin David to the wall." But David evaded
him twice over.[1]
. . . an evil spirit from the Eternal overpowered Saul as he sat
in his house, spear in hand. David was playing music, and Saul
tried to pin David to the wall with his spear. But David slipped
aside from Saul, and he drove the spear into the wall.[2]

It follows with certitude from this narrative that Saul
suffered from extremely painful psychic compulsions. His
case was therefore one of lucid possession.

As mentioned above, this is the sole case of possession
recorded in the Old Testament—we shall deal in the next
chapter with possession amongst the prophets and pseudo-
prophets. According to H. Duhm[3] the importance of belief
in evil spirits amongst the Jews in Old Testament times was
very slight. Their national separatism from the outer world
was in this respect very advantageous, keeping them free from
the more serious forms of infection by Babylonian and
Egyptian demonology.

Many an obscure form, amorphous survival and usage transformed in meaning, clearly shows that the Israelites had also had
their early demonic period and had several times come under the
influence of their neighbours; but these traces demonstrate equally
that belief in demons had no longer any individual and independent
life, and that its effects lingered with the same tenacity that we
observe amongst our own Protestants.[4]
On the other hand, since the destruction of the Israelitish and
then the Jewish state, the number of demons grew incessantly
and continued to augment right on into New Testament times
(under the influence of the Babylonian conception of the world).[5]

According to H. Loewe, belief in possession reigned
particularly in Galilee, whereas Palestine was immune from it.[6]

In the New Testament accounts of possession, the consequences of the influx of Babylonian demonology are extremely
obvious. Parallel with them are certain passages from
Flavius Josephus which also throw light on Jewish thera-
peutics. Of Solomon he relates:

God also enabled him to learn the art which expels demons,
which is useful and works cures for men. He composed charms
also by which diseases are alleviated. And he left behind him
forms of exorcisms, by which people drive away demons so that
they never return; and this method of cure is of very great value
unto this day: for I have seen a certain man of my own country,

[1] 1 Sam. xviii, 10 sq. (*ibid.*).　　　[2] 1 Sam. xix, 9 sq. (*ibid.*).
[3] Hans Duhm, *Die bösen Geister im alten Testament*, Tübingen, 1904.
[4] *Ibid.*, p. 31.　　　[5] *Ibid.*, p. 68.
[6] Herbert Loewe, *Encyclopædia of Religion and Ethics*, vol. iv, p. 613.

whose name was Eleazar, curing people possessed by demons in the presence of Vespasian and his sons and captains and the whole of his soldiers. The manner of the cure was as follows: he put a ring that had under its seal one of those sorts of roots mentioned by Solomon, to the nostrils of the demoniac, and then drew the demon out through his nostrils as he smelt it: and when the man fell down immediately, he adjured the demon to return into him no more, still making mention of Solomon, and reciting the incantations which he had composed. And Eleazar, wishing to persuade and show to the spectators that he had such a power, used to set a little way off a cup or basin full of water, and commanded the demon, as he went out of the man, to overturn it, and so let the spectators know that he had left the man.[1]

In his *Jewish War* Flavius Josephus speaks of a certain root (*bara*) which was sought after as a remedy against possession.

For the so-called demons—in other words, the spirits of wicked men which enter the living and kill them unless aid is forthcoming —are promptly expelled by this root, if merely applied to the patients.[2]

It seems that in ancient times, in the Semitic cilivizations of Palestine, possession as a whole had reached its most complete development. Bousset finds that "at all events belief in the devil together with an awakening dualism permeates late Jewish religion to a *very high degree.*"[3] He sees in the possession-beliefs of that time the result of a general established religious life—namely, that in all periods of transition when a people's highest faith weakens and is threatened with destruction, and before the somewhat higher new forms have as yet definitely developed, the more primitive old beliefs emerge from the lower depths of the popular mind.

Everywhere at the time of Hellenism and of the Roman Empire national religions were going bankrupt, and everywhere with a disquieting strength superstition, belief in spirits and ghosts, in the conjuration of spirits and in magic practices, in the power of names, the formulæ of sorcery, incantatory prayers, binding and loosing and other charms flourished luxuriantly.[4]

The particularly strong influence exercised on Judaism by belief in demons seems related to the deeply religious

[1] *Antiquities of the Jews*, book viii, chap. ii. (The Works of Flavius Josephus, Whiston's translation revised, A. R. Shilleto, London, 1900, vol. ii, pp. 79-80.)
[2] Josephus, *Jewish War*, vii, 186. (Loeb Classical Library, Josephus, vol. iii, p. 559.)
[3] Bousset, *Die Religion des Judentums in Neutestamentlichen Zeitalter*, 2nd edit., Berlin, 1906, p. 388.
[4] *Ibid.*, p. 387.

temperament of this people: almost the whole of its intellectual creativeness is concentrated on religion. By its religion alone it has become a world-power; in other forms of culture, science, art, philosophy, it is not to be compared with Græco-Latin antiquity. Even its poetry, in spite of certain great creative works, is poor regarded as a whole, and has never broken away from religion. Judaism has, of course, an essential importance from the point of view of social civilization, but this no longer belongs to the domain of the highest culture.[1]

To the religious impetus must be added the pathological tendencies of the Jewish people. These have long been recognized as indubitable in contemporary Judaism, a fact the more important to our subject as possession must be regarded as more nearly related to hysteria than to anything else, and hysteria is numbered amongst the affections to which the Jewish nation is predisposed.[2]

Let us pause to consider whether this disposition originates from social relations or from still deeper causes.

It is certain that life during the dispersion, the national conservatism of the Jews, the jealousy and ill-will called forth by the oppression of neighbouring peoples and the feelings of permanent aversion resulting therefrom, contributed in many cases to produce and develop neuroses and thus often to transmit an heredity of corresponding tendencies.[3] But it still appears questionable whether these environmental causes suffice to explain pathological tendencies. Quite as unconvincing are the suggestions of repeated degeneracy due to long-continued in-breeding and often betraying itself by external blemishes. All these reasons, not in themselves improbable, nevertheless lose some of their cogency when we consider the long series of Jewish monuments and observe the marked constancy of the racial type.[4] Those signs of degeneracy which are supposedly due to the age and in-breeding of the race exist already in the monuments of ancient Egypt, and to this physical constancy corresponds a moral

---

[1] Cf. Jos. Kohler, *Deutsche Literaturzeitung*, 1907, 3259.
[2] H. Oppenheim, *Lehrbuch der Nervenkrankheiten*, 6th edit., Berlin, 1913, vol. ii, p. 1393.
[3] Oppenheim adds to these reasons the growth of the spirit of industry fostered by unfavourable conditions of life.
[4] Cf. J. M. Judt, *Die Juden als Rasse*, Cologne, 1903.

one. All things considered, we are irresistibly driven to the conclusion that this is a people which unites in a quite peculiar manner and from the most remote times, an astonishing will to live with pathological tendencies, strong, as compared with those of other peoples, towards degeneracy.

These tendencies furnish a complete explanation of how it was possible for belief in demons to lead in Judaism to so many sicknesses as appears to have been the case. The history of possession amongst the Jews does not come to an end at the time of Christ, but is prolonged up to the present day.

In the third century A.D. we find evidence of Jewish possession and Jewish exorcisms in the great magic papyrus of Paris, the redaction of which goes back to about the year 300. The text[1] is the more interesting since its conclusion shows that it contains an exorcism applied to cases of genuine possession, whereas it is impossible to decide whether the majority of exorcisms handed down to us deal with real possession or a physical malady considered as such.

So far as the civilizations of the Far East in ancient times are concerned, I have so far only been able to obtain access to very scanty documents.

Some few particulars relating to ancient India may be found in a work of Jolly on old Hindu medicine, which can, however, barely be pressed into service. It appears from Jolly's information that in India also spirits have been imagined as able to enter into the human body, but for the most part we are again confronted by the interpretation of maladies of all sorts as possession.

> Children's ailments in particular were attributed to demoniacal influences, perhaps because this defenceless age was held to be particularly accessible to such influences and because the suddenness with which in children grave sickness succeeds perfect health could not be otherwise explained. . . . The general signs of a demoniacal attack are also enumerated. The child starts suddenly, he is frightened, he cries, bites himself and his nurse, his eyes are turned backwards, his teeth chatter, he groans, whines, yawns, knits his brows, clenches his teeth, twists his lips, frequently spits foam, grows thin, does not sleep at night, has swollen eyes, suffers from diarrhœa and hoarseness, smells of meat and blood, does not eat as before, does not take the breast; preliminary symptoms (*prodromi*) are fever and incessant tears.[2]

---

[1] Reproduced above, p. 101.
[2] Julius Jolly, *Grundriss der indo-arischen Theologie und Altertumskunde*, vol. iv, no. 10, Strasburg, 1901, p. 69.

There are also prevailing psychic symptoms by which possession is recognized. We have in India a degree of civilization where often the purely physical maladies are no longer considered as demoniacal in nature, but psychic disturbances, or at least many of them, are still so regarded. So far as the maladies of adults are concerned Jolly has established the following facts:

> The worst forms of dementia are attributed to a demoniac influence and consequently classed as possession (*bhutonmada*). Eight, ten, twenty, or " innumerable " demons and gods of madness are distinguished, who seize upon man when he transgresses the laws of religion, when he remains alone in an empty house or stops by night at a burial-place, etc. What spirit has entered into him may be discerned by his mode of behaviour. Thus the man possessed by a *Daitya* is spiteful, hot-tempered, proud; he calls himself a god, likes spirituous liquors and meat. He who is possessed by a *Gandharva* sings and dances, bedecks, bathes, and anoints himself. He who is possessed by a demon snake has red eyes, a fixed stare, his walk is tortuous and unsteady, he puts out his tongue, licks the corners of his lips, likes milk, honey and sweet things. He who is possessed by a *Yaksa* is voluptuous, lascivious, prodigal, talkative, and staggers like a drunkard in his walk. He who is possessed by a *Pisaka* is uneasy, gluttonous and dirty; he has no memory, runs hither and thither, tears his flesh with his nails and walks naked.[1]

At most only the last state described in this quotation may be considered as possession within the meaning of this work, but Jolly's scanty documentation is not adequate to a sure identification, and the sources on which he draws are Sanskrit works of which no translation is available. Further investigation from these works of the diffusion of possession in ancient India must therefore be left to orientalists.

The Atharva-Veda contains a mass of exorcisms of all kinds; in fact, so great a wealth that it recalls in the most striking manner the cuneiform Babylonian tablets referred to above, of which it is also reminiscent from another point of view. Just as we fail to find in the Babylonian tablets a completely satisfying attestation of the reality of possession in ancient Mesopotamia, so the Atharva-Veda has a similar disappointment in store for us. Amongst the multitude of exorcisms which it contains there is not one which might be cited with complete certainty as applying to true possession. It is possible that this is due to inadequate translation, for

[1] *Ibid.*, p. 122.

that of medical terms could not well be fully clear, but in the extensive extracts before me, published in *The Sacred Books of the East*, I have sought in vain for any evidence which might be regarded as satisfactory.[1] Rather than any other, reference might be made to the exorcism-hymn (VI, iii) which is entitled by the translator: *Charm against mania*. It runs thus:

> 1. Release for me, O Agni, this person here, who, bound and well-secured, loudly jabbers! Then shall he have due regard for thy share (of the offering), when he shall be free from madness!
> 2. Agni shall quiet down thy mind, if it has been disturbed! Cunningly do I prepare a remedy, that thou shalt be freed from madness.
> 3. (Whose mind) has been maddened by the sin of the gods, or been robbed of sense by the Rakshas, (for him) do I cunningly prepare a remedy, that he shall be free from madness.

In the translator's commentary it is said that the early Hindu scholiast here remarks that the rite in question is used for those possessed by demons.[2] Interpretation as true possession is, however, not free from doubt, for the reference may be to simple madness. The problem is to know whether the malady called " mania " by the translator is really mania or rather disturbances due to possession, but this too can only be resolved by orientalists, if indeed it be capable of real solution.

In the old legends of the life of Buddha, on the other hand, we find surer evidence of possession. Marvellous healing powers are attributed to his mother while she was pregnant of him, and possessed persons figure amongst those who were cured by her.

In the Lalita-Vistara, in the Gathas, it is said:

> Women and maidens, who happened to be afflicted by being possessed by demons, or by insanity, running about naked and covered with dust, regained their senses by the sight of Máyá, and, being endowed with memory, understanding, and correct notions, returned to their homes.[3]

---

[1] *Hymns of the Atharva-Veda* together with extracts from the Ritual Books and the Commentaries, translated by Maurice Bloomfield, Oxford, 1897 (*The Sacred Books of the East*, vol. xlii), p. 32.

[2] *Ibid.*, p. 519.

[3] *The Lalita-Vistara or Memoirs of the Early Life of S'a'kya Sinha*. Translated from the original Sanskrit by Ra'jendra'la la Mitra, Calcutta, 1881, pp. 110 sq. (chap. vi). Unfortunately, a note concerning the idea of possession which the translator had announced (as appears from the asterisk in the text) has been forgotten in the supplement. It might have thrown light on the idea of possession in the Hindu legend of Buddha.

Possessed persons also figure in the Hindu legends; the following narrative occurs in the forty-fifth and forty-sixth nights of the Cukasaptati:

There is a town of the name of Vatsamân, where lived a Brahman called Kecava who was wise, but poor. His wife, who was called Karagarâ (*i.e.*, poison-giver), behaved so ill towards everyone that even a demon, who lived on a tree in the house, fled into the desert for fear of her. Meanwhile the Brahman was no longer able to bear the wickedness of his wife and went away also. On the way to the desert the demon saw him and said to him: " I wish to-day to offer thee hospitality." When the Brahman heard this he was afraid. " Fear not," said the demon, " for I used to live upon a tree in thy house, but I fled to this spot for fear of Karagarâ, and since thou hast long had to do with me as my landlord I will do good to thee. Go thy way to the village of Mrigavati (that is to say, rich in gazelles); I will take possession of the daughter of the city, Mrigalotschanâ (signifying gazelle-eyed) and will not let myself be driven out by any exorcist; thou alone, when thou comest, shalt drive me out with a look." Having spoken thus the demon entered into the royal virgin. Meanwhile the Brahman went into the royal city Mrigavati and having heard the herald he went to the royal palace, but in vain he did all that magicians are accustomed to do and uttered his conjurations, the demon did not leave the maiden. When the Brahman saw that in no other way would the demon come out, he cried: " In the name of Karagarâ, come forth !" The demon replied: " See, I am coming forthwith !" and he immediately came out. Then the King gave to the Brahman the half of his kingdom and his daughter in marriage.

When the demon had come forth he went into the town of Karnavatî (that is to say, the town with ears) and took possession of the queen, who was the half-sister on the father's side of the above-mentioned Madana and who was called Sulotschanâ, signifying lovely-eyed. Greatly tormented by the demon, the queen became like a skeleton. Then the King, whose name was Satrughna (slayer of enemies), sent to the King Madana and begged him to send the magician Kecava. At the request of Madana and of his own wife the latter came to Karnavatî to the possessed queen. But when the demon perceived him he insulted and threatened him: " It is enough that I have done thy bidding once; now take care and look to thyself !" When the Brahman heard this he recognized that it was the same demon; then he approached and whispered in the queen's ear: " Karagarâ is following me here; I have only come to tell thee this !" When the demon learnt that Karagarâ was coming he was seized with fright and immediately left the queen. The Brahman, covered with honours by the King, made his way back to Mrigavatî.[1]

In the Dhaca-kumara-Caritam, a princess, according to Bastian, simulated possession by a spirit which her lover subsequently expelled.[2]

[1] *Pantschatantra-Caritam*, Fünf Bücher indischer Fabeln, Märchen und Erzählungen, Aus dem Sanskrit übersetzt mit Einleitung und Anmerkungen von Theodor Benfey, part i, Leipzig, 1859, pp. 519-521.
[2] A. Bastian, *Der Mensch in der Geschichte*, vol. ii, Leipzig, 1860, p. 557.

We shall now leave antiquity and pass to mediæval and modern times. In the foreground naturally stands Europe, concerning which information is most abundant, with extremely numerous and easily accessible literary sources.

As to the history and diffusion of possession in the Middle Ages, we are still ill-informed; all the spade-work is still to do.[1] But without further ado we may say that the Christian Middle Ages were filled with the phenomena of possession. It is not rare for religious biographies to contain descriptions of them, as is amply demonstrated by a glance through the *Acta Sanctorum*. I have consulted a large number of the sixty-one volumes as yet available; there is not one in which under the articles *energumeni* and *dæmones* cases of possession are not recorded. In passing, the reader should also see the volumes of Görres' *Mystik* which treats of possession and is largely based on the *Acta Sanctorum*.[2]

No one has made yet a complete collection of possession-episodes, and, moreover, it would hardly be worth while to search through literature for this purpose alone. Such a collection should be made incidentally by those studying the history of churches and religions, which involves acquaintance with great masses of literature.

We find the same stories of cures, which are already known to us from the New Testament and patristic literature, constantly repeated in the biographies and legends of the saints with a wearisome sameness.

H. Günter believes that there is a connection between certain legends of possession and the Talmud, in which he indicates analogous features.[3]

No useful purpose is served by confronting the reader with a multitude of cases; it is sufficient merely to adduce a few examples in chronological order. Owing to the complete similarity of the episodes it does not greatly matter whether some of them are or are not pure legend, for legend depicts in this connection nothing beyond what really occurred; the religious life of the Middle Ages models not only its bright

[1] The medical works on the epidemics of the Middle Ages (*e.g.*, Hecker, *Die grossen Volkskrankheiten des Mittelalters*, Berlin, 1865) also contain nothing, and the same is true of the social histories of that period.

[2] J. von Görres, *Mystik*, Regensburg, 1842, vol. iv, part i.

[3] H. Günter, *Die Christliche Legende des Abendlandes* (Religions-wissenschaftliche Bibliothek, vol. ii), p. 112.

but also its dark side on the time of Christ. Naturally this does not mean that the possessed voluntarily imitated the possession of the Gospels.

In the first place we will give a few cases of possession from the beginning of the Middle Ages, then three cases from the twelfth, thirteenth and fifteenth centuries. They belong to the lives of eminent personages: St. Augustine, Bernard of Clairvaux, Francis of Assisi and Norbert of Magdeburg. I have purposely chosen a few detailed cases; others are, as we have already said, easy to find by the hundred. In view of the great similarity of such stories, these examples must suffice, nor will the reader be long in crying " Enough ! " I do not, nevertheless, desire to content myself with the mere affirmation that cases are very frequent in the Middle Ages, and that their type is not distinguished from that of the New Testament. Their somewhat wearisome monotony offers striking proof of the stability of these phenomena in the Christian era.

The possession-cure traditionally attributed to St. Augustine takes us to the southern frontier of the Roman Empire, to Hippo, on the coast of what is now Algeria. Of the last days of Augustine when the Vandals were already besieging his bishopric (Augustine died during this siege) the following is related:

> I know also that this same priest and bishop was asked to offer prayers for these energumens, these sick persons, that he implored God with tears and that the demons came out of the men's bodies. In the same way also when he was ill and kept his bed they brought to him a sick man and begged him to lay on his hands that he might be cured. He replied that if it was in his power to do anything for him he would do it at once without fail. And the other said that he had been visited and that it had been said to him in a dream: " Go and see the bishop Augustine, so that he may lay on his hands and you will be saved." When he learnt this he made no delay in doing it and God immediately made of this sick man a healthy one.[1]

Now here are some cases from the life of Bernard of Clairvaux:

> The nameless Gaul, in book vii, chap. ix of his Acts, relates that when the holy man had been in charge of Clairvaux for several years, women obsessed by the demon were brought to him so that he might cure them. The day before the arrival of the saint the demon had taken to flight of his own accord saying that he could

---

[1] *Acta Sanctorum*, Augusti, vol. vi, p. 439 (August 28).

not resist Bernard, for the latter having up to that time remained
in the world and been sorely tempted by him against chastity but
without being in any way overcome, he who must obey in all things
would be delivered up to him.   This trophy and other like ones
being won from the common enemy by the grace of God, the saint
had the honours of the triumph.[1]

   . . . At Bar-sur-Aube there were two women whom the demons
tormented.   Then their parents brought them to the man of God
that he might cure them.   And as they were approaching the
gates of Clairvaux one of the devils said to the other by the mouth
of the woman that he must come out of that woman.   " And
why, then ?" replied the other demon.   To which the first
replied : " I can neither see Bernard nor hear his voice."   And on
the instant he left the woman who was immediately restored to
health.[2]

Without stopping they therefore led to him (at Milan) a woman
known to all, who had been tormented for seven years by an
unclean spirit, and they begged him in the name of God to order
the demon to depart and to restore the woman to health. . . .

Thereupon he was greatly disturbed and said that signs should be
given not to the faithful but to the heathen; having entrusted his
enterprise to the Holy Spirit and being imbued through prayer
with celestial strength, he overthrew Satan in the pride of his
strength, put him to flight and restored the woman to health and
quietude.[3]

On the third day the servant of God went to the Church of St.
Ambrose at Milan to celebrate the divine mysteries: an innumerable multitude awaited him there.   Between the ceremonies of
the masses, while the clerks were singing and he was seated near
to the altar, they pointed out to him a little girl who was greatly
tormented by the devil, begging him to come to the help of the
poor little thing and drive out from her this frenzied devil.   Having
heard the entreaties of those present, and seen the young person
grind her teeth and cry out in such a way that she was an object
of horror to all those who saw her, he had pity on her tender age
and suffered from the anguish of her suffering.   He therefore took
the paten of the chalice in which he was to celebrate the divine
mysteries, spilt the wine therein upon his fingers, praying inwardly
and trusting in the strength of God, and applied the saving liquid
to the child's lips, letting fall healing drops upon her body.   Immediately Satan, scalded, could not endure the virtue of this infusion.
Thanks to this urgent remedy from the Cross he came forth hastily,
all trembling, in a stinking vomit.   Then the girl being purged,
the devil in flight and discomfited, the church chanted to God the
praises due and after joyful acclamations the rejoicing people
remained still until the divine mysteries had been achieved.   Before
the eyes of all, the girl who had been saved was led home by her
people, and the man of God, jostled in the crowd, regained his
abode with difficulty.[4]

Ernaldus, one of the oldest biographers of St. Bernard,
further relates of his visit to Milan:

   Amongst those . . . who were tormented an old woman; a
citizen of Milan and formerly a respected matron, was propelled

---

[1] *Acta Sanctorum*, Augusti, vol. iv, pp. 106 sq. (August 20).
[2] *Ibid.*, pp. 248 sq.   [3] *Ibid.*, p. 239.   [4] *Ibid.*, p. 281.

by the crowd as far as the Church of St. Ambrose behind the holy
man; the devil had been within her for several years and was
already strangling her in such a way, as might be seen and heard,
that she was deprived of speech, ground her teeth and put out her
tongue like an elephant's trunk; she seemed not a woman, but a
monster. Her repulsive exterior, horrible face and fetid breath
attested the filthiness of Satan who inhabited her. When the man
of God saw her he knew that the devil was lodged and firmly fixed
in her, and that it would not be easy to expel him from a habitation
which he had possessed for so long a time. Turning towards the
people who were present in multitudes, he asked them to pray with
more fervour, and standing with the clerks and monks near to the
altar he commanded the woman to stay in the same place and remain
there. The latter, indeed, offered resistance, moved more by a
diabolic force than by her natural strength, and not without hurt
to others she kicked even the Abbot himself. The latter was full
of indulgence for these diabolic attacks; preparatory to the expulsion, he invoked with supplication the help of God, not in
indignation and wrath, but with a humble and quiet heart, then
proceeded to the sacrifice of the redeeming Host. Each time
that he made the sign of the cross with the sacred Host, turning
towards the woman, it was as if a strong athlete attacked the evil
spirit. For the wicked spirit as often as the sign of the cross was
directed against him testified by blows his access of rage, and
showed all his spleen in rebellious protest against the excitement
which he was made to endure.

Having completed the Lord's prayer the saint attacked the
enemy more vigorously. Placing the sacred body of Jesus on the
paten of the chalice and holding it above the woman's head, he
pronounced these words: "He is there, wicked spirit, thy judge,
the Almighty. Now resist if thou canst! He is there, who must
suffer for our salvation. Now," said he, "let the Prince of this
world be cast out! Here is the body which was taken from the
Virgin's body, stretched upon the cross, placed in the tomb, which
rose again from the dead and ascended to heaven in the presence
of the disciples. By the terrible power of His majesty I command
thee, evil spirit, to come out of His servant and dare to touch her
no more thereafter." More terribly despairing because he must
leave perforce and stay no longer, the demon's anger was the
stronger because of the few minutes which remained to him. Then
the holy father returned to the altar, completed the division of the
Host according to the rite, gave to his assistant the benediction
which is pronounced over the people, and immediately perfect
peace and health were restored to the woman. Thus the divine
mysteries are of such strength and virtue that the Evil One finds
himself constrained not to avowals but to flight. When the devil
had departed the woman whom the evil torturer had kept for so
long on a grid of torments, became once more mistress of her mind
and recovered her sense and reason; as her tongue had entered
again into her mouth she uttered thanksgivings, and having recognized her saviour fell prostrate at his feet. An immense clamour
arose in the church, everyone uttered loud cries to the honour of God,
the bells rang out, God was everywhere blessed, the homage passed
all bounds, and, melted with love, the nation venerated the servant
of God, whom it placed, if one may say so, above all men.

That which had happened among the Milanese was bruited
abroad, throughout Italy men spoke of the man of God, and it
was everywhere told that a great prophet had arisen, strong in

word and works, who in the name of Christ should cure the sick and deliver those possessed of the devil. His cures of sickness *already won for him* deep gratitude, but occasion more often arose to drive out demons, for there were more of the tormented who had recourse to his skilful aid and the operation of the greater powers obscured the lesser works.[1]

Ernaldus also hands down to us a conversation of Bernard with a demon:

He had already arrived at Pavia where the report of his virtues had preceded him. With very fitting pomp and rejoicing the happy town welcomed the man of such great fame; no delay would long have held in leash the anxiety of the people who, having heard tell of the miracles at Milan, desired to see a sign from him. Immediately behind him walked a peasant who had followed him from Milan leading a demoniac woman; he laid her at his feet relating in a tearful voice the torments which she endured. Without delay the devil betook himself to insulting the Abbot by the mouth of the wretched woman, and mocking the servant of God: " No," said he, " this eater of leeks, this devourer of cabbages shall not drive me away from my little bitch." Insults of this kind were thus hurled at the man of God so that, provoked by blasphemies, he might lose patience to endure the outrages and be put to confusion before all men at hearing himself harassed with vile words. But the man of God, understanding his wiles, mocked at the mocker and without himself punishing him but leaving it to God, ordered the demoniac to be led to the Church of St. Syrus. For he intended to give honour to the martyr for the cure which he was about to accomplish and to attribute to his virtue the first-fruits of the operations. But St. Syrus sent the affair back to his house; wishing to take nothing for himself in his Church, he desired that the whole work should be attributed to the Abbot. The woman was therefore led back to the Abbot's dwelling, while the demon said by her mouth: " Little Syrus will not drive me out, any more than little Bernard." Meanwhile the Abbot, having betaken himself to prayer, was beseeching God to save the woman. Then the Evil One, as if his wickedness had changed: " How gladly," said he, " would I come forth from this bitch ! I am so greatly tormented in her ! How gladly would I come forth ! But I cannot. . . ." Having been asked the cause: " Because the great Lord does not yet will it." " And who is the great Lord ?" " Jesus of Nazareth." To which the Man of God replied: " Where hast thou then known Jesus ? Hast thou seen Him ?" " I have seen Him," replied he. " Where hast thou seen Him ?" " In His glory." " And hast thou been in glory ?" " Yes, truly !" " And how hast thou departed therefrom ?" " Many of us fell with Lucifer. . . ." All these words were said in a lugubrious voice by the mouth of the old woman and were heard by all those present. Then the holy Abbot replied: " Wouldst thou not return to glory and be restored to thy first joy ?" In a changed voice and bursting into laughter in an extraordinary way the devil replied: " This is very late !" And he did not say another word. Then the man of God spoke

[1] Ernaldus, *Vita Bernardi Abbatis Claravallensis*, cap. iii, §§ 13-15 in Migne, *Patrologiæ Cursus completus*, vol. clxxxv, pp. 276 sq. Also *Acta Sanctorum*, Augusti, vol. iv, p. 282.

more earnestly, the Evil One withdrew vanquished, and the woman, restored to herself, uttered thanksgivings to the utmost of her power.

The man therefore departed with the woman, and rejoicing all the way over her salvation, returned to his house where friends awaited him. All those who heard the details of this exploit were filled with satisfaction, but soon the joy changed to tears because as soon as the woman reached the threshold of her house the devil entered into her afresh and with more hostility than usual began to rend the wretched creature frightfully. The unfortunate husband did not know which way to turn: what was he to do ? It seemed to him very dangerous to live with a demoniac and impious to abandon her. He therefore arose and taking his wife with him returned to Pavia. There as he did not meet the man of God he pushed on as far as Cremona, where he told him what had occurred and implored him with tears to lend his aid. The clemency of the Abbot did not repulse the pious request, but he commanded them to go into the church of his town (and before the body of confessors), to engage in prayer until he himself should come. Remembering then his promise, he went to the church with a single companion at the hour of twilight when others were going to bed, and passing the whole night in prayers he obtained from God that which he asked; and health having been restored to the woman he commanded her to return without anxiety to her house. But as he feared what had already occurred, the re-entry of the devil into her, he commanded that there should be fastened round her neck a notice bearing these words: " In the name of Our Lord Jesus Christ I command thee, demon, to dare to touch this woman no more." This command frightened the devil who was never afterwards minded to approach the woman after her return home.[1]

In Thomas of Celano's biography of St. Francis we read:

There was a brother who often suffered from a grievous infirmity that was horrible to see; and I know not what name to give it; though some think it was caused by a malignant devil. For oftentimes he was dashed down and with a terrible look in his eyes he wallowed foaming; sometimes his limbs were contracted, sometimes extended, sometimes they were folded and twisted together, and sometimes they became hard and rigid. Sometimes, tense and rigid all over, with his feet touching his head, he would be lifted up in the air to the height of a man's stature and would then suddenly spring back to the earth. The holy Father Francis pitying his grievous sickness went to him and after offering up prayer signed him with the cross and blessed him. And suddenly he was made whole, and never afterwards suffered from this distressing infirmity.[2]

At Città di Castello also there was a woman possessed by a devil; and when the most blessed Father Francis was there she was brought to the house in which he was staying. But she remained outside and began to gnash with her teeth, to make faces and to utter lamentable roarings, after the manner of unclean spirits; and many

[1] Ernaldus, *ibid.*, cap. iv, §. 21 sq.; Migne, *ibid.*, pp. 279 sq.; *Acta Sanctorum, ibid.*, pp. 283 sq.

[2] First Life, part i, chap. xxv (*The Lives of St. Francis of Assisi*, by Thomas of Celano, trans. by A. G. Ferrers Howell, London, 1908, p. 66).

of the people in that city of both sexes came up and besought St Francis for the woman; for that evil spirit had long vexed her by his torments and had troubled them by his roarings. Then the holy father sent to her a brother who was with him, with the intention of finding out whether it really was a devil, or only a woman's deception. When the woman saw the brother she began to mock him, knowing he was not St. Francis. The holy father was praying within, and when he had finished his prayer he came out; and then the woman began to tremble and to roll on the ground, unable to stand his power. St. Francis called her to him and said: " In virtue of obedience I bid thee go out of her, thou unclean spirit," and it straightway left her, doing her no hurt, and departed very full of wrath.[1]

Naturally episodes of possession also appear in the later legend of St. Francis of Assisi. Thus we read in the *Fioretti*:

How the demons could not endure the purity of the innocence and deep humility of Brother Juniper, doth clearly appear herein, that on a time a certain man possessed with a devil, contrary to all his wont and with antics most strange, sprang out of the way he was going in, and of a sudden set off running and fled by divers crossways for seven miles. And being asked by his kinsfolk, that with great anguish of spirit followed after him, wherefore he had fled away with such strange antics, he answered them: " The reason is this: because that mad fellow Juniper was passing by that way: not being able to endure his presence nor to look on him, I fled away into these woods." And certifying themselves of the truth thereof, they found that Brother Juniper had come along that way even as the devil had said. Wherefore St. Francis, when they brought to him those that were possessed to be healed, if the devils departed not straightway at his command, would say: " If thou come not out of this creature of God straightway, I will send for Brother Juniper to deal with thee "; and thereat the demon, fearing the presence of Brother Juniper, and not being able to endure the virtue and humility of St. Francis, would depart straightway.[2]

The case of a possessed woman who was exorcised by St. Norbert of Magdeburg (d. 1134) was very stubborn:

At first the devil mocked at him. Nevertheless the man of God did not permit himself in any way to give up and continued to command the unclean spirit to depart from God's creature. Thus driven to extremities, the devil cried out: " If thou wouldst that I come forth from hence, permit that I may enter into that monk in the corner over there," and he named him by his name. But Norbert said to the people: " Hear what he says and observe his wickedness: to outrage the servant of God this demon demands to possess him as a sinner worthy of this torment. But do not be indignant. It is just his cunning to vex the good and seek to outrage them as best he may." Thereupon he flung himself with the more earnestness upon the wicked enemy, who asked: " What wouldst thou then ? For thee nor for any other will I come

---

[1] *Ibid.*, pp. 68-69.
[2] *The Little Flowers of St. Francis of Assisi*, trans. by T. W. Arnold, London, 1899, pp. 234-35.

forth to-day. Behold! If only I call, the dark legions come to my aid. Eia, up, to the fight! These arches and vaults are about to fall upon you!" At these words the people took to flight, but the priest remained bravely and fearlessly in his place. Then the hand of the possessed seized his stole to strangle him with it. As those standing by rushed to frustrate her, he said: "Leave her! If God has given her strength she may do according to her will." At these words, all astonished, she of her own will withdrew her hands. Nevertheless the greater part of the day being spent, it was Norbert's counsel that she should be plunged into exorcised water and this was done. As she was fair-haired, the priest feared that this might permit her devil to retain his hold over her, and therefore had her hair cut. Thereupon the demon flew into a rage and cried out: "Stranger from France, stranger from France, what have I done to thee that thou shouldst not leave me in peace? All evil and misfortune be on thy head for tormenting me thus!"

Meanwhile night had fallen and when Norbert saw that the demon had not yet departed he commanded somewhat sadly that she should be led back to her father. On the following morning she was again brought to the mass. When he took off his alb and other vestments, the demon seeing this clapped his hands and cried out: "Ah, ah, ah! Now thou doest well! All day thou hast done nothing that has so pleased me. The day has passed undisturbed, and thou hast accomplished nothing." Dissatisfied, Norbert returned to his house and resolved to take no food until the sick woman should be cured. In fact, he passed the rest of the day and the night in fasting. As soon as day dawned he prepared to say mass. The girl was once more brought and the people hastened up to witness the combat between the priest and the demon. Forthwith Norbert ordered two brethren to hold the possessed fast not far from the altar; and when he came to the Gospel she was led to the altar itself and several passages from the Gospels were read over her head. The demon again roared with laughter at this and when the priest afterwards elevated the Host he cried out: "See how he holds his little god in his hands!" This made the priest of God shudder, and strong in the might of the Spirit he applied himself to attack the demon by prayer and torment him. Then the latter, full of anguish, cried out by the mouth of the girl: "I burn! I burn!" Again the voice howled: "I am dying! I am dying!" For the third time it uttered loud cries and repeated many times over: "I will go forth! I will go forth! Let me go!" The two brethren held her strongly, but the evil spirit would not let himself be bridled. Leaving behind him a trail of unspeakably stinking urine he escaped, abandoning the vessel which he possessed. She collapsed, was taken back to her father's house, took food and was soon entirely restored to health.[1]

Just as the saints cured the possessed during their lifetime, these powers were continued after death. Amongst the *Miracula* of the Emperor Henry the Saint (d. 1024) are found cures of possessed persons attributed to his body:

Three demoniacs, a man and two women . . . were cured, who did not cease to blaspheme the name of Henry, and at length

---

[1] Görres, *Die christliche Mystik*, Regensburg, 1842, vol. iv, part i, p. 332, from the *Acta Sanctorum*, June 6, c. viii, p. 834.

with horrible cries left the seats which they occupied. One of them, more obstinate than the others, long resisted the invocation of the holy name, when he knew that the remains were to be brought near him. Then as if Henry was coming in person, he said that he could not remain. Immediately with a great clamour he left the man whom he possessed. These things happened after mass on the very day when the remains arrived.[1]

. . . The demoniac woman had her hands tied with cords to the place previously indicated and was prevented from moving although she offered much resistance. The demon roared and writhed, shouting, away from Henry; then she was suddenly released from her torment. It seemed to her, as she related to those present, that she saw coming out of that place a white-haired personage with a long beard dressed in royal garments who by threats and blows drove away the evil spirit.[2]

Finally one more example from the thirteenth century. It is taken from the life of the Spanish saint Petrus Gonzalez (1190–1246).

Pedro Perez de Villela . . . had a son obsessed by a demon who for eleven consecutive days neither ate, drank nor slept. Adjured by exorcisms, the demon replied that no one would cause him to depart except Brother Pedro Gonzalez. The adolescent was led to the sepulchre of the holy Father with bound hands (rage would otherwise have prevented it). Prayers having been said by those who stood round him, the demon there and then withdrew. Maria Gonzalez of Valladerez was exceedingly tormented by a demon. For four days she remained without eating, drinking or speaking. When she was carried to the tomb of the saint the demon was expelled and she was restored to complete health. The daughter of Juan Palaez of Tobellum was possessed for two years by a demon and tortured almost every day. Having made a vow to the man of God she was at once delivered. The wife of Pedro Juan of Paramos was demoniac for two years and was cruelly tormented two, three, or even as many as five times a day. The family having made a vow to St. Pedro, the demon immediately left her.[3]

The following case belongs to the fifteenth century. It relates of St. François de Paule (1416–1508):

Antonius Mirenus says that when he arrived a woman of Anzitola was tormented by the evil spirit. She was surrounded, as is customary, by a crowd of men. Then the demoniac began to say: "Here is my enemy." The witness and many others turned and saw coming Brother Francis who entered the sacristy without paying any heed. And the following day when the demoniac was in the church certain of the brethren of St. Francis took upon themselves to conjure the evil spirit, who replied: "I care for none of you, save for St. Francis." In the last resort she was led into the sacristy where St. Francis was with certain noblemen, namely this same witness and others. He began to adjure

[1] *Miracula S. Henrici Imperatoris* (suppl. to the Life), *Acta Sanctorum*, July 3, vol. iii, p. 767.
[2] *Ibid.*, pp. 768 sq.   [3] *Acta Sanctorum*, Aprilis, vol. ii, p. 399.

the spirit and command him to leave the body of the poor creature, which spirit answered St. Francis with many words, and was obstinate. He said that he was the spirit of a woman who had died in the time of the wars of Duke Jean, that is to say twenty years before, and that in the beginning she had been a procuress and woman of evil life. Francis replied: " Why did you not confess ? You would not now be damned." At length after numerous discussions this same witness saw the woman go out to the sacristy delivered. She then returned home.[1]

These examples from the Christian Middle Ages will suffice. They should be taken in conjunction with the cases already mentioned on p. 8. It is evident that they are completely similar from whatever century they may come, and one might readily be substituted for another. The darker side of mediæval religious life bears the impress of the stability which characterized that period.

This is not merely true of Christian civilization; the mediæval *Kabbala* is also acquainted with possession. Bischoff speaks as follows in his *Einführung in die judische Mystik*:[2]

> Very interesting is the exorcism, according to Lurja,[3] of a spirit by which a woman was possessed. The spirit was the soul of a drunken Jew, who died without prayer and impenitent. Having wandered for a long time it was permitted to him to enter into a woman as she was in the act of blaspheming, and since that moment the woman (an epileptic-hysteric) suffered terribly. Lurja speaks to the tormenting spirit and treats him as Christian exorcists treat the devil; he reprimands him, makes him tell his story, etc. By means of the " Name " he at length obliges him to come forth by the little toe of the possessed, which the spirit thus handled does with his habitual vehemence.[4]

I have gathered much less information about non-European countries than about the European Middle Ages. This results not only from my slight personal knowledge of their literature but also from the comparative inaccessibility of the non-European literature of that period, as well as its lesser total extent. A story from Syria (ninth century) relates:

> A certain man was walking in the street at night past one of the fire-temples of the magi, which had some time previously fallen into ruins, when devils in the form of black ravens leapt upon him, entered into him, and brought on convulsions.[5]

---

[1] *Acta Sanctorum*, Aprilis, vol. i, p. 144.

[2] Erich Bischoff, *Die Kabbalah, Einfuhrung in die jüdische Mystik und Geheimwissenschaft*, Leipzig, 1903, pp. 87 sq.

[3] The main representative of the ethical-ascetic tendency of the Kabbala (1534-72).

[4] *Loc. cit.*, pp. 87 sq.

[5] E. A. Wallis Budge, *Thomas of Marga*, vol. ii, quoted by R. Campbell Thompson: *The Devils and Evil Spirits of Babylonia*, London, 1903, vol. i, p. 41 (Luzac's Semitic Text and Translation Series, vol. xiv).

On possession in Northern Africa, Leo Africanus, who towards 1492 visited the towns of that country, largely Mohammedan, writes as follows:

> There are in that country soothsayers of a kind called exorcists. It is believed that they have in the highest degree the power of curing the possessed, because now and then they succeed in doing so. If they do not succeed, however, they get out of the difficulty by saying that the spirit is unbelieving (disobedient) or that it is one of the heavenly spirits. . . . They describe certain characters and circles on the hand or on the forehead of the possessed and perfume him with many odours. Then they conjure the spirit and ask him how and through what part of the body he came, who he is, and what is his name, after which they command him to come forth.[1]

It is very noteworthy that in the Christian Middle Ages the spirit which speaks by the mouth of a possessed person should always be a demon, a devil. In modern times this is not so; possession still remains fairly frequent, but more and more it is the spirits of the dead who speak in the possessed. This clearly testifies to a certain weakening in demonological beliefs; men still believe in the existence of the devil—who in the interval has shrunk from a plurality of demons to a single one—but general opinion no longer takes sufficient account of him to allow him to play an appreciable part in the empirical life. It is only in spiritual establishments, especially convents of nuns—as well as in the epidemics of which we shall speak shortly—that the spirits which speak by the mouth of the possessed are still in the majority of cases demons.

The earliest works on the diffusion of possession date only from the time of the Renaissance.

Luther's influence does not seem to have been at all helpful; according to Kirchoff[2] his inflexible ideas long rendered difficult the right knowledge and treatment of maladies of the mind. He regarded all mental affections as possession,[3] and suicide as one of their consequences. In these circumstances he cannot, of course, have rejected the interpretation of true states of possession as such;[4] he rather personally undertook

[1] Leo Africanus, *Delle Navigazioni*, Raccolte de Ramuzio, vol. i, Venice, 1613, quoted by B. Heyne, *Ueber Besessenheitswahn*, p. 80.
[2] Kirchoff, *Beziehungen des Damonen- und Hexenwesens zur deutschen Irrenpflege*, " Allgemeine Zeitschrift für Psychiatrie," vol. xliv, pp. 329 sq.
[3] Grisar, *Luther*, Freiburg, 1912, vol. ii, pp. 235 sq.
[4] *Luthers Tischreden*. Erlanger edition of the works of Luther vol. lix, p. 289 and vol. lx, pp. 1-60, 75-80, 80-176, 285.

exorcisms of the possessed (1545). Here, as elsewhere, his position is opposed to that of the detested Catholic Church, and even runs counter to the doctrine of the apostles. Ecclesiastical exorcism appears to him a "display" of which the devil is unworthy. He himself does not set to work with exorcism, but with "prayer and contempt." Formerly, when exorcisms were first introduced, wonders were necessary to confirm the Christian doctrine; to-day this is no longer so. God himself knows when the devil is to depart, and man should not tempt God with these commands, but rather pray without ceasing until the prayer is heard.[1]

Amongst modern accounts, the epidemics of possession are of particular interest. Hitherto we have only dealt with isolated cases, but possession is not always manifested in this manner. Just as other psychic epidemics have occurred such as St. Vitus' dance (choreomania) and the Children's Crusade, possession has also manifested itself in epidemic form, without, however, assuming the same dimensions; in no case has it attacked more than some few dozen persons. Almost all epidemics have, moreover, broken out in convents of nuns or similar establishments where by reason of the close and perpetual contact the danger of psychic infection is particularly great. The ground was everywhere prepared by the fear of the possessing spirit passing from the possessed into the soul and body of the onlookers, and an idea of the risk run by these latter may be gathered from the fact that few exorcising priests remained entirely immune.

The available information on epidemics of possession which have occurred since the Renaissance in civilized Europe is collected in the work of L. F. Calmeil,[2] where early sources have been thoroughly utilized and quoted at length, and which is still authoritative on the subject. The work of K. W. Ideler,[3] Leubuscher,[4] and P. Richer[5] is in turn based on Calmeil's researches. It contains, partly in abridged form,

---

[1] Grisar, *Luther*, vol. iii, pp. 629 sq.
[2] L. F. Calmeil, *De la folie considérée sous le point de vue pathologique, philosophique et judiciaire*, 2. vols., Paris, 1845.
[3] K. W. Ideler, *Versuch einer Theorie der religiösen Wahnsinns*, Halle, 1848, vol. i, chap. viii.
[4] R. Leubuscher, *Der Wahnsinn in den vier letzten Jahrhunderten*, Halle, 1848, pp. 80 sq.
[5] P. Richer, *Études cliniques sur la grande hystérie*, Paris, 1885, Supplément.

good accounts of several of these epidemics, and as the documents are easily accessible I have for my own part decided to give no descriptions.

So far as I am aware there are as yet no corresponding researches dealing with the Middle Ages, owing no doubt to the fact that the materials, where they exist, must lie buried in manuscript form in the archives. Perhaps, moreover, documents are generally more plentiful in the subsequent centuries, thanks to the growth of interest in psychology since the Renaissance of Learning and the continuous influence of printing in facilitating and stimulating research. But naturally it may also be that veritable epidemics were lacking and only occurred after belief in the devil had reached its height in Europe—that is to say, in the time of the witch-craft trials extending from the thirteenth to the eighteenth century.

All the epidemics referred to in the following pages are taken from Calmeil except those for which I have indicated other sources. Those mentioned by him relate almost entirely to convents of nuns and detailed accounts are available in some instances. They took place at the following periods:

1491-1494, in a convent of nuns at Cambrai (county of la Marche, near Hammone).

1551, at Uvertet (Grafschaft of Hoorn).

1550-1556, in the cloister of Sainte Brigitte, near Xanten.

1552, at Kintorp, near Strassburg. The epidemic spread like a patch of oil, and seized several inhabitants of the town of Hammone.

1554, at Rome; an epidemic which affected eighty-four persons, amongst whom were twenty-four baptized Jewesses.[1]

1555, at Rome; eighty little girls in an orphanage.

1560-1564, at the Nazareth convent in Cologne.[2]

1566, at the Foundling Hospital in Amsterdam: thirty children (seventy according to another version) were attacked, the majority being boys.

1590, thirty nuns were possessed near Milan.

1598, a small epidemic at Friedeberg, in Neumark.[3]

---

[1] Esquirol, *Pathologie générale et spéciale et thérapeutique des maladies de l'esprit.*

[2] R. Leubuscher, *loc. cit.*, pp. 80 sq.

[3] A. Bastian, *Der Mensch in der Geschichte*, vol. ii, Leipzig, 1860, p. 565.

1594, eighty cases of possession at Friedeberg, Spandau and other places in the Mark of Brandenburg.

1609-1611, at Aix, in the convent of Ursulines.

1613, at Lille, in the convent of Sainte Brigitte. The possession of Aix had been heard of there, and several nuns had on the occasion of a visit, seen cases in that town, by reason of which one of them already began to feel herself possessed.

1628, at Madrid in a convent of nuns.

1632-1638, in the convent of the Little Ursulines at Loudun, whence the epidemic spread to several women of the town and also to Chinon, Nîmes and Avignon. In the last-named town Cardinal Mazarin cleverly arrested the progress of the epidemic by giving orders as soon as the first case occurred that no publicity should be given to the possessed persons.

1642, in a convent at Louviers (eighteen sisters).

1652-1662, in a convent at Auxonne.[1]

1670, at and around Mora (Sweden) amongst children.

1670, at Hoorn (Holland) in an orphanage, amongst children of both sexes under twelve years old.

1681, around Toulouse; this budding epidemic came to nothing owing to skilful measures taken by the authorities.

1687-1690, around Lyon (fifty sisters).

1732, in the district of Landes near Bayeux.

1740-1750 (it lasted ten years), in a convent at Unterzell, in Lower Franconia: only ten nuns indubitably attacked.[2]

In the nineteenth century several epidemics of possession are also known:

1857-1862, at Morzines, a little village in a region of Haute-Savoie remote from civilization: at least 120 people were attacked.

1878, at Verzegnis, in Friuli.

1881, at Plédran, in the neighbourhood of St. Brieuc.

1881, at Jaca, in Spain.[3]

The most famous of all these epidemics was that of Loudun. The documents concerning it are exceedingly abundant, the

[1] Horst, *Zauberbibliothek*, i, pp. 212 sq.; (A. Stoll, *Suggestion*, etc., 2nd edit., p. 425).

[2] *Ibid.*, iii, p. 165, v, p. 203, etc.

[3] For further details taken from the original documents, cf. Richer, *loc. cit.*, pp. 851-865.

most important being the *Histoire des Diables de Loudun,* already mentioned more than once.[1]

I have earlier called attention to the analogy between the general run of cases of possession, at least when isolated, and attacks of hysteria. Can this observation, about which doubt is no longer possible, be acceptably generalized ? Have all the possessed, even those affected in consequence of epidemics, been hysterical ? Naturally an affirmative reply has often been given, but we must approach the subject with scepticism; there is very little evidence to substantiate such a statement. At all events, the patients were not in all cases hysterical before in the same way as they appear to have been after the onset of possession. This state certainly gives most people occasion to regard it as hysteria, but such a diagnosis would only be justified if previous hysterical symptoms had existed; the mere fact that a person is attacked by a spiritual epidemic does not show that he is mentally unsound. It should rather be recognized as evident that psychically normal subjects may, when placed in a sufficiently favourable environment, succumb to psychic infection. The excitement and tension produced by the continual sight of the possessed and the fear of being oneself seized by the devil may produce an autosuggestive state such that similar psychic experiences begin to be manifested. No detailed researches into the genesis of such a state of autosuggestion yet exist, the conditions and chances of exact observation being as unfavourable as well may be, but its reality cannot be doubted. This acute suggestibility due to abnormal conditions is therefore the soil on which possession springs up, for it would be difficult to maintain that the possessed become hysterical at the moment when they are psychically contaminated and remain so until exorcism has been successfully accomplished, a theory which we should only be driven to adopt if it could be demonstrated that those who were attacked by the epidemic really presented all the symptoms of hysteria and were not simply and solely victims of certain epidemic phenomena of imitation.

[1] Cf. above, pp. 14, 51, etc. For a more complete study of the futile nature of magic and the iniquitous witchcraft-trials, cf. the *Acta Magica,* published by Johann Reichen, Halle, 1704. Finally, we should add the already oft-quoted autobiography of the heroine and originator of this epidemic: *Sœur Jeanne des Anges, Supérieure des Ursulines de Loudun,* Paris, 1887.

It is evident that this subject bristles with problems of mass-psychology which have not yet been subjected to really adequate study.

According to Esquirol, the famous French psychiatrist of the early nineteenth century, possession was often the subject of legal proceedings at the time of the Reformation. The devil was summoned " before a court of law, and the possessed were condemned to be burnt upon a pile. Doubly victims of the prevailing error, demonomaniacs were burned both as bewitched and as possessed, after a confession had been wrung from them that they had made a pact with the devil."[1]

This quotation is surprising. In the history of witch-craft, so far as I have studied it, I have met with no case of possession. Can it be that the explanation lies in a mere confusion between witches and possessed persons, permissible in the lay writer, but which we should not be asked to tolerate in a scholar such as Esquirol? His remarks on witchcraft trials and the battle waged against them transform this presumption into certainty. Moreover the cases of " demonomania " which he has reported are not all cases of possession in our sense of the world, but often mere hallucination and delusion. The only connection between witchcraft and possession lies in the fact that persons believing themselves bewitched often seem forthwith to have presented symptoms analogous to those of possession.

The not infrequent cases of zooanthropy found in the early Middle Ages show no slight resemblance to possession. The persons affected believed themselves to be wild animals, generally wolves (werewolves, lycanthropy), and behaved as such. They took refuge in the forests, let their hair and nails grow long, sometimes fell upon children whom they rent and devoured, in short behaved like savage beasts. There was also transformation into dogs (cynanthropy). But zoo-anthropy differed from true possession in that it produced, so far as we know, permanent states, whereas possession was never manifested except in fits.

It is true that we occasionally meet transitory zooanthropic states in epidemics of possession. Thus a writer, Dom Calmet,

[1] Esquirol, *Des maladies mentales considérées sous le rapport médical, hygiénique et médico-légal*, Paris, 1838.

relates of an epidemic which had attacked a German convent that the nuns believed themselves changed into cats, and at a certain time of day mewed and behaved as such.[1]

Another case is found in Luys:

> It had sufficed for a hysterical girl to pass a few days in the country for her to imitate in her fits the bark of big watchdogs and smaller dogs which she had seen there. When she was seized with a fit there was a curious succession of all sorts of barkings, which she uttered involuntarily.[2]

In Germany the influence, so noxious to civilization, of belief in the devil, owes its defeat principally to Christian Tomasius, who waged especial war against belief in witchcraft.

Belief in possession found its chief critic in Johann Salomon Semler,[3] the founder of the new Protestant theology.

Semler, who was the first seriously to tackle a survey of the Bible from the historical point of view, sees in the statements of the New Testament author relating to Jesus and the possessed no doctrine of healing, but ideas which, like many others, form part of the stock-in-trade of the time. He also finds a metaphysical difficulty: the alleged substantial indwelling of the devil appears to him impossible.

As early as 1767 Semler gauged the temper of his time to be such that a complete exposition of the history of possession would go far towards the general abolition of this belief, in so far as it still existed:

> If I desired to collect the thousands and thousands of stories of possessed persons and their cure, it would be a vast labour and would constitute a history of the devil in the Middle Ages. It would be of relatively large proportions, but would infallibly produce a happy, profound and lasting impression on all readers, inasmuch as they themselves, however simple-minded and credulous, would judge that it must be far from the truth. The frightful superstition which still brings forth many dark fruits would be very rapidly and generally weakened thereby.[4]

---

[1] Esquirol, *ibid.*; cf. also Calmeil, *loc. cit.*

[2] Luys, *Études de physiologie et de pathologie cérébrales*, Paris, 1874, p. 75. Taken from Briquet, *Traité clinique et thérapeutique de l'hystérie*, Paris, 1859, p. 322.

[3] J. S. Semler, *Commentatio de dæmoniacis quorum in Novo Testamento fit mentio*, 4th edit., Halæ, 1779. By the same author: *Umstandliche Untersuchung der dämonischen Leute oder sogenannte Besessenen nebst Beantwortung einiger Angriffe*, Halle, 1762.

[4] J. S. Semler, *Versuch einiger moralischer Betrachtungen über die vielen Wunderkuren und Mirakel in den älteren Zeiten zur Beförderung des immer besseren Gebrauchs der Kirchenhistorie*, Halle, 1762, p. 25.

Nicolai participated in the struggle against belief in possession by his *Allgemeine Deutsche Bibliothek,* which published many accounts of research on the subject of the possessed and the miracles of the New Testament.

These two were naturally not alone, but found many coadjutors.

The sceptical attitude of the enlightened and its social repercussion seem to have resulted in a marked falling-off in cases, readily explained by the auto-suggestive character of these states.

The conquests of enlightenment were not lost again. Schleiermacher, who was also profoundly hostile to demonology, considers possession as a sickness. Like Semler he takes liberties with any texts of the Gospels not in accordance with this theory, explaining that Christ would not in a general way have established the doctrine of the devil, but had merely made use of prevailing ideas to exorcise demons, " for he was always immediately intelligible and restricted himself to the use of ideas of the accepted type." Demonology, by admitting the existence of a great power of evil, must either imply a limitation of the divine omnipotence or else make Satan and evil a deliberate work of God, which is irreconcilable with the divine essence.[1]

The theologian Paulus, generally known as the adversary of Schelling, conceived at least Jesus' apostrophe to the demons at the moment of expulsion as a concession to the morbid ideas of the possessed themselves, a concession to which the doctor should lend himself for psycho-therapeutic reasons; but in other cases Paulus could not avoid the conviction that Jesus Himself had shared these ideas.[2] In Strauss we meet a completely critical impartiality and the abandonment of all striving after novelty of interpretation. He naturally rejects the theory of possession, and apart from his general scruples about admitting the existence of devils and demons, sees a further difficulty in the psycho-physical relation of the soul and body. However it may be con-

---

[1] Schleiermacher, *Das Leben Jesu,* complete works, vol. vi., Berlin, 1864, pp. 342 sq. Also in: *Der Christliche Glaube nach den Grundsätzen der evangelischen Kirche im Zusammenhang dargestellt,* §§ 44 and 55, *ibid.,* vol. iii, Berlin, 1835, pp. 209-222.

[2] Statement by Strauss in: *Das Leben Jesu,* 3rd edit., vol. ii, Tübingen, 1839, pp. 12 sq.

ceived, " no one could ever imagine how the bond which unites them can be loose enough for a strange consciousness to push its way in, and, dislodging that which belongs to the organism, take possession of the latter."[1]   On the other hand, of course, the orthodox opinion continued to prevail amongst other theologians.

Strauss already and very rightly recognizes the curative virtue of exorcism as autosuggestive, except that the word autosuggestion is naturally not found in his works:

> As the cause of such maladies was often really psychic or resident in the nervous system which may be wrought upon to an incalculable degree by the spiritual side, this psychological proceeding was not completely fraudulent, but thanks to the conviction induced in the patient that the demon possessing her would be unable for long to hold out against a magic formula, release from the malady was really effected.[2]

In another place Strauss further admits a certain telepathic action in Jesus' will:

> If the sick person conceived Jesus as the Messiah, and if his conception was acquired not merely according to rationalistic theory by communication from without, but by a personal magnetic sympathy, the words and will of Jesus to put the demons to flight also passed into him with immediate force and efficacy.[3]

Thanks to Semler, Schleiermacher and David Friedrich Strauss, belief in possession has in the Protestant world received its death-blow even if it is not completely dead.

Thus the general reaction of the romantics against the Age of Enlightenment was partially effective as regards belief in possession. In other words, Swabian romanticism of the school of Schelling reverted to belief in spirits, a reaction evidenced by the writings of Kerner and Eschenmayer which we have so often utilized (see above, pp. 9, 13, etc.). Its principal representative in the camp of the Catholic Church is Görres. But these authors cannot have exercised a very profound influence on the scientific views of the period: the latter maintained the conviction that possession is an abnormal psychic state and not the visitation of an individual by spirits of any description. Truth to tell, this conviction did not succeed in gaining a decisive victory; it rather seems that the number of cases of possession rose again in regions where they were once more taken seriously by persons in

---

[1] *Ibid.*, pp. 20 sq.   [2] *Ibid.*, vol. ii, pp. 26 sq.   [3] *Ibid.*, p. 31.

authority, showing particular increase in the very remote province of Swabia which inclines to a transcendental faith. I refer the reader to the publication issued by Kerner in the years 1831-38: *Blätter aus Prevorst.*

From Bavaria comes Baader's case.[1]

J. von Görres in his *Mystik* reports a case dating from 1830 in the diocese of Lüttich.[2]

In the forties of the nineteenth century occurs the case of possession described by Pastor Blumhardt. This also comes from Würtemberg.[3]

In France the eminent psychiatrist Esquirol (1772-1840) himself saw possessed persons and professes often to have observed a strong smell which they exhaled.[4]

Other examples of true possession in France are given in the biography of a modern Catholic saint who died in 1859, the curé of Ars, Jean-Baptiste-Marie Vianney. In his biography published by Alfred Monnin, we read:

> At different times and from various quarters there came to Ars persons who, in a more or less evident fashion, were possessed. Two of these unfortunates, a man and woman, are known to every-one in Ars; they often came and almost always found at the feet of Vianney relief and consolation in one of the most extraordinary and frightful of states.[5]

Colloquies between the curé and the possessing spirits are reproduced in detail.

The Westminster Review reported in 1860 the case of a nun in Paris who was possessed and had to be exorcised.[6]

That possession is a perfectly well-known phenomenon in England appears from the observations of Giraldus Cambrensis who saw analogous states in Wales.

> . . . A race of prophets who, when consulted, were agitated and tortured like men possessed. Their first answers were in-coherent, but the true revelations generally came to them in dreams in which, they said, they had received in their mouths milk and honey.[7]

---

[1] Cf. above, p. 14, 20 sq.

[2] J. von Görres, *Die christliche Mystik*, vol. iv, Regensburg, 1842, p. 287 sq.

[3] Cf. above, p. 15.

[4] According to Bastian, *Der Mensch in der Geschichte*, vol. ii, Leipzig, 1860, p. 561.

[5] A. Monnin, *Vie du Curé d'Ars J. B. M. Vianney*, Paris, vol. ii, chap. iii.

[6] According to A. Bastian, *loc. cit.*, vol. ii, p. 370.

[7] Quoted by A. Bastian, *Die Völker des östlichen Asiens*, vol. iii, p. 295.

Let us add to this a quotation taken by Bastian from another English author:

> The voice was often heard (1840). On one occasion it told them that Mary's (Jobson of Sunderland) own spirit had left her body and a new one had taken possession, making her frame a mere instrument or as it were a speaking-trumpet.[1]

The poet Walter Scott has written a little-known historical survey of demonology in England, under the title, *Letters on Demonology and Witchcraft*,[2] but it really deals throughout with magic and scarcely touches on possession.

An ecclesiastic on the Volga published in 1838 in the *Blätter aus Prevorst* an account of cases of possession in the interior of Slavonic Russia.

> Amongst the Russians, and especially the peasantry, there are astonishing psychological manifestations which may with good reason be called demoniac. . . . The upshot of conversations which I have had with an enlightened German who, knowing Russian perfectly, carries on a great trade with the Russians is as follows:
> These demoniacs fall with or without warning into a fit, have violent convulsions and generally break out into blasphemy. They cannot go into the churches without falling into this unhappy state immediately after the reading of the Gospel, and each divine word, each spiritual exhortation, every prayer throws them into a furious rage which is expressed by outrages and maledictions on God and Christ. When the fit has passed they are conscious of their deadly sin, are afflicted thereby and willingly castigate themselves. These unfortunate people number quite fifty, both of the male and female sex. They have a sickly look. The Russians call them the "tainted" (*Verdorbene*). At the consecration of a new Russian Church, when the bell is rung outside amongst the crowd to announce that the Gospel is being read, more than fifty men and women, old and young, will drop down and fall into this terrible state. . . .
> A father whose daughter, aged thirteen years, had fallen into this state spoke thus to the evil spirit during the fit: "What evil has my daughter done that you should seize her thus? She is a young and tender child." As if an evil demon made use of her mouth she replied: "Yes, but the young creature pleases me and I will not let her go."[3]

An author quoted by Bastian in 1875 relates the following of Greece:

> A very common complaint amongst these people (of Ithaca in the Ionian Isles) is hysterics, which appear in an infinite variety of shapes, often producing such extravagant gestures as to make

---

[1] *Ibid.*, p. 301, from the account of Dr. Reid Clanny.
[2] Sir Walter Scott, *Letters on Demonology and Witchcraft*, Murray's Family Library, 1830.
[3] *Blätter aus Prevorst*, ed. by Justinus Kerner, coll. 20, Stuttgart, 1838, pp. 173 sq.

the ignorant believe the patient possessed of the devil. In these cases the priest is called to frighten the demons and to send them to their lurking-places.[1]

From the American continent information concerning possession has only reached me in extremely slight quantity. For the time being it is only possible to wonder whether this is mere chance or whether possession in its usual forms has really been rare in America. The substantial mass of documents on states analogous to possession in that country does not lead us to suppose that conditions have become so unfavourable to the genesis of true possession. The strongly positive trend of American Christianity must also be considered, and I should be inclined for this reason to think that possession was not rare in the early days of the settlers, and that if the sources of North American social history were carefully explored they would afford divers proofs of this. Such research would, however, only be fruitful if carried out on the spot, for early American literature is well known to be only very sporadically represented in the libraries of Europe. This is particularly true of anything bearing on the religious life, and Eduard Meyer, for example, could not have written in Europe his *History of the Mormons*.[2] For the moment there is therefore a lacuna here.

A piece of evidence concerning early America which is not without interest is found in Scott's above-mentioned *Letters on Demonology and Witchcraft*; it enables us to obtain a glimpse of a prevailing mental constitution favourable to possession.

The first case which I observe, was that of four children of a person called John Goodwin, a mason. The eldest, a girl, had quarrelled with the laundress of the family about some linen which was missing. The mother of the laundress, an ignorant, testy, and choleric old Irishwoman, scolded the accuser; and shortly after, the elder Goodwin, her sister, and two brothers were seized with such strange diseases, that all their neighbours concluded they were bewitched. They conducted themselves as those supposed to suffer under maladies created by such influence were accustomed to do. They stiffened their necks so hard at one time that the joints could not be moved, at another time their necks were so flexible and supple, that it seemed the bone was dissolved. They had violent convulsions, in which their jaws snapped with the force of a spring-trap set for vermin.

---

[1] Quoted by A. Bastian, *Die deutsche Expedition an der Loanga Küste*, vol. ii, Jena, 1875, p. 204 note.
[2] Ed. Meyer, *Ursprung und Geschichte der Mormonen*, Halle, 1912.

Their limbs were curiously contorted, and to those who had a taste for the marvellous, seemed entirely dislocated and displaced. Amid these distortions, they cried out against the poor old woman, whose name was Glover, alleging that she was in presence with them, adding to their torments. The miserable Irishwoman, who hardly could speak the English language, repeated her Pater Noster and Ave Maria like a good Catholic; but there were some words which she had forgotten. She was therefore supposed to be unable to pronounce the whole consistently and correctly—and condemned and executed accordingly.

But the children of Goodwin found the trade they were engaged in to be too profitable to be laid aside, and the eldest, in particular, continued all the external signs of witchcraft and possession. Some of these were excellently calculated to flatter the self-opinion and prejudices of the Calvinist ministers, by whom she was attended, and accordingly bear in their very front the character of studied and voluntary imposture. The young woman, acting, as was supposed, under the influence of the Devil, read a Quaker treatise with ease and apparent satisfaction; but a book written against the poor inoffensive Friends, the Devil would not allow his victim to touch. She could look on a Church of England Prayer-Book and read the portions of Scripture which it contains, without difficulty or impediment; but the spirit which possessed her threw her into fits if she attempted to read the same Scriptures from the Bible, as if the awe which it is supposed the fiends entertain for Holy Writ, depended, not on the meaning of the words, but the arrangement of the page, and the type in which they were printed. This singular species of flattery was designed to captivate the clergyman through his professional opinions.[1]

It is clear that this story corresponds completely to European stories of possession. Whether Scott has any reason to recognize wilful fraud is the more difficult to discover as he does not give the source of this episode. But even if such were the case, there would obviously not be spontaneous invention on the part of the girl, but imitation of the phenomena of possession, well known even at that time, as the story shows, in America. Another story related by Scott[2] demonstrates that similar phenomena also appeared there in epidemic form.

Yet one more note on an American case in the nineteenth century. It is taken from Bastian:

Dr. Gray (a homœopathic doctor in New York) relates in the New York Journal (1852) that a spirit which tormented a blacksmith had told him " that until three weeks previously it had lived in the body of a naughty boy, and that while awaiting its return to hell it desired to amuse itself with this young man." But it promised not to molest him further and he thenceforward refused any further conversation.[3]

---

[1] W. Scott, loc. cit., pp. 421 sq.   [2] Ibid., pp. 422 sq.
[3] A. Bastian, Der Mensch in der Geschichte, vol. ii, pp. 558 sq.

These are the only cases of typical possession which I have as yet encountered in American literature. It is the more probable that their real number is not negligible, since modern American spiritualist literature contains extremely numerous accounts of similar states.

(ii.) IN THE PRESENT

Let us now deal with the more recent past.[1]

In the modern civilization of Central Europe there are three spheres in which belief in spirits still survives, as founded on possession.

The first is the strict Catholicism which takes its stand chiefly upon the past but also admits modern cases. " Why," asks Taczak, " must the Catholic firmly believe that possession is still possible to-day ?" And he replies: " Because the New Testament accounts of the words and acts of Jesus and His disciples establish as an indubitable fact that possession has existed in a numerous succession of cases and because that is the Church's conviction."[2]

Current Catholic views on possession have recently been the subject of a systematic general review in a large volume by Johann Smit: *De dæmoniacis in historia evangelica.*[3]

At bottom the demonological theory of primitive Christian times is immutably perpetuated by the Catholic Church. The change is only in the effective influence exercised by this conception, which has diminished. Affections which would formerly have been considered as demoniacal are now regarded as " natural," and there is a general weakening in the conviction that there exist demons and spirits of the dead who may be a source of danger to the living. Writings on practical theology show a unanimous tendency to warn the reader that possession should not be too readily admitted.

A case of possession is always a matter for the higher ecclesiastical authorities; it is, in a word, an event which has become very rare.

" When a state of possession declares itself as probable," says a modern Catholic pastoral theology, " the whole case should be

---

[1] Naturally all conclusions refer to the pre-war period.
[2] Th. Taczak, *Dämonische Besessenheit*, Dissertation, Münster, 1903, pp. 10 sq.
[3] Joh. Smit, *Disertatio exegetico-apologetica*, Romæ, 1913 (in Scripta Pontificii Instituti Biblici).

reported to the bishop and it should be left to his judgment whether the grand exorcism should be applied. Every priest has the right to use the simple exorcisms ordained in baptism and the other ecclesiastical benedictions without authorization by his superiors. But for major exorcism when it is to be accomplished publicly and solemnly, as well as for *Exorcismus in satanam et angelos apostaticos*, recommended by Pope Leo XIII (d.d. 18 Maii, 1890) episcopal authorization is always indispensable."[1]

" It is not," says Krieg, "unbelieving doctors who put us on our guard against credulity, but grave and pious men. And in recommending extreme prudence they do no more than repeat what theologians and eminent Churchmen like Bona have said. The prescriptions of the Church recommend it no less."[2]

And the Austrian Schubert expresses himself similarly:

> It cannot be contested that possession was often admitted when the state in question had an entirely natural cause.[3]

The best general survey from the modern Catholic point of view in all its aspects is found in the widely used *Handbuch der Pastoralmedizin* of Stöhr, in which we read:

> The possibility of maladies caused by demoniacal influences must be accepted by every Catholic believer as a fact beyond doubt. At the time of Christ it was a revealed truth: later the greatest doctors of the Church and her legitimate organs unanimously declared that this conception must be considered as an article of faith. So far as the present is concerned I believe, without being a professional dogmatist, that from the point of view of Catholic orthodoxy no one can advocate the contrary view. There are also demoniacal maladies radically different in their etiology from the pathological manifestations due to natural influences, and these human maladies are due, under God's will, to supernatural forces and the might of evil spirits. If we add yet a second thesis to this definition, namely, that the remedies of the Catholic church, sacraments and particularly exorcism, should be regarded as the most fruitful and the best authorized (although not infallible). we shall have exhausted in this difficult question the strict truths of the established faith, that is to say, what are for us the indubitable facts. As for the solution of many enigmas which the subject still presents, those curious for knowledge will have to seek it in the vast field of conjecture. Are demoniacal maladies frequent in our own time ? In the first centuries when the etiological knowledge of doctors was even slighter, if possible, than their therapeutic science, whole categories of slightly obscure maladies of a strange and at that time surprising character were summarily attributed to the influence of a supersensual power.[4]

These lines give an excellent *résumé* of the whole modern Catholic doctrine. No essential point is lacking. The reality

[1] J. E. Pruner, *Lehrbuch der Pastoraltheologie*, Paderborn, 1900, vol. i, p. 267.
[2] Aug. Stöhr, *Handbuch der Pastoralmedizin*, 4th edit., revised and dited by Ludwig Kannamüller, Freiburg, 1900, p. 425.
[3] The two cases observed by Stöhr himself are found *ibid.*, pp. 326 sq.
[4] *Ibid.*, pp. 426 sq.

of possession is not brought into doubt, at least as regards the past when it seems, given the inspired character of the Gospels, to be established by the cases related therein. So far as the present and even the more recent past are concerned, an effort is made to approximate to the non-Catholic point of view while still recognizing for dogmatic reasons the possibility of possession by evil spirits; belief therein is even required, but concrete individual cases are generally regarded with scepticism. It is obvious that such an attitude is one of compromise.

Stöhr himself has, as he relates, during twenty years of practice in hospitals and amongst private patients, had only two opportunities of forming an opinion at the request of a director of conscience on supposed possession. In both instances he reached in his medical capacity the conviction that there was no possession but a nervous condition. One of the two cases—it is related by him in fairly full detail— is so closely analogous to the ancient cases of possession that it may safely be said that in earlier times it would immediately have been taken for one.[1]

On what authority does Stöhr arrive at a different judgement ? Simply the fact that the possessed, on approaching any object which he considers as sacred, reacts by an access of rage, whereas according to the doctrine of the Church he ought only so to react to a genuinely consecrated object. In the truly demoniacal state the possessed, or rather the demon who is within him, ought to be capable of distinguishing hidden or completely invisible objects. It is only to authentic sacred things that the real demon responds by an outburst of fury. Now it may be said that if this criterion had been applied with full rigour in earlier times the Church would never have established a case of true possession.

It is the more surprising that Stöhr for his own part emphasizes that a devil may be capable of imitating all sorts of maladies; there would therefore, in a general way, be no medical criterion to distinguish natural maladies from those attributable to the demon. If, however, when it comes to the point he refuses in spite of this to recognize concrete

[1] Cornelius Krieg, *Wissenschaft der Seelenleitung*. Eine Pastoral-theologie in 4 Büchern, vol. i, Freiburg, 1901, p. 180.

suspected cases, such an attitude evidently arises from his sceptical turn of mind and would not have been condoned in him by any previous ecclesiastical writer.[1]

But the survival, at least in principle, of belief in possession means that the ground remains to some extent always prepared for the manifestation of such states. As a matter of fact they have become very rare in the Catholic world, for demonological ideas are no longer in the forefront of consciousness there and even retain no more than a theoretical value, having lost any particular importance *in concreto*.

The second spiritual territory where belief in possession is cherished is the right wing of Protestantism. As Schleiermacher was not successful in winning a sweeping victory, the same was true as regards negation of belief in the devil and consequently in possession. Even in 1894 a conference on the treatment of the insane gave rise to a lively debate between several ecclesiastics and psychiatrists on non-organic diseases of the mind in general and their interpretation in the sense of demonological ideas, and this was subsequently followed up in writing.[2] We might pursue the study of conservative Protestantism further, but should always meet with the same conceptions.

Finally the third domain where, at least in certain instances, this belief is maintained, is spiritualism, constituting as it does in the great civilized countries the sphere in which states of possession are still freely manifested. These states are frankly cultivated by spiritualism. As they are chiefly provoked and voluntary we shall study them in the following chapter.

Cases of possession of recent date are reported in France by Poulain who asseverates that he has personally assisted in the exorcism of the possessed.[3] The reader is moreover referred to several cases related above.[4]

As regards Germany I know no recent cases except in the south, in Würtemberg, well known in the romantic period

[1] Franz Schubert, *Grundzüge der Pastoraltheologie*, Gratz, 1913, p. 468.
[2] Georg Hafner, *Die Dämonischen des neuen Testaments*, Frankfurt a.M., 1894, Hans Laehr, *Die Dämonischen des neuen Testaments* (a reply to Pastor Hafner), Leipzig, 1894.
[3] A. Poulain, *La Plénitude des Grâces*.   [4] Pp. 107 sq., 109 sq.

for prevalence of possession, and in Catholic Bavaria. In 1911 two fresh cases were notified to me from Würtemberg by a student, but unhappily it was not possible to go and study them.

To Bavaria, at the end of the nineteenth century, belongs a case already cited more than once (pp. 15 and 23 sq.), the M. case.

Schilder has described in some detail a case of possession observed in 1911 at a neurological clinic in Halle[1] in which the patient conversed in a striking manner with the spirit possessing her. The case had no religious character. Schilder quite rightly does not consider it as hysteria, but as " approximating to schizophrenia. "[2] Treatment by hypnotism in Janet's manner was clearly not tried, neither was exorcism. Nevertheless it is impossible to relinquish the attempt to cure such patients by suggestion, however practised. What would have become of Janet's patients if he had not treated them by modernized exorcism ?

From Italy we have already cited a case.

In Europe possession is still encountered to-day in Russia, that is to say in the country where enlightened ideas have penetrated less than anywhere else into the lower strata of society. States of civilization are found there which in western Europe have long since receded into the past.

First, here is an account of possession from the north of Russia, amongst the Samoyedes. It comes from a learned Italian of the name of Cerletti. Unhappily I have not been able to lay hands on the original, but a detailed report exists in the *Journal de psychologie normale et pathologique*, from which I have borrowed the following particulars:

In the most northerly part of European Russia, particularly in the government of Archangel on the banks of the Lower Pechora, live Samoyedes; the men are almost entirely engaged in reindeer-breeding, hunting and fishing; the women perform the agricultural work neglected by the men. Education, very limited and derived entirely from pictures in the holy books, favours the development

---

[1] Paul Schilder, *Selbstbewusstsein und Persönlichkeitsbewusstsein*. Monographien aus dem Gesamtgebiete der Neurologie und Psychiatrie, ed. by A. Alzheimer and M. Lewandowsky, No. 9, Berlin, 1914, pp. 247 sq.

[2] *Ibid.*, p. 249.

of somewhat singular superstitious beliefs. Nevertheless the men are intelligent and active, showing, as do also their wives, a vivacious and expansive character in contrast to the brooding and fatalistic melancholy of the rest of the Russian population. The sanitary conditions are satisfactory, but for a long time past there has been observed in this population a special form of morbidity, particularly characterized by polymorphous convulsive fits, and known by the name of *Ikóta* or *Wistian*—i.e., *sobbing.*

Ikóta attacks, almost exclusively, the majority of married women; it is only found very exceptionally amongst men, children, old men and girls. As a general rule the girl of the Lower Pechora has shown no neuropathic disturbance up to the time of her marriage, when shortly afterwards, or usually *on her wedding day*, she is seized with a violent attack of convulsions.

The determining causes of these fits are very various. The spectacle of another woman in the throes of convulsions, the mere sight of a person or a given thing, the sound of a certain word, the inhaling of the smoke of a cigarette. Generally the fit is preceded by various symptoms: a feeling of giddiness, a feeling of constriction in the throat, oppression in the upper part of the chest or in the diaphragm, torpor in all the limbs. Some subjects declare that they have the sensation of a rat running all over the body and inflicting on the limbs innumerable and very painful bites.

Then comes the fit: a shrill cry, a fall, general convulsions, violent contortions of the limbs and trunk; the eyes roll in all directions, the teeth are ground, the hands are spasmodically contorted, tear the hair and rend the clothing. In other cases the subject flings herself upon the bystanders as if to attack them, upsets everything she can lay hands on, breaks the furniture and utters devilish cries. Sometimes during the fit she cannot speak a word; she emits a low, inarticulate bellow or a strident cry; in other cases she utters the most atrocious abuse, making use of obscene expressions. In less grave forms the patient can speak but does not answer questions, or else weeps and gives vent to frenzied laughter. In certain cases the fit is reduced to the emission of violent and entirely characteristic sobs. Sometimes the woman falls into an ecstasy or begins to predict the future, speaking in the name of the demon who has taken possession of her.

After the fit, which is of variable duration, there is a return to the normal state; nothing survives except at most a slight heaviness of the head, and no memory remains of what has occurred during the attack.

These morbid manifestations are connected with the prevailing superstitions of the country: the supernatural affection is a consequence of witchcraft; the demon enters into the body of his victim where he works a spell and brings on the various symptoms of the *Ikóta*. Wizards can produce all sorts of maladies notably madness, but the *Ikóta* is particularly communicated to married women and the most propitious day is the bridal day. In order to effect a cure the offices of another wizard are necessary, together with pilgrimages and prayers. But usually the possessed continues to suffer from the same fits until an advanced age.

In the majority of cases the somatic stigmata of hysteria are not found, nor is the so-called hysterical character. A very close pathogenic connection exists between the morbid condition and the superstitious idea; all the other etiological factors (natural conditions of nourishment, mode of life, etc.) may be

> This malady clearly consists in epidemic hysterical attacks with the extremely complex somatic symptomatology proper to the hysterical form of demoniacal possession, or *hystero-demonopathy*.[1]

I have it from a reliable Russian source that there is known throughout the rest of Russia a malady of the name of *ikóta* or *klikúschestvo*. It generally consists in a peculiar prolonged and obviously obsessive hiccupping (*ikóta* means nothing more than hiccupping), but may, in more serious cases, come to neighings, bleatings or other animal cries. The victims are also constrained to shout insults and use filthy words, and are subject to twitchings and contractions, wild writhings upon the ground, etc. In short, the picture is exactly the same as that offered by the possessed of western Europe. The malady affects only or almost exclusively women and is very common. It is considered as a form of possession. Naturally it only attacks the uneducated lower classes and is even characteristic of the particularly ignorant peasantry; it is a peasant woman's and not a townswoman's complaint. In other words, possession which is already almost considered as extinct in central and western Europe, is still very prevalent in Russia where it may readily be observed *in vivo*. We may confidently prophesy that its days there are also numbered; as the ideas more prevalent in the towns spread to the steppes it will rapidly retreat in a few decades, provided obviously that the general ideas of to-day concerning the life of the mind continue in the future to follow the same paths as heretofore and that a wave of spiritualism does not spread over the earth inclining it once more to belief in the existence of true possession. In such a case the remains of the old European demonology could hardly maintain their present rate of retreat.

The autosuggestive character of the *ikóta* is clearly attested by the manner in which this state is cured: by holy pictures, the exercises of the Church, the putting on of harness, or finally by immersion in holy-water on the day of the Epiphany.[2]

[1] Ugo Cerletti, *Sulle recenti concezioni dell' isteria e della suggestione a proposito di una endemia di posessione demoniaca*, in " Annali de l' Instituto psichiatrico della Università di Roma," vol. iii, no. 1, 1904. Detailed summary in " Journal de psychologie normale et pathologique," vol. ii, 1905.

[2] V. I. Mansikka, in the article " *Demons and Spirits* " of the Encyclopædia of Religion and Ethics, vol. iv, p. 626.

The German newspapers report the following recent case of possession from Russia.

> Batjushka Joann Kronstadtski is an illustrious Russian priest whom the orthodox population regard as a saint. Belief in the miraculous power of his prayers is so widespread that there is a constant stream of men moving towards Kronstadt to seek in prayer with the holy priest the cure of infirmities and help in need. His self-abnegation and the force of his personality, radiating confidence and hope, make this priest a phenomenon far beyond the ordinary. According to the *St. Petersburg Gazette* the metropolitan police headquarters have had intelligence of the following case. A short time ago a sick woman arrived in Petersburg. Her malady manifested itself in the fact, for example, that on hearing the church bells wherever she might be she at once fell down, began to cry out in a wild and terrible voice and was bathed in sweat. The same befell her every time a church procession took place, and from these signs her sickness was judged to be possession. She suffered from it for three years, all the while losing strength, to such an extent that her relations decided to have recourse to the last hope: to solicit the prayers of Father Joann of Kronstadt for the sufferer. To this end she was brought to St. Petersburg where on the 14th of March Father Joann celebrated the liturgy. During the administration of the Lord's Supper to the congregation she was led up to communicate also. She was immediately overcome by a fit, uttered cries, tore her face, and three strong men had to hold her. The priest Joann placed his hand on the sick woman, fixed on her a steadfast look and said in a loud and firm voice: " In the name of Our Lord Jesus Christ I command thee, Satan, to come forth !" The priest repeated these words several times. In the church, filled with devout worshippers, fell a deep silence. Nothing was heard except the words of power of the revered father: " Come forth, and come quickly !" Then the possessed uttered inarticulate cries and called out: " I am coming forth immediately !" This lasted for about three minutes. Then the cries ceased and the sick woman, shut-eyed and gasping, fell into the arms of those accompanying her. Father Joann turned towards her and said three times: " Open your eyes !" The sick woman executed the command slowly and with great effort. The father furthermore commanded her several times to cross herself. The first time she did it with a struggle, but afterwards more easily. After putting several questions to the woman the father gave orders to release her, saying: " Leave her, she is now completely cured !" and offered her the holy communion which she piously accepted. Later he caused her to be led forward once more and told her that she should thank God and remain in good health. This marvellous cure made the most profound impression on those present.[1]

From Slavonic Russia we shall now pass to eastern European Judaism. There too possession does not seem rare even to-day. Given the insistence on orthodox outlook which still persists in Russian Jewry together with marked

---

[1] Quoted by B. Heyne, *Ueber Besessenheitswahn*, Paderborn, 1904, p. 186.

exclusiveness towards the outside world, it is really not surprising that amongst these people, who represent as it were a survival of bygone antiquity within the modern world, possession should be far more prevalent than in western Europe. We possess an interesting narrative from a former member of the Russian ghetto, Jacob Fromer,[1] a Russo-Polish Jew, who was granted German nationality at the special request of the last German Emperor. In his autobiography, extremely interesting in other respects also, he gives us a sort of companion-picture to that of Solomon Maimon who shared his fate, a remarkable description of possession in the Polish ghetto:

> . . . A crowd assembled. " The dibbuk (possessed) is coming." A big, strong girl with disordered hair and an agitated face was rather dragged than led in by men and women. She begged to be taken back to the house and reiterated incessantly " I feel better already."
> Sights like this were not new to me. I had already often seen possessed persons at home and knew their fate. . . .
> The present case interested me very particularly. I had, as a matter of fact, learnt that the spirit inhabiting this girl was a *bachour* of great Talmudic learning. Having become an Epicurean through reading heretical works he had fled secretly from Bethamidrasch and succeeded in reaching Germany. There his co-religionists cared for him and enabled him to study. But in the course of time he revealed himself as so profound a heretic that it became too much for the German Jews and his protectors withdrew from him. He struggled for some time in the bitterest distress and was finally obliged to give up his studies. He took to drink, frequented dubious society, and was finally imprisoned. After that he was packed off to his own home. His parents would have nothing to do with a son who spoke German and dressed in European style. His co-religionists insulted, despised, and stoned him. In despair he went to the local clergyman and was baptized. But neither could or would the Christians do anything for him. Sunk in depravity and a physical and moral wreck through alcohol, suffering and privations, he was incapable of sustained work. The only help given to him took the form of permission to sit before the church amongst the beggars and eke out his miserable existence with alms. In the end he was unable to endure this life of shame: he drowned himself.
> When I heard the story of this unfortunate man related I was seized with a painful feeling which first became clear to me much later through the knowledge of the Buddhist saying: " Tat twam asi " (so art thou thyself). I knew that this girl was sick, deranged in mind, and that she had nothing to do with the dead man's destiny. Nevertheless mass-suggestion had so wrought upon me

---

[1] Jacob Fromer, *Ghetto-Dämmerung*. Eine Lebensgeschichte, 3rd edit., Leipzig, 1812, pp. 64 sq.

that I was anxious to learn by her mouth something about the
poor wretch's fate.

The wide and spacious room where the girl had been brought
and seated on a chair in the middle was filled with the serried
ranks of the crowd.   I had a good place, from which I could see
and hear everything.   She sat down, languid and exhausted, with
haggard, fearful eyes, and from time to time lamented, begging
to be taken back to the house because she was afraid of the wonder-
rabbi.   Her voice, weak and beseeching, inspired sympathy and
compassion.   Suddenly she sprang up and made efforts to remain
standing.

" *Silentium strictissimum* !"

I could not believe my ears.   It was a real man's voice, harsh
and rough, and the onlookers affirmed that it was exactly the voice
of the *meshoummed* (baptized man).   Not one of us knew the meaning of these words.   We only knew that it was a strange language
which the sick woman understood as little as ourselves.   " Ladies
and Gentlemen," continued she. . . .   Then she pronounced a
long, confused discourse with High-German turns of phrase, of
which I understood only that it greeted a festive gathering and
wished to draw attention to the meaning of the feast.

She broke off in the midst of the speech and burst into a frightful
laugh which made us shudder to the marrow. . . .   I was as if
thunderstruck.

A murmur arose: " The rabbi is coming !"

The crowd drew aside respectfully to make room for the new
arrival.   A short, rotund little man came in sight, dressed from
head to foot in white.   Around the long white silk *talar* which fell
to his feet was swathed a wide white sash, and his head was covered
with a white silk *strcimel* (fur-trimmed hat).   The full cheeks hung
like peaches in his face with its complexion of mingled blood and
milk, while long and bushy eyebrows overhung his eyes.   In one
hand he held a *shofar* (horn) and in the other a *loulaf* (frond of
palm).   He entered at a run, chanting Hebrew verses, and followed
by a secretary and servants, until, arrived in front of the girl, he
handed the loulaf and shofar to the secretary and lifted up his
eyebrows with his hands.   From his coal-black eyes shone a light
like the sparkle of a diamond; the girl was unable to sustain his
look, and lowered her eyes in confusion.   Two lighted tapers were
brought and the rabbi began his address.   " In the name of the
42 letters of the God with long sight, which has indeed no end;
in the name of the lesser and greater celestial families; in the
name of the chiefs of the bodyguard: Sandalfon, Uriel, Akatriel
and Usiel, in the name of the potent Metateron surrounded with
strength, awe-inspiring, vouchsafing salvation or damnation, I
adjure thee, abject spirit, outcast from hell, to reply to my words
and obey all my commands !"

Stifling heat prevailed in the room.   Through the wide, high
windows fell the rays of a burning August sun which flooded the
rapt faces of the crowd.

" What is thy name ?" the rabbi asked the sick woman in a loud,
harsh voice.   " Esther," replied the girl softly and faintly, trembling all over.   " Silence, thou *Chazufe*" (impudent woman), cried
the rabbi.   " I asked not thee but the dibbuk."

There was a long silence.

" Wilt thou, or wilt thou not, reply ?" resumed the rabbi,
making as if to strike the girl with the loulaf.   " Do not strike
me !" implored the man's voice.   " I will reply."   " What is thy

name ?" " Christian Davidovitch." " *Jemach shemo*" (may his name be blotted out), spat the rabbi stopping his ears. " I would know thy Jewish name." " Chaim." " And what was thy mother's name ?" " Sarah." " Chaim ben Sarah," commanded the rabbi, " relate what occurred after thy death."

The dibbuk told a long story. After death he had been cast out of hell with insults and opprobrium. He wandered for a long time, but could no longer remain without habitation and finally entered into a pig.

" How like a meshoummed !" murmured the entranced on-lookers.

That was not too bad. When the pig was slaughtered he passed into a horse, where he had a very poor time. It was a draught-horse, which had to work hard, receive many blows, and never eat his fill. At length he decided to try man. The occasion was propitious. He knew that Esther had illicit relations with a young man, and watched the moment when she abandoned herself to his embraces; at that instant he was permitted to enter into her. He ended his narrative by begging not to be driven out; in life and after death he had suffered so greatly that they should have pity on him and grant him a little rest.

This prayer appeared to make no impression on the rabbi. With an air of asperity he took the shofar from the hand of his secretary and put it to his mouth. But what is this ? In spite of all his efforts he was unable to make any sound. Some minutes passed in anxious waiting. The rabbi put forth all his strength, sweat poured from his brow, and still no sound was heard. He gave up the attempt and remained for some instants plunged in deep meditation. Suddenly his face cleared; an inspiration of genius appeared to flash across his brow; he whispered something in his secretary's ear, and the latter went away quietly and returned with a piece of wax. The rabbi snatched it from his hands and stopped the two openings of the refractory instrument. He tested carefully whether the closure was complete, then burst into a triumphant laugh, saying: " Now see, accursed Satan, how thou canst get out !"

He raised the other shofar to his mouth. Now everything went smoothly.

Tekio ! and a clear, forthright blast rang out.

Teruo ! A resounding noise rent the air.

Shevorim ! The notes gushed forth in rapid succession.

Tekio gedolo ! This time it was a long and piercing sound.

Abbela Srallok ! burst forth the man's voice suddenly with the same strident laughter as before.

Abbela was the rabbi's name; Srallok is a coarse insult. The rabbi changed colour and shook with rage and excitement; he had never yet encountered such impudence. But he recovered his self-control rapidly, seized the loulaf and struck the girl violently in the face with it. Then an incredible thing happened: the girl had freed her hands with lightning speed and before anyone could prevent her she dealt the rabbi two resounding boxes on the ears.

A panic followed. The frightened crowd uttered cries and oaths, storming and weeping with excitement. Never had the like been seen. Nevertheless strong arms had seized the sick girl, the rabbi struck her so furiously with the loulaf that her face streamed with blood; she collapsed with a terrible cry and became unconscious. At this moment a noise was heard at the window as if it had been struck by a small stone. Everyone rushed towards it and dis-

14

covered in one pane a hole of the size of a pea through which aperture the spirit had fled. The girl was carried out.

After this scene I was as if transformed. I had come there as an unbeliever, an atheist, ostensibly to study on the spot superstition, religious dementia. The experiences of an hour had sufficed to overthrow like a house of cards the independent ideas which I had acquired by years of study, trials and struggles. In vain I told myself a thousand times that the girl was ill, that she had been in touch with the dead man in his lifetime and might have imitated his voice and manner of speech. In vain I asserted that the rabbi had executed an illusion with involuntary comic effect. Before me were thousands of men, older, more experienced, wiser than I. They all believed in the existence of the dibbuk, they had seen the spirit come out, they had heard the impact on the window and seen the hole in the pane. They all attested that the rabbi had times without number cured incurable sicknesses, recalled the dead to life, and brought to light inscrutable mysteries.

Now that I am committing these thoughts to writing I can, if I wish, call these men fools. What is there to prevent me ? I am sitting alone in my room, I have paper and pen and can think and write what I please. But at that moment I found myself like a single and tiny intelligence amongst thousands of stronger ones which weighed me down, absorbed me and carried me away. My brain had almost ceased to work, I gave myself up entirely to the sensations and emotions which assailed me so powerfully.

This narrative, which offers in other respects no peculiar psychological features, leaves the noise and the hole in the window unexplained. It is naturally insufficient to make us admit a parapsychophysical phenomenon, for it is not established that no hole existed previously and a pre-arranged revolver-shot is not, moreover, beyond the bounds of possibility.

As mentioned above, American spiritualistic literature furnishes a great abundance of recent cases of possession, but as they are generally of a nature to imply voluntary and partly induced phenomena I shall discuss these accounts in the next Part. I except one case where the spontaneous nature of the state is abundantly evident: the so-called Watseka Wonder. It has had an enormous publicity in America, since to all appearance the spirit of a dead child had passed into the organism of a girl friend. I give the case as W. James has produced it in his *Psychology*. I have unfortunately not yet been able to obtain access to the original.

Lurancy was a young girl of fourteen, living with her parents at Watseka, Ill., who (after various distressing hysterical disorders and spontaneous trances, during which she was possessed by departed spirits of a more or less grotesque sort) finally declared herself to be animated by the spirit of Mary Roff (a neighbour's daughter. who had died in an insane asylum twelve years before) and insisted on being sent "home" to Mr. Roff's house. After a week of "home sickness" and importunity on her part, her parents agreed, and the Roffs, who pitied her, and who were spiritualists into the bargain, took her in. Once there, she seems to have convinced the family that their dead Mary had exchanged habitations with Lurancy. Lurancy was said to be temporarily in heaven, and Mary's spirit now controlled her organism, and lived again in her former earthly home.

The girl, now in her new home, seemed perfectly happy and content, knowing every person and every thing that Mary knew when in her original body, twelve to twenty-five years ago, recognizing and calling by name those who were friends and neighbours of the family from 1852 to 1856, when Mary died, calling attention to scores, yes, hundreds of incidents that transpired during her natural life. During all the period of her sojourn at Mr. Roff's she had no knowledge of, and did not recognize, any of Mr. Vennum's family, their friends or neighbours, yet Mr. and Mrs. Vennum and their children visited her and Mr. Roff's people, she being introduced to them as to any strangers. After frequent visits, and hearing them often and favourably spoken of, she learned to love them as acquaintances, and visited them with Mrs. Roff three times. From day to day she appeared natural, easy, affable, and industrious, attending diligently and faithfully to her household duties, assisting in the general work of the family as a faithful, prudent daughter might be supposed to do, singing, reading, or conversing as opportunity offered, upon all matters of private or general interest to the family.

The so-called Mary whilst at the Roffs would sometimes "go back to heaven" and leave the body in a "quiet trance"—*i.e.*, without the original personality of Lurancy returning. After eight or nine weeks, however, the memory and manner of Lurancy would sometimes partially, but not entirely, return for a few minutes. Once Lurancy seems to have taken full possession for a short time. At last, after some fourteen weeks, conformably to the prophecy which "Mary" had made when she first assumed "control," she departed definitely and the Lurancy-consciousness came back for good. Mr. Roff writes:

"She wanted me to take her home, which I did. She called me Mr. Roff, and talked with me as a young girl would, not being acquainted. I asked her how things appeared to her—if they seemed natural. She said it seemed like a dream to her. She met her parents and brothers in a very affectionate manner, hugging and kissing each one in tears of gladness. She clasped her arms around her father's neck a long time, fairly smothering him with kisses. I saw her father just now (eleven o'clock). He says she has been perfectly natural, and seems entirely well."

James adds:

My friend Mr. R. Hodgson informs me that he visited Watseka in April, 1889, and cross-examined the principal witnesses of this case. His confidence in the original narrative was strengthened by what he learned; and various unpublished facts were ascertained, which increased the plausibility of the spiritualistic interpretation of the phenomenon.[1]

[1] William James, *The Principles of Psychology*, London, 1891, vol. i, pp. 397 sq. The source is E. W. Stevens' book: *The Watseka Wonder*, Chicago, 1887. Stevens had followed the whole case as a

In the other continents conditions are quite different from those prevailing in the principal countries of Europe and America, and possession is manifestly still an extremely frequent phenomenon, even in the lands of ancient civilization. This naturally results from the fact that such civilization is less highly developed than in the majority of European countries or those formed on the European model (America, and the civilized parts of Australia and Africa). In particular the education of the masses is much more restricted, and the old religious ideas exercise a power which, generally speaking, they have long since lost in Europe.

But possession is not confined to these lands; it is also encountered in other regions, although information about such cases is scanty. The majority of documents dealing with them come from countries where civilization is sufficiently advanced to permit the existence of an extensive literature, but, on the other hand, has not penetrated the lower strata of society to a degree where rational criticism destroys primitive ideas.

From the Near East comes an account by Curtiss concerning some cases of possession at Nebk, in Syria:

> Suleiman, a Protestant teacher of Nebk, had from his wife the following account of the expulsion of an evil spirit which inhabited a young girl of her acquaintance. "The holy man commanded the spirit to come out of her. He replied: 'I will depart by her head.' 'If you do so,' replied the holy man, 'you will kill her.' 'Good, then I will depart by her eye!' 'No, you would kill her!' At length the spirit declared himself willing to depart by her toe, which was accepted." A child was subject to epileptic fits. He felt the spirit come upon him. The sheik struck the child a blow on the shoulder so violent that it made a wound through which the spirit came forth.

Curtiss adds the following remark:

> Baldensprenger mentions a similar case in Palestine:[1] "On December 31st, 1891, our nearest neighbour was possessed by a shape dressed in white. . . . Dumb with fright, she ran into the house but could make known only by signs that something extraordinary had occurred. Immediately a sheik (priest) was fetched from the neighbouring sakmet, Abu Derwish, who brought

doctor. More extensive extracts from the original will be found in Myers' work: *The Human Personality and its Survival of Bodily Death*, London, 1907, vol. ii, pp. 360-68. Steffens' account had been published in the *Religio-philosophical Journal* (1878). Hodgson's account also appeared in that journal (December 20th, 1890).

[1] *Quarterly Statement*, London, 1893, pp. 214 sq.

his holy books—magic books—and who, by way of beginning the cure, gave the patient a violent cut with a whip. Having lit a fire which was to burn all the time, he began to question her: Who art thou? The spirit replied by the mouth of the woman: A Jew.—How hast thou come hither?—I was killed on this spot. From whence art thou?—From Nablus.—When wast thou murdered?—Twelve years ago.—Come forth from the body of this woman!—I will not!—Very well. I have fire here and shall burn thee.—How must I come forth, by the eye, the nose, or where? After long preambles the spirit, in a horrible convulsion of the whole body and of the legs came out by the great toe. The woman fainted from exhaustion and subsequently recovered her speech."[1]

Cases of possession seem to have occurred very frequently amongst the primitive lower classes of India. The documents here are far more plentiful than anywhere else, so that I shall only quote a very small number, which can readily be supplemented from literature.

The missionary R. Fröhlich, whom I had asked for fuller particulars, writes:

The external character of possession which I have studied amongst Christian women (and which I have heard described in connection with heathen ones) is a circular movement of the whole trunk upon the hips, at first slow, then quicker, and finally so furious that the hair is loosed from its knot and lashes like a whip. The person then sits down on the ground with legs folded under her. In the case of which I was an eye-witness the circular movement lasted for hours. At times she wished to get up and leave the house; it was not without difficulty that three men were able to hold her. This circular movement, called the *swami* dance, that is the dance of God, was accompanied by an incessant half-singing stream of speech, corresponding to the rhythm of 3/4 time. She spoke of herself in the third person as " my child," " my pearl," " my treasure," " my flower," and never wearied of reiterating the assurance that " he " would not give up nor let go " his pearl." She often repeated also: " It burns . . . it burns . . . the name of Jesus burns me . . . but I have permission . . . for five days more. . . . Until then I will not leave my pearl. . . . I will not leave her. . . . I will not leave her. . . !"
After the specified number of days (each day she accurately reduced it by one) the phenomena ceased. Until then they were reproduced every evening at six or nine o'clock and lasted until midnight or three a.m. To the question addressed to her by an onlooker: " Who are you, then, you who are speaking?" The woman replied: " I am *Murugen*." Once when she wished to rush out she cried: " Let me go out. . . . I must go out. . . . *Kali* is waiting for me . . . over there in the corner." (Kali is a village divinity like Murugen.) In childhood the woman had been vowed by her father to Murugen. Later the father had become a Christian with all his family, and the woman was married to a Christian but had become inwardly estranged from Christianity. After such

---

[1] Curtiss, *Ursemitische Religion im Volksleben des heutigen Orients*, Leipzig, 1903, pp. 172 sq.

nocturnal manifestations she declared when questioned that she remembered nothing, and behaved quite normally until towards six o'clock or later the fit came upon her again.

The case of the other Christian woman which I was able to witness personally was ephemeral. It was on the occasion of a visit to the village parishes. The woman had been baptized long before, but had relapsed into paganism, then had recently to all appearances returned to the Christian congregation. She was before her hut. The native clergyman was speaking to her, but she was distracted, made no reply, and suddenly falling on her knees, squatted with an absent air. " Say the Creed, I will show you how !" cried the black pastor. She recited the first article after him word for word, always in the squatting position. But when he came to the words " and in Jesus Christ " she became completely mute and began slowly to execute a circular movement with the trunk. Then the pastor had a vessel of water brought and vigorously sprinkled her head and face with it; he flung the cold water in her face and over her head by handfuls so that it resounded like slaps. The success of this remedy was to arrest the circular movement. The woman remained sitting and we were obliged to go. The pastor had often seen similar things: " They can no longer pronounce the name of Jesus when the influence is upon them," said he. He was of opinion that if they could be brought to force themselves to do it the state would cease. When that was not possible he used the successful cold water cure just described. . . .

These are all the observations which I have had the opportunity of making.

To this document may be added another taken from the annals of an English mission:

In . . . the ceded districts of South India there is an important village, that we shall call Verapalli, attached to which is a large pariah-Christian community. To this place there came, comparatively recently, a severe epidemic of cholera.

What can the foreigners know of the ways of Maremma, the awful ? Cattle innumerable are slaughtered in sacrifice. Some poor ignorant person, usually a woman, becomes, as it is called, a " Shivashakti," that is, becomes possessed, to the complete alteration of her character, by, as the people believe, some demon-goddess. She rises, rushes suddenly for the nearest mangora-tree, and crams her mouth with its leaves. These she chews and spits out as she runs shrieking frightfully up and down the village street, predicting the death of its inhabitants.

This extraordinary phenomenon, explain it how you may, is known in every village in the ceded districts, and probably also over all India. It would be impossible to conceive anything better calculated to foster the spirit of hopeless terror that contributes so greatly to the fatality of the disease.

The epidemic in Verapalli was unusually severe and lasted long. As the days passed a striking circumstance became daily more marked. Though in the caste and chucklers' (a pariah caste) houses the disease claimed its victims, the Christians—though the buildings all closely adjoined—remained unaffected. This, too, again, explain it as you may, is quite a usual circumstance, so common, indeed, that it is remarked upon by the other castes.

Now, in the village there lived a person of much wealth and evil influence, called Venkatareddy. . . . To this man it seemed a matter of grave injustice that the Christians should escape the fate that was afflicting so heavily all the others. . . .

He called the "Shivashakti" of the place, in this instance a poor shepherd woman, and induced her to exert her supposed malignant powers against the Christians, to pass on to them the dread disease that the other castes might go free.

On the dreaded evening the Christian community divided into four bands, and under trees in the four corners of their hamlets, all night prayer meetings were held, not prayer meetings for quiet devotion by any means: for hours they made their part of the village resound with loud singing and strong praying.

All heathen rites, like that about to be performed, are recognized as works of darkness, and it is not till the moon hides its kindly face that they may begin, so it was long after midnight before the procession started.

The Shivashakti went first, closely followed by Venkatareddy and his friends. Close behind them crowded half the village. Torches were carried, whose flickering, smoky flame made the strange scene yet more fearsome.

The woman, an awful figure, staggered ahead, as one possessed. Her black hair tumbled loose over her starting eyes, her face horribly contorted, her fingers clutching like claws. Her blood-curdling yells were clearly heard above the din of the drums.

Slowly the procession pursued its way towards the boundary. Within, the Christians redoubled the vigour of their hymns and prayers. All at once the wretched woman stops, rigid with sudden terror. "See," screams the Shivashakti: "There He stands, God Jesus, with hands outstretched, protecting His people, as a shepherd does his lambs. Back, back; He is a great God, I dare go no farther. If I do, I die."

But Venkatareddy is in no mood to accept defeat. Far too drunk, probably, to understand, he blocks the way, roughly catching hold of her. Then he pushes her, and eventually, in tipsy desperation, beats her with his fists.

With the fury of a tiger the woman turns upon him, shrieking madly. "The curse of Mysooramma be upon you. It is not me you struck but her. By to-morrow evening may Maremma grip you."

When the words of the curse reached the stupefied brain, the great brutal fellow collapsed. He had to be helped to his home, spent the night in deadly fear, and by sundown of the next day the curse had come true. The cholera goddess had claimed another victim.

The tale passed over the countryside, and on its way made an impression greater than many sermons.[1]

Bastian also gives particulars of exorcism in India and Ceylon which seem to come from a foreign source:

The temple of Hur-hureshvuru at Conkan, whose healing current of air (waren) is attributed to the *Bhuiroba*, is particularly visited by pilgrims suffering from the nervous affection called *pishachu-copudruvu*, or devil's ill (unfortunately this affection is not further described). After a few days the patients are subjected to a course of ceremonies which begins with all sorts of exercises and salt

---

[1] *Chronicles of the London Missionary Society*, March, 1911.

baths (in the pool at high tide) and ends by the application of the usual stimulants to excite the imagination and overstimulate the nerves: the dazzling glare of camphor flames, the scent of repulsive-smelling flowers, clouds of smoking incense, and a deafening janizary-music of bells, cymbals, gongs, drums, sirens mingling their violent discords, tinkling, rattling, clapping and howling without interruption. The patients, epileptics or hysterics, are subjected to this treatment and an artificial state of epilepsy and hysteria is created in which the presence of the tormenting demon is recognized. This latter is evoked by the power of the priest and is only exorcised by him, by means of the power conferred over them (the patients) at his approach by order of Bhuiroba. The priest questions the evil spirit and demands his expulsion. The latter trembles at the imperious words and angry look. He replies to questions according to impressions received from his tender infancy and perhaps asks as sole favour that he may be allowed to leave his citadel with all the honours of war and may be promised the observance of the usual ritual. (This is so arranged in order to fill the purse or stomach of the priest.) At length the demon announces his retreat, the patient falls senseless, and when he recovers consciousness finds himself in most cases completely cured.[1]

Another of Bastian's narratives –it cannot unfortunately be ascertained with certainty whether it originates from him or from another traveller—makes it perfectly clear that the state of possession is first revealed by the procedure of exorcism or by approach to the temple where it is practised. It is evident that the maladies which the patients bring there are chiefly nervous phenomena of another kind. The reader will remember Kerner's doctrine of the " hidden demon " who must first be brought to light.

Pilgrims from all parts of Ceylon visit the temple of the demon Vakula Bandara Devijo at Alutnuvera at all seasons to be cured of demoniacal possession when it resists other means. It is principally women who believe themselves to be under this influence. To dance, sing or cry out without cause, to tremble and jerk the limbs or be subject to frequent and prolonged fainting fits, are considered as the symptoms of a case of possession. From time to time women who think they find themselves under this imaginary influence try to run away from their homes, pouring forth insults and abuse or biting and tearing their flesh and hair. Sometimes the fits last only an hour, sometimes fit after fit occurs in rapid succession, sometimes they only overtake the women on Sunday nights and Wednesdays, or once in three or four months, but always at the time when a demoniacal ceremony takes place. On such occasions the conjurations of the *catladiya* bring a passing relief, but it seems that no conjuration is capable of ensuring a permanent cure; no resource therefore remains except the temple, Gala kap-pu dewale.

[1] Ad. Bastian, *Ueber psychische Beobachtungen bei Naturvolkern.* Schriften der Gesellschaft für Experimental-Psychologie zu Berlin, ii, Leipzig, 1890, pp. 20 sq.

If the woman is two or three miles from the temple it is believed that she is overcome by the demoniacal influence and she approaches the temple in a wild and excited condition; no one can then stop her and she would rather tear anyone opposing her to pieces than stay her progress. She walks faster and faster as she nears the sacred place. Once arrived, she takes refuge in a corner and sits trembling and whimpering, or else entirely speechless and blank, as if overcome with fear, until the *capua* begins his exorcisms. Sometimes she goes quietly to the temple without showing any demoniac signs and the influence begins with the exorcism. The principal room of the temple is divided into three parts by curtains; in the middle is the sanctuary of the god. The capua stands before the outer curtain with the woman confronting him. After the sacrificial offerings have been brought the priest turns towards the god behind the curtain, enumerates the gifts and tells him that such a woman of such and such a village has come to seek for aid against a demon. During this time the woman trembles and shudders, with intermittent outcries. The capua then puts questions in the following way: " Wilt thou, O devil, leave this woman instantly or must I punish thee for thine impudence ?" Thereupon it may happen that the patient replies, shaking with fear: " Yes, I will go at once !" But generally the request is at first met by a refusal. Then the capua takes a bamboo in his right hand and administers to the woman a smart shower of blows, repeating his questions and threats. When a good number of blows has been meted out she generally replies: " Yes, I will go away at once !" She then ceases to tremble and shake and resumes possession of her reason in cases where she had lost it, while her friends congratulate themselves on the happy issue of the cure. (Cf. Dandris de Silva.)[1]

Examples of possession in Siam are also found in Bastian, according to whom purely physical maladies often give rise to this diagnosis and psychic possession of the true kind follows in consequence of the exorcisms performed to expel the demon.

Bastian raises the question of whether the Siamese doctors are capable of driving out the demons which have entered into a possessed person and how they set about it. He writes:

> To this question we must reply that the doctors (*Mo*) believe themselves perfectly capable of driving out demons. So far as exorcisms are concerned, I have seen possessed persons behave in a very singular manner. Some laugh, others weep, some become mute, others act like madmen. All this is unconscious, for the possessed know nothing of themselves. When a doctor is called in to treat them he begins by blessing a piece of areca nut and giving it to them to eat. This should serve as a preliminary test to see whether there is really demoniacal possession or some other malady. In cases of possession the patients experience giddiness or begin to vomit, cry out loudly, groan, or close their eyes and remain mute. By these signs it is easily and surely recognized that

---

[1] *Ibid.*, pp. 21 sq.

a demon has entered. Then the doctor takes a thread of cotton which he has blessed and ties it round the neck of the possessed. This is designed to make sure of the demon and bind him. Then potent charms are pronounced to menace the demon which has taken possession of the person. Sometimes the demon grows uneasy. He laments, cries out and asks pardon, saying: " I will come out without doing her any harm." The doctor then subjects him to an examination in order that he may make himself known: " Whence comest thou, companion (*mung*) ? What wouldst thou here ? Dost thou need anything ?" As a rule the demon who has taken possession of the patient's body now gives his name and replies that he desires this or that. But the doctor then generally takes rods and deals him a rain of blows, after having bound him by charms so that he cannot escape. This puts the demon in a fright and he cries out: " I am going ! I am going !" The doctor then bids him farewell and at the instant when the demon comes forth the possessed falls to the earth and remains there about three hours without saying a word. When she begins to come to her senses the bystanders ask her: " Did you know anything when just now you were in a state of possession ?" She replies that she was not possessed, but only felt slightly indisposed and disturbed in mind. For that reason the Siamese firmly believe that the doctors are capable of driving out the *phi pisal* from the human body. Whether this exorcism of the phi pisat is founded to any extent on fact I cannot state with certainty ; I can only speak from hearsay.[1]

Finally a case from Burmah.

Dr. Mason mentions a prophet who was converted to Christianity.

He could say nothing of his first impressions, but said that it had seemed to him as if a spirit spoke and he had to give an account of what it had said.

Dr. Mason then relates the following anecdote:

Another individual had a familiar spirit that he consulted and with which he conversed; but, on hearing the Gospel, he professed to become converted, and had no more communication with his spirit. It had left him, he said; it spoke to him no more. After a protracted trial I baptized him. I watched his case with interest, and for several years he led an unimpeachable Christian life; but, on losing his religious zeal, and disagreeing with some of the Church members, he removed to a distant village, where he could not attend the services of the Sabbath, and it was soon after reported that he had communications with his familiar spirit again. I sent a native preacher to visit him. The man said he heard the voice which had conversed with him formerly, but it spoke very differently. Its language was exceedingly pleasant to hear, and produced great brokenness of heart. It said, " Love each other; act righteously—act uprightly." with other exhortations such as he had heard from the teachers. An assistant was placed in the village near him, when the spirit left him again; and ever since he has maintained the character of a consistent Christian.[2]

---

[1] Ad. Bastian, *Die Völker des östlichen Asiens*, vol. iii, pp. 800 sq.
[2] Mason, *Burmah*, p. 107, quoted by A. Lang, *The Making of Religion*, 2nd edit., London, 1900, p. 130.

Whereas there is generally a lack of detailed accounts of possession from foreign countries those coming from Mongol civilization are very abundant and in some cases especially circumstantial. Here also it is particularly the lower and uneducated classes which are attacked by possession.

In China possession finds a quite peculiar support in the general belief, strongly impressed on the consciousness of the Chinese people, in the survival of man after death. This forms the basis both of ancestor-worship and of the conviction that it is possible, thanks to specially gifted persons called mediums, to enter into immediate communication with the souls of the dead and also with the gods. The Chinese people in general profess spiritualistic belief, as we shall see still more clearly below. A missionary writes:

> Possession is here in the country a daily occurrence which attracts no attention. . . . Ordinary neo-Christians often demonstrate with complete success the power of belief and the efficacy of holy water, with which they drive out the wicked enemy.[1]

A number of accounts of possession in China are to be found, particularly in the writings of the Christian missionaries. There is, moreover, a special book on the subject apparently not without interest and often quoted in English and American literature. This too is the work of a missionary named John L. Nevius.[2] Unfortunately I have not, owing to the war, been able to obtain a copy of this book, but have had to content myself with the information contained in a review in the Proceedings of the Society for Psychical Research[3] and in Andrew Lang.[4] It appears from Nevius' observations that Chinese possession to some extent resembles the European variety more closely than does that of Japan, for it is not, like the latter, often attributable to the spirits of animals. Nevius, who counted forty years of active missionary work in China, found diabolic possession an everyday phenomenon amongst the Chinese, and although he did not himself observe a single case, succeeded in collecting vast

[1] Herz-Jesu Bote, hg. vom Steyler Missionshaus, July, 1801, quoted by Stützle, *Das griechische Orakelwesen*, part ii, Progr. des Gymn. zu Ellwangen, 1890-91, p. 66.
[2] John L. Nevius, *Demon Possession and Allied Themes*, 2nd edit., London, 1896.
[3] *Proc.* S.P.R., xiii, 1897-98, pp. 602 sq.
[4] Andrew Lang, *The Making of Religion*, 2nd edit., London, 1900, chap.vii: *Demoniacal Possession*.

stores of information concerning these states and their interpretation by the natives. Those attacked by possession
showed themselves as a rule extremely reserved towards him,
as a stranger.

A Chinese mountaineer of the name of Know related to
Nevius that he had himself experienced a state of possession. He was actually busied in preparing for a service
to the domestic god Wang Muniang when one night the
divinity appeared to him in a dream and announced that she
had taken up her abode in his house. After a few days he
was seized with inner disquiet to which was added a crazy
impulse to play. He then had a sort of epileptic attack
followed by a state of mania with homicidal impulses. The
" demon " announced his presence and demanded to be
adored like a god. As soon as his wishes had been deferred
to, he once more disappeared. During several months the
demon reappeared from time to time and promised to cure
the mental affections. Know remarks that " over many maladies he was not master and only appeared able to cure those
which were caused by spirits." When the sick man was
converted to Christianity the demon vanished, saying, " That
is no place for me."

In several of the cases of possession described the spirit
claims to be identical with that of a dead man. In other
cases, however, as in Japan, he gives himself out as one of
the lower animals, such as a fox.

According to Nevius, Chinese states of possession fall into
three groups according to symptoms: (1) The automatic,
continuous and consistent action of a new personality which
calls itself *shieng* (spirit) and designates the sick man as *hiang
to* (incense-burner, medium); (2) the possession of knowledge and intellectual capacities which the sick man does not
command in his normal state and which cannot be explained
by pathological hypotheses; (3) a complete change in the
moral character of the sick man.

As with one single exception Nevius is obliged to rely on
outside evidence, his statements taken singly are naturally
not of great weight, but in any case he makes it quite plain
that the states known as trance are very frequent in the part
of China where he worked, far more so than in present-day
European civilization.

Nevius' work is supplemented in a remarkable manner by an older narrative. In 1862 a French missionary, Monseigneur Anouilh, wrote in a letter:

> Would you believe it? The villages have been converted! The devil is furious and is playing all sorts of tricks. During the fortnight's preaching which I have just completed there have been five or six cases of possession. Our catechumens with holy water drive out the devils and cure the sick. I have seen some marvellous things. The devil is a great help to me in converting the heathen; as in the time of Our Lord, although the Father of Lies he cannot help speaking the truth. For instance, one poor possessed man executed innumerable contortions and shrieked aloud: " Why dost thou preach the true religion ? I cannot bear to have my disciples taken away by thee." " What is thy name ?" asked the catechist. After some refusals, " I am the envoy of Lucifer." " How many are you ?" " We are twenty-two." Holy water and the sign of the cross delivered this demoniac.[1]

This passage reflects a feeling of triumph such as is only paralleled by the early Christian exorcists still struggling with pagan antiquity.

The same may be said of an eminent English woman missionary in China, Mrs. Howard Taylor, née Geraldine Guiness, whose book *In the Far East* had already enthralled me when I was at school and which I unexpectedly found many years afterwards in the literature of this subject. In the biography of a follower of Confucius converted to Christianity, Pastor Hsi, she gives an account of several cases of possession. It is evident from her statements that, at least in the parts of China known to her, it must be very frequent. The most important of her accounts are the following:

> Always receptive and intelligent, she (Pastor Hsi's wife) had grasped the truth with clearness. Her life had brightened and her heart enlarged, until it seemed as though she would become her husband's real fellow-worker and friend.
>
> Then suddenly all was changed; and her very nature seemed changed too. At first only moody and restless, she rapidly fell a prey to deep depression, alternating with painful excitement. Soon she could scarcely eat or sleep, and household duties were neglected. In spite of herself, and against her own will, she was tormented by constant suggestions of evil, while a horror as of some dread nightmare seemed to possess her. She was not ill in body, and certainly not deranged in mind. But try as she might to control her thoughts and actions, she seemed under the sway of some evil power against which resistance was of no avail.
>
> Especially when the time came for daily worship, she was thrown into paroxysms of ungovernable rage. This distressed and amazed

---

[1] Gaume, *L'eau bénite au XIXme siècle*, 3rd edit., Paris, 1866.

her as much as her husband, and at first she sought to restrain the violent antipathy she did not wish to feel. But little by little her will ceased to exert any power. She seemed carried quite out of herself, and in the seizures, which became frequent, would use language more terrible than anything she could ever have heard in her life. Sometimes she would rush into the room, like one insane, and violently break up the proceedings, or would fall insensible on the floor, writhing in convulsions that resembled epilepsy.

Recognizing these and other symptoms only too well, the excited neighbours gathered round, crying:

" Did not we say so from the beginning ! It is a doctrine of devils, and now the evil spirits have come upon her. Certainly he is reaping his reward."

The swing of the pendulum was complete, and in his trouble Hsi found no sympathy. There was not a man or woman in the village but believed that his wife was possessed by evil spirits, as a judgement upon his sin against the gods.

" A famous ' Conqueror of Demons,' " they cried. " Let us see what his faith can do now."

And for a time it seemed as though that faith could do nothing. This was the bitterest surprise of all. Local doctors were powerless, and all the treatment he could think of unavailing. But prayer; surely prayer would bring relief ? Yet pray as he might the poor sufferer only grew worse. Exhausted by the violence of more frequent paroxysms, the strain began to tell seriously, and all her strength seemed ebbing away.

Then Hsi cast himself afresh on God. This trouble, whatever it was, came from the great enemy of souls, and must yield to the power of Jesus. He called for a fast of three days and nights in his household, and gave himself to prayer. Weak in body, but strong in faith, he laid hold on the promises of God, and claimed complete deliverance. Then without hesitation he went to his distressed wife, and laying his hands upon her, in the name of Jesus, commanded the evil spirits to depart and torment her no more.

Then and there the change was wrought. To the astonishment of all except her husband, Mrs. Hsi was immediately delivered. Weak as she was, she realized that the trouble was conquered. And very soon the neighbourhood realized it too.

For the completeness of the cure was proved by after events. Mrs. Hsi never again suffered in this way. And so profoundly was she impressed, that she forthwith declared herself a Christian and one with her husband in his life-work.

The effect upon the villagers was startling. Familiar as they were with cases of alleged demon-possession more or less terrible in character, the people had never seen or heard of a cure, and never expected to. What could one do against malicious spirits ? Yet here, before their eyes, was proof of a power mightier than the strong man armed. It seemed little less than a miracle.[1]

Another case reported by Mrs. Taylor is one of the rare ones which ended in death:

To the head doctor (in the hospital of the provincial capital T'ai-yüan where Hsi sometimes found himself) was brought one

---

[1] Mrs. Howard Taylor, *One of China's Christians*, London, 1903, pp. 14-16.

day a young woman . . . suffering from what her husband described as " an evil spirit." The doctor went into the matter carefully, but could find no physical explanation of the distressing symptoms. She seemed wholly given up to evil; and the violence of the paroxysms into which she was thrown was so great that life itself was imperilled.

After prescribing what he hoped might help her, the doctor . . . suggested that Hsi . . . should be invited to visit their home.

* * * * *

There was no mistaking the excitement and confusion that prevailed on their arrival. The girl was in one of her terrible seizures, and had to be held down by half a dozen neighbours to prevent injury to herself and those around her. Calling the family together, Hsi briefly explained that he, like themselves, could do nothing, but that the God he worshipped was the living God, who could perfectly heal and deliver.

* * * * *

After public prayer for God's blessing, Hsi was taken to the room from which the cries and confusion proceeded. Immediately he entered, there was a lull. The girl saw him, ceased struggling, and in a quiet, respectful way asked him to take a seat.

Astonished, the onlookers cried at once that the spirits had left her.

" No," answered Hsi, who could tell from her eyes that something was wrong, " she is as yet no better. The devil is merely trying to deceive us."

The girl was still friendly, and tried to make the polite remarks usually addressed to strangers; but Hsi went over, and laying his hands on her head, simply and earnestly prayed in the name of Jesus, and commanded the evil spirits at once to come out of her.

Suddenly, while he was still praying, she sprang to her feet with a terrible cry, rushed out into the courtyard, and fell to the ground unconscious and to all appearances dying.

" Alas ! she is dead. You have killed her now !" cried the startled friends.

But Hsi quietly raised her. " Do not be alarmed," he said. " The spirits are gone. She will soon be all right."

Recovering in a little while from what seemed a heavy swoon, the young woman came to herself, and was soon restored to a perfectly normal condition.

For some time the husband, full of gratitude, attended the services at the mission chapel and made a half-hearted profession of Christianity; but sad to say it was not the real thing with him or any of the family. As long as Hsi remained he went now and again to see him, carrying some little present to express indebtedness and thanks.

At last one morning he returned from such a visit bringing with him a packet of confectionery that was meant for Hsi.

" Why have you brought back the present ?" cried his wife as he entered the courtyard.

" The scholar has left the city," he replied, " and is on his way home to the south of the province."

Scarcely were the words spoken when the poor girl relapsed into the old condition. In the midst of most terrible convulsions, foul language and blasphemies streamed from her lips. She seemed possessed by a more fearful power of evil than before.

" He is gone; he is gone !" she cried. " Now I fear no one. Let

them bring their Jesus. I defy them all. They will never drive us out again, never."
This continued for a few terrible days, until exhausted by the strain, she died.[1]

Animal possession occurs quite frequently in China. Von der Goltz relates:

> In the organ of the Protestant missionaries in China, the *Chinese Recorder*, the Rev. G. Owen published in 1887 several interesting articles on the "five great families" from which the following summary is taken. In the North of China it is generally believed that many animals possess the secret of immortality. In order to attain immortality they must acquire experience for eighty years, and if they continue still further they may enter into men and render them possessed. The persons in question, mostly women, completely lose their individuality and become the mere tools of the possessing animals. If, for example, it is a fox, the possessed woman gives up her own name to take that of the fox-spirits,[2] and also adopts the habits of foxes. Possession by monkeys is also known; the persons so bewitched have a predilection for liquor. Mr. Owen knew a young person of good family who was possessed by a monkey. She called herself Housan, Monkey III, and was able during her possession to drink endless quantities of liquor without showing the least sign of drunkenness. The possessed remain either for a short time, one or two years, or else their whole lifetime in that state. For the most part they have no bodily derangements, but if the possession is an act of vengeance on the part of the animal the victim feels terrible pains against which all remedies are powerless. They have acquired the gift of second sight and often do a good business with soothsaying. Others have power to cure the sick and in many cases carry on a lucrative medical practice. It is not generally necessary for them to see their patients or to be told their sickness; they fall into a half-sleep or are seized by an ecstasy in which they see everything and prescribe the necessary remedies. There are also a number of professional mediums who can be possessed at will.[3]

From China let us pass to Japan.

In Japan belief in spirits is also extraordinarily widespread, but it seems that, contrary to what might at first sight be supposed, the influence has come rather from the Malays than the Chinese. The belief in spirits and the literature which it has produced is so great that research suffers rather from superabundance than from lack of materials. A Japanese writer remarks that " the difficulty of collecting

[1] *Ibid.*, pp. 94-97.
[2] The Fox family consists of three divisions, at the head of which stand three brothers: Fox I, Fox II and Fox III.
[3] V. d. Goltz, *Zauberei- und Hexenkünste in China* (Mitteilungen der deutschen Gesellschaft für Natur- und Völkerkunde Ostasiens, vol. vii (1893-97), p. 22.

materials for an article about ghosts is that there are so many of them."[1]

Possession by a large number of animals is known. That produced by foxes is the most frequent, but there is also possession by cats, badgers, dogs, monkeys, and snakes, as well, of course, as by non-animal spirits. The various kinds of possession are not equally frequent in different parts of Japan; sometimes one, sometimes another predominates.[2]

Possession is so widespread in Japan that there is a religious sect, the Nichiren, which has made exorcism its particular task. Near Tokyo in the village of Nalayama is a famous temple of this sect where possessed persons of all kinds assemble in periodical retreats for the purpose of exorcism.[3]

We owe some detailed accounts of Japanese possession to an ex-professor of medicine at the University of Tokio who died some years ago, E. Bälz, who during a residence of many years in that country had opportunity for personal observation of a number of cases.[4] He declares them to be " of exactly the same character as those described in the Bible."[5] Although this phenomenon may be known throughout eastern Asia, it apparently does not arise in epidemic form. " In those parts possession is very widely disseminated in China, Japan and Korea. There are only isolated cases, infectiousness is slight, and the hysterical and erotic factor is in complete regression."[6] This absence of epidemics of possession would be, if generally confirmed, very interesting from the point of view of racial psychology; it would reveal a profound disparity between the suggestibility of various races, since extraordinarily dense populations like that of China, very conservative in intellectual matters, present all the conditions likely to foster psychic epidemics.

This low degree of suggestibility would be closely and very comprehensibly bound up with the further fact, of such great psychological importance, that in Mongol civilization ecstasy is practically non-existent and has never played an important part in the history of religion. In the language of Paulhan's

[1] *Encyclopædia of Religion and Ethics*, vol. iv, p. 608.
[2] *Ibid.*, p. 610.   [3] *Ibid.*, p. 612.
[4] E. Bälz, *Ueber Besessenheit* (Verhandl. d. Ges. deuts. Naturforscher und Aerzte, Conf., 78 [1906]), Leipzig, 1907.
[5] *Ibid.*, p. 120.   [6] *Ibid.*, p. 129.
15

characterology, these people belong to the " types produced by the predominance of systematic inhibition (masters of themselves, reflectives)."[1]

According to Bälz, Japanese possession is characterized by the fact that it is not produced by a human or demonic spirit but by an animal one. In eastern Asia various animals are accused of entering into man: the tiger, the cat, the dog, but especially the fox. This last was originally the symbol of a divinity, but supplanted it long since and became itself an object of veneration.[2]

From the psychological point of view this phenomenon, as we have already said, presents no fresh difficulty for our solution. The state is one of automatic and obsessive imaginary identification (*Einfühlung*) with animal personalities, a very naïf affair, for the animals are credited with intelligence and even with human speech.

> The duration of the malady differs widely from one case to another.
> Many foxes remain only for a day, play all sorts of malicious tricks, frighten their hosts and those around by their speech and actions, and then disappear. Others take up their abode and stay for years, making themselves felt from time to time and braving all the exorcisms and expulsions of priests or any other persons.[3]

In Indo-China it is the ox which, according to Marie,[4] takes the place of the fox; in Niam-Niam the boa-constrictor.

We reproduce below two cases observed by Bälz. In both the patient remains as a rule fully conscious, but in the first case this consciousness disappears during the more violent fits, so that it may serve at the same time as a good example of this phenomenon.

> I have several times had the opportunity of observing personally these cases of possession by foxes. I once had a possessed woman in my university clinic at Tokio for four weeks.
> She was forty-seven years old, strong, sad-looking, born of a well-to-do peasant family; she was in good physical health, had scarcely an hereditary blemish, and was not very intelligent. Eight years previously she had been with friends when someone related that a fox had been driven out of a woman in a village and was now seeking a new abode. People must be careful! This unfortunately stuck in the peasant-woman's mind and the same evening when the door was opened unexpectedly she felt a prick

---

[1] F. Paulhan, *Les caractères*, 2nd edit., Paris, 1902, pp. 23-31.
[2] Bälz, *loc. cit.*, p. 129.   [3] *Ibid.*
[4] Marie, *Bulletin de l'Institut général psychologique*, vol. vi (1906), p. 78.

in the left side of the chest. It was the fox. From that moment onwards she was possessed. In the beginning the sinister guest contented himself with occasional stirrings in her bosom, and mounting into her head criticized by her mouth her own thoughts and made mock of them. Little by little he grew bolder, mingled in all conversations, and abused those present. By night he led the poor woman a hellish life. She went to all the exorcists, for instance to the *hoiny*, that is to say wandering mendicant monks from the mountains (corresponding exactly to the *orpheotelestes*) who went about the country and specialized in the cure of possession. All in vain! The priests of other sects and pilgrims of all sorts of temples were equally impotent. While she told us, with tears in her eyes, about her sufferings, the fox announced himself. At first there appeared slight twitchings of the mouth and arm on the left side. As these became stronger she violently struck with her fist her left side which was already all swollen and red with similar blows, and said to me: "Ah, sir, here he is stirring again in my breast." Then a strange and incisive voice issued from her mouth: "Yes, it is true, I am there. Did you think, stupid goose, that you could stop me?" Thereupon the woman addressed herself to us: "Oh dear, gentlemen, forgive me, I cannot help it!"

Continuing to strike her breast and contract the left side of her face, she said to the fox: "Be quiet, brute! Are you not ashamed before these gentlemen?" The fox replied: "Ha, ha, ha! I ashamed? And why? I am as clever as these doctors. If I were ashamed it would be for having taken up my abode in such a stupid woman!" The woman threatened him, adjured him to be quiet, but after a short time he interrupted her and it was he alone who thought and spoke. The woman was now passive like an automaton, obviously no longer understanding what was said to her; it was the fox which answered maliciously instead. At the end of ten minutes the fox spoke in a more confused manner, the woman gradually came to herself and was soon back in her normal state. She remembered the first part of the fit and begged us with tears to forgive her for the outrageous conduct of the fox.

Similar fits came on from six to ten times a day or even more. They did not occur in sleep or else she awoke when one was imminent. I had her carried into a room with a glass wall so that I could observe her at any moment without her knowledge. Things always took the same course, only varying in degree of violence and in duration. When she was alone the fit still began with convulsions, the blows on the left breast and the colloquy between the mistress of the house and her guest. Any psychic excitement, such as the doctor's visit or a remonstrance from the clinic, paved the way for a fit.

In view of the woman's poor level of intelligence and the rest of her character, it was astonishing to see the cleverness of speech, the witty and ironic language, so unlike the patient's own, which the fox displayed. (He never tried to speak in foreign tongues.) Once when I entered the room with some students and was putting various questions to the fox, the latter suddenly cried out in his mocking way: "Look here, Professor. You might do something more intelligent than trying to entice me by your questions. Don't you know that I am really a gay young girl, although I live in this old frump? You should rather pay court to me (die Kur machen) properly. These young gentlemen over there (pointing to the students) don't seem to want anything of me, and moreover I am pleased with you. But I have had enough for to-day. Good-bye!" And he departed, while the room resounded with the laughter of the bystanders.

Once I gave a narcotic to the patient, and as might have been anticipated, the first unpleasant whiffs of chloroform sufficed to bring on a fit. The struggle of the two egos lasted until loss of consciousness supervened. But the fox had the last word, and when the patient came round it was he who spoke first complaining that he had been ill-treated.[1]

My efforts to effect a cure by verbal and other suggestion, by hypnosis, electric treatment, etc., were fruitless. The sick woman had passed through the hands of so many famous suggestionists, priests and exorcists of all kinds, that I in turn could do nothing in this direction. Her malady had taken the form of a regular periodic delusion[2] to which she sought gradually to accommodate herself. Between the fits she was in full possession of her senses, although timid. Her memory had not suffered essentially, and there were in general no signs of degenerescence.

It should be observed that the fox does not openly refuse to go, but attaches conditions to his departure. He desires, for instance, that certain food should be placed for him in such a place, and if this is promised leaves the body exactly at the stated time.[3]

We shall recall Bälz' case already cited (pp. 106 sq.) The facts related about possession by the *tengu* spirit are remarkable. In contrast to possession by other spirits, possession by him appears to have no trace of maleficent or diabolic character.

> When a man is obsessed by a *tengu*, he merely becomes preter-naturally learned or solemn, reading, writing, or fencing with a skill that would not be expected from him. Exorcism is of little importance. For possession by evil spirits, foxes, badgers, and the like, there are many forms of exorcism in vogue, the sect of Nichirin being especially noted for its labours in this kind of healing.[4]

It is evident from the general character and mutual consistency of these statements that we cannot explain them away as representing no more than that particular aptitude for harbouring a spirit by which the Greeks explained the gift of poetry as the inspiration of Apollo or a Muse. There must clearly be in the case under discussion a sudden and

[1] Same story in *Wiener klinische Wochenschrift*, 1907, pp. 982 sq.

[2] This expression does not seem to me happy. The phenomenon is not regular nor can we designate by the name of delusions the transition of these compulsions from semi- into complete somnambulism. This is contrary to the whole of current terminology and would also be inappropriate. The woman's belief in the possibility of possession and in her own affection by a demoniacal being is by no means a delusion. She only shares the ideas of her environment.

[3] Bälz in *Verhandlungen der Gesellschaft deutscher Naturforscher und Aerzte*, 78. Versammlung (1907), pp. 129 sq.

[4] A. Lloyd, *Encyclopædia of Religion and Ethics*, vol. iv, p. 612.

abnormal increase in certain capacities. Unfortunately the accounts are so laconic that it is impossible to gather a more precise idea of the real facts. I must, however, at least mention these peculiar statements so that someone else may perhaps elucidate the matter by local investigation. Possession is no more a new phenomenon in Japan than elsewhere; it is rather very old. The earliest case known to me dates back to the year 1565. It is to be found in Görres, who has taken it from a book by Delrio, *Disquisitiones Magicæ*, from whence it may in turn be traced to the stories of the missionaries.

At Bungo, in Japan, so the missionaries relate, a certain family had in 1565 already been possessed for a hundred years; the malady was handed down as hereditary from generation to generation. The father had spent all his fortune in attempts to placate the gods, but instead of ceasing the evil had rather increased. A son, aged thirty years, was possessed to such a point that he recognized neither father nor mother and took no food for fifteen days. At the end of this time a Father of the Society of Jesus came to see him and commanded him to say the name of the Archangel Michael. When this name was pronounced he was seized with a great trembling and his limbs were convulsed in a manner which alarmed the bystanders. But after he had invoked the Father, the Son, and the Holy Spirit he was suddenly delivered from the demon.

A few days later his sister was seized by the demon who spoke by her mouth. At certain moments when she had heard a sermon in the abbey, she wished to be converted to the Catholic faith; but if she drew near the font and made the sign of the cross, she fell to trembling and had violent convulsions. Joining her, the Father prayed earnestly; she herself strove to pronounce the name of Jesus and the Archangel; but her mouth only shut the more obstinately. At length she suddenly began to sing: " If we reject Xaca and Amida, no one is left to adore; there is nothing blameworthy in serving them nor others like them."

One day the Father was assisting in divine service in the presence of many Christians and of the possessed woman. At the end of the service he asked her how she was. " Never better !" replied she. But when he commanded her to say the name of St Michael she recommenced to tremble and grind her teeth. Thereupon the demon declared that he wished to come forth, but since he had now possessed the family for so many years he would leave it with regret. Once more commanded to pronounce the name, she replied that it was extremely difficult, then bursting into tears and bitter complaints she cried: " I do not know where to begin nor which way to turn !" The Christians then all fell to prayer and when that had lasted for some time the demon at length gave up his prey. Then she asked for a drink. When she was reminded to invoke Jesus and Mary, she pronounced the two names with such sweetness that those present thought they heard the voice of an angel.[1]

---

[1] J. v. Görres, *Die christliche Mystik*, Regensburg, 1842, vol. iv, part i, pp. 86 sq. from Delrio, *Disquisitiones magicæ*, i, vi, c. ii, p. 980.

The phenomena of possession are also very prevalent in present-day Egypt. They are met with in all classes of society except the intellectual middle classes; in so-called high society exorcisms and their variants count amongst the day's diversions. It is a very remarkable fact that possession in Egypt is not a survival of the old manifestations, but appears to have been introduced from Abyssinia a few decades ago; at least Lane, who in the nineteenth century studied conditions in Egypt very closely and described them with equal thoroughness, says nothing on this subject. According to Macdonald the *Zar* was still unknown there even in 1880.[1]

The general phenomena of possession in Egypt reveal no special peculiarity, and in fact bear a strong resemblance to those of the European Middle Ages. This is not true of the formulæ of exorcism known up to the present, which as compared with Christian exorcisms clearly attest a lower level of religious development. Like all the other procedure of Egyptian exorcism, they strongly recall the primitive rites of the same nature.

The most detailed description of the Egyptian *Zar* is found, according to Macdonald, in a book on harem life written by a lady (an Oriental ?) whom he styles Mme. Ruchdi Pacha.[2] This name is not to be found in bibliography. Probably the reference must be (although the name is spelt several times in the same way by Macdonald) to Rachid Pacha, a lady who, under the pseudonym of Richa Salina, published *Harems et musulmanes*, Lettres d'Egypte (Paris, 1902). Unfortunately I have not been able to procure this book, and it is for this reason that I give extracts from other accounts.

The orientalist Kahle was present in person at an exorcism about which he has really very little to tell, but he succeeded in taking a photograph. He met whole carriage-loads of sick persons returning from the ceremony—the best proof of the prevalence of the malady. There are in Cairo a series of sanctuaries where regular exorcism of the Zar is practised, and the well-to-do have it done at home. Exactly as in Christianity there are different forms of exorcism,

[1] E. W. Lane, *Manners and Customs of the Egyptians of To-day*, London, 1836. Dr. B. Macdonald, *Aspects of Islam*, New York, 1911, p. 332.

[2] *Ibid.*, pp. 330 sq.

complete and abbreviated, only in Egypt their length is a matter of money.

> The duration of the exercises varies. Where there are ample means the ceremony is apt to be prolonged, and not infrequently lasts three and even seven nights. On the last night the principal ceremony takes place. The *shêcha* (exorcist) and other onlookers pass the whole of this night in the patient's house and on the following morning accomplish the solemn sacrifice in which the exorcism reaches its crux. But as a general rule one night or at most two are considered sufficient; the ceremony begins in the evening and lasts until the following day. . . . The regular exorcisms of the Zar which take place in the sanctuaries are much simpler and last only a few hours.[1]

The Zar is not confined to Egypt, but is apparently to be found in the Near East. A more exact description of the Zar in Arabia, especially at Mecca, was given by Snouck Hurgronje thirty years ago, and in view of the stability of these states in the East his account might still apply. It appears from this document that the Zar at Mecca is frankly epidemic. Almost all the women are affected, but with a fairly mild form; for according to Snouck Hurgronje possession at Mecca has degenerated in an astonishing fashion and become a kind of pastime for the women. As the customary local exorcism conduces to satisfy woman's love of dress it is quite comprehensible that the desire to be stricken by the Zar should have become very general. But it is perhaps doubtful whether all that occurs can be considered as mere play-acting on the part of the women. Snouck Hurgronje seriously underrates the importance of autosuggestibility and does not observe that there are many cases where these phenomena are called forth by the will and then follow their course passively. He nevertheless conveys the definite impression that Zar-possession at Mecca involves no serious psychic suffering. According to Snouck Hurgronje men are " generally not troubled " by the Zar.[2]

Here is this author's account:

> Another genus of spirits which afford the women plenty of occupation are the Zar. The fight with the Zar displays at once the darkest and the happiest side of the Meccan women's life. . . . From infancy they hear so much talk of the Zar that any specific maladies which overtake them generally appear as the domination

---

[1] P. Kahle, *Zar Beschwörungen in Aegypten*, in the review *Der. Islam*, vol. ii, 1912, pp. 9 sq.

[2] Snouck Hurgronje, *Mekka*, The Hague, 1889, vol. ii, p. 125, note

of a Zar over the patient's will. Sometimes this domination declares itself in the fact that the woman is thrown to the ground at certain moments and remains there for hours with her whole body in convulsions. Sometimes she seems to suffer from a definite malady which now and then disappears suddenly leaving nothing but pallor and widely open eyes; sometimes the patient is wild and raging in her fits. Scientists, doctors and men in general, are always inclined to resort either to the pharmacopœia or to religious exorcism against diabolic power; the female relatives and friends, on the contrary, will hear of nothing but calling in an old woman accustomed to dealing with the Zar, a *shechah-ez-Zar*, and in the end they get the better of all resistance. . . .

The shechah does not question the patient herself, but the Zar who inhabits her body; it sometimes happens that the conversation takes place in the ordinary manner and is thus understood by everyone present; but frequently the questioners use the Zar language which no man can penetrate without the shechah's interpretation. At bottom the results of such conversations present little variety. On the reiterated injunction of the shechah the Zar declares himself ready to depart on a certain day with the usual ceremonies, if in the interim certain stipulations have been fulfilled. He demands a new and beautiful garment, gold or silver trinkets, etc. As he himself is hidden from all human perception, nothing can be done except carry out his wish and make gifts of the specified objects to the sick body which he inhabits; it is touching to see how these evil spirits take into account the age, tastes and needs of the possessed. On the day when the departure is to take place the patient's women friends, invited for the purpose, come in the afternoon or evening and are offered coffee or sometimes a concert of flutes. The shechah and the slaves who are to accompany her in her operations with the drum and a sort of chant, are entertained with them and prepare for the work in hand. . . .

The patient puts on the clothing demanded by the Zar; the slaves of the shechah drum a particular magic march which anyone with a little experience can immediately distinguish from other music. The shechah handles the body of the possessed according to the rules of her art, and all sorts of strange usages are added which render this pagan game still more shocking to pious men of learning; for example, a lamb is sacrificed and the forehead and other parts of the body of the. possessed are smeared with its blood. Each method of treatment has its prescribed external signs by which the breaking of the charm is evidenced: the possessed must dance, sway her body, or else faint and this is the moment when the muttering shechah declares that the Zar has departed. This sometimes happens only on the second or third night. . . .[1]

Particularly interesting is Snouck Hurgronje's declaration that the Zar appears not only amongst the Arabs of Mecca but also amongst persons of all nationalities residing in that city. That town contains subjects and even whole colonies of a very large number of Mohammedan peoples, the majority of whom have been induced to settle there for

[1] *Ibid.*, pp. 124-128.

religious reasons, particularly the desire to live in the immediate vicinity of the holy places; but also by such material
considerations as the hope of a lucrative existence. Amongst
all of these peoples manifestations of the Zar occur, indeed
they bring them in with them, so that the appearance of
these phenomena amongst numerous peoples through occurrence amongst their representatives at Mecca seems assured
at one blow.

> Zar appear amongst all the nations represented at Mecca, for
> although in their own countries they may bear other names, they
> soon adopt the one customary here. Nevertheless there subsist
> national differences which must also be taken into account in
> treatment. There are, for example, exorcisms of the Zar in the
> Maghrib,[1] Soudanese, Abyssinian, and Turkish manner which can
> only be employed in specific cases; but it cannot be gainsaid that
> verification of the Zar's nationality almost always leads the she-
> chah who has been called in to the conclusion that her method
> has been the right one.[2]

According to Klunzinger also possession is not rare in any
part of the Mohammedan world. States of rapture or ecstasy
" are also attributed to the djinns, who suddenly make themselves master of a person, change his clothes or ride him and
speak and act through him." Klunzinger mentions later
certain dances or *zikr* which are continued to the point of
frenzy, but there is nothing in his description authorizing us
to regard them as possession. It must therefore remain
indeterminate whether these dances are really phenomena of
possession, whereas this can be positively affirmed of the Zar
which he also describes.

Here is the description of the Zar, or as he calls it, the Sar.
It is evident from his narrative that exorcism is rather the
cause of possession than a weapon used to combat it, and his
account vividly recalls certain cases of the Romantic period
which we have already met and where possession is first induced in the patient by the doctor's treatment.

> The " Sar," a certain djinn, is the potent genius of sickness
> and principally attacks women. Where a woman shows symptoms
> of any malady the causes of which are not as clear as daylight, it is
> the Sar who is to blame. . . . It is at once made known that to-

---

[1] Under the name of Maghrib countries the historians of Arabia
include the western parts of the Mohammedan world, that is to say
Northern Africa (with the exception of Egypt) and Spain. *Maghrib*
means *west* in Arabia.

[2] Snouck Hurgronje, *Mekka*, vol. ii, p. 125.

day the Sar is with such and such a one; but this must be on a Saturday, Tuesday or Thursday. A crowd of women and girls stream into the house of the patient and are offered *busa*, the half-fermented Arab beer, the favourite drink of the Abyssinians together with sheep's tripe. Then they sing, beat cymbals and dance the Sar-dance. The women in a squatting position or with legs bent under them sway their trunk and head backwards and forwards as in the zikr. Soon some of them become possessed and leap around dancing madly. All this is under the direction of the shechah of the Sar, who is a person known for her tendency to dance ecstatic dances; in most cases it is a female slave who earns large sums in this way. As soon as she and the others are in ecstasy, the somnambulist is questioned as to the means of curing the sickness. The remedy always consists in a plain silver finger-ring, thick, without stones, or more rarely in bracelets or anklets, and as soon as the greedy Sar is satisfied with this gift the malady disappears. Faith in success is so great that many sacrifice their last penny to obtain the silver ornament and meet the very considerable cost of entertaining the multitude of female guests.

Like the tarantella of the Middle Ages the Sar is infectious; one woman after another rises up in the Sar-gathering and is involuntarily gripped by the dance, boys and even men who are here and there admitted to these orgies being no exception. In many cases the features are altered, they strike their faces, bang their heads against the walls, weep, howl, try to strangle themselves and are restrained only with difficulty. They give themselves out as other persons, saints, and particularly the Sar itself. They are asked what they want, are shown a silver ring, henna-paste or busa. They cast a furious glance upon these objects, seize them suddenly with a wild grip, put on the ring, grasp the henna-paste in the fist, or drink the busa. This suffices as a rule to satisfy and quiet the Sar; the possessed wipes the sweat from her and now talks composedly and reasonably as before. On a day fixed by the Sar the fit is often renewed and ends like the first with the satisfaction of an often strange wish.

These states are not mere simulation, as may be clearly seen; for otherwise why should the possessed wound themselves, often dangerously ? It is acute delirium or ecstasy. The spiritualist calls these persons " mediums," the believer in animal magnetism calls them " magnetized."[1]

The Zar derives, as we have already observed, from Abyssinia. As early as 1868 the English traveller Plowden speaks as follows of those possessed by the Zar.

These Zars are spirits or devils of a somewhat humorous turn, who, taking possession of their victim, cause him to perform the most curious antics, and sometimes become visible to him while they are so to no one else—somewhat I fancy after the fashion of the " Erl King." The favourite remedies are amulets and severe tom-toming, and screeching without cessation, till the possessed,

---

[1] B. Klunzinger, *Bilder aus Oberägypten, der Wüste und dem roten Meere*, Stuttgart, 1877, pp. 388 sq. An excellent work of great literary charm giving a clear idea of these countries and their natural features.

doubtless distracted with the noise, rushes violently out of the house, pelted and beaten, and driven to the nearest brook, where the Zar quits him, and he becomes well.[1]

To rationalist objections that there are no Zar spirits the Abyssinian Christians reply, exactly like the orthodox European Christians, that there were possessed persons in the time of Jesus and that they still exist in their country, even if these supernatural phenomena no longer occur in Europe.

M. J. de Goeje refers to the narrative of a French traveller, J. Borelli, who writes:

> To all their superstitions the Abyssinians add a particular fear of evil spirits, especially " Bouddha " and " Zarr."
>
> The person who proclaims himself possessed rises in the middle of the night, rolls upon the ground and utters inarticulate cries. After one or two hours of contortions he is exhausted and remains lying as if inanimate. The most efficacious remedy then consists in taking a hen and swinging it round the head of the possessed, subsequently throwing it upon the ground. If the hen dies at once or soon afterwards it is a good omen; the Zarr or Bouddha has passed into the body of the fowl and caused it to perish. If the hen survives this ill-treatment it is clear that the demon has resisted and has remained in the patient's body; another attempt must be made.
>
> The Zarr has numerous followers, and in certain localities is the object of a sort of worship. He has incarnations, and various forms and names. In the neighbourhood of Ankoboer the evil spirit, for reasons quite unknown to me, is designated by the name of " Waïzero Encolal," that is to say literally " Miss Egg." At certain periods of the year the initiates of the Zarr unite and shut themselves up for three days and nights, indulging in practices as mysterious as they are grotesque. In these assemblies the Zarr does not fail to appear to his pious votaries.[2]

It is regrettable that the accounts in my possession do not permit of an assured judgement as to the relationship of this Zar-possession to the facts reported by Tremearne. Are they essentially the same phenomena, or else manifestations of possession which, as such, show some natural psychological resemblance, but without genetic or ethnological connection ?

[1] W. C. Plowden, *Travels in Abessinia and the Galla Country*, with an account of a mission to Ress Ali in 1848, London, 1868, p. 259. Cf. also pp. 264 sq.

[2] J. Borelli, *Ethiopie méridionale*, Paris, 1890, p. 133.

CHAPTER VII

ARTIFICIAL AND VOLUNTARY POSSESSION AMONGST PRIMITIVE PEOPLES. SO-CALLED SHAMANISM

A general survey of the whole body of known cases of possession shows that, in addition to the two principal forms, somnambulistic and lucid, it falls into other important divisions, since, while many cases are characterized by extraordinary excitement and even fury, others are comparatively quiet. The first have made by far the more stir, and we too have given them our principal attention. But they are not the only ones; there are also more tranquil states, several of which we have learnt to know, and which are also rightly styled "possession," inasmuch as to the casual and unscientific observer they seem to consist in the domination of the individual by a strange, intruding soul. This soul is either that of a demon, of a dead (or quite exceptionally a living) man, or in some cases of a beast.

From the standpoint of the history of religion the somewhat calmer cases of possession are of much greater importance than the violent ones. That is to say, they are often not simply endured, however and wherever they may chance to occur, but are or were systematically provoked over wide stretches of the habitable globe. Such deliberately produced states of possession are now designated as Shamanism—we shall see with what degree of justification.

To primitive people the possessed stand as intermediaries between the world of men and the spirit-world; the spirits speak through their mouths. It is therefore no wonder that as soon as men realized that states of this kind could be voluntarily induced, free use was made of the fact.

The accounts of ethnologists show beyond a doubt that the *psyche* of primitive peoples is much less firmly seated than that of civilized ones. In my *Einführung in die Religions-*

psychologie,[1] I have already mentioned in this connection a narrative by Thurnwald.[2] I shall again reproduce it here because of its importance in the present connection:

> As an example (of the case with which autosuggestion can change the personal consciousness amongst primitive people) I might relate how one young man mocks another by saying "I *am* so-and-so," not "I am *like* so-and-so." An incident which occurred showed me how far such an identification may go. At Buin my landlord Ungi lay stretched out one day looking deeply agitated on a great wooden cask in the chiefs' room which I had rented. When I asked what was the matter, he told me that he was ill. Questioning him further I learnt that often, without more precise localization, he was " ill all over." I gave, as usual when I could not gather anything specific, aloe pills. On the following day he still lay there. Then my servants told me that Ungi was ill because his wife was ill. By further questioning I learnt that she had a bad wound; so I now gave Ungi bandages and sent the man home to his wife with them. After a few days he was well, for his wife had recovered. This is a case of identification with the sufferings of another person, of physiological sympathy.

This narrative shows how unstable is primitive personality, how easily it succumbs to autosuggestion, which never exercises the same kind of influence on civilized man.

The following episode may also serve as an example of primitive autosuggestibility. Bastian relates of Siam:

> When the growers sieve the rice (*Kadong fat*) they like to amuse themselves by letting a young person who does not yet understand the cleansing of the rice through the hand-sieve (*Kadong*) take part. Before they give the hand-sieve over to the boy or girl they secretly call the female demon (*Phi*) of the sieve to enter into it, and she then works upon it so powerfully that the holder of the sieve twists his body into the most strange and wonderful positions, always swaying in measure with the others the while, which causes the greatest amusement and merriment. Those who have often taken part in the rice-sieving cannot be infected by the demon, for they keep their movements too much under voluntary control for this influence to act upon them.[3]

It must, moreover, be admitted that civilized people show a high degree of autosuggestibility in certain circumstances. By way of example we may quote the peculiar psychic intoxication to which in certain places (*e.g.*, Munich and Cologne) a large part of the population falls victim on a given day of the year (Carnival).

[1] Berlin, 1917.
[2] R. Thurnwald, *Ethnologische Studien an Südseevölkern*, Leipzig, 1913, p. 103.
[3] A. Bastian, *Die Völker des östlichen Asien*, vol. iii, Berlin, 1867, p. 28.

Abnormal suggestibility characterizes the following cases cited by Bastian as examples of the imitative instinct:

> In Tunis a maidservant was present when someone clapped. Actuated by the spirit of imitation, she threw away the carafe she was carrying in order to do the same. When she saw dancers she joined in with them.[1]
>
> In an hysterical affection (in Siam) which is also known in Burmah and is there called *yaun*, the sufferers involuntarily imitate all the movements which they see made by other people. If anyone raises an arm or scratches himself they do the same. An old woman carrying a jar of oil passed behind an ox; as the latter began to urinate the old woman took the jar and poured the oil out in a similar stream.[2]

There are even examples of the most extreme degree of autosuggestion, autosuggestive suicide. The English observer Mariner, who gives an impression of particular trustworthiness, has already communicated a case of this kind from the Tonga Islands:

> These imaginations, however, have sometimes produced very serious consequences; to give an instance: on one occasion a certain chief, a very handsome young man, became inspired but did not yet know by whom; on a sudden he felt himself very low-spirited, and shortly afterwards swooned away; when recovered from this, still finding himself very ill, he was taken to the house of a priest, who told the sick chief that it was a woman, mentioning her name, who had died two years before, and was now in Bolotoo (paradise) that had inspired him; that she was deeply in love with him, and wished him to die (which event was to happen in a few days) that she might have him near her: the chief replied that he had seen the figure of a female two or three successive nights in his sleep, and had begun to suspect that he was inspired by her, though he could not tell who she was. He died two days afterwards. Mr. Mariner visited the sick chief three or four times, at the house of the priest, and heard the latter foretell his death and the occasion of it.[3]

We should certainly consider this story incredible were there not other similar accounts of death by autosuggestion.[4] In this connection our first thought is of the old stories such as that of Ananias and Sapphira in the Acts. A case has also come down to us from the fifteenth century. These would in themselves hardly furnish sufficient basis for a considered judgement, but there are more recent accounts of the same kind which put the matter beyond all doubt. We are indebted to Klaatsch for bringing them to light.

---

[1] *Ibid.*, p. 288.   [2] *Ibid.*, p. 295.
[3] W. Mariner, *An Account of the Natives of the Tonga Islands*, ed. J. Martin, London, 1817.
[4] Unhappily, I have not been able to obtain access to the whole of this literature.

This is what he says concerning the belief of the Australian aborigines that both the living and the dead can effect this strange form of death from a distance:

> Ability to exercise influence at a distance naturally varies, like the exhibition of strength in hand-to-hand fighting. There are men who are particularly feared by reason of their dangerous powers. These are wizards. . . .
> The strength of the belief in long-distance influence is attested by the " death-madness," " thanatomania," as Roth aptly calls it, found amongst the Australians. If a savage believes himself struck from afar, he lies down and slowly dies in consequence of the psychic affection. There is only one remedy, that is the counteracting of the influence by another wizard of the same kind.[1]

In another place Klaatsch continues:

> This singular phenomenon (thanatomania) has been unanimously established by observers studying the life and customs of the aborigines in the most various regions of Australia. As regards the South where the race is already partly extinct and partly degenerate, we have the accounts of missionaries and of the oldest colonists.
> For the Adelaide district we have the careful observations of the Rev. G. Taplin, a missionary of Point McLeay.[2] For Southern Queensland the excellent memoirs of Tom Petrie furnish a rich fund of information. This latter arrived in 1837 as a child at the place where Brisbane stands to-day, and established very friendly relations with the aborigines who have now completely disappeared.[3] These old accounts confirm the new. . . .
> Not only the living but also the spirits of the dead may exert influence to cause death from a distance.[4]

Unfortunately, I have not so far been able to procure the original narratives to which Klaatsch refers.

These accounts are also entirely confirmed by Eylmann, who has made a prolonged sojourn in South Australia and lived with the people as one of themselves.[5]

Analogous cases are also known in northern Asia. A modern Russian investigator relates of the people of the Orotcha:

> Once upon a time a man of Orotcha was returning home at night by moonlight and the country was everywhere covered with a thick

[1] H. Klaatsch, *Die Anfänge von Kunst und Religion in der Urmenschheit,* Leipzig, 1913, p. 45.
[2] G. Taplin, *The Narrinyeri, an Account of the Tribes of South Australian Aborigines,* Adelaide, 1878.
[3] T. Petrie, *Reminiscences of Early Queensland, recorded by his Daughter* (dating from 1837), Brisbane, 1904.
[4] H. Klaatsch, *Die Todes-Psychologie der Uraustralier in ihrer volks- und religionsgeschichtlichen Bedeutung,* in Festschrift zur Jahrhundertfeier der Universität Breslau, Breslau, 1911, pp. 405 sq.
[5] E. Eylmann, *Die Eingeborenen der Kolonie Südaustralien,* Berlin, 1908.

mantle of snow. Suddenly he saw one of his souls jump aside and run off (it is generally believed in Siberia that man has several souls and these are conceived as very material). It had gone. Seized with mortal fear he hurried home as fast as possible, and once arrived took to his bed with high fever and remained there for two days and nights until the shaman was fetched. This latter shamanized, caught the fugitive soul and reinstated it in the man's body at the end of operations lasting for almost six hours, whereupon the patient arose on the following morning completely cured.

Other cases might also be cited.[1]

Given their high degree of autosuggestibility, it is not surprising that primitive races are very prone to mental derangements of an autosuggestive character. The number of mental troubles cured by all sorts of magic procedure is quite astonishing, and all these must, of course, be purely autosuggestive. Unhappily we are not yet in a position to say whether they are simply hysterical; this can only be suggested when the complaint is not merely a psychic malady of autosuggestive origin, but shows the typical complex of symptoms. Autosuggestive derangement alone would not seem to me adequate to justify the diagnosis of hysteria, which would only be legitimate in the presence of other symptoms. We are faced with exactly the same problem as arose earlier in respect of epidemics of possession.

Judging by the available information, it is by no means certain that hysteria is always present. It rather appears that the matter is often simply one of a higher general and " normal " degree of suggestibility on the part of primitive peoples, or at least many of their number. Their general psychological resemblance to the child-mind is here manifested, and just as no class of schoolchildren attacked by an epidemic of trembling should without further ado be roundly designated as hysterical, the same holds good of primitive people. Both children and savages show a greater degree of suggestibility than do normal adults without this constituting hysteria properly so called.

It is high time that suggestibility and autosuggestibility amongst primitive races were studied more narrowly. The

---

[1] Detailed information as to sources will be found in G. Tschubinow, *Beiträge zum psychologischen Verstandnis des sibirischen Zauberers*, Dissertation, Halle, 1914, p. 17.

question is of general importance from the standpoint of racial psychology and ethnology.

As regards possession, the autosuggestibility of primitive races makes itself felt in the marked frequency with which states of this nature are deliberately provoked. As soon as they are expected by the person concerned they obviously come on with great readiness.

This artificially provoked possession amongst primitive peoples raises a number of psychological problems, combining as it does in a remarkable way deliberate play-acting with spontaneous psychic development. It should certainly not be supposed that the " artificially " possessed behave in all respects like persons under the influence of spontaneous possession. The close, or even the merely superficial observer, provided he troubles to think for a moment, at once perceives that they generally carry out a definite " programme." The details of what they do are fixed by custom. They first accomplish a certain sacrifice after certain ceremonies, then they turn to certain persons and speak to them likewise in a sense which is in the main predictable. All this shows that their conduct is largely " studied "; projects conceived in the normal waking state produce their effect in trance. A casual observer might perhaps immediately conclude that we are not dealing with cases of possession at all, but merely with fraud. Such a conception cannot, however, be defended, the very numerous accounts placing beyond dubiety that the states of the shamans are generally not fraudulent but entirely abnormal in character, a fact often confirmed by the abnormal physiological state. We have therefore no option but to admit the existence of an abnormal state, the phenomena of which are nevertheless often determined by the anterior waking consciousness. Moreover in somnambulistic states the ordinary psychic life is by no means entirely blotted out, speech and its comprehension, as well as a number of cognitions and memories from the waking state, being as a rule perfectly preserved. If the normal psychic life had completely disappeared, a man on falling into a somnambulistic state would be like a new-born child.

The second surprising phenomenon is that with many races possession is preluded by sudden collapse. It is certain that this is intimately associated with the profound modi-

16

fication occurring in the psychic structure, but unfortunately we are not for the moment in a position to say more on the subject; far too little is known of psycho-physical relations.

Artificial possession by animals is also known, the masked dances of primitive peoples often furnishing occasion for it. The participants generally represent various animals, from which they are not as a rule clearly distinguished by the spectators, but are rather regarded as identical with them. In the eyes of the onlookers they do not represent the animals, they *are* the animals. But the dancers are, at least for a time, not only one with the animals in the eyes of the by-standers, but also in their own, they identify themselves with them. The question before us is to know the nature of this change of personal consciousness. Is it purely intellectual— that is to say, does the dancer merely think himself identical with the particular animal, or does his personality really suffer a profound change ? Only in the second case could we speak of possession.

What are the real facts of the matter ?

Unfortunately no fully satisfactory answer can be given, as information is deficient on a number of points. There are innumerable accounts of the manner in which the dances are executed, in what order, with what figures, how many dancers, etc., and much has also been written concerning the masks worn by the dancers, with which moreover the ethnological museums are filled. On the other hand, ethnologists have almost always neglected to obtain information about the psychological state of the dancers during the performance. It is only from meagre and casual remarks that the student can occasionally draw inferences on this subject, and even then without any conviction of standing on firm ground, since the ethnologists themselves have paid no attention to the points under discussion. In this connection we must once more deprecate the fact that ethnology confines itself to somewhat superficial aspects and lacks the deeper questioning spirit of psychology.

For my own part I presume that the original state of things is possession, but that later the dances have in many cases been transformed into simple representations. Frazer[1] is obviously right, moreover, in seeking in these ritual dances

[1] J. G. Frazer, *The Golden Bough*, vol. vi, London, 1913.

the origins of the drama. Between true possession and mere studied participation in rehearsed performances of a stereotyped nature there are of course innumerable stages, just as amongst modern actors the psychic state differs widely in individual cases; in many it approaches possession, in others performance is completely detached and apparently the outcome of intellectual calculation.

There can be no question of an exhaustive treatment of voluntary possession in the following pages. I shall give and elucidate material accumulated with the passing years, and even quote documents *in extenso*, as no one can be expected to investigate the widely scattered evidence on the spot, and such a collection is as yet nowhere available. This evidence, in spite of its fragmentary nature, will permit us to form a clear conception of the part which may be played by the phenomena of possession. The nature of the states themselves is not everywhere alike, depending as it does entirely on the autosuggestive expectation of the possessed.

I shall begin with the primitive peoples, the pigmies, amongst whom a kind of Shamanism is found concerning which the available information is unfortunately still scanty in the extreme.

Martin has collected the accounts of Shamanism amongst the pigmy races of the interior of the Malay Peninsula.[1] The shamans are there designated by the name of *poyangs.*

" The dignity of poyang is generally hereditary, that is to say that supernatural gifts are transmitted from father to son."[2] But this is not a simple, I might say legal, transmission of office; inspiration is necessary before any man can become a poyang. In other words, only an outstandingly autosuggestible individual can become a shaman; those not possessed of this quality to a sufficient degree are excluded from the beginning.

An investigator of the first half of the nineteenth century, T. J. Newbold, describes the consecration in detail as follows. Underlying the proceedings is the idea that the soul of the dead shaman has passed into a tiger and that this latter appears to his descendants.

---

[1] R. Martin, *Die Inlandstämme der malayischen Halbinsel*, Jena, 1905.

[2] *Ibid.*, p. 959.

The corpse of the Poyang is placed erect against the projection near the root of a large tree in the depth of a forest, and carefully watched and supplied with rice and water for seven days and nights by the friends and relatives. During this period the transmigration (believed to be the result of an ancient compact made in olden times by the Poyang's ancestors with a tiger) is imagined to be in active operation. On the seventh day, it is incumbent on the deceased Poyang's son, should he be desirous of exercising similar supernatural powers, to take a censer and incense of Kamunian wood, and to watch near the corpse alone; when the deceased will shortly appear in the form of a tiger on the point of making the fatal spring upon him. At this crisis it is necessary not to betray the slightest symptom of alarm, but to cast with a bold heart and firm hand the incense on the fire; the seeming tiger will then disappear. The spectres of two beautiful women will next present themselves, and the novice will be cast into a deep trance, during which the initiation is presumed to be perfected. These aerial ladies thenceforward become his familiar spirits, " the slaves of the ring," by whose invisible agency the secrets of nature, the hidden treasures of the earth are unfolded to him. Should the heir of the Poyang omit to observe this ceremonial, the spirit of the deceased, it is believed, will re-enter for ever the body of the tiger, and the mantle of enchantment be irrevocably lost to the tribe.[1]

The soul of the dead man is only provisionally incarnated in the tiger, and when the inspiration has been successfully accomplished it passes from thence into the new shaman.

In other cases an innate and unusual gift may confer the right and possibility of rising to be poyang of a community, or else instruction by a known and tried poyang confers a title to the exercise of the office.[2]

For the purpose of exorcising the sick, the poyang enters voluntarily into an abnormal condition.

The exorcisms take place at night: fire, incense, and various herbs and roots possessed of marvellous properties are used. The *besawye* or ceremony of exorcism consists in the burning of incense and muttering at midnight of magic formulæ over the herbs, the most important of these being Palas, Subong, Krong, Lebbar, and Bertram, and finally in conjuring the spirit of the mountains. If the operation is successful the spirit descends, plunges the exorcist into a state of unconsciousness (possession), in which he imparts to him what the latter desires to know.[3]

This ceremony resembles in many respects the one in use amongst the Malays, and the methods adopted, the burning of incense, dancing, music and noise are the same as we encounter everywhere in Shamanism. The essence of the whole procedure is that through the incense, dancing, etc., and through autosuggestion the pawang falls into an unconscious state in which he is able not only to drive out spirits but reply to any questions put to him. The loss of

---

[1] T. J. Newbold, *Political and Statistical Account of the British Settlements in the Straits of Malacca*, London, 1839, vol. ii, p. 388.
[2] According to Martin himself, p. 960.   [3] *Ibid.*, p. 961.

consciousness is considered as possession and consequently the replies are not those of the pawang but of the spirit who has entered into him and now speaks by his mouth.[1]

These descriptions are naturally very far from clear and show *how necessary it is for ethnologists to possess a more thorough knowledge of psychology.* There can be no question of loss of consciousness. From the first description one would be inclined to postulate a sort of state in which the shamans lose all contact with the outer world; according to the second, on the other hand, there appears to be a certain mutual intercourse with the bystanders, since questions are put to the shaman and he replies. A further contradiction is that in the first description we are apparently dealing with auditions on the part of the shaman, the spirit imparting communications to him, whereas according to the second there is veritable possession. Naturally the two cannot co-exist, but the shaman might sometimes have mere visions and auditions and sometimes fall into a state of possession. The expression " loss of consciousness " must simply mean that the individual concerned is not " known to himself " but that he has become somnambulistic, and that the normal individuality is apparently replaced by that of the invading spirit.

As we have already remarked, voluntary possession includes many cases of the animal variety. Martin relates of the pigmies of the Malay Peninsula:

> . . . Bound up with these ideas is also another that wizards are able to change themselves into various animals and in this new form to harm their fellow-men, even devouring their flesh. The most celebrated and also the most frequent is self-metamorphosis into a raging tiger; this has numerous analogies in different parts of the world and beyond all doubt rests on autosuggestion. Skeat and Laidlaw obtained from a B'lian at Ulu Aring the following description of the procedure requisite to the achievement of this metamorphosis:
> " You go," he said, " a long way into the jungle " (usually, he added, into the next valley), " and there, when you are quite alone, you squat down upon your haunches, burn incense, and making a trumpet of your hand blow some of the smoke of the incense through it, at the level of your face, in three directions. You then repeat this process, holding your hand close to the ground; all you now have to say is, ' Yĕ chop ' (' I am going abroad '), and presently your skin will change, the stripes will appear, your tail will fall down, and you will become a tiger. When you wish to return say, ' Yĕ wet ' (' I am going home '), and you will presently return to your natural form."[2]

[1] *Ibid.*, p. 963.
[2] W. W. Skeat, *The Wild Tribes of the Malay Peninsula* (" Journal of the Anthropological Institute of Great Britain and Ireland "), London, vol. xxxii, p. 137.

In a rather more detailed description which Skeat has recently given[1] it is also stated that in squatting the B'lian leans forward, rests upon his hands and rapidly moves his head from right to left. This exercise combined with the inhalation of the smoke is certainly not without influence on the production of autosuggestive ecstasy. Moreover, the whole of this procedure recalls that often used in exorcism of the sick, when the Malay pawang by the force of autosuggestion flings himself about and covers the body of the sick person in the manner of a tigress.[2] Here it is, of course, the tiger-hantu (hantu = spirit) which has passed into the pawang, not the wizard who changes himself into a tiger.[3]

Amongst many dwarf races possession seems to be generally non-existent. Thus I find in Ed. II. Man's account[4] of the pigmies of the Andamans, in other respects so interesting, no mention of analogous states. He merely remarks that in dreams certain individuals enter into relation with the spirit-world, but nothing indicates that spirits may speak by the mouth of a living man. We also read in M. V. Portman:

They have much faith in dreams, and in the utterances of certain " wise men " who, they think, are able to foretell the future and know what are the intentions of the Deity, and what is passing at a distance. Like all such " priesthoods " this superstition is used by the " wise men " to enhance their powers and comforts, and to obtain articles they wish for from others without any real compensation.[5]

This observation is too summary to warrant any conclusions as to the existence of possession.

The information concerning Shamanism amongst the pigmies as, indeed, all other aspects of their life, is extremely scanty. I must associate myself with the urgent request made from the standpoint of religious psychology by P. W. Schmidt that a rapid and thorough study of these small and fast-disappearing peoples should be undertaken before it be too late. Given their general position in the history of human evolution it is of the highest importance to acquire a more precise knowledge of their extraordinary states of religious excitement.

Closely allied to the pigmies are the Veddas of Ceylon,

[1] Same title, London, 1905, vol. ii, p. 228.
[2] Cf. Maxwell, *Shamanism*, 1883, p. 226, and Skeat, *Malay Magic*, 1900, p. 443.
[3] Martin, *loc. cit.*, p. 961.
[4] E. H. Man, *On the Aboriginal Inhabitants of the Andaman Islands*, London (1884 ?)
[5] M. V. Portman, *A History of our Relation with the Andamanese*, 2 vols., Calcutta, 1899.

concerning whose states of possession some very interesting information is available. The great work of the cousins Sarasin[1] which focussed upon them the attention of the German scientific world, contains nothing on this subject, but we are indebted to two English researchers named Seligmann for some very valuable accounts.[2] It emerges from these that the Veddas are very familiar with ritual possession, in which every one of their communities has a man trained to be a professional expert. This shaman falls into possession at the time of their ceremonial dances, thus making it possible to communicate with spirits, particularly the souls of the dead. But there is not only the professional shaman; other Veddas, especially the kinsfolk of those most recently dead, may become possessed, showing that the required autosuggestibility is not confined to certain individuals. Nevertheless, as we shall see, there are persons who are not susceptible to possession.

> In each community there is one man called *kapurale* or *dugga-nawa*, who has the power and knowledge requisite to call the *yaku*, and in the ceremony of presenting the offering called *Nae Yaku Natanawa* (literally the dancing of the *Nae Yaku*), this man calls upon the yaka of the recently dead man to come and take the offering. . . . The dugganawa becomes possessed by the yaku of the dead man who speaks through the mouth of the shaman in hoarse, guttural accents, declaring that he approves the offering, that he will assist his kinsfolk in hunting, and often stating the direction in which the next party should go.
>
> Each shaman trains his successor, usually taking as his pupil his own son or his sister's son (*i.e.*, his actual or potential son-in-law). Handuna of Sitala Wanniya learnt from his father. At Henebedda we were told that a special hut was built in which the shaman and his pupil slept, and from which women were excluded. It seems probable that this is only done among Veddas who have come under Sinhalese influence, as among them, but not among the wilder Veddas, women are considered unclean, and there was no isolation of the shaman and his pupil at Sitala Wanniya.
>
> Sella Wanniya of Unawatura Bubula was instructed by his father, and during his apprenticeship he resided with him in a hut into which his mother was not allowed to come.
>
> The pupil learns to repeat the invocations used at the various ceremonies, but no food is offered to the yaku. At Sitala Wanniya we were told that the shaman recited the following formula, explaining to the yaku that he is teaching his pupil: " May (your) life be long ! From to-day I am rearing a scholar of the mind. Do not take any offence at it. I am explaining to my pupil how to give this offering to you."

¹ P. and F. Sarasin, *Die Veddas*, in Ergebnisse naturw. Forschungen auf Ceylon in den Jahren, 1884-86, vol. iii, Wiesbaden, 1893.

² C. G. Seligmann and Brenda Seligmann, *The Veddas*, Cambridge, 1911.

The yaku understand that although the formulæ invoking them are recited they are not really being called, and so the pupil does not become possessed while learning, nor do the yaku hurt him. The pupil avoids eating or touching pig or eating fowl in the same way as the shaman, and Sella of Unawatura Bubula stated that while learning he avoided rice, coconuts and *kurakan*, eating especially the flesh of the sambar and monitor lizard.[1]

The shaman exercises complete control over his pupil and, we believe, does not usually train more than one disciple. We heard of one instance in which a shaman, considering his pupil unfit, advised him to give up all idea of becoming a shaman. This happened among the Mudigala Veddas, apparently between twenty or thirty years ago. No man, however highly trained, is accounted, the official shaman of a community during his teacher's life, although with his teacher's permission he will, when he is proficient, perform ceremonies and become possessed by the yaku. . . .

Besides the shaman one or more of the near relatives of the dead man may become possessed, but this though common is not invariable. The yaka leaves the shaman soon after he has promised his favour and success in hunting, the shaman often collapsing as the spirit departs and in any case appearing in an exceedingly exhausted state for a few minutes. However, he soon comes round, when he and all present, constituting the men, women and children of the group, eat the offering, usually on the spot on which the invocation took place, though this is not absolutely necessary, for on one occasion at Sitala Wanniya a rain squall threatened, the food was quickly carried to the cave a few hundred yards distant from the dancing ground.[2]

It must be emphasized that according to the Seligmanns the possession of the shamans is not of a somnambulistic character:

The method of invocation of the yaku is essentially the same in all Vedda ceremonies; an invocation is sung by the shaman and often by the onlookers, while the shaman slowly dances, usually round the offering that has been prepared for the yaku. Sometimes the invocations are quite appropriate and either consist of straightforward appeals to the yaka invoked for help, or recite the deeds and prowess of the yaku when he too was a man, as when Kande Yaka is addressed as " continuing to go from hill to hill (who) follows up the traces from footprint to footprint of excellent sambar deer." But at other times the charms seem singularly inappropriate; probably in many of these instances they are the remains of old Sinhalese charms that have not only been displaced from their proper position and function, but have been mangled in the process, and have in the course of time become incomprehensible. As the charm is recited over and over again the shaman dances more and more quickly, his voice becomes hoarse and he soon becomes possessed by the yaka, and although he does not lose consciousness and can co-ordinate his movements, he nevertheless does not retain any clear recollection of what he says, and only a general idea of the movements he has performed. Although there is doubtless a certain element of humbug about some of the performances, we believe that this is only intentional among the tamer Veddas accustomed to show off before visitors, and that among the

---

[1] *Ibid.*, pp. 128 sq.   [2] *Ibid.*, pp. 129 sq.

less sophisticated Veddas the singing and movements of the dance soon produce a more or less automatic condition, in which the mind of the shaman, being dominated by his belief in the reality of the yaku, and of his coming possession, which acts without being in a condition of complete volitional consciousness. Most sincere practitioners whom we interrogated in different localities agreed that although they never entirely lost consciousness, they nearly did so at times, and that they never fully appreciated what they said when possessed, while at both the beginning and end of possession they experienced a sensation of nausea and vertigo and the ground seemed to rock and sway beneath their feet.

Some men, including Handuna of Sitala Wanniya, whom we consider one of the most trustworthy of our informants, said that they were aware that they shivered and trembled when they became possessed, and Handuna heard booming noises in his ears as the spirit left him and full consciousness returned. He said this usually happened after he had ceased to dance. We could not hear of any shaman who saw visions while possessed or experienced any olfactory or visual hallucinations before, during, or after possession. The Veddas recognize that women may become possessed, but we only saw one instance of (alleged) possession in a woman, which occurred at a rehearsal of a dance got up for our benefit on our first visit to Bendiyagalge, during which we are confident that none of the dancers were really possessed. Although we did not see the beginning of this woman's seizure we have little doubt that there was a large element of conscious deception in her actions, for when we became aware of her she was sitting bolt upright with her eyes shut and the lids quivering, apparently from the muscular effort of keeping them tightly closed, while opposite her was Tissahami the Vedda Arachi muttering spells over a coconut shell half full of water with which he dabbed her eyes and face.[1]

It is particularly interesting from the point of view of psychology to know up to what point the Veddas participate voluntarily and of set purpose in the genesis of possession. The Seligmanns are of opinion that the states are intermediate, neither quite passive nor entirely voluntary, and unquestionably not purely assumed. They have probably hit the mark. The more exact analysis of this remarkable blending remains a task for the future demanding a deeper insight than we now possess into the relationship between active and passive psychic phenomena, especially as conditioned by the mentality of primitive peoples, so essentially different from that of the civilized.[2]

[1] *Ibid.*, pp. 133 sq.
[2] It is interesting to note that the Seligmanns wondered whether hysteria were not present amongst the Veddas. They reached the following conclusion: " There was nothing about the general behaviour of all the Veddas with whom we came into contact that suggested a neurotic or hysterical tendency. The graver stigmata of hysteria, which would warrant a diagnosis of functional disease, were also absent, and the Veddas, even when ill, were in no sense fuss-makers or inclined to magnify their ailments in the way so many Melanesians do " (*The Veddas*, p. 135, note).

It is not suggested that the conscious element is entirely absent from the Vedda possession-dances, it is impossible to believe that such a sudden collapse as that occurring in the Henebedda *Kiri-koraka* ceremony (when Kande Yaka in the person of the shaman shoots the sambar deer), followed by an almost instantaneous recovery, is entirely non-volitional, and the same holds good for the pig-spearing in the Bambura Yaka ceremony at Sitala Wanniya. We believe that these facts can be fully accounted for by a partial abolition of the will, that is to say, by a dulling of volition far short of complete unconsciousness. The shaman in fact surrenders himself to the dance in the fullest sense, and it is this, combined to a high degree with subconscious expectancy, which leads him to enact almost automatically and certainly without careful forethought the traditional parts of the dance in their conventionally correct order. Further, the assistant, who follows every movement of the dancer, prepared to catch him when he falls, may also greatly assist by conscious or unconscious suggestion in the correct performance of these complicated possession-dances. Again, we do not think there can be any doubt as to the non-volitional nature of the possession, by the yaku, of the bystanders, near relatives of the dead man, which may take place during the Nae Yaku ceremony.

One remarkable fact may be chronicled here—viz., that we have never met a Vedda who has seen the spirit of a dead man, that is to say, no Vedda ever saw a ghost, at least in his waking hours.[1]

Nor did the Nae Yaku regularly make their presence known in any other way than by possession, though some Veddas translated the minor noises of the jungle into signs of the presence of the yaku. These facts also seemed to militate against the idea that any considerable part of Vedda possession is a fraud, deliberately conceived and perpetrated, for knowing, as many Veddas do, of the frequency with which the Sinhalese see " devils " and " spirits " of all sorts, nothing would appear easier, if fraud were intended, than for a shaman to assert that he could see the spirits which every Vedda believes are constantly near him.[2]

The facility with which the Veddas become possessed is quite astonishing, the accounts recalling those given by Mariner of the natives of the Tonga Islands. There is no need for preparatory autosuggestion; suddenly, as if at a given signal, the change in the state of consciousness takes place:

When the Maha Yakino are invoked to cure sickness a basket is used in which are put a bead necklace and bangles and the leaves of a *na* tree. The Shaman becomes possessed and raises the basket above the patient's head and prophesies recovery.[3]

The Nae Yaku are the spirits of the dead, they must report themselves to Kande Yaka as the chief of all the yaku and from him obtain permission to help the living and accept their offerings. Kande Yaka comes to the Nae Yaku ceremonies since the spirits of the dead could not be present without him. It was definitely stated that the spirits of the dead did not become yaku until the fifth day after death, but my informant knew nothing of the state of the spirits during this period though it was surmised that

---

[1] *Ibid.*, p. 135.   [2] *Ibid.*, p. 136.   [3] *Ibid.*, p. 166.

at least part of the time would be passed in seeking Kande Yaka or in his company, though there was no idea as to where Kande Yaka had his being. It was, however, stated that the spirits of the dead were in the hills, caves and rocks. The Nae Yaku including the spirit of the dead man are invoked on the fifth day after death. An offering is made of coconut milk and rice, if these are obtainable, but if not one consisting of yams and water is substituted. The shaman dances, holding in his hand a big ceremonial arrow for which no special name could be elicited, while the remainder of the community gather round. The shaman invokes the Nae Yaku and also Kande Yaka and Bilindi Yaka. The shaman becomes possessed and is supported lest he fall while the spirit of the deceased promises that yams, honey, and game shall be plentiful. He then sprinkles coconut milk or water from the offering on the relatives of the deceased, as a sign of the spirit's favour. One or more of the relatives of the dead man may also become possessed. The shaman gives the relatives water and yams, putting their food into their mouths himself while he is possessed, and it appeared that this might cause the relatives to become possessed. At the end of the ceremony he asks the Nae Yaku to depart to where they came from and the spirits leave the offering.[1]

We consider that the beliefs so far described represent the first stratum or basis of the Vedda religion and to be of its original substance.[2]

With a single possible exception the dances of the Veddas are ceremonial and are performed with the object of becoming possessed by a yaka. . . . The majority of the ceremonial dances described in this chapter are pantomimic, and so well illustrate the objective manifestations of the condition of possession that little need be said on this subject, though it may be well to repeat our conviction that there is no considerable element of pretence in the performance of the shaman. The sudden collapse which accompanies the performance of some given act of the pantomime, usually an important event towards which the action has been leading up, is the feature that is most difficult to explain. According to the Veddas themselves it occurs when a yaka suddenly leaves the individual possessed, but it does not invariably accompany the cessation of possession, and it may equally occur when the individual becomes possessed. . . . This can be explained as the result of expectancy, they expected to be overcome by the spirit of the deceased, and in fact this happened. In this connection we may refer to a Sinhalese " devil ceremony " which we witnessed in the remote jungle village of Gonagolla in the Eastern Province. One of us has described this ceremony elsewhere, but we would here specially refer to the condition of the Katandirale or " devil dancer " when dealing with the dangerous demon Riri Yaka. Although he took special precautions to prevent the demon entering him, that is to say to avoid possession by the demon, he almost collapsed, requiring to be supported in the arms of an assistant, as under the assaults of the yaka he tottered with drawn features and half open quivering lips and almost closed eyes. Yet avowedly he was not possessed by the demon, but on the contrary was successful in warding off possession. His whole appearance was that of a person suffering from some amount of shock and in a condition of partial collapse, while the rapidity with which he passed into sleep immediately Riri Yaka, and his almost equally dreaded consort Riri Yakini

---

[1] *Ibid.*, p. 151. [2] *Ibid.*, p. 153.

had left him, also favour the genuine character of his sufferings, concerning which he said that although he had never completely lost consciousness he had been near doing so and had felt giddy and nauseated. During the condition of partial collapse the dancer's face was covered with sweat and so felt clammy, but this may only have been the result of his previous exertions; his pulse was small and rapid and was certainly over 120, though the conditions prevented it being accurately counted. Here we have a condition only a degree short of possession, occurring in an individual who not only hoped and expected to avoid being possessed by the spirit whom he invoked to come to the offering, but took elaborate precautions to prevent it. Had he become possessed it would have been a disaster which would have led to his illness and perhaps death, and would certainly have frustrated the object of the ceremony. Here there can have been no desire to lose consciousness, yet as the result of anticipation of the attack of the yaka the katandirale came near collapse.

This in our opinion throws a flood of light on Vedda possession and the collapse which may take place at its beginning, but it does not exactly explain the collapse often experienced when a yaka leaves a person. But here we may seek assistance in the idea of anology; when a spirit leaves the body, collapse and unconsciousness, permanent (death) or temporary (swoon, fainting fits or sleep), ensue. When the yaka leaves the body which for the time it has entirely dominated, what more natural than that collapse should occur or be feigned by the less honest or susceptible practitioners? There is no doubt that the Vedda ceremonies make considerable demand on the bodily powers of the dancers, but this is not so great as in the case of the Sinhalese devil ceremony of Gonagolla, since the Vedda ceremonies are of shorter duration—none we saw lasted over two hours and the majority certainly did not take so long. In spite of this we noted, after more than one ceremony, that the shaman was genuinely tired, and this was the case at Sitala Wanniya, where Kaira appeared actually exhausted at the end of the Pata Yaka ceremony.[1]

When the yaka enters the person of a shaman it is customary for him to inspect the offerings, and if he is pleased—which is almost invariably the case—he will show his pleasure. This is usually done by bending the head low over the offering, then springing away and shouting "Ah! Ah!" while taking short deep breaths. The natural outcome of the yaka's gratitude is a promise of favours to the community. When prophesying good luck, the shaman places one or both hands on the participant's shoulders, or if he carries an *aude* or other sacred object, the shaman holds this against the latter's chest, or more rarely, presses it on the top of his head. His whole manner is agitated and he usually shuffles his feet, speaks in a hoarse somewhat guttural voice, taking short deep breaths, and punctuates his remarks with a deep "Ah! Ah!"[2]

A whole series of ceremonial dances executed by the Veddas is very exactly described in the Seligmanns' book, and what is more interesting, it also contains a number of photographs of these dances in which shaman becomes possessed or falls on his back.[3]

[1] *Ibid.*, pp. 209 sq.   [2] *Ibid.*, pp. 211 sq.   [3] *Ibid.*, chap. ix.

Far more copious than our information about the pigmies is that relating to the shamanistic states of primitive peoples of normal stature, with which we shall now deal.

Let us first say a few words on African shamanism which the ethnologist Frobenius has studied at first-hand in Central Africa.[1] But his description is not at all clear, so that we have merely a rough sketch. Here, too, the distinguishing feature is belief in spirits which take possession of men and speak by their mouth. From Frobenius' accounts it is necessary to distinguish clearly, as already remarked, two sorts of possession, voluntary and involuntary. The first has already been discussed and we shall now pass to the second. Possession appears as a rule to consist in visionary apparitions. The chief means of provoking it is music.

Sometimes possession is desired and the demon is conjured and asked to grant it, but sometimes the latter invades the man's body of his own initiative and free will. Then the priest can speak to the demon by the mouth of the possessed, communicate with him and hold consultations. This requires music before all things, generally the simple guitar, sometimes the Soudanese violin, the " goye." Rarely, and then only in the Sahara, have I heard it said that the drum was used.[2]

Owing to the fact that the demons exercise a free and premeditated choice of their preferred ones, the shaman is elected and must carry out his mission often against his will. He is seized by the spirit and suffers possession by him.[3]

The elders of the Bori have strange sacred instruments, namely, the woman a sacred calabash; a *korria* =mborri; a little bow with arrows. When an old woman (especially the Magadja) wishes to speak with one of the spirits of the Bori who are always in the bush, the following people form the circle: (1) the old woman—*i.e.*, the Magadja—who sings and strikes the calabash; (2) the young Adjingi who usually makes the offering; (3) the old Adjingi . . ., who before the ceremony has bathed his eyes with a *magani* (a magic drug) because he would otherwise be unable to recognize and above all to see the Bori which inspires or enters the circle; (4) and lastly, the guitar-player; for in order to obtain inspiration, the possession which is sought and petitioned, it is necessary that a *Maimolu* or guitarist should play the airs prescribed by Bori custom. This group of four is gathered in a room, and performs the musical rite. Meanwhile the Bori people are seated outside the door awaiting what will take place, that is to say what Alledjenu (summoned by the magic circle of the four persons forming the ring) will seize one of their number and cast him to the ground. For one of those who are seated waiting without will be thrown down by an *iska* (*i.e.*, wind, spirit), coming from the place where the four are sitting. The man overthrown will then be able to

[1] Leo Frobenius, *Und Afrika sprach* . . ., vol. ii, Berlin, 1912, chap. xi.
[2] *Ibid.*, vol. ii, p. 249.
[3] *Ibid.*, p. 249.

say what will happen (*i.e.*, he will prophesy). The course of events is as follows:

The four persons are gathered in the room. No one dances. The Maimolu repeats to the guitar the names of all the Alledjenu and converses for a few minutes with each of them. Meanwhile the Magadja is seated on the ground and beats the calabash. She pronounces the names of the Alledjenu with her lips at the same time as they are sounded on the guitar. The Adjingi sits in the place of honour on a fine skin and has a large quantity of kola-nuts before him.

When in the enumeration of the Alledjenus the name of the Salala (Djengere) who is their chief is pronounced, the Adjingi, because the Salala is his personal Alledjenu (it is clear that Adjingi =Djengere) distributes the kola-nuts amongst those present (and apparently those outside also), after which the Alledjenu who has been evoked enters the circle.

According to the account in my possession, the Alledjenu does not possess any of the four members of the circle, but no doubt comes into the room after the summons of the Djengere and the sacrificial sharing-out of the kola-nuts, " through the Magadja." No one can see or recognize him except the old man whose eyes have been previously bathed with the magic brew of magani. He sees the Alledjenu come forth from the circle (if I have understood rightly, from the Magadja) and pass through the room and the people outside.

As soon as the old man has seen the Alledjenu appear to go out he tells the young Adjingi that the Alledjenu has come, and names him by his name. For his part the Alledjenu, before going out, pays all honour to the elder, presenting him with kola and saying: " Now let me know everything that happens." This occurs in the room.

When the Alledjenu, invisible to other eyes, has crossed the room of the four and gone outside where the whole Bori community is gathered beneath the open sky, he takes a man or a woman, according as he likes them personally or favours them on this day, and possesses him. *The Alledjenu will only descend upon whom he pleases.* He fells this man or woman to the earth. When the person is so strongly affected that he becomes as if insane, the people insult the Alledjenu. (The insults in question are not, however, very serious. They shout: " You are behaving badly !" " Do not think that you are amongst animals !" " We will give you nothing to eat, so that you may die." " You do not behave like a friend," etc.) When, however, the Alledjenu goes gently to work and leaves the possessed merely stupid and dazed, the members of the tribe praise him and say: " You are our friend ! We thank you ! We thank you ! We thank you !"

The possessed is then led into the house in which the four form a circle. The rhythmic music is continued. When the somnolence of the possessed has lasted for an hour, he begins to speak to the Adjingi. But it is not the man who speaks, it is merely his voice, and this is changed, for it is the Alledjenu who speaks by his mouth. He speaks about all public concerns, and particularly things which will come to pass (thus prophesying the future). He often tells of a great misfortune which is to occur in the future, but adds by what sacrifice the calamity may be averted and to which Alledjenu the sacrifice should be offered. The Adjingi hears all this from the mouth of the possessed.

When he has heard everything he goes out to the assembled

people of Bori and repeats what the Alledjenu has said through the possessed. The people of Bori shout: " The King must be told ! The King must be told !" Then the Adjingi places himself at the head of the procession while all the people follow after. They proceed towards the King's dwelling, where the Bori shout that the King must hear them. The King's pages go in and tell him that the Bori people with the Adjingi are without. The King comes out.

The people salute the King. Then, in the olden times, the latter flung himself at the feet of the Adjingi, the elder of the tribe, and did him honour. The Adjingi commanded the King to arise and asked him: " Shall I tell you what the Alledjenu has said to us ?" The King replied: " Can I act against the will of the Alledjenu ? Must I not hear from the Alledjenu all that they say to you ? Why will you not repeat what he has said to you ?" Thereupon the Adjingi relates everything which the Alledjenu has said in the circle. The King must then collect from the people all that is necessary to cover the cost of the sacrifice and levies a Toussa (tax) on everyone. . . .[1]

In this account, to which many others might be added, we see clearly how the possessed incarnates the spirit: the latter enters into him and speaks by his mouth. He possesses plenary authority, so that the King himself bows before him. Possession here constitutes an essential, even the principal part of the religion, and Frobenius aptly speaks of a " religion of possession." This is, in fact, no rare phenomenon, but the religion of the Bori, according to Frobenius' information, is disseminated over *a very great part of Central Africa*. He believes it to come from the East and even from Persia whence it travelled by way of Palestine to the countries of the East African coast. " It passes across the Middle Nile through the Sudan to the Niger, acquires there in the Hausa triangle a particularly marked, localized and self-referent development of strength, and then dies away towards the east coast."[2]

Besides Frobenius we owe detailed information on the Bori religion to the English investigator Tremearne, already mentioned above, although he writes as an ethnologist and there is reason to regret that he has not envisaged matters from the psychological standpoint proper. This is the more to be deplored as his numerous photographs show that he acquired a comprehensive knowledge of these strange customs and would have had unique opportunities for obtaining psychological data of a remarkable nature. The information which Tremearne has collected on possession-dances among the Hausa peoples is extensive, but on the genesis, course,

[1] *Ibid.*, pp. 258-260.   [2] *Ibid.*, p. 270.

and extinction of possession he vouchsafes practically nothing. It is always the same with ethnologists; they seek rather to accumulate facts and describe customs than to offer psychological explanations.

According to Tremearne the Bori is older than Islam amongst the Hausa races. He considers these dances as pre-Islamic,[1] and immediately related to the Semitic cults of ancient Carthage and Babylon.[2] Amongst the Hausas dances were originally a method of treatment for mental diseases and each of them represents a kind of sickness. In later times this form of treatment was practised by a special class composed of men and women of bad reputation known as Karua. Still later young people, particularly girls, who had not turned out well or who had criminal or morbid tendencies, came under the influence of the Bori. It was admitted that they were under the control of evil spirits which must be driven out. To be accused of Bori is therefore not necessarily a disgrace although many men regard it as a reproach against their wives if the latter have been concerned in it.

According to the explorer Richardson, Bori must have degenerated long ago, for one evening in the year 1850 he writes:

" I found that one of our negresses, a wife of one of the servants, was performing *Boree*, the ' Devil,' and working herself up into the belief that his Satanic Majesty had possession of her. She threw herself upon the ground in all directions, and imitated the cries of various animals. Her actions were, however, somewhat regulated by a man tapping upon a kettle with a piece of wood, beating time to her wild manœuvres. After some delay, believing herself now possessed, and capable of performing her work, she went forward to half a dozen of our servants who were squatting on their hams ready to receive her. She then took each by the head and neck, and pressed their heads between her legs—they sitting, she standing —not in the most decent way, and made over them, with her whole body, certain inelegant motions not to be mentioned. She then put their hands and arms behind their backs, and after several other wild cries and jumps, and having for a moment thrown herself flat upon the ground, she declared to each and all their future— their fortune, good or bad."[3]

After the conquest of the Hausa states by Islam at the beginning of the nineteenth century, Bori was, according to

[1] Tremearne, *Hausa Superstitions and Customs*, London, 1913, p.146.
[2] Ibid., *The Ban of the Bori*, London, 1919.
[3] Tremearne, *Hausa Superstitions . . .*, p. 146; from Benton, *Notes on Some Languages of the Western Sudan*, p. 15.

Tremearne, forbidden in the large towns but continued to flourish in the small ones and villages. Later, by a kind of bribery of the native authorities, it found its way back into the large centres. In the regions under British government the bribe then became a legal tribute to the Bori practitioner, but in the latter years of the war serious steps were taken towards the complete suppression of these strange ceremonies and it was explained to Tremearne that they no longer occurred. For this reason he found it impossible to take further photographs of Bori, at least in northern Nigeria, where repression seems to have been completely successful. Even in 1913, however, he produced two sketches. It is true that they are of no great significance.[1]

In Italian Tripolitania Tremearne later succeeded in obtaining from the authorities, who showed a sympathetic understanding, permission for the celebration of the Bori rites which otherwise no longer occur, and was able to study them very carefully. We are, however, entitled to believe that the natives no longer regard them with their former seriousness, as they would hardly otherwise have lent themselves to such a performance in the presence of a European. In consequence Tremearne was able to take a number of photographs which he published in 1914 in his new book. The photographs which we possess of primitive states of possession are unfortunately all too few in number.

Let us hear how he describes the whole spectacle:

> The master of ceremonies is called the *Uban Mufane*; he takes charge of the offerings of the spectators, but they are afterwards divided amongst the musicians (a violinist, and a man who drums on an overturned calabash), and the dancers. A mat is usually spread in front of him, so that those onlookers who wish to give money will know where to throw it—though it is not refused should it fall elsewhere.[2]

After all sorts of other ceremonies have been accomplished a goat is slaughtered. Similarly a red cock is sacrificed. Then:

> Immediately some of the dowaki began yelling, and certain ones of them flung themselves upon the ground and began drinking the blood, these being Mai-Ja-Chikki, Kuri, Sarikin Pawa, Jigo, and Jam Maraki. Others smeared their faces and clothes—and their instruments also, in the case of the musicians—with the blood,

---

[1] *Ibid.*, p. 148. The pictures are near the title-page.
[2] *Ibid.*, p. 530.

17

and the Arifa, having scooped some of it up, sprinkled those near her. The first of the Bori had now mounted, and the persons possessed were forcibly conducted into the dancing-space.

The first to appear were Kuri (Haj Ali), Jam Maraki (Khamcis), and Mai-Ja-Chikki (Khadeza).[1] A few other dowaki became possessed as fresh bori arrived upon the scene or got their turn, as the case might be. . . .[2]

Often a particular dancer will have kola-nuts poured into his or her mouth. . . . Soon after the musicians have commenced, some of the dancers begin to go round and round in a circle with shuffling steps, the hips swaying from side to side, and in a few minutes the strains of the violin and the scents used by the dancers take effect. The eyes become fixed and staring, the dancer becomes hysterical, grunts or squeals, makes convulsive movements and sudden rushes, crawls about, or mimics the actions of the person or animal whose part he is playing, and then jumps into the air, and comes down flat on the buttocks, with the legs stretched out in front horizontally, or with one crossed over the other. The dancer may remain rigid in that position for some time, often until each arm has been lifted up, and pressed back three times by one of the other performers.

This may be the end of that particular dancer's part, but often he will continue to act up to his name, his words and actions being supposed to be due to the spirit by which he is possessed, and if it is not clear which spirit it is, the chief mai-bori present will explain, or the performer himself may do so. Finally, in most cases, the dancer will sneeze, this evidently being for the purpose of expelling the spirit. Sometimes, not content with the dashing on the ground, the dancers will claw their chests, tear their hair, or beat various parts of their bodies, and even climb trees and throw themselves down, but all deny that they feel any pain while possessed, whatever they do. Sneezing expels the spirit, as has been said, but it is some days before the effect of the seizure wears off, even if no serious injury has been done, the appropriate diet meantime being kola-nuts and water.[3]

The spirits are all summoned by the incense, and expelled by the sneezing, and if any character becomes offensive to the spectators (as did Jato at Tripoli) the Arifa will touch the mount on the back of the neck and under the chin, so as to make him or her sneeze and so get rid of the spirit. The performers, as has been said, are supposed to act involuntarily and unconsciously, in fact, to be " possessed " in every sense of the word.[4]

The performances went on until six a.m. next morning, though from six p.m. until midnight only the ordinary dancing was indulged in. Again next day, about two-thirty p.m., it recommenced, and a similar programme was performed, though there were no sacrifices. A third day completed the rites.[5]

The number of spirits which cause possession is very great—Tremearne counts several dozen—and the dancers' gestures are completely different according to the spirit which

---

[1] The names in brackets are those of the dancers representing the spirits.
[2] Tremearne, *The Ban of the Bori*, p. 287.
[3] Tremearne, *Hausa Superstitions*, pp. 530 and 532.
[4] Tremearne, *The Ban of the Bori*, p. 288.   [5] *Ibid.*, p. 287.

they represent. These spirits are of very various origin; some come from Islam, others are peculiar to the negro world. In the performances they are incarnated by the participants and the latter act as if they were the spirits in question. Unfortunately it is not clearly apparent from Tremearne's numerous accounts at what stage possession proper comes on. It is evident that for some time the participants voluntarily play the part of the spirits and subsequently fall into possession, so that this latter stage is only an intensification of the voluntary ones.

A few examples will serve to illustrate the actual conduct of the actors. The best idea is really conveyed by the numerous photographs published by Tremearne.

There is, for example, the Bori Malam Alhaji. He is a scholar and a pilgrim. He pretends to be old and trembling, as if counting little pellets with his right hand, holding meanwhile in the left a book which he reads. He walks bent double, with a crutch, and is all the time tired out and coughing. He is present at all the marriages of the Bori sect. He is always clothed in white.[1]

Another spirit is Dan Galladima. He is the son of a prince. There is also Janjare.

> The dancer puts on a large cloth, which comes over his head. He walks along slowly, head bent, and then crossing his feet, he sits down. He is then approached and saluted by everyone. He is the highest judge of the sect, appeals being brought to him from the court of the Wanzamie. If he agrees with the decision of the latter, he remains seated, if not, he jumps up and falls down three times, and then he gives his decision. The tsere consists of the full attire of a prince—viz., a blue robe and trousers, white turban, shoes, and scent.[2]
>
> Janjare or Janzirri—? from Khanziri, a hog. The same as Nakada. Sometimes, if not forcibly prevented, the person possessed, naked, except for a monkey-skin, will rush about devouring or rubbing his body with all kinds of filth, and pushing an onion or tomato into the mouth is the only cure. On other occasions he hops round a few times, then puts a stick between his legs for a hobby-horse, and prances. Finally, he simulates copulation, falls to the ground, and pretends to sneeze.[3]

Another spirit is called Be-Maguje:

> The dancer wears a loin-cloth, a quiver, and a bag in which are tobacco and a flint and steel. He carries an axe on his shoulder, a bow in his hand, and smokes a long pipe. He walks along,

---

[1] Tremearne, *Hausa Superstitions*, p. 534.
[2] *Ibid.*, p. 536.　　　　　　　　　[3] *Ibid.*, p. 537.

mimicking a pagan (the performance takes place in a Mohammedan district), and presently lights his pipe with a spark from his flint (the Hausas now use imported matches). He then calls out " Chewaki Tororo (two common pagan names) bring beer," and on a person bringing him some, he drinks greedily, letting the beer run down his chin. He then gives back the calabash of beer, relights his pipe, and moves off.[1]

A spirit of sickness, still clearly recognizable as such, is Nana Ayesha Karama:

> Nana Ayesha Karama is said to be a grandchild of Yerima. She has a farm of her own. She gives sore eyes and smallpox, the proper sacrifice being speckled fowls. Although young, she is by no means innocent, as her song shows. At the dance, she wears white, red, and pink cloths on her body, and two head-cloths, one tied on each side. She rushes about, claps her hands, waves a cloth in the air, and then sits down and scratches herself, and lets her head fall first on one side and then on the other, afterwards resting it upon one hand. If not given sugar then she cries, but if she receives enough she becomes lively again, and dances around once more, until she sneezes and goes.[2]

The most interesting part of Tremearne's narrative consists in the statement of one Haj Ali, a follower of the Bori cult, the principal passages of which I shall quote. It shows that we are here confronted to some extent by non-somnambulistic possession.

> Haj Ali was taken as a slave to Egypt, and one day while with his master Ibrahim at Sarowi, Nakada (also called Jato and Janzirri) took possession of him, and he foretold that on the third day his master would be summoned before the chief of the district, Tanta. On the departure of the bori, the listeners told Haj Ali what he had said, and asked him what he had meant, but he then remembered nothing of it, and simply told them that Nakada had mounted him, and that it must have been that spirit speaking through his mouth. A female Hausa slave who knew the wisdom of the bori, corroborated, and the people then became anxious, for clairvoyance is well known to the Arabs, and when on the third day the district head's messengers arrived, they were terrified. However, the master, instead of being disgraced as he had feared, was given a post under the Government, and so Haj Ali had great honour, was taken to Mecca, and later on received his freedom.[3]

> Haj Ali told me that when the bori first takes possession of him, he feels cold all over, and his limbs become so rigid that the other Masu-Bori have to cense them forcibly before he can move—I did not see them do this, however, it was not done on the first day, so far as I could see, though as each mount possessed was seized and forcibly pushed by several Masu-Bori through the crowd into the ring, it may have escaped my notice. He is not sure how or where the spirit enters; he says that it sits on his neck with its legs on his shoulders, and yet it is inside his head. But sneezing brings

[1] Ibid., p. 538.   [2] Tremearne, The Ban of the Bori, p. 377.
[3] Ibid., p. 257.

it out, though whether by the mouth, nose, or eyes he is not certain, because all parts may be affected. "A bori is like the wind, it is everywhere, so who can tell just where it goes in or out? One knows that it is there, and that is all." The dancer nearly always has to wait some time for the spirit to get properly up, to settle down in the saddle, as it were, and he often glides around the ring or to and fro in it —this being supposed to be the bori floating in the air—or rather making his mount do so. At other times the mount became rigid, as has been stated.

Sometimes, he says, the women do not become possessed, and then it is evident that some enemy has put a hairpin or something made of iron into their hair, or in their head-coverings, for the bori do not like iron. When this is supposed to be the case, a boka will commence to dance, and will jump and fall three times, on the last occasion managing to seat himself just in front of the women. He then abuses them, and, having ordered them to put their heads forward, he feels about to find the neutralizing influence, and upon its removal they immediately become possessed.

According to Abd Allah, at midnight on the last night of the rites, before the spirits have come again, the Sarauniya sits down almost opposite the mai-gimbiri (the player on the guitar), and sets fire to a pot of incense in front of her, while a candle is lighted in front and on each side of him. . . . And then, the bori spirits having reappeared, the dancing begins again, and lasts until dawn. Most of the people then go home for good, but the most influential of the Masu-Bori will sleep in the dakin tsafi that night, and sacrifice a white hen at midnight. That ends the rites, and the dancers recover as best they can, the effect lasting for several days in many cases, a diet of kola-nut being the best pick-me-up, which, on account of its stimulating properties, is regarded as being almost magical.[1]

The following accounts also show the astonishing suggestibility of the Tripolitan natives, in spite of the fact that they live on the outskirts of civilization:

I am told that Kuri's mount must beat himself the proper number of times with the pestle or stick, otherwise he will suffer afterwards. One night, some years ago, not long after his arrival in Tunis, Haj Ali was taken by a friend to one of the other bori houses, and after a time Kuri mounted him, and he began to dance. The people there, not knowing him, gave him a big log to dance with, and he began to knock himself about so badly that they became afraid that he would kill himself, and stopped him. The friend argued with them, saying that he would answer for Haj Ali's safety, but all in vain, and the drummers changed their call. The friend then took Haj Ali home, and he was so ill for four days that he could not rise. On learning what was the matter, the then Arifa ordered her own drummers to go to the house, taking a pestle with them, and on their arrival Haj Ali arose, got through the remainder of his performance, made up the required number of thuds upon his body and was quite well immediately.

No mount must be given a drink during seizure, else he will vomit afterwards, and perhaps be so bad that he will die, so they say; but directly after the bori has gone, the mount may have a few sips of

---

[1] *Ibid.*, pp. 288 sq.

water. The vessel is not entrusted to him, however, a special person (Fagge or Mai-Ruwa) brings it and holds it to his lips. Kola-nuts are the proper stimulant to be taken afterwards, but, as there are so few in North Africa, coffee is drunk instead.

During seizure a mount may have his arms stretched backwards three times; this is in order to render them supple and so avoid any injury to them ! If a bori is treating his mount too severely, the other Masu-Bori clasp the mount in their arms (if it be a woman), or put his head under the arm of one of them (if a man), and hold him while begging the bori to be more gentle, especially in the presence of his " children "—the other Masu-Bori. If the spirit still persists, the mount's neck and chin are touched, and the spirit " is sneezed away."[1]

Persons also fall voluntarily into a state of possession in order to heal the sick. Tremearne begged further details from Haj Ali:

Asked to describe an actual case, he said that he went with another man, his assistant, at the beginning of the year to see a child thus afflicted, and fixed a day when they would return and divine. At the appointed hour they came, and Haj Ali, having wrapped a cloth tightly round his waist, and squatted down by the incense, began to rub his right hand round and round on the ground, fingers bent slightly downwards, and then to turn it over " so as to call the spirits out of the earth " and, apparently, to mesmerize himself. Soon he began to breathe heavily, and suddenly he grunted and yelled, and it was evident the bori had entered his head. Then the other man asked the bori who he was and he replied " I am Kuri." Then the assistant said, " O Father Kuri, So and So is ill, will you tell me in what he has offended ?" Kuri replied: " He threw hot water upon the Yayan Jidderi, and they have made his eyes sore." Then the other said: " O Father Kuri, will you not cure him." And Kuri asked: " What will you give me if I cure thee ?" The assistant (having consulted the father) said: " We will sacrifice a he-goat to you." Then Kuri touched his left shoulder (i.e., that of his horse, Haj Ali),[2] his right shoulder, and then his forehead, and replied: " Very well, he will recover." Apparently, Kuri then summoned the guilty bori (who had not responded to the summons of the incense), and arranged with him to forgive the child. Kuri then left Haj Ali, and he and the assistant went home neither going near the patient until several days afterwards, when they were sent for. On arriving at the house they found the child much better, and then they said : " You must now offer up the sacrifice which you promised." This was done, and the cure was complete.

---

[1] *Ibid.*, pp. 292 sq.

[2] Possession is imagined as a ride on horseback. The Bori rides the possessed, " he mounts him." This image has already been used. We read in Fritz Langer, *Intellektualmythologie*, Berlin, 1916, p. 252: " Amongst popular beliefs we meet the image of the horseman. . . . It is connected with the idea of possession, ' The devil rides so-and-so ' is a well-known metaphor still encountered to-day. (Cf. Grimm, *Mythologie*, i, p. 384: ' The devil has listened to you and ridden you; as Satan, so the nightmare: nightmare- or hobgoblin-ridden.') A man who is ridden by the devil is, in fact, possessed by the devil, and in the same way he may be ridden by a demon, a witch, etc., whither the malignant power wills."

Before the Mai-Bori summons Kuri he is paid between two and five francs. On the child's recovery he gets more money, and perhaps cloths for Kuri, or whichever bori has responded, as well. He gets the liver of the animal sacrificed and also a share in the flesh. Each Mai-Bori specializes in certain spirits, and Haj Ali would always be ridden by Kuri or Ma-Dambache. . . .[1]

Bastian gives the following accounts from an unknown source:

At the festival of the Aissaoua, in memory of the miracle of their establishment at Algiers (under the standard of the marabout Mohammed Ben-Ais-Sa) the Mokadanni, or chief of the Sect, utters prayers for the fulfilment of which each of the Aissaouas prays according to his desires (health, fecundity, etc.), while the choir accompanies him as do the women in the gallery. To the rhythm of the tambourines, in which snakes are imprisoned, the Zikr dancers whirl with violent movements, placing pieces of hot iron on their hands, arms and tongue, and when they fall exhausted to the earth they are reanimated by persons treading on their stomachs. . . . They imitate the voices of lions and camels into which they believe themselves transformed, and tear thorny cacti with their teeth.[2]

It is not without interest to compare with these modern accounts an earlier one from Africa. The geographer O. Dapper has given a detailed and circumstantial description of Africa in the second half of the seventeenth century. He relates the following of lower Ethiopia, or South Africa as it is called to-day:

. . . These images of devils or idols are made by various masters who are called Enganga Mokisie. Their chief instrument is a tree-trunk and they make the images when they have reached a suitable age and are afflicted with disabilities or maladies, which takes place in the following manner.

In the first place the said Engango Mokisie or rather devil-exorcist persuades someone to it; and this man then summons together his whole family, which is in some cases very numerous, and all his neighbours. Then they erect for him who desires to make his devil-image a hut of palm-leaves which must serve him as dwelling for the whole duration of the work. But it lasts for fifteen days during which he must have nothing to do with anyone and in the first nine days must not even speak.

On either side of his mouth he has a parrot-feather and when someone greets him by clapping the hands he may not reply in the same way, but holds in his hands a small log, oblique, very deeply hollowed out in the middle, having a small hole on the top and with a handle behind. It has also at the end a carved man's head; he strikes it with a wand in token of respect. The exorcist habitually has three of these wands, one large, one small, and one of intermediate size.

When all is finished a tree-trunk is brought on to a level clearing

---

[1] Tremearne, *The Ban of the Bori*, pp. 259-60.
[2] A. Bastian, *Der Mensch in der Geschichte*, vol. ii, Leipzig, 1860, p. 151.

where there is no tree or other growth. The relations and neighbours form a circle here; the tambourine-player who is in the middle begins to play, the exorcist to chant, and everyone accompanies him at the top of his voice. This chant is designed to praise the idols, solicit their aid, celebrate their divinity, etc. The initiator of the work, if he be not infirm, himself dances round the trunk. And this lasts for two or three days: during which time nothing is heard of the devil.

The exorcist now brings himself to the attention of the initiator, which is done by means of a hideous voice while he is as yet invisible. Then the drumming, which began with the singing and dancing towards evening at about four o'clock and ends in the morning, leaves off for a while, and the exorcist taps on the aforementioned small log, mumbles a few words and makes at the same time some red and white spots on his own body and that of the initiator, namely on the temples, around the eyes, on the pit of the stomach as well as on all the limbs according as he (the initiator) is handled harshly or gently by the Evil One.

When he is possessed he looks terrible, he leaps and behaves in a terrifying manner, cries out in an unearthly voice, takes glowing coals in his hands and bites them without taking harm. Sometimes he is taken unseen from the midst of all the spectators, led away by the devil into the wilderness to a solitary place where he bedecks himself round the body with a girdle of green herbs and remains two or three hours or even sometimes two or three days. During this time his friends seek him most diligently, but cannot find him, this search being assisted by the incessant beating of drums. As soon as the possessed hears the drums he returns towards them and is led to their accompaniment back to his house. Leaping and dancing goes on until everything is accomplished.

At length the exorcist asks the devil within the possessed, who is stretched out as if dead, what shall be offered to him. The devil replies by the mouth of the possessed and makes known what should be done. Then the man begins once more to sing and dance until the devil comes forth, after which he is often sick unto death. Something is afterwards done to his arm so that he may always remember what has been laid upon him.

When these men swear, they swear by the ring; namely, that the devil who allows them to wear many rings may strangle them inasmuch as what should be believed is not true. Therefore they do not swear lightly, or else it must be true: and although a few light-minded persons do not pay much heed, they nevertheless hold strictly to what they have promised, even though they should perish on the spot, as has often occurred. When the devil speaks by the mouth of the possessed, as is frequent, the latter is greatly tormented, is thrown from side to side and foams at the mouth. . . . In various other ways all the other devil-images or Mokisien are made, with which the King surrounds himself in great quantities, but for the sake of brevity we will not go further into the matter.

When someone amongst them falls ill they often employ these methods for several days and invoke the devil while dancing until he enters into the sick man. Then they ask him why this man is sick, if he has infringed his commands, and more questions of the same kind. The devil replies by the patient's mouth and advises that certain gifts be offered so that he may recover his health.[1]

---

[1] O. Dapper, *Umständliche und eigentliche Beschreibung von Africa und denen dazu gehörigen Königreichen und Landschaften*, etc., Amsterdam, Anno MDCLXX, pp. 530 sq.

As may be seen, states of possession amongst primitive races have also shown no change during the passage of centuries. These people are not, however, always disposed to show unquestioning belief in all the phenomena; amongst them are sceptics who in some cases, where the state of a possessed person is not entirely sincere, obviously give him an embarrassing time. Andrew Lang relates:

> The Zulus admit " possession " and divination, but are not the most credulous of mankind. The ordinary possessed person is usually consulted as to the disease of an absent patient. The enquirers do not assist the diviner by holding his hand, but are expected to smite the ground violently if the guess made by the diviner is right; gently if it is wrong. A sceptical Zulu, named John, having a shilling to spend on psychical research, smote violently at every guess. The diviner was hopelessly puzzled; John kept his shilling.[1]

Information concerning the possession-religions of Africa is far less complete than that relating to the Malay Archipelago. The religion of this latter region is purely spiritualist. In the eyes of its inhabitants the world is peopled by spirits able to enter directly into men, and this belief is not even in the background of consciousness—it is dominant. Possession, thanks to which the living establish contact with the spirit-world, is not in any way rare—it is an everyday manifestation. The belief in particular gods is of entirely secondary importance as compared with the belief in spirits.

The worship of spirits and the fear which underlies it, fills the religious life of the Bataks and all the animist peoples. It pervades daily life down to its minutest details: at birth, baptism, betrothals, marriage, the building of houses, seedtime and harvest the spirits play their part; in the felling of trees, the foundation of a village, in war, trade, smithery, agriculture, it is necessary before all else to satisfy them. With them are shared lodging and board, they have their part in all the possessions of the living, they are omnipresent and everywhere demand consideration.[2]

We are indebted to the missionary, J. Warneck, for very adequate information concerning this religion. His researches owe their great value to the fact that he has elicited detailed accounts from the native converts themselves, and

---

[1] A. Lang, *The Making of Religion*, 2nd edit., London, 1900, p. 141.
[2] J. Warneck, *Die Religion der Batak*, Göttingen, 1909, p. 68.

published their stories in a form which preserves the impression of spontaneity.[1]

Warneck's works are particularly concerned with the Bataks of Sumatra, but the observations on their religion hold good for all the islands of the Indian Ocean.

It appears from the statements of the natives that beside regular mediums other persons may also be possessed on occasion. As regards the facility with which possession may be induced in the mediums the accounts are not in entire agreement; according to one, they prepare themselves by fasting and by abstinence from all irrelevant thoughts, that is by a sort of concentration and expectation; according to another, the mere beating of the drum appears sufficient to bring on possession. In reality the procedure differs according to the individual concerned. Men and women are alike possessed, and there are also fraudulent imitations of possession for reasons of self-seeking. The possessing spirit is not a demon presumed to inhabit the human sphere, but always the spirit of a dead person who has sometimes reached a high degree in the world beyond; the possessed imitates the gestures of the defunct in a manner so striking that oftentimes the relations burst into tears. In certain cases possession is also multiple: several spirits speak by the mouth of the possessed and carry on a conversation, now friendly, now hostile, according to the relationships which existed in their lifetime.

This is the only case known to me of plural possession amongst primitive peoples. During possession the mediums are inaccessible to the strongest sensations of heat and taste (*e.g.*, live coals, pepper). Their social function consists in providing a means of questioning the spirits as to the future, asking their advice and imploring their protection direct. Moreover, the whole Batak repertory of ideas concerning the divine world of the hereafter and the destiny of men after death is bound to repose on the communications which the spirits make by the mouths of the mediums. The many narratives of the natives are interesting, inasmuch as they show how strongly the mediums are gripped by their state and also the fact that they die early, particularly when chosen

[1] In conjunction with Warneck's work see *Die Lebenskräfte des Evangeliums*. Missionserfahrungen innerhalb des animistischen Heidentums, 3rd edit., Berlin, 1908, and the study *Der bataksche Ahnen- und Geisterkult*, "Allgemeine Missions-Zeitschrift," 1904.

by spirits who hold high rank in the Beyond. Possession is preceded by a vision of the spirit which is about to enter into the medium.

Accounts of the parapsychic performances of the mediums are not susceptible of subsequent proof. In certain cases mediums must copy the dead very exactly in all their gestures without having known them, and must in addition possess intimate knowledge of them which could not have been acquired in a normal manner. Finally, they must give proof of capacities which they do not possess in the waking state, such as ability to read.

The statements of the natives are naturally insufficient to demonstrate the actual occurrence of parapsychic phenomena. In certain cases their non-existence is practically certain, as, for instance, when a native writes that the medium reads, although he has never learnt to read, a magic book just as the possessing spirit had been accustomed to do in his lifetime. This must naturally refer to somnambulistic hypermnesia of things which the possessed has often heard read. A native also states that the words of the possessed are sometimes true and sometimes false. It cannot for the moment be said whether there is a residuum of objective parapsychic phenomena, but given the frequency with which they are mentioned an examination on the spot is much to be desired.

Finally, it is also interesting to know that autosuggestive measures are used against possession when it comes on undesired.

In order to afford the reader a first-hand glimpse into this curious world I shall now give a series of quotations from Warneck.[1] It is first necessary to explain the meaning of certain words used in them. *Begu* means spirits in general, *sumangot* the spirit of an ancestor who has attained high rank in the spirit world through the worship rendered to him by his descendants. If he mounts a degree higher he is called a

---

[1] I refer mainly to documents communicated by Warneck, because they are essentially composed of accounts gleaned from the natives. These are not by any means the only ones we possess, many others being fully utilized in a great work by G. A. Wilken, *Het Shamanisme bij de Volken van den Indischen Archipel*, which appeared in " Bijdragen tot de Taal Land en Volken Kunde van Nederlandsch Indie," Vidfje Volgreeks, Tweede Deel, 1887, pp. 427-497. The reader is referred to this work for supplementary information.

sombaon. The possessed are called *hasandaran*; not everyone can attain this condition. The *datu* are wizards.

By way of introduction, here are some observations by Warneck:

> The *begu* invoked (that of a person recently dead) often descends upon a medium and says: " Oh, poor mother, I have received your offering and heard your wish. But what is to be done ? Men are wholly dependent on him who has sent them. But only take good care of this our child and all will be well with him."
>
> The *begu* . . . have a need to communicate with the world of men. With this object they choose a man or woman as medium. In the ancestral ceremonies or family festivals the ancestor descends on the medium whom he has chosen. This is called marsiaran or hasandaran. Shamanism is an essential part of the Batak spiritualist civilization. Generally, but not always, the music of the five Batak drums, with their five different tones, must resound, whereby the transformation will be provoked not by particular melodies but by different rhythms. They the spirit suddenly seizes his medium whose personal consciousness disappears, as the Bataks say, and is replaced by that of the deceased. Those present seek to assure themselves that they are not dealing with an impostor, and he is there for subjected to a severe cross-examination. When he has established his authenticity, the deceased says what is in his mind or answer the questions of his descendants. In all circumstances the thing demanded by the begu through his medium must be brought. The person who serves as medium is much fatigued by the paroxysm, and not seldom falls ill after the performance; it is said that such people do not make old bones. They are, however, held in high esteem. It is not possible to become a hasandaran of one's own initiative not through study, as the datu can, but the spirit himself seeks out his medium and his choice is unpredictable. Whereas the datu (wizard) charges dearly for his skill, the medium receives nothing. In so far as this puzzling manifestation can be explained it is certain that apart from an element of trickery the possessed man finds himself in a state of insensibility and eclipse of personal consciousness. The Batak Christians who were formerly mediums return to this state in certain cases *against their will*, which renders them profoundly unhappy afterwards. The inner life of the possessed is invaded by forces which he cannot control, which suspend both will and thought and replace them by an extraneous power. This state in a person otherwise completely sane has nothing to do with epilepsy or other nervous affections, for those who suffer from mental troubles are well known and clearly distinguished from the shamans; no one of the diseases of the mind found amongst the Bataks presents the same symptoms. The incarnated spirit uses a peculiar language the vocabulary of which is partly periphrastic and partly archaic. Sometimes the state of ecstasy takes possession of a man when no one has given it a thought, not even himself.
>
> It is generally ancestors who thus enter into communication with their descendants. Nevertheless, the begu of a . . . murdered man sometimes sets forth, much against the will of his assassins, to seek a medium and then to make himself exceedingly unpleasant. Here at least the wish is not father to the thought.[1]

---

[1] *Ibid.*, pp. 8 sq.

The following testimonies are of particular value as having been written down at Warneck's instigation not by foreign observers but by the christianized natives:

The begu of a dead person cannot converse directly with the living because he has no body. This is why he must borrow the body of a living person when he desires to converse with his descendants. He therefore chooses for the purpose someone according to his liking. The begu who is incarnated borrows, as it were, the body and voice of the human medium. In this medium he reproduces exactly his own manner while living, as well as his mode of dress and deportment. This is why the relations are often unable to restrain their tears when the deceased is recalled so vividly to their memory, when they hear his voice without, nevertheless, seeing his face. The medium excites belief by reason of the likeness in behaviour.

The medium sees the face of the begu when the latter descends upon him. The begu mentions his name, all his family relationships and the occupation followed in his lifetime. He makes known hidden details of his past life, and when these show verisimilitude the relations believe that they are really dealing with the begu of the deceased. He elucidates secret family affairs. When someone is ill the possessing begu is asked whether he will live or die. In times of epidemic, when death is all around, the begu is invoked and offerings brought to him so that he may afford protection. In cases of childlessness, the begu is questioned through his medium to know whether this will be a permanent condition, and is also consulted as to where lost or stolen things may be found. When anyone is lost the begu is asked in what direction search should be made.

The begu's words are sometimes true, sometimes false, "like stones thrown at night" (i.e., they sometimes hit and sometimes miss). True, the heathen say that the mediums are not always genuinely possessed; there are some who simulate possession because they see that mediums are held in esteem and receive offerings.

When a medium is asked how a begu enters into him, he gives the following account: he sees the begu approach, it feels to him as if his body were dragged away, his feet grow light and begin to jump. He sees men very small and reddish, the houses appear to whirl round. During the trance the begu does not remain continuously in the medium; he sometimes leaves him in order to take a turn. It often happens that after the ending of possession the medium is ill, and sometimes he dies. It is then said that "the begu comes to fetch him."

When a medium's begu is a person of consequence, his fate is a painful one; the mediums and the great datu (wizards) seldom reach old age.

Many Bataks converted to Christianity say that it is wrong to regard possession as mere trickery, for if it were how could the possessed know the secret affairs of the deceased, matters often going back three generations? It is true that now when many have become Christians, the begu are afraid to come because of the true word of God which is amongst the Bataks.

When a begu desires to take possession of someone who is unwilling, the latter seeks to prevent him in the following manner: he burns dung in his vicinity, and when the begu arrives this puts him to flight. When a begu has taken possession of a man but

has not yet spoken he is begged with fair words to express himself
distinctly. The begu of outcasts or suicides cannot choose a
medium, for they are an abomination to men and begu alike.
When two or three begu take possession of their mediums at the
same time they often quarrel if they were already enemies in their
lifetimes. But if they were friends they treat one another amiably
and with courtesy.

A medium is one thing, a person once accidentally possessed by a
begu quite another. . . . This latter may be no matter whom;
the former when he has been chosen by a begu, becomes a regular
medium as soon as the customary drumming has been executed.
When the heathen desire to make a sacrifice to the *sumangot* of
their ancestor because the datu has declared it necessary, the
medium first puts his *tondi* (his soul) into the log, which means
that the chosen man avoids all thought of other things; he fasts
for some days, he wastes away, for the begu already has him on
the hook. Then he grows sick, for the begu is now upon him.
Often when the medium is ill this furnishes the occasion for drum-
beating owing to the belief that the begu is preparing to come to
him: when the drumming has begun the people dance and the
medium jumps about. His steps resound, he takes burning coals
from the hearth and puts them in his mouth. When he is offered
palm wine, ginger or other delicacies, he gulps them down, cries
aloud or sings in a nasal voice. But he is not yet trusted; to know
whether he is really the grandfather's sumangot he is asked:
" Who are you, grandfather ?" Then the medium announces the
grandfather's relationships and his private affairs, and demands the
dishes which he preferred in his lifetime. When these things are
recognized as true he inspires confidence and is then asked for
advice. He announces what people should do in order to win
good luck or to get rid of an illness; he also foretells misfortune.
So far as the medium's utterances are concerned, there are some
who merely confine themselves to chatter about things which they
know; some have a slightly studied language; and yet others really
receive their words from the begu. It is through mediums that
the Bataks have learnt the manners and customs of the begu; they
know that the begu have houses, hold markets, need food and
sacrifices, etc.

Sometimes a man takes a wife from a far country. Then the
grandfather of the man who went to seek her takes possession of her
without ever having known her. When she has called him by his
name she is asked to give proofs. " Who are your relations ?"
She is also asked to tell things which are only known to the family.
The medium makes correct replies, although the woman cannot
have known anything about these matters. Sometimes the begu
of a datu takes possession of a woman. The latter has never learnt
Batak writing, but if she is given a magic book she reads it fluently
in a singing voice, exactly as the datu did in his lifetime.

There was formerly in Silindung a famous datu named Ompu
Djarung. After his death none of his descendants were datu for
four generations. But someone of his line having learnt magic,
the defunct took possession of an ignorant and taciturn woman.
When she had become a medium she called the man who had
learnt magic and taught him the magic charms, the choice of days
and other magic arts. The disciple gave her a book of sorcery in
old Batak script, and she was at once able to read and interpret
it although she had never been to school and did not know the
magic books. Everyone marvelled at this. . . .

There are many of them (*sombaon—i.e.*, ancestors who have reached the summit of the hierarchy in the spirit-world); for all the woods and great trees are peopled with sombaon. Every time when another sombaon is invoked he descends upon his own medium. It then sometimes lasts for a month.[1]

The begu of a man who has been done to death in a horrible fashion for the purpose of working a certain magic spell sometimes takes possession of a man, but never of a woman. When he descends upon him it is a terrible spectacle. He strips himself of all clothing down to the loin-cloth passing between his legs; crams his mouth with live coals, drinks great quantities of dirty water in which washing has been done, picks up the remains of rice which lie about on the mats and devours them like an animal. As offering he demands dressed meat, palm wine and salted meat. When he has received all this he begins to speak. On entering into the medium he generally cries: " I say it, I say it, I say it !" He announces his name, the way in which he has been killed, together with the name of his murderer. The frightened people reply: " Not that, grandfather ! You ought not to say it !" For if he proclaims it his late master or relatives may come to know of the fact that he has been killed with molten lead, and this would arouse strife. Sacrifices are offered to the *pangulubang* (the murdered man) every year. If this is not regularly done he brings misfortune on those responsible for the arrangements; often the whole family is exterminated or the children born without bones. This begu is a terrible one.[2]

When the cult of the sumangot is celebrated there is a feast with music, sacrifice, dances, etc. Warneck says:

> . . . Thereupon the master of ceremonies begins to dance, then the nearest relatives, then the mediums, male or female. These latter are purified by the usual methods and the people cry: " Visit your host, oh grandfather, so that he may announce prosperity to us, to us your descendants." Then the sumangot takes possession of his medium. He is given *piri* (?) to unseal his lips. He gives his name, and asks why the whole orchestra is playing. The master of ceremonies then tells him about the sick man's malady and the datu's verdict. The sumangot replies by the medium: " If this is so you have recognized your fault (in having remained for a long time without sacrificing); the sickness of my grandchild will be healed, but you must still do this and that." Everyone is joyous and relieved because the medium has spoken thus and feels complete faith in his utterances.[3]

We will supplement with this passage from another of Warneck's works:

> This is what happens on the arrival of the spirits. The whole family assembles to honour a great ancestor and question him on a matter of importance. First, music is made for a long time on four different instruments. The monotonous rhythm, the melody based essentially on measure, have a certain fascination. Suddenly a medium dashes forward and becomes another man. He sees the soul of the ancestor coming towards him in its erstwhile form.

[1] *Ibid.*, pp. 89 sq.   [2] *Ibid.*, pp. 93 sq.   [3] *Ibid.*, p. 104.

He no longer has any consciousness of his own body, he feels that he is the deceased whose inner life dominates his own. Those present appear to him small and reddish. He begins to leap and dance convulsively when the rhythm carries him away, always sustained by that muffled music until everything whirls around him and he stops exhausted and flecked with foam. He is given palm wine and betel and interrogated. First of all he asks for a certain kind of drum music which is an indispensable condition to the manifestation of the spirit. . . . It is characteristic that the medium is terribly exhausted by this agitation. He not seldom falls ill and dies in consequence, and it is said that such people never grow old.[1]

It is also significant that the invading spirit uses a particular language which strikingly recalls ancient Batak. The words of this special language are . . . in part cautious circumlocutions . . . and in part quite strange words. That a medium should previously have practised this language is generally out of the question. As a rule the drum must be beaten in order that the soul of the deceased may come, but in certain cases it comes spontaneously upon a man at a moment when no one was giving it a thought. While the spirit is in him the possessed loses personal consciousness and behaves exactly like the deceased. Cases exist in which the medium has had no knowledge of the man whose soul entered into him.[2]

Mediums have often announced things and names which they could not possibly have known of themselves. A short time before the first Europeans arrived in the country various mediums foretold in a circumstantial manner that a new era was opening for the country of the Bataks and what it would mean to them.[3]

It is certain that conversion to Christianity cures a number of possessed persons by the feeling which it confers of greater security against the attacks of demoniac powers.

At Sumatra and Nias the Christians have dared when confronted with the possessed to command the evil spirit to come forth quietly in the name of Jesus, and it was thereupon clear to them that the demon left the unfortunate man.[4]

Warneck is of the opinion that this state of possession defies explanation. It must, however, be added that, in so far as there is no question of secondary parapsychic manifestations, these phenomena present no difficulty to the psychologist. They are, as we have seen, completely and even easily explicable.

From the foregoing accounts it is obvious that possession amongst the Bataks is perfectly consistent with the general picture of the less violent forms. The only thing which is not absolutely clear is whether the possessed really fall into

---

[1] J. Warneck, *Der bataksche Ahnen- und Geisterkult*, "Allgem. Missions-Zeitschr.," 1904, vol. xxxi, p. 74.

[2] *Ibid.*, p. 76.

[3] Warneck, *Die Lebenskräfte des Evangeliums*, Berlin, 1908, 3rd edit., p. 63.

[4] *Ibid.*, p. 229.

complete somnambulism. It is surprising they that retain a certain memory of their state.

Of considerable importance are the states of possession artificially induced amongst the inhabitants of the Malay Peninsula (the Bataks of the Island of Sumatra are also Malays).

Most of the information relevant to our subject is given by Skeat, the most detailed of whose accounts I reproduce below. It very obviously, as Martin has already remarked,[1] shows a strong resemblance to matter relating to the pigmy races of the Malay Peninsula cited earlier in this work. The analogy extends even to the wizard's name; amongst the pigmies he is called the *poyang*, amongst the Malays *pawang*. The ceremonial of the incense-burning is also reminiscent, but most important of all, the soul which forcibly enters into the possessed is amongst the Malays as amongst the pigmies that of a tiger. It is impossible without further research to say anything more about the genealogical relationship existing between the two. In all likelihood priority rests with the Malays, the pigmy races being so barren from the psychic point of view that they are probably the imitators.

While in the Malay Peninsula, Skeat had the rare opportunity consequent on the sickness of his Malay collector's brother, of being present at the exorcism of a sick man. This was carried out, in accordance with stereotyped traditional forms, in the immediate vicinity of the patient who was lying on a mat. The invocation of the spirit, which in this case was that of a tiger, was not conducted by the shaman but by his wife. I shall pass over all non-essentials and confine myself to the principal points in Skeat's narrative which alone concern us here.

> Meanwhile the medicine-man was not backward in his preparations for the proper reception of the spirit. First he scattered incense on the embers and fumigated himself therewith, " shampooing " himself, so to speak, with his hands, and literally bathing in the cloud of incense which volumed up from the newly replenished censer and hung like a dense gray mist over his head. Next he inhaled the incense through his nostrils, and announced in the accents of what is called the spirit-language (*bhasa hantu*) that he was going to " lie down." This he accordingly did, reclining upon his back, and drawing the upper end of his long plaid *sarong* over his head to completely conceal his features. The invocation was not yet ended, and for some time we sat in the silence

---

[1] Cf. above, p. 244.

18

of expectation. At length, however, the moment of possession arrived, and with a violent convulsive movement, which was startling in its suddenness, the " Pawang " rolled over on to his face. Again a brief interval ensued, and a second but somewhat less violent spasm shook his frame, the spasm being strangely followed by a dry and ghostly cough. A moment later and the Pawang, still with shrouded head, was seated bolt upright facing the tambourine player. Then he fronted round, still in a sitting posture, until he faced the jars, and removed the yam-leaf covering from the mouth of each jar in turn.

Next he kindled a wax taper at the flame of a lamp placed for the purpose just behind the jars, and planted it firmly on the brim of the first jar by spilling a little wax upon the spot where it was to stand. Two similar tapers having been kindled and planted upon the second and third jars, he then partook of a " chew " of betel-leaf (which was presented to him by one of the women present), crooning the while to himself.

This refreshment concluded, he drew from his girdle a bezoor or talismanic stone (*batu pĕnawar*), and proceeded to rub it all over the patient's neck and shoulders. Then, facing about, he put on a new white jacket and head-cloth which had been placed beside him for use, and girding his plaid (*sarong*) about his waist, drew from its sheath a richly wrought dagger (*k'ris*) which he fumigated in the smoke of the censer and returned to its scabbard.

He next took three silver 20-cent pieces of " Straits " coinage, to serve as *batu buyong*, or " jar-stones," and after " charming " them dropped each of the three in turn into one of the water-jars, and " inspected " them intently as they lay at the bottom of the water, shading, at the same time, his eyes with his hand from the light of the tapers. He now charmed several handfuls of rice (" parched," " washed," and " saffron " rice), and after a further inspection declared, in shrill, unearthly accents, that each of the coins was lying exactly under its own respective taper, and that therefore his " child " (the sick man) was very dangerously ill, though he might yet possibly recover with the aid of the spirit. Next, scattering the rice round the row of jars (the track of the rice thus forming an ellipse), he broke off several small blossom-stalks from a sheaf of areca-palm blossom, and making them up with sprays of champaka into three separate bouquets, placed one of these improvised nosegays in each of the three jars of water. On the floor at the back of the row of jars he next deposited a piece of white cloth, five cubits in length, which he had just previously fumigated. Again drawing the dagger already referred to, the Pawang now successively plunged it up to the hilt into each of the three bouquets (in which hostile spirits might, I was told, possibly be lurking). Then seizing an unopened blossom-spathe of the areca-palm, he anointed the latter all over with " oil of Celebes," extracted the sheaf of palm-blossom from its casing, fumigated it, and laid it gently across the patient's breast. Rapidly working himself up into a state of intense excitement, and with gestures of the utmost vehemence, he now proceeded to " stroke " the patient with the sheaf of blossom rapidly downwards, in the direction of the feet, on reaching which he beat out the blossom against the floor. Then turning the patient over on to his face, and repeating the stroking process, he again beat out the blossom, and then sank back exhausted upon the floor, where he lay face downwards, with his head once more enveloped in the folds of the *sarong*.

A long interval now ensued, but at length, after many convulsive twitchings, the shrouded figure arose, amid the intense excitement of the entire company, and went upon its hands and feet. The Tiger Spirit had taken possession of the Pawang's body, and presently a low, but startlingly life-like growl—the unmistakable growl of the dreaded " Lord of the Forest," seemed to issue . . . This part of the performance lasted, however, but a few minutes, and then the evident excitement of the onlookers was raised to fever pitch, as the bizarre, and, as it seemed to our fascinated senses, strangely brutelike form stooped suddenly forward, and slowly licked over, as a tigress would lick its cub, the all but naked body of the patient —a performance (to a European) of so powerfully nauseating a character that it can hardly be conceived that any human being could persist in it unless he was more or less unconscious of his actions. At all events, after his complete return to consciousness at the conclusion of the ceremony, even the Pawang experienced a severe attack of nausea, such as might well be supposed to be the result of his performance. Meanwhile, however, the ceremony continued. Reverting to a sitting posture (though still with shrouded head), the Pawang now leaned forward over the patient, and with the point of his dagger drew blood from his own arm; then rising to his feet he engaged in a fierce hand-to-hand combat with his invisible foe (the spirit whom he had been summoned to exorcise). At first his weapon was the dagger, but before long he discarded this, and laid about him stoutly enough with the sheaf of areca-palm blossom.

A pause of about ten minutes' duration now followed, and then with sundry convulsive twitchings the Pawang returned to consciousness and sat up, and the ceremony was over.[1]

A sudden collapse with loss of consciousness such as occurs amongst the pigmies is also observed amongst the Besisi of the Malay Peninsula who are of full stature. These have a special ceremony designed to summon the spirits. The most profound darkness together with smoke, music and muffled sing'ng, are the means used to induce an abnormal state.

As the incantation (which consisted of an invocation to the spirits) proceeded, one of the spirits commenced to give evidence of his descent, by taking possession of one of the company, who presently fell down apparently unconscious. While he was in this state (of possession) questions are put to him, apparently by anyone desiring to do so. The required information having been given, the possessed person was restored to consciousness by the inhaled smoke of the burning incense, which, I was assured by one of the company, will always " restore him immediately."[2]

[1] W. W. Skeat, *Malay Magic*, being an introduction to the folklore and popular religion of the Malay Peninsula, London, 1900, pp. 440-444.
[2] W. W. Skeat and C. O. Blagden, *Pagan Races of the Malay Peninsula*, London, 1906, vol. ii, p. 307.

Possession by the spirits of animals is also found amongst the Malays, for example a monkey dance.

The " Monkey Dance " is achieved by causing the " Monkey spirit " to enter into a girl of some ten years of age. She is first rocked to and fro in a Malay infant's swinging cot (buayan), and fed with areca-nut and salt (pinang garam). When she is sufficiently dizzy or " dazed " (mabok), an invocation addressed to the " Monkey spirit " is chanted (to tambourine accompaniments), and at its close the child commences to perform a dance, in the course of which she is said sometimes to achieve some extraordinary climbing feats which she could never have achieved unless " possessed." When it is time for her to recover her senses she is called upon by name, and if that fails to recall her, is bathed all over with cocoa-nut milk.[1]

On the subject of autosuggestive animal possession Selenka also relates the following of the Dyaks of Borneo:

Much was also told us of hypnotic states. These appear spontaneously or may be artificially provoked by such means as pulling a man's head hither and thither for a quarter of an hour by the corner of a handkerchief bound round it, a treatment designed to produce in the medium the illusion of being a monkey. The hypnotized person then behaves like a quadrumane, until the manang (medicine-man) delivers him from the charm. The name of this violent game is " calling down the monkey." According to the Resident Tromp, illusions are also produced in which the hypnotized person believes himself to be a bird and behaves accordingly.[2]

Let us now leave Asia and pass to the shores of the Pacific Ocean.

From the South Seas we have a relatively very accurate description of shamanistic states in the Tonga Islands of Polynesia by the English observer Mariner. It is found amongst the extremely interesting and informative travel books previously mentioned.[3]

Mariner remarked that the interrogation of the gods by priests under the influence of possession is of frequent occurrence in the Tonga Islands. It is noteworthy that the concomitant noisy drumming which generally serves to provoke inspiration is completely absent. The priests fall through the mere autosuggestion of a waiting period into divine possession which seems as a rule to last for some con-

---

[1] Skeat, *Malay Magic*, p. 465.
[2] Emil and Lenore Selenka, *Sonnige Welten*, Ostasiatische Reise-Stizzen; Wiesbaden. 1896, p. 78.
[3] W. Mariner, *An Account of the Natives of the Tonga Islands in the South Pacific Ocean*, ed. by John Martin, 2 vols., London, 1817.

siderable time. The status which they enjoy is regulated according to the divinity speaking through them; they are even identified with him during the period of inspiration, and the King as well as the people treat them with submission. The Tonga islanders have already attained a height of religious development where human distinctions of rank are as nothing in presence of the divinity.

As soon as they are all seated, the priest is considered as inspired, the god being supposed to exist within him from that moment. He sits for a considerable time in silence, with his hands clasped before him; his eyes are cast down, and he remains perfectly still. During the time that the victuals are being shared out, and the cava being prepared, the matabooles sometimes begin to consult him; sometimes he answers them, at other times not; in either case he remains with his eyes cast down. Frequently he will not answer a word till the repast is finished, and the cava too. When he speaks, he generally begins in a low and very altered tone of voice, which generally rises to nearly its natural pitch, though sometimes a little above it. All that he says is supposed to be the declaration of the god, and he accordingly speaks in the first person as if he were the god. All this is done generally without any apparent inward emotion or outward agitation; but sometimes his countenance becomes fierce, and, as it were, inflamed, and his whole frame agitated with inward feeling; he is seized with an universal trembling; the perspiration breaks out on his forehead, and his lips, turning black, are convulsed; at length tears start in floods from his eyes, his breast heaves with great emotion, and his utterance is choked. These symptoms gradually subside. Before this paroxysm comes on, and after it is over, he often eats as much as four hungry men, under other circumstances, could devour. The fit being now gone off, he remains for some time calm, and then takes up a club that is placed by him for the purpose, turns it over and regards it attentively; he then looks up earnestly, now to the right, now to the left, and now again at the club; afterwards he looks up again, and about him in like manner, and then again fixes his eyes upon his club, and so on for several times: at length he suddenly raises the club, and, after a moment's pause, strikes the ground, or the adjacent part of the house, with considerable force: immediately the god leaves him. . . .[1]
Some of the natives are such adepts at this sort of mysterious conversation with the divinities, that they can bring on a fit of inspiration whenever they feel their mind at all so disposed.[2]

How strong the tendency towards states of possession finally becomes is evidenced by this observation of Mariner's:

It is customary to take a sick person to the house of a priest, that the will of the gods may be known. The priest becomes immediately inspired, and remains almost constantly in that state while the sick person is with him. If he does not get better in two or three days he is taken to another priest.[3]

---

[1] W. Mariner, *An Account*, etc., pp. 106-108.
[2] *Ibid.*, p. 112.   [3] *Ibid.*, pp. 112 sq.

Unlike the generality of shamanizing peoples, the Tonga possessed have acquired, as we observe, a certain consciousness of their state, so that we have in them a rare case of lucid possession amongst primitive races. Mariner has obtained interesting information directly from a possessed man, and his account, although brief, is searching. It is the only document which I can quote adducing personal evidence on a state of lucid possession, and from the point of view of interest ranks with Surin's testimony, with which we have already dealt.

> Now we are upon this subject it may not be amiss to mention that Finow's son, who at this period of our history was at the Navigator's Islands, used to be inspired by the spirit[1] of Toogoo Ahoo, the late King of Tonga, who it may be recollected was assassinated by Finow and Toabo Neuha. When this young chief returned to Hapai, Mr. Mariner, who was upon a footing of great friendship with him, one day asked him how he felt himself, when the spirit of Toogoo Ahoo visited him; he replied that he could not well describe his feelings, but the best he could say of it was, that he felt himself all over in a glow of heat and quite restless and uncomfortable, and did not feel his own personal identity as it were, but felt as if he had a mind different from his own natural mind, his thoughts wandering upon strange and unusual subjects, although perfectly sensible of surrounding objects. He next asked him how he knew it was the spirit of Toogoo Ahoo ? His answer was " There's a fool ! How can I tell you *how* I knew it ? I felt and knew it was so by a kind of consciousness; my mind told me that it was Toogoo Ahoo."[2]

This passage clearly shows the inner transformation of the personal consciousness and also the lucidity of states of possession amongst the Tonga natives. They feel themselves transformed into the divinity which speaks by their mouth, they are no longer masters of themselves, their thoughts " wander." The passive nature of the states is also manifested. The cause of the compulsion does not emerge as clearly as in Surin's case, because the natives do not resist divine possession as did the Christian energumens the demoniacal variety. Nevertheless, the abnormal and passive nature of the psychic phenomena is evident; the divine presence invades the man, it is not created by him.

Possession is not always confined to the priests; other persons, even the King, have similar states. " King Finow " used occasionally to be " inspired by the ghost of Mooimooi,

---

[1] The souls of deceased nobles become gods of the second rank in Bolotoo (Mariner).
[2] *Ibid.*, vol. i, pp. 111-112.

a former King of Tonga,"[1] but " he was not strictly considered a priest on that account." Mariner recollects no chief who was a priest; for although Tali y Tooboo inspired him the King was not on that account regarded as a priest, " those only, in general, being considered priests who are in the frequent habit of being inspired by some particular god."[2]

The lack of any exciting music might lead us to doubt the genuineness of the whole performance, but such a thought is negatived by the description. Mariner himself raised the question of authenticity and replied without hesitation in the affirmative. What is still more important, it sometimes happens that the divine consultation must be interrupted because the priest cannot attain to a state of possession. Admissions of this nature were made to Mariner and he has preserved them to us as a testimony of an entirely unique nature to which I know no parallel in literature.

> Mr. Mariner frequently associated with them, watched their general conduct, and enquired the opinion of all classes of the natives respecting them; and after all, has no reason to think that they combine together for the purpose of deceiving people.[3]
>
> It might be supposed that this violent agitation on the part of the priest is merely an assumed appearance for the purpose of popular deception; but Mr. Mariner has no reason at all to think so. There can be little doubt, however, but that the priest, on such occasions, often summons into action the deepest feelings of devotion of which he is susceptible, and by a voluntary act disposes his mind, as much as possible, to be powerfully affected: till at length, what began by volition proceeds by involuntary effort, and the whole mind and body becomes subjected to the over-ruling emotion.[4]
>
> Mr. Mariner, indeed, did once witness a rare instance of a man who was disappointed in this particular: finding himself, as he thought, about to be inspired, some cava was brought to him (as is usual on such occasions), but, in a little while he was obliged to acknowledge that the god would not visit ; at which all present were greatly surprised, and so the cava was taken away again.[5]

False prophecies by possessed persons are also accepted without any particular scandal:

> When a priest is inspired, he is thought capable of prophesying, or, rather, the god within him is said sometimes to prophesy; those prophecies generally come true, for they are mostly made on the probable side of a question, and when they do not come to pass as expected, the priest is not blamed, but it is supposed the gods for some wise purpose have deceived them; or that the gods, for

[1] W. Mariner, *An Account* . . ., vol. i, p. 112.
[2] *Ibid.*, vol. ii, p. 145.   [3] *Ibid.*, vol. ii, p. 146.
[4] *Ibid.*, vol. i, pp. 110 sq.   [5] *Ibid.*, vol. i, p. 112.

aught they know, have since changed their mind, and ordered matters otherwise; or that the god who inspired the priest spoke prematurely without consulting the other gods.[1]

Unlike those of the Sandwich Islands, the priests of the Tonga Islands do not form a special body. Only so long as the god is within them are they raised above the people. On the other hand, there is a certain degree of heredity in the priesthood, probably for the simple reason that the priest's son is exposed in a high degree to the influence of suggestion; it is possession which first makes him a priest and not the converse. At bottom there is therefore a specific and lasting priesthood.

> In regard to the priests, their habits are precisely the same as those persons of the same rank; and when they are not inspired, all the respect that is paid to them is that only which is due to their private rank. . . . It most frequently happens that the eldest son of a priest, after his father's death, becomes a priest of the same god who inspired his father.[2]

There appears to be no profound general psychic difference between the priests and the other men of the same race. Mariner has observed that:

> . . . If there was any difference between them and the rest of the natives, it was that they were *rather* more given to reflection, and somewhat more taciturn, and probably greater observers of what was going forward.[3]

A second detailed account of possession in the South Sea Islands dates from the end of the last century. This, too, comes from the pen of an English investigator and is found in his book on the Melanesians.[4] Whereas Mariner's information related to a group of Polynesian islands, Codrington has studied the Melanesians. The states of possession are not of the same nature; in Melanesia it is visibly the somnambulistic form which predominates. The methods by which they are provoked are also more complicated than the simple auto-suggestion of the Tonga islanders. A particularly interesting fact is that the Melanesians distinguish clearly between diseases of the mind and possession, just as do the Ba-Ronga in Africa. Possession may be desired or else undesired and morbid; the former variety may be spontaneous or artificially provoked. A further remarkable fact is the conscious

[1] *Ibid.*, vol. ii, pp. 145-46. [2] *Ibid.*, vol. ii, p. 145.
[3] *Ibid.*, vol. ii, p. 146.
[4] Codrington, *The Melanesians*, Oxford, 1891.

identification of the possessed with the spirit who fills him, a phenomenon which clearly indicates that the possession is at least partly lucid in form.

Codrington remarks concerning certain Melanesian spirits:

> There is often difficulty in understanding what is told about them, because the name Nopitu is given both to the spirit and to the person possessed by the spirit, who performs wonders by the power and in the name of the Nopitu who possesses him. Such a one would call himself Nopitu; rather speaking of himself, will say not "I," but "we two," meaning the Nopitu in him and himself, or "we" when he is possessed by many. He would dance at a festival, such as a kolekole, as no man not possessed by a Nopitu could dance. He would scratch himself, his arms or his head, and new money not yet strung would fall from his fingers; Vetpepewu told me that he had seen money fall from a Nopitu at a kolekole—bags full. One would shake himself on a mat and unstrung money would pour down into it.[1]

Of spontaneous possession we learn the following:[2]

> The knowledge of future events is believed to be conveyed to the people by a spirit or a ghost speaking with a voice of a man, one of the wizards, who is himself unconscious while he speaks. In Florida the men of a village would be sitting in their kiala, canoe-house, and discussing some undertaking, an expedition probably to attack some unsuspecting village. One among them, known to have his own *tindalo* ghost of prophecy, would sneeze and begin to shake, a sign that the tindalo had entered into him; his eyes would glare, his limbs twist, his whole body be convulsed, foam would burst from his lips; then a voice, not his own, would be heard in his throat, allowing or disapproving of what was proposed. Such a man used no means of bringing on the ghost; it came upon him, as he believed himself, at its own will, its *mana* overpowered him, and when it departed it left him quite exhausted.[3]
>
> A party would be sitting round an evening fire, and one of them would hear a voice as if proceeding from his thigh, saying: "Here am I, give me some food, I am hungry." He would roast a little red yam, and when it was done fold it in the corner of the mat on which he was sitting. In a little while it would be gone, and then the Nopitu would begin to talk and sing in a voice so small and clear and sweet, that once heard it never could be forgotten; but it sang the ordinary Mota songs, while the men drummed an accompaniment for it. Then it would say: "I am going"; they would call it, and it was gone. Then a woman would feel it come to her, and sit upon her knee; she would hear it cry "Mother! Mother!" She would know it, and carry it in a mat upon her back like an infant. Sometimes a woman would hear a Nopitu say "Mother, I am coming to you," and she would feel the spirit entering into her, and it would be born afterwards as an ordinary child. Such a one, named *Rongoloa*, was not long ago still living at Motlav. The Nopitu, like other spirits, were the familiars only of those who

---

[1] *Ibid.*, p. 153.
[2] These accounts of spontaneous cases belong logically to Chap. V.
[3] *Ibid.*, pp. 209 sq.

knew them, and these were often women. If a man wished to know and become known to a Nopitu, he gave money to some woman who knew those spirits, and then one would come to him.[1]

It is difficult to separate the practice of magic arts from the manifestation of a ghost's or spirit's power in possession; because a man may use some magic means to bring the possession upon himself, as in the case of prophecy, and also because the connection between the unseen powerful being and the man, in whatever way the connection is made and works, is that which makes the wizard. Yet there is a distinction between the witchcraft and sorcery in which by magic charms the wizard brings the unseen power into action, and the spontaneous manifestation of such power by the unseen being; even though there may be only a few who can interpret, or to whom the manifestations are made. In a case of madness the native belief is that the madman is possessed. There is at the same time a clear distinction drawn by the natives between the acts and words of the delirium of sickness in which as they say they wander, and those which are owing to possession. They are sorry for lunatics and are kind to them, though their remedies are rough. At Florida, for example, one Kandagaru of Boli went out of his mind, chased people, stole things and hid them. No one blamed him, because they knew that he was possessed by a tindalo ghost. His friends hired a wizard who removed the tindalo, and he recovered. In the same way not long ago in Lepers' Island there was a man who lost his senses. The people conjectured that he had unwittingly trodden on a sacred place belonging to Tagaro, and that the ghost of the man who lately sacrificed there was angry with him. The doctors were called in; they found out whose ghost it was by calling on the names of dead men likely to have been offended, they washed him with water made powerful with charms, and then burned the vessel in which the magic water had been under his nose; he got well. In a similar case they will put bits of the fringe of a mat, which had belonged to the deceased, into a cocoa-nut shell, and burn it under the nose of the possessed. There was another man who threw off his malo and went naked at a feast, a sure sign of being out of his mind; he drew his bow at people, and carried things off. The people pitied him, and tried to cure him. When a man in such condition in that island spoke, it was not with his own voice, but with that of the dead man who possessed him; and such a man would know where things were hidden; when he was seen coming men would hide a bow or a club to try him, and he would always know where to find it. Thus the possession which causes madness cannot be quite distinguished from that which prophesies, and a man may pretend to be mad that he may get the reputation of being a prophet. At Saa a man will speak with the voice of a powerful man deceased, with contortions of the body which come upon him when he is possessed; he calls himself, and is spoken to by others, by the name of the dead man who speaks through him; he will eat fire, lift enormous weights, and foretell things to come. In the Banks' Islands the people make a distinction between possession by a ghost that enters a man for some particular purpose, and that by a ghost which comes for no other apparent cause than that being without a home in the abode of the dead he wanders mischievously about, a *tamat lelera*, a wandering ghost. Wonderful feats of strength and agility used to be performed under the in-

---

[1] *Ibid.*, p. 154.

fluence of one of these "wandering ghosts"; a man would move
with supernatural quickness from place to place, he would be heard
shouting at one moment in a lofty tree on one side of a village,
and in another moment in a tree on the opposite side, he would
utter sounds such as no man could make, his strength was such
that many men could hardly master him. Such a man was seized
by his friends and held struggling in the smoke of strong-smelling
leaves, while they called one after another the names of the dead
men whose ghosts were likely to be abroad; when the right name
was called the ghost departed, but sometimes this treatment
failed.[1]

This is the manner in which the Melanesians set about
invoking the spirits, that is to say for the purpose of inducing
possession artificially:

This has been described by a native under the name of *Na tamet
lingalinga*, by which name those who are subjected to the ghostly
influence are called. It is done, he writes, on the fifth day after
a death. There was a certain man at Lo who took the lead, and
without whom nothing could be done; he gave out that he would
descend into Panoi, the abode of the dead, and he had with him
certain others, assistants. He and his party were called simply
"ghosts" when engaged in the affair. The first thing was to
assemble those who were willing to be treated in a *gamal*, a public
hall, perhaps twenty young men or boys, to make them lie down
on the two sides, and to shake over them leaves and tips of the
twigs of plants powerful and magical with charms. Then the
leader and his assistants went into all the sacred places which
ghosts haunt, such as where men wash off the black of mourning,
collecting as they went the ghosts and becoming themselves so
much possessed that they appeared to have lost their senses,
though they acted in a certain method. In the meanwhile the
subjects lying in the *gamal* begin to be moved; those who bring
as they say the ghosts to them go quietly along both sides of
the house without, and all at once strike the house along its whole
length with the sticks they carry in their hands. This startles
those inside, and they roll about on the ground distracted. Then
the "ghosts" enter in with their sticks, and in this performance each
is believed to be some one deceased, one Tagilrow, another Qata-
wala; they leap from side to side, turning their sticks over to be
beaten by the subjects on one side and the other. The subjects
are given sticks for this purpose, and as they strike the stick the
ghost "strikes," possesses, them one after another. In this
state the sticks draw them out into the open place of the village,
where they are seen. They appear not to recognize or hear any
one but the "ghosts" who have brought this upon them, and who
alone can control them and prevent them from pulling down the
houses; for they have a rage for seizing and striking with anything
—bows, clubs, bamboo water-vessels, or the rafters of the houses—
and their strength is such that a full-grown man cannot hold a
boy in this state. After a time the "ghosts" take them back into
the *gamal*, and there they lie exhausted; the "ghosts" go to drink
kava, and as each drinks he pours away the dregs calling the name
of one of the possessed, and the senses of each return as his name

[1] *Ibid.*, pp. 218 sq.

is called.   It is five days, however, before they can go about again. This was done once after a Christian teacher had come to Lo, and two of his scholars whom he let go to prove that it was a deception were possessed.[1]

In New Guinea possession has a bearing on all important circumstances affecting either the individual or the family. Ancestor-worship is practised there, and the natives have the portraits of their ancestors carved in wood in their houses. These are made the object of a certain cult with sacrifices, but this is not all; natives endowed with a particular aptitude plunge themselves when occasion arises into a state of possession before these ancestors in order to ask their advice on important questions.   The ancestor-gods are induced to speak not by efforts to obtain from the wooden images some utterance which is afterwards interpreted, but by persuading the ancestor dwelling in the image to enter into the body of a living man and thus pronounce real words.   The head of the household or else a professional sorcerer acts as medium.

A Dutch writer describes as follows the manner in which these images of ancestors are questioned through the agency of possessed persons.

> When anyone is sick and wishes to know the means of cure, or when anyone desires to avert misfortune or to discover something unknown, then in presence of the whole family one of the members is stupefied by the fumes of incense or by other means of producing a state of trance.   The image of the deceased person whose advice is sought is then placed on the lap or shoulder of the medium in order to cause the soul to pass out of the image into his body.   At the moment when that happens, he begins to shiver; and encouraged by the bystanders, the soul speaks through the mouth of the medium and names the means of cure or of averting the calamity.   When he comes to himself, the medium knows nothing of what he has been saying.   This they call *kor karwar*, that is, "invoking the soul"; and they say *karwar iwas*, "the soul speaks."   The writer adds: "It is sometimes reported that the souls go to the underworld, but that is not true.   The Papuans think that after death the soul abides by the corpse and is buried with it in the grave; hence before an image is made, if it is necessary to consult the soul, the enquirer must betake himself to the grave in order to do so.   But when the image is made, the soul enters into it and is supposed to remain in it so long as satisfactory answers are obtained from it in consultation.   But should the answers prove disappointing, the people think that the soul has deserted the image, on which they throw the image away as useless. Where the soul has gone, nobody knows, and they do not trouble their heads about it, since it has lost its power.[2]

[1] *Ibid.*, pp. 224 sq.
[2] F. S. A. de Clerq, *De-West en Noordküst van Nederlandsch Nieu-Guinea*, in "Tijdschrift van het Kon. Nederlandsch Aardrijkskundig

Amongst the Vindessi of New Guinea the idea of possession is particularly connected with the conception, so frequent amongst other primitive races as well as this one, of a double soul existing in man. According to their belief, every human being has two souls. When a woman dies they believe that two souls pass into the other world, but when it is a man only one does so; the other may enter into a living person, generally a man but occasionally a woman. A man who has thus become possessed is considered as a medicine-man or a woman as a medicine-woman.

> When a person wishes to become a medicine-man or medicine-woman, he or she acts as follows. If a man has died, and his friends are sitting about the corpse lamenting, the would-be medicine-man suddenly begins to shiver and to rub his knee with his folded hands, while he utters a monotonous sound. Gradually he falls into an ecstasy, and if his whole body shakes convulsively, the spirit of the dead man is supposed to have entered into him, and he becomes a medicine-man. Next day or the day after he is taken into the forest; some hocus-pocus is performed over him, and the spirits of lunatics, who dwell in certain thick trees, are invoked to take possession of him. He is now himself called a lunatic, and on returning home behaves as if he were half crazed. This completes his training as a medicine-man, and he is now fully qualified to kill or cure the sick.[1]

The great work on New Guinea edited by Neuhauss is remarkable for a complete absence of reference to possession as well as to Shamanism. The only thing possibly relating to these subjects concerns certain " fits of madness." There are cases in which single individuals are out of their mind for hours, or more rarely days at a time, and inclined to commit grave acts of violence. The missionary Ch. Keysser says: " This state is considered to result from a mysterious influence exercised by spirits."[2] This remark is unhappily too vague for us to deduce from it with safety that the natives regard these states as true possession. In the Fiji Islands each tribe contains a family on whom alone it is incumbent to become inspired or possessed from time to time by a holy spirit.

> Their qualification is hereditary, and any one of the ancestral gods may choose his vehicle from among them. I have seen this possession, and a horrible sight it is. In one case, after the fit

Genootschap," Tweede Serie, x (1893), quoted by J. G. Frazer, *The Belief in Immortality and the Worship of the Dead,* vol. i, London, 1913, p. 309 (Gifford Lectures, St. Andrews, 1911-12).
[1] J. G. Frazer, *ibid.,* p. 322.
[2] R. Neuhauss, *Deutsch Neu-Guinea,* vol. iii, Berlin, 1911, p. 79.

was over, for some time the man's muscles and nerves twitched and quivered in an extraordinary way. He was naked except for his breech-clout, and on his naked breast snakes seemed to be wriggling for a moment or two beneath his skin, disappearing and then suddenly reappearing in another part of his chest. When the *mbete* (which we may translate " priest " for want of a better word) is seized by the possession, the god within him calls out his own name in a stridulous tone: " It is I ! Katouivere !" or some other name. At the next possession some other ancestor may declare himself.[1]

Of the Southern Islands of the Pacific Ocean Ellis writes:

Appearing to the priest in a dream of the night, though a frequent, was neither the only nor the principal mode by which the god inti- mated his will. He frequently entered the priest, who, inflated as it were with the divinity, ceased to act or speak as a voluntary agent, but moved and spoke as entirely under supernatural in- fluence. In this respect there was a striking resemblance between the rude oracles of the Polynesians and those of the celebrated nations of ancient Greece.

As soon as the god was supposed to have entered the priest, the latter became violently agitated, and worked himself up to the highest pitch of apparent frenzy, the muscles of the limbs seemed convulsed, the body swelled, the countenance became terrific, the features distorted, and the eyes wild and strained. In this state he often rolled on the earth, foaming at the mouth, as if labouring under the influence of the divinity by whom he was possessed, and in shrill cries, and violent and often indistinct sounds, revealed the will of the god. The priests, who were attend- ing, and versed in the mysteries, received, and reported to the people, the declarations which had been thus received.

When the priest had uttered the response of the oracle, the violent paroxysm gradually subsided, and comparative composure ensued. The god did not, however, always leave him as soon as the com- munication had been made. Sometimes the same *taura*, or priest, continued for two or three days possessed by the spirit or deity; a piece of native cloth, of a peculiar kind, worn round one arm, was an indication of inspiration, or of the indwelling of the god with the individual who wore it. The acts of the man during this period were considered as those of the god, and hence the greatest atten- tion was paid to his expressions, and the whole of his deportment.[2]

America has a surprise in store for us. Up to the present not one single account of spontaneous possession amongst the American aborigines has reached me ! Even the great travel- books of such distinguished explorers as K. von den Steinen,[3] Preuss,[4] and Koch-Grünberg[5] are completely empty of them.

[1] Private letter of the Rev. Lorimer Fison to J. G. Frazer, *The Magic Art*, London, 1911, vol. i, p. 378.
[2] W. Ellis, *Polynesian Researches*, 2nd edit., London, 1832-36, i, p. 372.
[3] K. von der Steinen, *Durch Zentral Brasilien*, Leipzig, 1884. *Unter den Naturvölkern Zentral-Brasiliens*, 2nd edit., Leipzig, 1897.
[4] K. Th. Preuss, *Nayarit-Expedition*, Leipzig, 1912.
[5] Theodor Koch-Grünberg, *Zwei Jahre unter den Indianern*. Reisen in Nordwest Brasilien, 1903-05, 2 vols., Stuttgart, 1910.

Accounts of shamanistic possession are also more rare in the ethnological literature of America than elsewhere. The literature on the dances of the American natives is to-day far richer than that concerning the other races of the globe, but it is only accidentally that we meet a remark from which some information may be gleaned as to the subjective state of the dancers.

We find, for example, in Koch-Grünberg's work a few short observations on the masked dances of the South American Indians, in which animals are often represented.

> At the root of all these mimetic performances lies the idea of a magic influence. They are designed to secure for the village and its inhabitants, the plantations and all the country round, blessings and fertility, and also to serve as indemnity to the dead in whose honour the feast is given. Inasmuch as the dancer seeks by gesture and action to imitate as faithfully as possible the being whom he desires to impersonate, he identifies himself with the latter. The mysterious force residing in the mask passes into the dancer, makes him himself a potent demon and renders him capable of driving out demons or rendering them favourable. In particular the demons of growth, the spirits of animals which play a part in it and the animal-spirits of hunting and fishing must by mimetic gestures be conjured up within the reach of human power.[1]

> All the masks represent demons. The Indian's imagination peoples the whole of nature with good and evil spirits which hold potent sway over life and death. . . . This search for a personified cause of all joys and sorrows finds its expression in the masked dances. In these are shown, speaking and acting, all the spirits with their following of animals from earth, air, and water which, however, again represent demons and typify various classes of animals, sometimes with appropriate mimicry.

> The demon is in the mask, he is incorporated in it. To the Indians the mask *is* the demon. When I questioned the Kobéua as to the meaning of this or that mask they always said: " This one is the butterfly, the aracu fish, the makukú," etc., and never, "This is the mask of the butterfly," etc. The demon of the mask passes for the time being into the dancer who wears it. On the morrow of the feast of the dead when the masks are consumed by fire, the demons leave their transitory abode and betake themselves to Taku, the paradise of masks, or to their dwelling-place situated on some other mountain or in a torrent. . . .

The demons are invisible to ordinary mortals. Only the medicine-man can see them and speak to them by virtue of his magic powers.

> As for this invisible part of the mask, the Kobéua called it the " maskara-anga " (soul of the mask), in order to make its essential nature as clear as possible to me. Just as the human soul is invisible in the body, animates it and departs after death to Makö-

[1] *Ibid.*, vol. ii p. 196.

lami, the Beyond of all Kobéua souls, so with the " death "—*i.e.*, the incineration of the mask—the invisible power which dwelt in it during the feast, leaves the visible husk and retires to its own dwelling-place. This unseen force is the demon. " All the masks are *abochökö* (demons); all abochökö are lords of the masks," says the Kobéua.

The conception of Taku as the paradise of masks may have arisen from analogy with the human Beyond.

> The incineration of the mask is founded on the same belief as the cremation of the mortal remains of the dead, on the fear of an unwelcome return of the demon with whom it is not desired to have further dealings after the feast of the dead. When certain masks are preserved or made over into bags this must be regarded as a sign of decadence.[1]

These are the principal passages in which Koch-Grünberg refers to the psychology of masked dances. It results categorically that the natives' conception of these dances is entirely along the lines of possession. But that is all; to assume that the dancers really fall into abnormal states seems to me definitely hazardous, and in my opinion Koch-Grünberg's further general description tends to the opposite conclusion. The details of sudden collapse, sudden onset and cessation of possession which have already become familiar to us in the Indian and Malay Peninsulas are completely lacking; we rather gain the impression that the dances run their course in a certain psychic equilibrium and are not distinguished *toto genere* from the " performances " of civilized peoples. This at least appears to be the position to-day. Whether it has always been so is another question, to which no reply can be given without a systematic examination of the accounts of the early travellers for data concerning the masked dances of the American natives. It is conceivable that abnormal psychic phenomena have ceased under the influence of civilization, since even the Indian and Malay natives are now no longer untouched by it.

At the time of the colonization of America we have, in fact, a description by a Spanish priest (Las Casas) of epidemic possession amongst the Indians of Brazil. He writes:

> (To the Indians in the neighbourhood of Cape San Augustin) came from time to time, at intervals of several years, wizards from a great distance who pretended to bring the divinity with them. When the time for their return arrived the roads were

---

[1] *Ibid.*, vol. ii, pp. 178 sq.

carefully cleansed and the people welcomed them with feasts and dances. Before they entered the village the women went in pairs from house to house and confessed aloud the sins of which they had been guilty towards their husbands or mutually with them, and entreated pardon as if they were at death's door. When the wizard in holiday attire arrived at the village he entered a darkened hut and erected in a suitable spot a calabash shaped like a man. He then stood by the calabash and announced in a changed voice, assuming that of a child, that they need no longer trouble to work and go to the fields, for the food-plants would prosper of themselves and they would never lack nourishment. Bread would come into the huts of its own accord, the ploughs would cultivate the fields of themselves, the bow and arrows would hunt game in the forests for their masters unaided. They would, moreover, slay many enemies. The old women would grow young again and marry their daughters well. By these and other similar falsehoods the wizard deceived the people, making them believe that there was in the calabash something divine which told him these things. As soon as he had come to the end of his predictions everyone began to tremble, particularly the women who were seized with violent shudderings of the whole body so that they seemed possessed by the devil. They threw themselves to the ground foaming at the mouth and the wizard thereupon induced them to believe that the happiness they desired was coming upon them and that they shared in the goodwill of the pretended gods.[1]

It is very surprising that the literature on the North American Indians should contain nothing relating to possession. I have most carefully perused numerous volumes of the Bureau of American Ethnology's Annual Report without finding anything of importance. It is certainly not to be believed that the investigators would have given no account of true states of possession had they met phenomena of this kind. Even in the thick *in-quarto* volume of James Mooney[2] on the frankly epidemic politico-religious movement, accompanied by visions and dances, of the Sioux Indians in the nineties of the last century, there is nothing whatever about states of possession. Could a wave of excitement of this intensity have come and gone without any such phenomena if the memory of them had existed in the popular mind ? The matter which has hitherto come my way is insufficient to convert me to the view that the phenomena of possession have played no part in the religious life of the American aborigines.

It is only on the north-west coast of America that pos-

[1] Otto Stoll, *Suggestion und Hypnotismus in der Volkerpsychologie*, 2nd edit., Leipzig, 1904, p. 131.
[2] James Mooney, *The Ghost-Dance Religion*, Ethnol. Report, Washington, vol. xiv, 1896.

session is known to me with certainty. The ethnologist Adrian Jacobsen in the course of a work on the secret societies of the Indians of this region in which masked dances play an essential part, relates the following:

> In each tribe intelligent and, as they pretend, inspired men take upon themselves the representation of the gods. They form secret associations so that their hidden arts and doctrines, their masquerades and mimicries may not be betrayed by the profane to the general public. . . .
> There were and still are hundreds of masks in use each of which represents a spirit from the legends. In the performances they enter separately or in groups, as is indicated by the legend to be enacted, and those wearing masks are no longer regarded by the awe-struck crowd as actors and persons representing the gods but as the gods themselves descending from heaven to earth. Each actor must therefore execute exactly what legend relates of the spirit. If the actor wears no mask, as often happens amongst the Hametz (devourers or biters) or the Pakwalla (medicine-men) the spirit whom he represents has entered into his body and the man possessed by the spirit is on that account not responsible for his actions while in that state.[1]
> Amongst the secret societies mentioned the Hametz are the most highly regarded and the most renowned. . . .
> Under the name of Hametz the Quakjult and neighbouring races designate in each village certain men (and also sometimes women) who practise a sort of cannibalism. The right to become a Hametz can apparently only be acquired by high birth or marriage into families possessed of this privilege. The Hametz must, moreover, be inspired by the spirit whom he represents in the dance. This inspiration occurs only in winter. For several days previously the Hametz, stark naked, is led by his companions from door to door in the village, as I have myself seen at Fort Rupert in 1881. There is reason to believe that the preparation of at least some of the Hametz demands four years during which they must wear under the left arm and on the right shoulder a specially prepared red-dyed ring of cedar-bark. During the last four months they must live alone in the forest.[2]
> My brother writes me the following on the subject of a Hametz feast. . . .
> The Bella-Coola Indians call the Hametz Alla-Kotla after the spirit by whom they generally profess to be inspired. When the novice is inspired by the spirit Alla-Kotla he thinks he hears a roaring like that of a storm: the earth is shaken by the potent voice of Alla-Kotla. The postulant is seized by the spirit and carried into the air or the bowels of the earth where he is almost stifled by the lack of air and where there are deep precipices. No one knows whither Alla-Kotla goes in these journeys and no one may track him.
> On his return to the surface of the earth the spirit commands the novice to bite those present in the dance-house, otherwise he will be devoured by the spirit.

---

[1] J. Adrian Jacobsen, *Geheimbünde der Küstenbewohner Nordwest-Amerikas*. In: Verhandlungen der Berliner Gesellschaft für Anthropologie, Ethnologie und Urgeschichte, 1891, p. 384.

[2] *Ibid.*, pp. 386 sq.

Another spirit, Sek-seik Kallai, who is present at these feasts, inspires men to dance. Nus-Alpsta is the third spirit present on these occasions. He seems to be an envoy of Bek-bek Kwallanit, but he wishes nothing but evil to men and seeks to trip the dancers up. The novice recognizes him easily by his growling which resembles that of a bear. All this is taught to the postulant by his master the old Hametz months before the performance. The exhortations as to the rules to be observed are made with a degree of zeal and earnestness such as is hardly equalled in our religious instruction.[1]

The novice's first appearance is generally without a mask. The Hametz wears round his neck several rings of cedar-bark and often around his head a narrow circle, from the front of which hang strips of cedar-bark half covering his face, which is painted black. The head is thickly bestrewn with eagle's down, and the wrists and ankles also adorned with rings of cedar-bark. Some renowned Hametz in whose honour slaves were formerly slain or who to-day, when men may no longer be put to death, have at least bitten a large number of persons, wear either a ring round their neck with carved wooden death's-heads or else a covering adorned with them and worn over the shoulder during the dance. The Hametz dances in a half-squatting position. His arms are turned outwards with hands upwards and he stretches them out to right and left, imparting to the hands and fingers a constant quivering movement. The dance is mainly composed of leaps to right and left. The eyes are turned upwards so that little more than the white is visible, the mouth half open, the lips drawn backwards, and the Hametz utters inarticulate sounds like a prolonged ah! The dance consists of four parts with appropriate and different chants.

During the last chant the four Hametz who always accompany him, and who dance with him, hand him two dance-rattles of a particular shape, with handles differing from those of the ordinary ones used in dancing. As a rule they represent death's heads or human faces, but are sometimes also carved in the shape of man-headed frogs. Especially in a Quakjult village I found human faces cut into rattles, the tongues hanging out, to signify, as an Indian explained to me, the thirst for blood. His companions also have each a rattle. At the end of the fourth dance the Hametz casts off the coverings from his body, flings himself upon the chosen victim and bites off from his chest and arms small pieces of flesh. Not infrequently dangerous wounds result from the proceeding; I have, for example, seen a man with deep scars who had been on his back for six months as a result of the bites he had received. Another died because an over-zealous Hametz had bitten him right through the throat.

My brother who was present at a Hametz feast in 1887 writes me as follows: " At the first feast the Hametz and his companions danced four different dances to an uninterrupted tune. At the end of the fourth dance the spirit took possession of him and he became as if mad, tore off his dancing-dress and howled like an animal as he flung himself on an Indian near by. The latter defended himself with all his strength, but the Hametz seemed to possess supernatural power. He threw him to the ground and bit a piece of flesh out of his arm. Meanwhile the four companions formed around the victim a circle so close that he could hardly be seen. The Hametz behaved in the same way with four other

[1] *Ibid.*, p. 388.

spectators, whereupon almost all the others fled. The Hametz accompanying him tried to quiet him but without success for he had fallen into a veritable frenzy. In the end the shaman or medicine-man was fetched who managed to calm him after a quarter of an hour.

My brother describes the scene as the most shocking imaginable. The frenzied man's eyes were bloodshot and his glance demoniacal.[1]

The savage character of this form of possession recalls the demoniacal fits of the Middle Ages. It is, however, almost the only case I know.

There appear to be no accounts whatever concerning the half-civilized peoples of ancient America. H. Beuchat's comprehensive and masterly work on the civilizations existing at the time of the European invasion contains no information of importance about religious states resembling possession. We find only the following which relates to the priests of Peru:

> The priests who uttered the oracles . . . performed shamanistic ceremonies. They drank chicha, inhaled the smoke of narcotic plants, danced and leapt until they fell down in a trance. On recovering from their ecstasy they gave forth the oracles in a language incomprehensible to the uninitiated.[2]

In Eduard Seler's study of sorcerers and sorcery in ancient Mexico also it is merely stated that there were sorcerers who provoked visions and ecstatic states by means of certain narcotics, amongst which tobacco played the leading part.[3] But there is no proof that possession arose in these states. The only thing which might suggest it is the fact that " at least in certain ceremonies " the priest of a god appeared in the latter's vestments. It should, however, be observed that the same applied to the god's consecrated victim.[4]

No other evidence concerning primitive and half-civilized America has reached me. The cause of this paucity of documentation is not altogether clear; does it in fact result merely from one of the hazards of research into sources, or is possession really less frequent amongst the American peoples than in other parts of the world ? I cannot for the

---

[1] *Ibid.*, pp. 390-92.

[2] H. Beuchat, *Manuel d'archéologie américaine* (Amérique préhistorique—Civilisations disparues), Paris, 1912, p. 419.

[3] Ed. Seler, *Altmexikanische Studien, Museum fur Völkerkunde*, vi, parts 2-4, Berlin, 1899, pp. 42 sq.

[4] *Ibid.*, p. 45.

moment help feeling that this latter supposition is the correct one; the lack of relevant documents in American ethnological literature is altogether too surprising.

If this impression were confirmed by further and more thorough research, we should naturally be faced with the problem of explaining this differentiation between the primitive peoples of the Old and New Worlds.   Is it possible that the structure of the personality is more solid amongst the American primitives, *i.e.*, the Red Indians ?   The general impression which they produce is not out of keeping with such an idea, but no definite reply can be given except as the result of exact psychological research, a thing still in its infancy as relating to primitive races.

CHAPTER VIII

THE SHAMANISM OF THE NORTH ASIATIC PEOPLES IN ITS RELATIONSHIP TO POSSESSION

WE shall now pass to the countries from which the word " Shamanism " originates, as it was first generally used in connection with their sorcerers.

We should expect to find the phenomena of possession at their height, both as regards intensity and general prevalence, in these lands. Whether this expectation is justified and in what measure remains to be seen. We must first pass in review the relevant literature.

V. M. Mikhaïlowsky published in 1892 in the *Transactions of the Russian Royal Society of Natural History, Anthropology and Ethnography* a large number of accounts of Shamanism amongst the peoples of Asiatic Russia: Tunguses, Yakuts, Samoyedes, Ostiaks, Tshuktsh, Koriaks, Kamchadals, Giliaks, Mongols, Buriats, Altaians, Kirghiz, Teleutes, etc.[1] He has come to the following conclusions:

> Throughout the vast extent of the Russian Empire, from Behring's Strait to the borders of the Scandinavian Peninsula, among the multitudinous tribes preserving remains of their former heathen beliefs, we find in a greater or less degree Shamonist phenomena. Despite the variety of races and the enormous distances that separate them, the phenomena which we class under the general name of Shamonism are found repeated with marvellous regularity.[2]

I shall now give some descriptions, both ancient and modern, taken from German literature, which I have found more accurate than any other. It is noteworthy that the data furnished by the more recent travellers are much superior

---

[1] Engl. trans. in *The Journal of the Anthropological Institute* of *Great Britain and Ireland*, vol. xxiv (1895), pp. 62-100 and 126-158. *Shamanism in Siberia and European Russia, being the Second Part of* " *Shamanstvo* " (from the 12th vol. of the Proceedings of the Ethnological Section of the Royal Russian Society, etc., 1892, in Russian). Unfortunately most of the sources to which it refers are likewise in Russian.

[2] *Ibid.*, p. 158.

to those of the earlier ones, but as a matter of fact, accounts satisfying all the requirements of the psychologist are still to seek.

The travellers of the eighteenth century, the "Age of Enlightenment," could not do enough to show the shamans as mere charlatans or impostors. Their accounts are therefore devoid of information.[1]

With the romantic period the corresponding deepening in the scientific spirit resulted in the abandonment of the rationalistic view of Shamanism as mere trickery, in fact the change of attitude even went too far in the opposite direction. To-day the *bona fides* and psychological genuineness of a considerable proportion of shamanistic states is generally recognized, but on the other hand it is universally held that not all manifestations of the shamans are authentic and that imposture goes hand in hand with abnormal phenomena. It is reserved for future investigators to indicate the exact division between the two and above all to determine by close study up to what point both genuine phenomena and trickeries are common property, or differ from one shaman to another. Given the continual melting away of primitive conditions before the " sun " of civilization, it is much to be desired that such researches should be carried out very urgently and under the auspices of the state. Amongst the numerous scientific tasks which it will be easier to execute in the Russia of the future than in that of the past is the investigation of the religious life of its highly diversified populations.

Wrangel, a late eighteenth-century traveller remarkable for his scrupulous accuracy, was the first, or one of the first, to declare the shamans to be more than impostors and play-actors. In certain circumstances they would endure ill-treatment rather than go back in any way on their words.

> It is not infrequent for the shaman to be severely beaten in order to induce him to change an unwelcome pronouncement; sometimes this little domestic remedy helps, but the shaman often has firmness enough to stand by his opinion, a fact which infallibly raises him in the public esteem to a marked degree.[2]

---

[1] By way of example the author here gives a quotation from the works of J. G. Gmelin, *Reise durch Sibirien* (Göttingen, 1752) which is, as he states, entirely lacking in precision and psychological interest (R. Sudre).

[2] F. von Wrangel, *Reise längs der Nordküste von Sibirien und auf dem Eismeere in den Jahren* 1820-1824, ed. with a foreword by C. Ritter

Almost all those who up to the present have expressed an opinion on the shamans have represented them as unqualified impostors of a crude and vulgar kind, whose ecstasies are nothing more than an illusion created for base purposes of gain. From all that I have been able to observe in the course of my journeyings in Siberia, both here and in various other places, this judgement appears to me harsh and unjust. At least it is entirely partial and only applicable to charlatans who travel about under the name of shamans and excite the people's wonderment by all sorts of apparently supernatural tricks, such as grasping a red-hot iron, walking on it, running long needles through their skin, etc., in order to extract money from them.

Anyone who has observed a *true* shaman at the height of ecstasy will certainly . . . admit that he is neither able to practise deception, at least at that moment, nor desirous of doing so, but that what is occurring to him is a consequence of the involuntary and irresistible influence of his intensely stimulated imagination. A true shaman is certainly a very remarkable psychological phenomenon. Every time that here or elsewhere I have seen shamans operate they have left on me a dark impression which was long in fading. The wild glance, blood-shot eyes, raucous voice which seemed to come forth with extreme effort from a chest racked by spasmodic movements, the unnatural convulsive distortion of the face and body, and even the bristling hair, and even the hollow sound of the magic drum—all this gives to the scene a horrible and mysterious character which has gripped me strangely every time, and I understand very readily how uneducated and crude children of nature see in it the sinister work of evil spirits.[1]

Wrangel also disputes the existence of any scholastic association amongst the shamans. He believes in the absolute independence of each individual, and explains what they have in common by the impression of external nature which is common to all the dwellers in one region.

The true shamans belong to no particular caste, they form no corporation for the accomplishment of a common aim, but arise as it were singly and remain isolated. Amongst the people men are born endowed with an ardent imagination and excitable nerves. They grow up surrounded by the belief in spirits and shamans. The apparently supernatural ecstasy of these latter, the mystic nature of their whole being, makes a profound impression on the young man. He also desires to attain to this communion with the extraordinary, the supramundane, but there is no one to show him the way, for the oldest shaman does not know how he himself found it. It is from his own inner depths that by contact with the great and sombre nature surrounding him that he must derive knowledge of the incomprehensible. Solitude, reclusion from human society, vigil and fasting, stimulants and narcotics excite his imagination to the highest pitch; now he sees the apparitions and spirits of which he has heard tell in his early youth; he regards them with

---

(38th and 39th vols., Magazin von merkwürdigen neuen Reisebeschreibungen =14th vol. of the new Magazine), Berlin, 1839, vol. i, p. 285.

[1] *Ibid.*, pp. 286 sq.

firm and unshakable belief. At length he is consecrated shaman —i.e., proclaimed in the stillness of the night with certain solemnities, the traditional practices, the magic drum, etc. This brings him no increase of knowledge, no change in his spiritual, his inmost being, it is a mere ceremony touching the outer man. What he henceforward feels, does and says, is and always remains the result of his own inner mood—he is no cool and deliberate impostor, no vulgar charlatan.[1]

Castrén relates of the Ostiaks:

> Anyone can accomplish such ordinary sacrificial ceremonies, but when general sacrifices must be offered to the gods and their counsel asked on behalf of the race or a single individual, the priest or shaman is indispensable, for he alone can open the hearts of the gods and converse with them. But to the shaman the magic drum is an indispensable instrument. Ordinary sounds cannot penetrate to the ears of the gods; the shaman must conduct the conversation by means of song and drumming. Then the image of the god placed before him begins to speak, his words being nevertheless understood by the shaman only.[2]

The description of the Samoyede sorcerers is still more sharply characterized:

> When a *tadibe* (as the shaman is called amongst the Samoyedes) is properly initiated into his calling, he provides himself with a drum and a special costume. . . . Thus attired the sorcerer sits upon the ground to ask the counsel and help of the *tadebstios* (spirits). In this he is assisted by a tadibe less deeply initiated than himself in his art. At the beginning of the ceremony the more experienced tadibe beats the drum and sings a mystic and terrible melody accompanied by words. The other tadibe forthwith joins in and both sing the same air, like our Finnish rune-singers. Each word and each syllable are indefinitely prolonged. When after a short prologue the conversation with the spirit begins, the superior tadibe becomes mute and strikes only lightly on his drum. Presumably he is listening for the reply of the tadebstios. Meanwhile the assistant continues to sing the last words uttered by the Master. As soon as the latter has finished his mute conversation the two tadibes break into a wild howl, the drumming grows in strength and the words of the oracle are announced. . . .
>
> When, for example, a reindeer has strayed the melody is very simple. The tadibe first invokes the spirit, and one of their number said that he used the following words:

> Come, come,
> Spirits of sorcery !
> If you come not
> I shall come to you.
> Waken, waken,
> Spirits of sorcery !
> I have come to you,
> Waken from sleep.

---

[1] *Ibid.*

[2] M. Alexander Castrén, *Nordische Reisen und Forschungen*, vol. i., Reiseerinnerungen aus den Jahren 1838-1844. St. Petersburg, 1853, p. 291.

The tadebstio replies:

> Say with what
> You are concerned.
> Why do you come
> To disturb our rest ?

> (*These words are also sung aloud.*)

The tadibe continues:

> Came to me
> Lately a Nienets (Samoyede),
> This man who
> Earnest entreats me.
> Away has his reindeer gone
> Therefore have I
> Now come unto you.

According to my Samoyede only one tadebstio customarily replies to this invitation. When they come in numbers one says one thing and another another, so that the tadibe does not know which to listen to.

The tadibe then asks his attendant spirit to seek for the reindeer. " Seek it, seek it well, so that the reindeer may not be lost." The tadebstio naturally obeys the command. Meanwhile the tadibe exhorts him to search very thoroughly and not to cease until the reindeer has been found. When the tadebstio returns the tadibe adjures him again to speak the truth. " Do not lie: if you lie things will not go well. My comrades will despise me. Say only what you have seen. Speak both good and ill. Speak one word only. If you say much without clearness or precision it will do me harm," etc.

Then the spirit names the place where he has seen the reindeer. . . . We should not forget to say that before the conjuration the tadibe enquires all the circumstances of the loss of the reindeer, when and where it happened, whether the Samoyede supposes that it has been stolen, who are his neighbours and whether there is not an enemy amongst them, etc. If the person concerned cannot give all the necessary information the tadibe takes his drum and questions the spirits, then interrogates the Samoyede again, and continues thus until he has convinced himself as to the facts by means of the Samoyede's own declarations. Perhaps this conviction now and then takes form during the state of exaltation as a dream or magnetic vision; so much is certain, that the tadibe believes he has received the pronouncement of the oracle from the mouth of the tadebstio appearing to his imagination.

In addition to the collected, devout, and mutually consistent accounts given by the tadibes of these circumstances one thing fills me with particular conviction, that is the fact that the sorcerer often admits either that he cannot call up the tadebstio or cannot constrain him to give a reasonable reply, and this even in cases where he might with ease have fabricated some acceptable augury. It gave me pleasure to put the honesty of the tadibes to the proof in this way.[1]

---

[1] *Ibid.*, vol. i, pp. 192 sq.

Unfortunately Bastian's information concerning the Buriat shamans is entirely lacking in precision, which is the more regrettable since as one of the few ethnologists possessed of a deep interest in and knowledge of psychology he was highly qualified to furnish detailed psychological observations. He relates:

> . . . During the sacrificial ceremonies there is an outburst of ecstasy. The shaman's soul fares forth to unite with the spirits of the dead and receive from them in the kingdom of shadows the desired instruction. The body which all this time lies on the ground as if deprived of soul, is insensible to pain and performs during the absence of consciousness all those singular tricks which serve in the people's eyes as attestations of a true prophet: the shaman leaps into the fire with impunity, grasps a red-hot iron in his hands . . . and draws hot knives over his tongue until the hut is filled with the smell of burnt flesh, etc.[1]

From this description it results at least that the shamans fall into " ecstasy," into a " second " or somnambulistic state. Bastian's expression concerning the " absence of consciousness " is naturally false.

It may be assumed that the shamans, owing to the dangers to health consequent on their manner of life, must become nervously deranged. The majority of investigators have so completely taken for granted the essential nature of Shamanism as to pay no attention to the general psychic state of the shamans. It is therefore of the utmost value that the traveller Pallas has given on this point information showing that the shamans are often sensitive to an extreme degree.

> It should be noted as highly remarkable that many Samoyedes, particularly the sorcerers, show a peculiar form of timidity which seems to be caused in part by the excessive tension and excitability of fever, the action of the northerly climate, their mode of life, and an imagination warped by superstition. I know from reliable accounts that similarly excitable people are found amongst the Tunguses and inhabitants of Kamchatka. Major Islenief has assured me that it was the same amongst the Yakuts and I have observed it myself, although to a lesser degree, amongst the Buriats and the Tatars of the Ienissei. An unexpected touch on the side, for instance, or any other sensitive spot, a call, an unforeseen whistle or any other sudden manifestation of a startling nature puts these people beside themselves and almost into a frenzy. Amongst the Samoyedes and Yakuts who seem to manifest this excitability in the highest degree (since the whole of the former people will show in emergencies a pusillanimity quite beyond the normal) this frenzy goes so far that without knowing what they are doing they seize the first axe, knife or weapon which comes to hand and seek,

---

[1] A. Bastian, *Ein Besuch bei den burätischen Schamanen*, in " Geographische und ethnologische Bilder," Jena, 1873, p. 406.

if they are not restrained by force and all lethal weapons removed from their reach, to wound or kill whoever is the cause of their fright or happens to be near. When they cannot work off their rage in this way they gesticulate, shout, roll upon the ground and behave absolutely like raving madmen. In such cases the Samoyedes have an infallible means of bringing people to themselves: they set fire to a piece of reindeer skin or a tuft of its hair and make the patient inhale the smoke; the latter immediately falls into a sort of languor and sleep which often lasts for twenty-four hours, after which he recovers the full use of his senses. This is a remedy which reveals still more clearly the source of the ill.[1]

In considering this timidity due regard must be had for the more acute affectivity of primitive peoples. Pallas' description recalls that which the cousins Sarasin give of the Veddas, both peoples showing a similar character - timid and easily provoked. It must, however, be remembered that the Veddas are isolated pigmy primitives of the lowest degree of civilization, whereas the peoples explored by Pallas are on an essentially higher plane. In any case one thing is clear—that the shamans are much more excitable than the rest of the population. In an episode cited by Pallas in the same place a young Samoyede sorcerer went almost raving mad because a black glove had been put on his hand, a case which gives a glimpse of mental states so morbid, so acutely susceptible to illusion, that they can only with difficulty be paralleled. Observe, moreover, the particularly unreasoning character of the terror. The sight of the gloved hand arouses in the shaman the fear that it is a bear's paw, without it occurring to him in the least that this hand is at the disposal of his will and that moreover, a single paw not connected with a whole bear can offer no danger. The general state of the shaman is so precarious and emotionally excitable that he almost loses sight of reality.

Bastian's account of the Buriat shamans is also perfectly consistent with the idea that it is highly nervous individuals —men or women—who are automatically regarded as called to the profession of shaman, and that the whole training which they have thereupon to undergo—it lasts for nine years—leads to the enhancement of their neurotic condition.

In order to attain to the condition of shaman it is necessary to have the right disposition of mind which is called *Ug garbul*. The

---

[1] P. S. Pallas, *Reise durch verschiedene Provinzen des russischen Reichs in einem ausführlichen Auszuge*, part iii, Frankfurt, 1778, pp. 84-86.

signs of such candidature are considered to be: frequent fainting-fits, excitable and sensitive disposition, taciturnity, moroseness, love of solitude and other symptoms of a susceptible nervous system. When these signs appear in a child the parents apply to the chief shamans, men or women (Buge-Udagan), who forthwith seek to propitiate the spirits by sacrifices and prayer.[1]

As a rule the ability to become a shaman is hereditary in certain families, and this must be so since magic practices can only achieve success by the help of deceased ancestors.[2]

Mikhaïlowsky adds the following to the accounts of other travellers:

> It is not everyone who can become a shaman. Individuals are designated for it either, as amongst the peoples of Siberia, by heredity, or else by reason of a particular disposition which manifests itself in a child or young man chosen by the gods for their service. Amongst the Transbaikalian Tunguses the man who wishes to become a shaman explains that such and such a deceased shaman has come to him in a dream and commanded him to be his successor. Before becoming a shaman, moreover, the candidate shows himself " weakly, as if dazed, and nervous." According to the accounts of the Tunguses of Turukhansk the man destined to become a sorcerer sees in a dream the devil " *Khargi* " executing shamanistic practices. . . . The Yakut shamans and shamankas (a degenerate form of shaman) do not hold their magic gifts by heredity although it is the tradition that when a conjuror of spirits appears the honour remains in the family. They are predestined to serve the spirits whether they will or no. " Emekhet," the guardian spirit of the dead shaman, seeks to enter into one of the deceased's relations. He who is to become a shaman begins to rage like a raving madman. He suddenly utters incoherent words, falls unconscious, runs through the forests, lives on the bark of trees, throws himself into fire and water, lays hold on weapons and wounds himself, in such wise that his family is obliged to keep watch on him. By these signs it is recognized that he will become a shaman. An old shaman is then summoned to whom has been entrusted knowledge of the dwelling-places of such spirits as live in the air and under the earth. He teaches his pupil the various kinds of spirits and how they are invoked. Amongst the Yakuts the consecration of a shaman is accompanied by certain ceremonies: the old shaman leads his pupil up a high mountain or into the open fields, clothes him in shaman's robes, provides him with the tambourine and drumstick, places on his right nine pure youths, on his left nine pure maidens, then gives him his own robe and placing himself behind the new shaman makes him repeat certain words. Before all else he commands that the candidate abjure God and all that is dear to him inasmuch as he promises to devote his whole life to the demon who will fulfil his requests. Then the old shaman tells where the various demons live, which sicknesses they cause and how they may be propitiated. Finally, the new shaman slays the animal destined for sacrifice, his clothing is sprinkled with the blood and the flesh is eaten by the spectators.[3]

It is even said that amongst the Tunguses the future shamans are chosen before they are two years old. The

[1] Bastian, *loc. cit.*, p. 402.
[2] *Ibid.*, p. 406.   [3] Mikhaïlowsky, *loc. cit.*, pp. 85 sq.

criterion is *inter alia* convulsions.[1]	At the beginning of its third year the child is taken by an old shaman.

According to the accounts of the natives to which Radloff refers in his description of Shamanism in the Altaï, men become shamans purely and simply by a sort of inspiration, without receiving any kind of instruction.

> The aptitude for Shamanism and its lore is hereditary and handed down from father to son, also in special but rare cases from father to daughter. The future shaman receives no preliminary instruction or teaching from his father, and does not prepare himself for the profession; the shamanistic power falls upon him suddenly, as a sickness grips the whole man. The individual destined by the power of the ancestors to become a shaman suddenly feels in his limbs a languor and lassitude which manifest themselves in violent trembling. He is seized with violent and unnatural yawning, feels a heavy weight upon his chest, is suddenly moved to utter inarticulate cries, is shaken by feverish shiverings, his eyes roll rapidly, he dashes forward and whirls round like one possessed until he collapses covered in sweat and rolls on the ground a prey to epileptic convulsions. His limbs are numbed, he seizes everything he can lay hands on to swallow it involuntarily. . . . After a little while what he has swallowed comes out again dry and unchanged. . . . All these sufferings grow continuously worse until the individual thus tormented at length seizes the drum and begins to shamanize. Then and then only is nature appeased, the power of the ancestors has passed into him and he can now do no other, he must shamanize. If the man designed to be a shaman opposes the will of the predecessors and refuses to shamanize, he exposes himself to terrible afflictions which either end in the victim losing all his mental powers and becoming imbecile and dull or else going raving mad and generally after a short time doing himself an injury or dying in a fit.[2]

If it is true that the shamans, when they have become so by inspiration, receive no other instruction, this arises simply from the fact that as descendants of shamans they are fully instructed from youth up. It would otherwise be impossible for them duly to accomplish the shamanistic functions.

According to Mikhaïlowsky also it is neuropathic persons, pathological from infancy, who become shamans, undergoing a preparation of several years which constitutes a regular neuropathic training. Here are some details concerning the Buriat shamans:

> The dead ancestors who were shamans customarily choose amongst their living descendants a boy who shall inherit their

[1] Gustav Klemm, *Allgemeine Kulturgeschichte der Menschheit*, vol. iii, Leipzig, 1844, p. 105. Also Georgi, *Bemerkungen auf einer Reise im russischen Reiche*, vol. i, pp. 275 sq.
[2] W. Radloff, *Aus Sibirien*, Lose Blätter aus dem Tagebuche eines reisenden Linguisten, vol. ii, Leipzig, 1884, pp. 16 sq.

power. This child is recognized by several signs: he is often pensive, a lover of solitude, he has prophetic visions and is occasionally subject to fits during which he remains conscious. The Buriats believe that the child's soul is then amongst the spirits who teach him. . . . If he is to become a white shaman he goes to the abode of the spirits of the west, a black shaman to the spirits of the east. In the palaces of the gods the soul learns under the guidance of the dead shamans all the secrets of the shamanistic art; it impresses upon its memory the names of the gods, their abode, the forms with which they should be worshipped and the names of the spirits subject to the great gods. After undergoing trials the spirit returns to the body. Every year the mental tendencies are accentuated; the young man begins to have fits of ecstasy, dreams and swoons become more frequent. He sees spirits, leads a restless life, goes from village to village and tries to shamanize. In solitude he gives himself up whole-heartedly to shamanistic practices in no matter what place, forest or hillside, beside a blazing fire. He invokes the gods in a strange voice, shamanizes, and often falls senseless. His friends follow him at a certain distance and watch him to see that he takes no harm.

So long as the future mediator between gods and men is fitting himself for his impending duties, his parents or relatives apply to an experienced shaman to ask help for him, they call upon the gods and bring them offerings, imploring that their son or kinsman may pass safely through the trials. If the future shaman belongs to a poor family the community contributes towards supplying animals for the sacrifice and the objects necessary for the rites. The preparation lasts for several years, its length depending on the young man's aptitudes. As a general rule no one becomes a shaman before the age of twenty years.[1]

Wrangel, otherwise so reliable, surprises us by advancing an entirely individualistic conception of the shamans.

What the shamans and their partisans believe and practise is not something invented by a man and handed on to other men; it springs up in the breast of each individual through the impression of the surrounding objects. As these surroundings are alike all over the Siberian deserts, as their half-wild dwellers stand only on the threshold of enlightenment, so also are these impressions more or less general and the same for everyone. Each man sees and feels for himself; but without any communication there prevails a certain resemblance amongst the fruits of the imagination, and the personal belief of each becomes the common belief of the people. It is, in my opinion, just because such a belief is, so to speak, the creation of every individual and therefore particular and dear to him that they have endured up to the present and will continue to endure so long as these children of nature rule over the tundras, forests and gulfs, so long as the same setting continues to produce upon them the same impressions.[2]

It must be said that this theory is completely untenable. The uniformity of shamanistic states cannot in any way be explained by the homogeneous character of nature in Siberia;

[1] Mikhaïlowsky, loc. cit., p. 87.
[2] Wrangel, loc. cit., vol. i, pp. 285 sq.

it arises from the impression which the shamans make on their fellows. Even if the young shaman-to-be received no instruction of any kind from an old shaman and neglected all special education he nevertheless knows the nature of the shamanistic states, he sees shamans before him and hears them speak. Wrangel has not had sufficient regard for these facts, which are nevertheless in themselves entirely sufficient to explain the typical resemblance amongst the shamans. The impression of nature matters little if at all. It may be true that the consecration of the shamans brings no new metaphysical knowledge to the initiates, but it would certainly not be possible if there were not some connection between the shamans, and according to Wrangel's own statement the novices learn the exorcism of spirits from the older shamans ! The disciples learn from them how to fall into the " ecstatic " state, and that is certainly something more than " a mere ceremony touching the outer man."

The social importance of the shamans is extremely great. They combine in their person the priest, the sorcerer, and the physician, and are everywhere summoned when a misfortune is to be averted, either from an individual or from the whole population.

The shamans are—and this is consistent with their mysterious powers—intimately connected with the life and customs of the Siberian natives which are concerned with the most important interests of a race on a low level of development. In the simple life of the peoples of Northern Asia the shaman plays a prominent part; with few exceptions he occupies amongst his compatriots a situation of exceptional importance. Only amongst the Tshuktsh the shamans, according to Litke, are not honoured, and their function is restricted to curing the sick and performing conjuring-tricks. The Yakuts have absolute faith in their sorcerers, whose mysterious operations performed in circumstances of a highly exciting nature throw the half-savage people into a state of terror. It is not surprising that they should be afraid of the shamans. But fear outweighs respect, and the Yakuts are persuaded that their shamans, possessed by spirits, do not die by the will of the gods and are unworthy of the angel of death which is sent to them. They slay one another mutually by the sending of their demons.

The Tunguses whose country adjoins that of the Yakuts have still, as in Wrangel's time and in spite of the growing influence of Christianity, great confidence in their shamans and these latter assist at the burial of Christian Tunguses. The Ostiaks show great respect towards their doctors and diviners. In Southern Siberia the Buriats honour their shamans; the white shamans in particular are generally respected and beloved, the black shamans and shamankas are unloved, but greatly feared. Nevertheless, according to certain authors, a doctor loses the regard in which he is held if the patient whom he is attending happens to die.

The respect and fear felt towards the shamans must also necessarily be manifested by outward signs: gifts of honour fall to their
lot, they perform the most important functions and receive from
their fearful compatriots handsome material rewards for the benefits
which they are supposed to confer.   In the feasts of the Yakuts
the shamans take the highest rank, even a prince kneeling before
an Oyun on such occasions and receiving from his hands a cup of
kumiss.   Nevertheless the Yakut shamans have no particular
privileges in everyday life and are in no way distinguished from
their compatriots.[1]

Such is apparently the general picture of north Asiatic
Shamanism from the psychological point of view.   Is it, or is
it not, a state of possession ?

Strangely enough, we must unhesitatingly answer in the
negative.   The original Shamanism does not in any way
consist, at least generally speaking, in possession, but rather
in mere visual phenomena.   The shamans of northern Asia—
and also of northern Russia-in-Europe in so far as shamans
have been known to exist there—do not aspire to states
analogous to possession, but to visions: in the so-called
ecstasy they desire to see the spirits and hear them speak.
Contact with the spirit-world is not achieved by these peoples
as amongst the Bataks, where the spirits descend on chosen
persons and speak to the assembled hearers by their mouths,
but by " states of trance " in which they appear to the
shamans and impart to them communications which these
latter announce to their compatriots on their return from the
dream-like state to the waking one.

This theory is also confirmed by Radloff's description,[2]
the most detailed account given by a German investigator
of the shamanistic ceremonies, but unfortunately much too
long to be reproduced here.

The ceremony begins with an appeal and invocation to the
spirits.   Then the shaman appears to set off on a journey
through the various regions of the heavens—according to the
belief of these peoples the heavens are composed of various
regions.   The shaman seeks as best he may to give a vivid
picture of this journey, and also makes the spirits talk, that
is to say he speaks in their stead.   It is as if an actor played
several scenes single-handed and impersonated various
characters in turn.   Up to this point Shamanism recalls
true possession, but when we realize that everything takes

[1] Mikhaïlowsky, *loc. cit.*, pp. 131 sq.   [2] W. Radloff, *op. cit.*

place in a pre-determined order, that the words of the spirits are fixed in advance, we shall be reluctant to admit true possession, and shall rather believe that these are stereotyped ceremonies. Nevertheless there is no doubt that such set performances are the echo of earlier true phenomena of possession. What to-day is stereotyped was once spontaneous and involuntary.

It is surprising that in spite of this the shamans even now fall into quite abnormal states of excitement, the wildness of which recalls those of the energumens.

From the highest god the shaman learns " whether the sacrifice is favourably received or not; he also receives from him the best predictions as to whether the weather is set or what its changes will be, bad harvest, failure of crops, whether Uelguen (the god in question) expects still further offerings and of what kind."[1] Unfortunately Radloff does not expressly say in what manner the shaman obtains this information, whether by acoustic or visual hallucinations or else whether he himself speaks in place of the god. Radloff speaks of a " conversation " with Uelguen without it being possible for us to know whether the shaman hears the god speak in his own imagination or whether there is a dialogue in which he speaks alternately in his own name and in the god's. If this latter hypothesis were true, which I do not believe to be the case, the reality of true possession in shamanistic conjurations would be demonstrated.

That there is nothing more than a mere audition of words is almost established by what Radloff relates of shamanistic practices amongst the Kirghiz converts to Mohammedanism. He remarks that " after the meal it is the custom for the *baksa* (shaman) to make known what he has learnt . . . from the spirit."[2]

All that has hitherto been said of Siberian Shamanism is based on the German literature concerning Siberia. The Russian literature is far more extensive but remains inaccessible to me, although it may to some extent be replaced by a dissertation of the University of Halle published shortly before the war by a young Russian ethnologist called Tschubinow. It was to have appeared in extended form in Krüger's *Arbeiten zur Entwicklungspsychologie*, and contains

---

[1] *Ibid.*, vol. ii, pp. 49 sq. [2] *Ibid.*, vol. ii, p. 62.

a review of the Russian literature of the subject. Up to the present this is the most thorough work which has appeared in German on Siberian Shamanism, but unfortunately it does not pursue in further detail the question, all-important so far as we are concerned, of the extent to which states of possession occur. Broadly speaking, Tschubinow's text and arguments produce the same impression as the writings of German travellers.

Tschubinow also gives a description of a typical shamanistic performance,[1] from which the reader is at first inclined to believe that the shamans are possessed and that spirits do indeed speak by their mouths. This would nevertheless be a fallacy, for scrutiny of the other evidence reveals that there is no spirit-speech of the kind so abundantly known to us from primitive regions; the shaman practices something much more like ventriloquism. Thus the spirits do not speak through him as through the possessed, but he imitates them voluntarily.

> " The shamans of the Tshukshs and Koriaks utilize ventriloquism in such a way that the demons utter articulate sounds, incomprehensible to the spectators, the sense of which the shaman sums up from time to time. The shamans in their way achieve—especially amongst the Tshukshs—the most impressive effects." " The sounds make themselves heard somewhere very high up, approach little by little, seem to pass like a hurricane through the walls, and finally vanish into the bowels of the earth."[2]

There can naturally be no question of true possession in these performances; ventriloquism is clearly the artificial substitute for true possession which is wanting. The Siberian shaman appears to be a relatively late religious phenomenon.

The following description shows very plainly the extent to which the whole performance is pre-arranged.

> Amongst the more highly developed peoples he (the shaman) is the only actor—the centre of general attention and of dramatico-religious interest. He arranges the dialogue so as to appeal to the audience on their sentimental side, and combines the various poetic measures and other modes of expression in such a manner as to render the finest shades of meaning while at the same time producing a general impression of unity. The prosody and music of the songs are very strictly prescribed, even when the text is improvised and variable.[3]

[1] G. Tschubinow, *Beiträge zum psychologischen Verständnis des sibirischen Zauberers*, Diss., Halle, 1914, pp. 34-38.
[2] *Ibid.*, pp. 55 sq.   [3] *Ibid.*, p. 57.

This recalls the accounts of the Vedda shamans.

It is obvious that the manifestations of the Siberian shamans are not all identical in character, the excitement to which the shaman works himself up making it inevitable that individuals who lack stability should fall into abnormal states. Even if to all appearance it is visionary states which pre-ponderate, there is naturally no reason why the phenomena of possession should not also be produced on occasion. But as Siberian Shamanism is now no longer anything more than a sort of play-acting, this occurs much more rarely than amongst the primitive peoples, with whom everything is still genuine and where visions and possession have not yet given rise to theatrical performances. In Siberian Shamanism we have a very interesting primitive form of dramatic spectacle, more primitive than history enables us to discover in the Græco-Roman world, and yet more recent and highly de-veloped than that of the Shamanism intimately connected with true possession of most other primitive peoples.

Tschubinow repeatedly speaks of "states of trance," without defining more clearly the meaning of this expression. We must understand it as denoting somnambulistic or at least pseudo-somnambulistic states in which the shaman is insensible to the ordinary stimuli of the outer world— words addressed to him, etc.

> The sorcerer loses all sense of reality when by inhaling smoke or smoking tobacco, as well as fixing his gaze upon the hearth-fire, he has reached a state bordering on intoxication. He begins to get into touch with the invisible powers and sometimes falls into a trance. . . .[1] In this state the shaman sees and hears the spirits and converses with them.[2]

Nevertheless many of Tschubinow's data seem to leave open the possibility that possession occurs in many cases amongst the Siberian shamans. Thus a sudden collapse of the shaman is not unknown. " Sometimes on the appearance of the spirit the shaman falls to the earth as if struck by lightning."[3]

The exact manner in which the shaman gets into touch with the spirits is said by Tschubinow to be unexplained:

> When the sorcerer has changed the drumming to a new measure he begins to sing a conjuration; then the spirits of the ancestors

---

[1] *Ibid.*, p. 48.   [2] *Ibid.*, p. 51.   [3] *Ibid.*, p. 57.

approach. Our knowledge of these operations is unfortunately very imperfect and existing literature still fails to explain them in any way.[1]

It is of the highest interest that in the neurological clinic of Tomsk in 1909 Doctor W. W. Karelin observed in a shaman of the Altaï the following physiological changes when he was shamanizing:

> The shaman's pulse increased from 80 to 100 before the magic action, to 200 afterwards, the respiration from 20-24 to 36, the temperature from 36·5 to 38·7.[2] The muscular strength showed a marked augmentation in the right hand and a slight one in the left. The reflexes of the legs, which were generally very weak, disappeared completely after the magic action.[3]

The word shaman is, moreover, often understood, even by Ehrenreich, in a sense so wide as to embrace persons who induce in themselves sleep and dreams by artificial means.[4]

If in spite of their wide divergence the genuine states of possession of other peoples are generally included under the name of Shamanism, this is at bottom a misuse of words, an application of the term to states which are entirely distinct from true Shamanism. Perhaps nothing is more significant of how little psychology has hitherto come into its own in ethnological works; it has not been observed that completely different things have been falsely identified. Once the word Shamanism has been adopted into the language as embracing possession—and this has become quite usual not only in German but also in English literature—it is very difficult to divorce it from this association again. In future it will be necessary to bear clearly in mind that true Shamanism is something quite distinct from possession-Shamanism.

So far as north Asiatic Shamanism is concerned the most important problem arising and the investigation of which I should like to commend to Russian researchers as the persons most nearly interested, is a close psychological study of the shamans, not only during shamanistic phenomena, but also at other times. The thorough individual observation of a single shaman might readily be worth more than the whole

---

[1] *Ibid.*, p. 49.

[2] *I.e.*, a rise in temperature of more than 2 degrees due to essentially psychic causes (36·5 is a surprisingly low temperature).

[3] *Ibid.*, pp. 66 sq.

[4] P. Ehrenreich, *Beiträge zur Völkerkunde Brasiliens* in Veröffentlichungen aus dem Königl. Museum für Völkerkunde, Berlin, 1891, vol. ii, part i, p. 33.

mass of " casual " travellers' tales. The neuropsychic constitution of the shaman requires elucidation, as well as the
manner in which the shamanistic states come on. How far
does his will intervene in their production and cessation ?
Are the phenomena which occur akin to somnambulism or is
memory complete ? What is the history of the shaman's
youthful development ?

As Shamanism is dying out it is high time that such
investigations were undertaken. If there is much delay the
opportunity will have vanished for ever.

CHAPTER IX

ARTIFICIAL AND VOLUNTARY POSSESSION AMONGST THE HIGHER CIVILIZATIONS

(i.) IN THE PAST (THE GRÆCO-ROMAN WORLD)

IN the Græco-Roman world religious possession did not, so far as we are aware, constitute one of the primordial elements of life. It was still unknown to Homer, and in more recent times was brought into Greece from Asia and Thrace, producing phenomena analogous to possession which persisted in a greater or less degree down to the Christian era. Even in the cult of Apollo which had in turn replaced an older worship at Delphi, inspiration was introduced at a late date, and even then from Dionysiac worship.

The vehicles of manifestations resembling possession in the ancient world are almost exclusively women. We must consider on the one hand the " seeresses " and on the other the participants in the cult of Dionysos.

The foremost of the prophetesses of Greek antiquity is Cassandra; yet it is remarkable that in Homer she as yet possesses no gift of vision, or at least there is no mention of it, either in the *Iliad* or *Odyssey*.

She first appears as a seeress in Æschylus' *Oresteia*, but is in no way possessed; she beholds the future in visions. Thus Lykophron does not show her as possessed in his poem *Alexandra*. When she says " I " it is of herself that she speaks, it is not Apollo speaking through her mouth. He has conferred on her the gift of reading the future, but it is always she who prophesies and speaks, distinguished from others only by the gift of foreseeing future events.[1] Cassandra cannot therefore be regarded as the poetic prototype of Greek religious possession.

Amongst the possessed prophetesses of historic times the most eminent is the Pythoness.[2] The seeress of Delphi is

[1] Lykophron's *Alexandra*.
[2] Amongst the books which I have handled the richest in documentation is the very profound work of von Stützle: *Das griechische*

mentioned innumerable times, but we can form no clear and certain picture of her inspirations; everything is wrapped in obscurity and contradiction. Unfortunately little is known about her; there exists no eye-witness's description designed to hand down to posterity a detailed knowledge of the Delphic priestess. Much of the information given by existing documents is, moreover, disputed.

The priestess was originally a maiden from the surrounding countryside who must keep her virginity. Later, after a priestess had fallen victim to a sexual assault, a fifty-year-old woman was chosen. She was—at least in Plutarch's time (second century A.D.)—required to undergo no training.

In early times the Pythoness only gave replies on one fixed day in each year; later, when the influx of visitors increased, it was one day a month. The replies were given at once and uninterruptedly, and at its zenith the oracle was even in constant activity, two Pythonesses alternating regularly while a third was in readiness to assist them.[1] In Plutarch's time it was once more sufficient, owing principally to the terrible depopulation of Greece, for the Pythoness to give her utterances once a month, for now as formerly pilgrims came but seldom to consult the oracle. According to Plutarch a preliminary sacrifice was, moreover, necessary, and only when the sacrificial animal at once trembled and whined did the priests lead in the Pythoness.[2]

It is generally thought[3] that the Pythoness, when an oracle was demanded, made lustral ablutions, and then wearing a golden headdress, clad in long robes and her head encircled with laurel-leaves, went into the Adyton, drank from the spring Kassotis and chewed laurel-leaves. She seated herself upon a tripod above a cleft in the rock from whence arose in-

---

Orakelwesen und besonders die Orakelstatten Dodona und Delphi, in Programm des Kön. Gymnasiums zu Ellwangen, 1886-87 and 1890-91, also the article on Delphi in the *Realenzyklopadie der Klassischen Altertumswissenschaft* of Pauly, new edit. by Wissowa, vol. iv, Stuttgart, 1901. Cf. also for later times, particularly since the imperial period, G. Wolff, *De novissima oraculorum aetate*, Berolini, 1854.

[1] Paul Stengel, *Die griechischen Kultusaltertümer*, 2nd edit., Munich, 1898, p. 65.

[2] Plutarch, *De orac.* (Plutarch's *Morals*, trans. by Several Hands, W. Taylor, London, 1718, vol. iv, *Why the Oracles cease to give Answers*).

[3] Cf. Stengel, *loc. cit.*, pp. 65 sq., and C. W. Goettling, *Gesammelte Abhandlungen aus dem klassischen Altertum*, vol. ii, Munich, 1883, pp. 59 sq.

spiring vapours, then fell into a state of enthusiasm in which, apparently under the influence of Apollo, she foretold the future and gave counsel either in plain words or more often by dark sayings. Near her stood a προφήτης to whom those consulting the oracle imparted their questions either verbally or in writing.

The state of inspiration into which she fell was one of great excitement. Unhappily we know very little about it, as is clearly demonstrated by the summary statements of philologists.

P. Stengel comes to the following conclusion:

> Owing to the gaseous emanations arising from the gulf, the Pythoness was thrown into an ecstasy. She then pronounced more or less consecutive words which were rendered by the priests into often very bad hexameters or later into other poetic metres also, and imparted to the questioners. Sometimes the replies were given in prose. The Pythoness must often have found herself in a state which rendered her incapable of reasoning, and it was then the duty of the priests to see what they could make of her words and outcries. But deliberate fraud was certainly rare. It may have occurred in isolated cases and a Pythoness is even reported to have been deprived of her office because she was alleged, on receipt of a bribe, to have given a false oracle. But in the hey-day of the oracles the Pythoness and the priests themselves believed, as a general rule, that the god spoke in her; and even if these men, wily, and for the most part well-informed as to the circumstances of the questioners, showed moreover all possible circumspection and were content to speak darkly and ambiguously where not sure of their ground, it would be impossible to explain the extraordinary regard which the oracle enjoyed for centuries by an attempt to posit repeated fraud. Lysandros made attempts at corruption at Delphi, at Dodona, and in the seat of the Ammonian oracle, but was everywhere frustrated and finally betrayed.[1]

Bergk also can say no more than this:

> The questioner received immediately by the mouth of the inspired seeress a sentence in verse which fitted only the case in question and which the prophets subsequently interpreted. . . . What part was played by real inspiration in these utterances no one can say, but naturally as time went on the advice of the priests together with pre-arranged plan must have loomed larger and larger, and it seems probable that in later times real poets in the service of the sanctuary lent their aid to put the replies into metrical form.[2]

Erwin Rohde thus describes the Pythoness:

> . . . There (at Delphi) the Pythoness, a virgin priestess, prophesied under the intoxicating excitement of the vapours issuing from a cleft in the rocks above which she sat on a tripod; she was filled

---

[1] P. Stengel, loc. cit., p. 65.
[2] Bergk, Griechische Literaturgeschichte, vol. i, Berlin, 1872, p. 335.

with the god himself and his spirit. The god, as was believed, entered into the earthly body, or else the priestess' soul, " loosed " from her body, apprehended the divine revelations with the spiritual mind. What she then " with frenzied mouth " foretold, was spoken through her by the god. When she said " I " it was Apollo who spoke to whomsoever it concerned. That which lived, thought. and spoke in her so long as she was in frenzy, was the god himself.[1]

It will immediately be observed, however, that it is straining all these descriptions to construe the " perception " of revelations as signifying acoustic visionary states, while the speech in the first person in the name of Apollo indicates possession.

The inadequacy of modern philologists' descriptions of the Pythoness arises unhappily from the poverty of ancient documentary sources. These nevertheless stretch over a long period of time and continue far into the Christian era, but contain very little definite information. A few examples will demonstrate this. Amongst the most ancient is a remark of Heraclitus (born c. 500 B.C.) found in Plutarch:

> Now the Sibyl " from her frenzied mouth," to use the expression of Heraclitus, lets fall words which are anything but merry, ornate and painted; and yet for a thousand years, thanks to the gods, her voice has resounded through the centuries.[2]

According to Bergk[3] these words indubitably apply to the Pythoness, of whom Plutarch also remarks " that she does not perfume herself with scented oils, nor does she descend into the sanctuary draped in a crimson mantle."[4]

Strabo relates:

> It is said that the oracle is a spacious grotto in the depths of the earth with a narrow opening. From it arises an inspiring vapour. Over the mouth of the grotto stands a tripod on which the Pythoness mounts, and breathing in the vapour gives forth prophecies either in verse or otherwise; but the latter also are put into measure by poets in the service of the temple.[5]

But no author is more disappointing than Plutarch (born A.D. 46), in spite of the fact that during the years 95-125 he was one of the priests of the oracle. Three of his writings

---

[1] E. Rohde, *Psyche*, vol. ii, 2nd edit., Freiburg, 1898, pp. 60 sq.
[2] Plutarch, *De Pyth. or.*, c. 6 (a translation will be found in Plutarch's *Morals*, trans. by Several Hands, London, 1718, *Why the Pythian Priestess ceases to deliver her Oracles in Verse*, p. 104).
[3] Bergk, *op. cit.*, vol. i, Berlin, 1872, p. 343.
[4] Plutarch, *De Pyth. or.*, c. 6.
[5] Strabo, *Geography*, ix, 419. (There is a translation with notes by H. C. Hamilton and W. Falconer, 3 vols., 1854-57.)

relate to it: *On the Cessation of Oracles, On the Eî at Delphi, On the Pythian Responses, why no longer given in Verse.* We expect to gather from him a mass of details, but this hope is completely frustrated; he says so little on the subject that it has been possible to argue that he never had access to the sanctuary where the Pythoness gave forth her oracles. However that may be, his three writings on the Delphic oracle are surprisingly empty of positive information.

The early conceptions of the effect of the vapour and the " entry " of Apollo into the seeress were often of a very primitive nature, resembling some of the ideas on demoniacal possession which we have already encountered. They have persisted up to the latest times, and some of them emerge with particular distinctness.

The Christian author Chrysostom (d. 407) writes:

> Of this priestess, the Pythoness, it is now said that she sat with parted thighs on the tripod of Apollo and the evil spirit entered her from below passing through her genital organs and plunged her into a state of frenzy, so that she began with loosened hair to foam and rage like one drunken.[1]

Similarly we read in Origen:

> It is said of the Pythian priestess, whose oracle seems to have been the most celebrated, that when she sat down at the mouth of the Castalian cave, the prophetic spirit of Apollo entered her private parts, and when she was filled with it, she gave utterance to responses which are regarded as divine truths.[2]

Apart from the fact of the spirit of Apollo being alleged to enter the Pythoness' womb, Origen is particularly shocked at her state of excitement.

> It is not the part of a divine spirit to drive the prophetess into such a state of ecstasy and madness that she loses control of herself.[3]

The Hellenism of the later period had already found the idea that Apollo introduced herself into the Pythoness' organism and really spoke by her mouth unacceptable. Many sought to give a materialistic explanation to the whole thing by means of winds and emanations from the earth, as we see from Plutarch.

Others took a middle course, admitting the operation of

---

[1] Chrysostom, *Homilies on the First Epistle to the Corinthians,* XXIX, chap. xii, 1.
[2] Origen, *Against Celsus,* vii, 3 (Ante-Nicene Library, " Writings of Origen," trans. Crombie, vol. ii).
[3] *Ibid.*

the vapours on the mind, but seeing the directing hand of the gods in this phenomenon.

Of the above-mentioned conception, already traditional in antiquity, an important feature is to-day disputed: the vapour which is alleged to have emanated from the rocky cleft. Oppé has sought in a searching criticism of these ancient accounts to demonstrate[1] that at Delphi there was never any cleft in the earth over which the Pythoness' tripod was set and from whence arose an intoxicating exhalation. No information concerning it is to be found amongst ancient writers, and Oppé believes it to be a legend of late origin, which, however, was so universally believed that even Plutarch, who as a Delphic priest was fully acquainted with the true facts, said nothing in his writings directly to contradict it, but nevertheless expressed himself in such a fashion as conveyed beyond doubt to the initiated that he knew nothing of the existence of this fissure.

Oppé's hypothesis is consistent with the fact that the French excavations at Delphi have revealed no trace of the existence of any cleft in the earth in the temple of Apollo, although they have been very thorough and pursued to a great depth. Perdrizet, a collaborator of Homolle, the director of excavations, speaks as follows of the results obtained:

> Amongst the monuments of the Pythian enclosure the temple of Apollo had, as may readily be understood, aroused the greatest expectations. How was the Adyton placed? What ought we to think of the prophetic fissure the emanations from which intoxicated the Pythoness? It is established that it never existed except in the imagination of the devout and of poets. No cleft yawned in the rocks beneath the Adyton, no vapour ever arose in that spot from the bowels of the earth, the foundations of the temple hid nothing mysterious; the subterranean chambers upon which it was built were hollowed out at the time of its foundation with the sole object of economizing materials.[2]

As, however, is so often the case in philological questions, Oppé's arguments have not proved conclusive. The extremely judicious English scholar Farnell[3] judges, and it

---

[1] A. P. Oppé, *The Chasm at Delphi*, in the "Journal of Hellenic Studies," vol. xxiv, 1904, pp. 214-40.

[2] Perdrizet, *Die Hauptergebnisse der Ausgrabungen in Delphi*, in "Neue Jahrbücher für das klassische Altertum," vol. xxi, pp. 29 sq.

[3] L. R. Farnell, *The Cults of the Greek States*, vol. iv, Oxford, 1907, p. 181. The author is dealing particularly with Plutarch's third work: *Of the Cessation of Oracles*.

seems to me with justification, that Plutarch's data are entirely compatible with the existence of a fissure. In any case he (Plutarch) believed, as emerges clearly from § 5, in the existence of an exhalation which caused the Pythoness to be inspired, even although he does not directly say that it arose from a fissure. Nor can it, moreover, be demonstrated that Plutarch ever gained admittance to the room in which the Pythoness gave forth her oracles. Similar fissures are still to-day found in the neighbourhood of Delphi.

A traveller named Pomtow believes that he has discovered " at certain spots on the new carriage-road, particularly in places where, when it was driven last autumn, changes in the configuration of the ground resulted, ice-cold draughts of air accompanied by vinegary smells arising from rocky fissures or hollows in the ground." He adds that " the clefts in the limestone mountains which were known in antiquity still exist to-day." Curtius has also come upon sultry air and rapidly changing warm and cold currents.[1]

A fresh difficulty is introduced into the whole question by the statement of Dion Cassius (third century)[2] that Nero caused several men to be thrown into the cleft, a story which has not yet been taken into account in the discussions on the subject and which would have necessitated a relatively wide fissure. Diodorus of Sicily (first century B.C.), moreover, relating the well-known legend of the origin of the fissure according to which a troop of goats having come into the vicinity of this cleft in the earth became so excited that the goatherd ran up and, under the influence of the vapours, fell into a state of enthusiastic excitement—represents it as so great that men might have been engulfed in it. Diodorus states that the tripod was a protecting erection to prevent the Pythoness from falling into the gulf.[3]

The statements of Dion Cassius and Diodorus evidently complicate the issue still further, and even throw it into confusion. As to the reality of the tripod there appears to

[1] See Stützle, loc. cit., ii, p. 14, for further details on the statements of Pomtow and Curtius.
[2] Dion Cassius, History of Rome, lxxviii, 14.
[3] Diodorus, Bibliotheca Historica, xvi, 4-5.

318 THE DISTRIBUTION OF POSSESSION

be no doubt. According to Zozimus (fifth century) it was carried off from Delphi with other objects in the reign of Constantine and brought to Constantinople where it was to be seen.[1] Moreover a tripod is found sculptured on the frieze of the ancient Treasury of Delphi which the French excavators have brought to light. Judging by a plaster reproduction in the Archæological Institute of Tübingen it is very high, but not very wide.

The question arises as to whether more precise information on the size of the tripod can be gathered from literary or archæological sources. If Diodorus' statements are accurate it must have been of considerable size and strongly built. Fr. Lübker's *Reallexikon des Klassischen Altertums*[2] states without any indication of source: " Over the cleft (in the ground) stood a colossal wooden tripod cased in gold, on which rested a fitting designated λέβης, φιάλη, κύκλος, or ὅλμος, Latin *cortina*. It was a perforated platform, horizontal or slightly hollowed, on which the prophesying priestess seated herself in a sort of armchair." Thus the Pythoness would have sat not immediately but indirectly on the tripod. The artist who sculptured the frieze mentioned above can hardly have had such a conception, as the tripod he depicts is not large enough.

Having regard to the geological conditions of the country where earthquakes have not infrequently occurred, it is conceivable that a once-existent fissure should have closed up again with the lapse of time, so that from the geological point of view the question is undecided. We should, however, ask ourselves whether the late occlusion of a crevasse could not be detected from its effects on the building; this should have been the case with a cleft of any size—at least, in so far as the occlusion extended to the surface of the earth. Homolle, the director of the French excavations at Delphi, speaks expressly in a memoir of dislocations suffered by the foundations of the temple and which indicate a very violent earthquake.[3]

The enigma becomes complete with Ponten's declaration in

---

[1] See Stützle, *loc. cit.*, part ii, p. 49 (cf. p. 311, note 2).
[2] Seventh edit., Leipzig, 1896, p. 304.
[3] Homolle, *Le Temple de Delphes, son histoire, sa ruine*, in " Bulletins de correspondance hellénique," vol. xx, 1896, p. 731.

1914, affirming the existence of a fissure. He writes of the temple of Apollo:

> Only the foundation-walls subsist, and in the midst yawns a dark crevasse over which sat the Pythoness when she gave forth the oracles.[1]

Has a fissure once more opened on the spot ? Unfortunately the official French excavations at Delphi are not yet complete. The geological aspect of the problem should also most certainly be followed up; Philippson's opinion given from this standpoint is completely negative,[2] but it would be of the first importance to subject the question of the true nature of earth-vapours causing psychic excitement to a thorough and final investigation. Do gases of this nature really exist and might they emanate at Delphi ?

Of the effect produced by the mastication of laurel-leaves there is nothing circumstantial to be said. It was a customary practice on the part of all seers.[3] The water of the Delphic springs also possesses—to-day, at least—no intoxicating properties. Goettling writes:

> I have tasted the five poetic springs of Greece: the charming fountain of Pirene at Acrocorinth where according to the legend Pegasus was caught, the two springs sacred to the Muses of Helicon, Hippocrene and Aganippe, the spring Kassotis and the Castalian spring at Delphi. Each time I hoped, having drunk of so poetic

---

[1] J. Ponten, *Griechische Landschaften. Ein Versuch künstlerischer Erdbeschreibung*, Stuttgart, 1914, p. 159.
I have written to J. Ponten to ask him if he could fathom this strange contradiction. He replied that he was a poet and not a scholar, although a lover of knowledge. " The crevasse in that place (it stands out clearly in the picture) is so much a part of the landscape, and particularly of that of Delphi, that error would be justified, at least from the artistic standpoint. I clearly remember having studied the matter from the geological point of view also, and as I did not find on the spot in the homogeneous mass of limestone rocks any natural cause for the production of vapours, I had at the time doubts about the author of the statement. I also remember that he did not admit the existence of any kind of volcanic or plutonic vapours because local observation was too completely irreconcilable with these, but believed in the existence of another noxious vapour, perhaps sulphuretted hydrogen. I contented myself with this explanation, for it is dangerous to try to probe the depths of mythology in too rationalistic a spirit. . . ." The contradiction which we have pointed out therefore remains unsolved.
[2] Philippson, Article on the geology of Delphi in Pauly-Wissowa's Realenzyklopädie, see also Oppé's *Mitteilungen aus einem Privatbrief Philippsons, loc. cit.*, pp. 233 sq.
[3] I made at Locarno experiments in chewing fresh laurel-leaves, but without results of any interest.

a stream, to have fair dreams at least by night. But not at all; I always slept merely the sleep of the just. I cannot bring myself to think that the " Nordic curse " as Schiller called it in an excess of poetic superstition, can have paralyzed the operation of these springs on the constitution of a barbarian whereas on the Greeks it was quite otherwise. But all these poetic mountain springs of Greece are really nothing more than the purest, most limpid and virgin water of the Nymphs.[1]

Let us now consider the nature of the psychic state of the priestess during inspiration. Is such inspiration founded on fact or not ? While it would be difficult to demonstrate in particular cases, it seems indubitable that inspired states did exist in a general way, as without them the important historical rôle played by Delphi would be quite inexplicable.

The reality of a state of possession in the priestess is principally indicated by the fact that the word " I " in her utterances always designated Apollo.

The Pythoness speaks in the name of the god himself, this is why she greets Lycurgus with the words ἐμὸν κατὰ πίονα νηόν. In the same way we read in an oracle in Pausanius, ii, 26, 7, considered, however, to be spurious: Φλεγυῆς ἔτικτεν ἐμοὶ φιλότητι μιγεῖσα.[2] In the oracle dating from the time of the first holy war in Pausanius, x, 37, 6, we read: ἐμῷ τεμένει[3] and in Æschines' Ctesiphon θεοῦ τεμένει.[4] Æschines is thinking, moreover, of a quite different oracle, which is why this sentence which later scholiasts have inserted in that place may well be genuine.[5]

Also in the reply given to Crœsus we read:

Sec, I count the sand, I know the distances of the sea,
I hear even the dumb and understand those who are silent.[6]

Similarly in the late Greek novel Æthiopica the author Heliodorus (third century) makes Apollo speak through the mouth of the priestess in the first person of " my temple " (νηὸν ἐμόν).[7]

This first person supposes that the Pythoness was, at least originally, in a state of inspiration, later traditional abuse of this form of speech by the priests being only comprehensible as a secondary occurrence. Naturally it is false

---

[1] C. W. Goettling, loc. cit., p. 60.
[2] Pausaniæ Descriptio Graeciæ, ii, 26, 7.
[3] Ibid., x, 37, 6.　　　　[4] Æschines, Against Ctesiphon, 112.
[5] Bergk, loc. cit., p. 335.　　[6] Herodotus, Historiæ, i, 47.
[7] Heliodorus, Æthiopica, ii, 35.

to say with Bergk that the Pythoness when uttering the oracle spoke in the name of the god; it was rather the god himself who spoke through her.

Perhaps the above-mentioned quotation from Origen, according to which the Pythoness when giving the oracle was in a state where she was no longer mistress of herself: ὡς μηδαμῶς αὐτὴν ἑαυτῇ παρακολουθεῖν, may be regarded as evidence for the existence of somnambulistic possession.

As proof that the priestesses underwent states of the most acute excitement we may adduce Plutarch's statement that these affected them so greatly that they died young. We have already found the same allegations concerning inspired persons among the Bataks.

From all that has hitherto been said we are driven to conclude that the states under discussion are autosuggestive. It is regrettable that we do not know more of the manner in which a new Pythoness was chosen by the priests from the environs of Delphi. It was apparently by no means the first comer who was chosen. Always supposing, therefore, that the Pythoness did not play a merely fictitious part, should we not suppose that persons with psychic gifts were passed in review? It must have been the same as amongst primitive peoples where not everyone can become a shaman and where Mariner's data clearly demonstrate the existence of states of possession purely autosuggestive in character. To all appearances drinking at the Castalian spring, chewing laurel-leaves, sitting upon the tripod, and finally being exposed to the hypothetical current of air, are compatible with such interpretation along the lines of suggestion.

An event of which Plutarch had personal experience, or at least authentic information, confirms the extreme auto-suggestibility of the Pythoness. He relates that a Pythoness who had sinned against the law of chastity and who in spite of certain unfavourable preliminary omens insisted on officiating as seeress, fell into a state of abnormal excitement and died after a few days.

> She went down into the Hole against Her will, but at the first Words which she uttered she plainly shewed by the Hoarseness of her Voice that she was not able to bear up against so strong an Inspiration (like a Ship under Sail, opprest with too much Wind) but was possesst with a dumb and evil Spirit; and finally, being horribly disordered, and running with dreadful screeches towards

the Door to get out, she threw herself violently on the Ground, so that not only the Pilgrims fled for fear but also the High Priest Nicander, and the other Priests and Religious which were there present; who entering within a while, took her up, being out of her Senses; and indeed she lived but few days after. For these Reasons it is, that Pythia is obliged to keep her body pure and clean from the Company of Men, there being no Stranger permitted to converse with her.[1]

This story recalls that of Ananias and Sapphira in the Acts of the Apostles.

Such a death by autosuggestion cannot be regarded as impossible; there are in existence, as already mentioned, several similar narratives.[2]

The most serious difficulties arise from what is known of collaboration by the priests in the giving of oracles. They received the pilgrim's request and officially formulated the oracle in its final shape, serving also as intermediaries between the consultants and the Pythoness. It must often have happened that the latter's words were difficult to understand or even incomprehensible, so that the priests had first to elucidate them. To what extent they had any personal share in the utterance of the oracles we shall never know, however much we would give to do so.

It should be emphasized that the idea of the Pythoness speaking incomprehensible words is not general, at least in later times. In the above-quoted *Æthiopica* of Heliodorus we read:

> As we were by the altars and the young man was beginning the sacrifice while the priest read prayers, the Pythoness uttered the following words from the interior of the sanctuary . . . (whereupon follow six perfectly intelligible verses).[3]

A close perusal of the texts will not reveal much more than this. The result is unsatisfactory enough in all conscience, for to put it plainly we are confronted, if the priests did not really intervene, with a woman in an acute state of excitement yet simultaneously filled with intuition of the highest order, to whom the whole of Greece lent ear. In the other event we should have to posit a college of priests possessed of very profound insight into the political and cultural

---

[1] Plutarch's *Morals*, trans. by Several Hands, pub. W. Taylor, London, 1718, vol. iv, *Why the Oracles cease to give Answers*, p. 59.
[2] Cf. Stadelmann, *Tod durch Vorstellung (Suggestion)* in "Zeitschrift für Hypnotismus," vol. iii, 1894-95, pp. 81 sq.
[3] Heliodorus, *Æthiopica*, i, 35.

relations of Greece, but which had for centuries practised what was in essence the fraud of inspiration. If the oracles were founded on no inspired utterances of the Pythoness, this deception of the whole of Greece must be regarded as a feat of supreme cunning.

Amongst nineteenth-century investigators Goettling argues —not, however, without self-contradiction—the point of view that the college of priests, to which every request had to be submitted a considerable time in advance, carefully supplied the reply and merely had it enunciated by the Pythoness. " What the Pythoness said was the outcome of mature consideration."[1] Why then did she often speak words hard to understand ?

Goettling tries, it is true, to clear her of the imputation of fraud:

> Even if, therefore, these Delphic oracles were attributed to a god, Apollo, as his revelations, this was a profound and beautiful thought the complete truth of which is inherent in man's nature; for our own moral will, as it emerges after earnest, conscientious reflection, is also God's will. It is his revelation.[2]

In spite of all the fair words in which Goettling clothes these facts they nevertheless remain a deception if the Pythoness uttered in a well-simulated state of inspiration oracles previously dictated to her by the priests. It is difficult to reconcile such trickery with the high moral regard in which the oracle was generally held.

The sentences attributed by literature to the Delphic oracle have to the best of my knowledge been merely collected[3] and not subjected to any critical study, so that the genuine ones really emanating from Delphi have not been distinguished from the false.

Wilamowitz attributes a high value to some of these utterances. Of the Delphic ones, " of which we possess not a few genuine examples from the sixth century onwards," he remarks:

> This poetry, the foundation of which is and remains Homeric, but which declines into patchwork imitation from imperial times onwards, is in part of high merit, and the periphrasis and typical

---

[1] C. W. Goettling, loc. cit., vol. ii, p. 59. Cf. p. 62.
[2] Ibid., p. 62.
[3] Epigrammatum Anthologia palatina, vol. iii (2nd edit.), ed. Cougny, Paris, 1890, pp. 464-533. A new collection will appear in the Poetarum græcorum fragmenta of Wilamowitz.

turns of speech or metaphors (such as the introduction of animals, wolf, bull, dragon) have exercised a marked influence on lyric poetry and tragedy.   In this domain also the Greeks, starting with Homer, invented a fixed style and maintained it for a thousand years.[1]

Amongst the oracles of later times is found one of no less standing than the poem on Plotinus (A.D. 204-270) which Porphyry gives in the twenty-second chapter of his biography. According to him the poem was uttered in reply to the question put by Amelius as to where the soul of Plotinus had gone since his death.   Such a work cannot naturally be the interpretation of senseless words uttered by the Pythoness; it presupposes, moreover, a real knowledge of the works of Plotinus and their meaning.   If authentic, it shows to what heights, both ethical and spiritual, the Delphic priesthood had attained at this epoch (third century A.D.).   It must, however, be added that this authenticity is contested on the grounds of the length of the poem.

The importance of Delphic possession from the point of view of politics and civilization has often been proclaimed.

> The foundation of colonies, one of the most magnificent achievements of the Greek nation, was especially directed by the Delphic priesthood.   The institutions and laws of the states were under the protection of the oracle.   Generally speaking, nothing of importance was undertaken without consulting the gods; thus before the beginning of a war counsel was sought almost regularly.   But the influence of this oracle on worship and the religious life was no less felt; Delphi was at all times the highest authority in these matters. Art and poetry also, and generally speaking all the higher aspects of civilization, owed to the oracle progress in manifold directions.[2]

Curtius goes even further.

> All that European Hellas became from the ninth century (B.C.) onwards, and all that happened there, the stamp of national character imprinted on every manifestation of intellectual life, on religious and moral outlook, the constitution of states, architecture and sculpture, music and poetry, was essentially the outcome of the influence of Delphi as was also the deliberate opposition to the barbarians.[3]

For the most part the authority of Delphi was undisputed. It is highly remarkable that Plato himself recognizes this

---

[1] U. von Wilamowitz-Moellendorf, *Die griechische Literatur*, 9th edit., Berlin, 1907, p. 42.
[2] *Bergk, loc. cit.*, vol. i, p. 338.   Cf. Stengel, *loc. cit.*, p. 67.
[3] E. Curtius, *Griechische Geschichte*, 6th edit., Berlin, 1887, vol. i, p. 549.

oracle and considers it as invested with the highest authority. He believes in its divine nature as in that of the other oracles.

> . . . We owe our greatest blessings to madness (διὰ μανίας) if only it be granted by Heaven's bounty (θεία δόσει). For the prophetess at Delphi, you are well aware, and the priestess of Dodona, have in their moments of madness done great and glorious service to the men and the cities of Greece, but little or none in their sober mood.[1]

Other thinkers, particularly the Stoics and Neo-Platonists, have adopted the same point of view. Chrysippus even gathered together a vast collection of Delphic oracles.[2]

At the time when the Roman Republic came to an end the oracle was no longer accredited.[3] As regards the past, however, the genuineness of Delphic prophecy appeared indubitable.

> This, therefore, remains and cannot be denied unless we falsify the whole of history, that during many centuries this oracle was genuine.[4]

In his *De divinatione* Cicero makes his brother Quintus say that unlike what happened in the olden days the oracles uttered at Delphi no longer prove true:

> Never would this temple of Delphi have been so celebrated, so illustrious, and so loaded with gifts by all peoples and kings, if the whole world had not proved the truth of its oracles. For a long time past all this has changed and its glory has diminished because the truth of the oracles has grown less, whereas without their great truth it would never have enjoyed such fame.[5]

In another place where he himself, who does not believe in the oracle but holds it to be a deception of the priests, is speaking, we read:

> . . . for . . . the oracles of Delphi have ceased to be given, not only in our day but for a long time past, since nothing could be more despised.[6]

---

[1] Plato, *Phædrus* (trans. Everyman Series, " Five Dialogues of Plato," p. 228).
[2] Cicero, *De divinatione*, i, 19.
[3] Cf. Lucan, *Pharsalia*, v, pp. 111 sq. Some details concerning the decadence and rehabilitation of the oracle of Delphi will be found in L. Friedländer, *Darstellungen aus der Sittengeschichte Roms*, 8th edit., vol. iv, Leipzig, 1910, pp. 176 sq.
[4] Cicero, *loc. cit.*, i, 19, p. 38.
[5] *Ibid.*, i, 19, pp. 37 sq.
[6] *Ibid.*, ii, 57, p. 117.

In imperial times the fame of Delphi flourished once more. How general the recognition of the oracle had become in later times is shown by the fact that Celsus (c. A.D. 178) was in a position to reproach the Christians with the lack of belief in it as a grave shortcoming.

> They set no value on the oracles of the Pythian priestess, of the priests of Dodona, of Clarus, of Branchidæ, of Jupiter Ammon, and of a multitude of others: although under their guidance we may say that colonies were sent forth and the whole world peopled."[1]

The oracle seems to have fallen into desuetude at the time of Constantine and was officially closed by Theodosius in A.D. 390. Under Nero, who, it is said, had men slain over the sacred gulf, it had already discontinued its activity for some time.[2]

It seems as if at a later date the Adyton, the preservation of which would have been of supreme interest to us, fell victim to the destructive fury of the Christians—

> . . . thoroughly and apparently deliberately destroyed, so that in spite of unusually deep excavations nothing has been established as to the actual seat of the oracle. The statement of Pausanius, however, that the prophetic spring in the Adyton was fed from the spring *Kassotis* seems to be corroborated; the channels visible to the south of the temple served to regulate the discharge of the water.[3]

It would nevertheless be completely erroneous to believe that the Christians regarded the oracles as priestly trickery or morbid psychic exaltation; there can be no question of this. Like the non-Christians they believed them to be inspired, but held that the spirit who produced inspiration was not divine but a demon. With these reservations belief in oracles had sprung up once more amongst them with the rehabilitation of the oracle's reputation in imperial times. Since Christianity conceived the spiritual powers behind the oracle as of a demoniacal and fiendish nature, it consequently identified them with the demons of the δαιμονιζόμενοι and the insane, with the result that all mental afflictions once more appeared as provoked by demons.

Friedländer[4] makes the following general statement:

> The Christian writers also, who asserted that with the advent of the Saviour into the world the might of the false gods had been

---

[1] Ante-Nicene Library, Writings of Origen, *Against Celsus*, vol. ii, bk. vii, chap. iii.
[2] Cf. P. Stengel, *loc. cit.*, p. 67.
[3] Baedeker, *Greece*, 4th edit., London, 1909, p. 149.
[4] Friedländer, *loc. cit.*, p. 177.

destroyed, that sorcery, by means of which they had so long lent speech to images of wood and stone, had lost its power and its oracles were silenced:[1] even they were obliged to recognize that the demons in the temples of the oracles once more uttered true prophecies and wholesome warnings and also worked cures; but truth to tell, only in order by these apparent benefits to do the greater injury to those whom they turned aside from seeking the true God by the insinuation of false ones.[2]

They explained the fact of demons knowing the future by stating that as former servants of God they were acquainted with his designs.[3]

Again it was in possession that the ancient religious beliefs found such strong support that the Christians could not get away from it except by refusing to recognize these gods as such and designating them as evil demons. Thus Minucius Felix makes Octavius say:

> Saturn, Serapis, Jupiter, and whatsoever demons you worship, when overcome by pain confess what they are; they certainly would not lie and bring disgrace upon themselves, especially when any of you were present. You may believe their own testimony that they are demons, when they confess the truth about themselves; for when adjured by the only true God, against their will, poor wretches, they quake with fear in men's bodies, and either come forth at once or gradually disappear, according as the faith of the sufferer assists or the grace of the healer inspires.[4]

Apollo and the Muses also seem to have spoken occasionally by the mouth of the possessed and confessed themselves as demons, which was rejoicingly hailed by the Christians as confirmation of their non-divine character.[5]

> There exist certain wandering unclean spirits who have lost their heavenly activities from being weighed down by earthly passions and disorders. So then these spirits, burdened with sin and steeped in vice, who have sacrificed their original simplicity, being themselves lost, unceasingly strive to destroy others, as a consolation for their own misfortune; depraved themselves, they strive to communicate error and depravity to others; estranged from God, they strive to alienate others by the introduction of vicious forms of religion. Poets know these spirits as "demons" . . .[6]
>
> Now these unclean spirits, the demons, as the magi and philosophers have shown, conceal themselves in statues and consecrated images, and by their spiritual influence acquire the authority of a present divinity. At one time they inspire the soothsayers, at another take up their abode in the temples, sometimes animate

---

[1] Arnobius, *Adv. Gentes*, i, 1; Eusebius, *Præp. Evang.*, v, 1; Prudentius, *Apothcosis*, pp. 435 sq.
[2] Tertullian, *De Anima*, c. 46.   [3] Lactantius, *Inst. div.*, ii, 16.
[4] Minucius Felix, *Octavius*, cap. 27, C.S.P.C.K., Translations of Christian Literature, series ii.
[5] Theophilus, *Ad Autolyc.*, ii, 8, quoted by Harnack, *loc. cit.*, p. 151.
[6] Minucius Felix, *loc. cit.*, cap. 26.

the fibres of the victims' entrails, direct the flight of birds, control the lots, compose oracles, enveloped in a mist of untruth. For they both deceive and are deceived; being ignorant of the pure truth, to their own destruction they are afraid to confess that which they do know. Thus they weigh down men's minds and draw them from heaven, call them away from the true god to material things, disturb their lives and trouble their sleep; stealthily creeping into men's bodies, thanks to their rarefied and subtle nature, they counterfeit diseases, terrify the imagination, rack the limbs, to compel men to worship them; then, sated with the fumes from the altars and the slaughter of beasts, they undo what they have tied themselves, so as to appear to have effected a cure. They are also responsible for the madmen, whom you see running out into the streets, themselves soothsayers of a kind but without a temple, raging, ranting, whirling round in the dance; there is the same demoniacal possession, but the object of the frenzy is different.[1]

Tatian (second century) also has not the slightest doubt as to the genuineness of the Pythoness' inspiration. In his eyes, however, Apollo is no " god " but a " demon," and thus a creature of evil.[2]

The Christian writer Theophilus even shares the belief in possession amongst the poets and holds it to be not divine but demoniacal. Homer, Hesiod, and the other Greek poets—

> . . . spoke according to imagination and delusion, inspired not by a pure but by a deceitful spirit. This was clearly demonstrated by the fact that other persons controlled by a demon often and up to the present time are exorcised in the name of the true God, and that then the deceitful spirits themselves confess that they are demons who were once active in those poets.[3]

Thus Origen (b. 185) holds the Greek oracles—even in contradistinction to certain other pagan conceptions—to be not fraud but purely and simply the work of evil spirits. There are certain aspects of the state of possession which he refuses to recognize as divine and to which he attributes a demoniacal character. The believer in oracles bases his belief on the supernormal and prophetic nature of the utterances, as well as on the involuntary manner in which they are made by the prophetess. Origen, on the contrary, cannot get beyond the alleged manner, incompatible with Christian modesty, in which Apollo enters into the Pythoness and her general derangement of mind. The facility with which the demons can be expelled from the possessed also seems to

---

[1] Minucius Felix, *loc. cit.*, cap. 27.
[2] Tatian, *Oratio ad Græcos*, 18.
[3] Theophilus, *Ad Autolyc.*, ii, 9.

him evidence of the demoniacal character of the oracles, an argument in which the identity of the states of the δαιμονι- ζόμενοι with those of the Pythoness is assumed, whereas it should certainly be subject to prior demonstration. The exorcisms, however, applied only to the possessed and not to the inspired givers of oracles, and it should also be noted that inspired Christians likewise suffered from grave mental troubles. Origen here shows a surprising ignorance of the psychological character of these states; is it possible that he never saw anyone under the influence of inspiration? His arguments run:

> . . . it would be possible for us to gather from the writings of Aristotle and the Peripatetic school not a few things to overthrow the authority of the Pythian and the other oracles. From Epicurus also, and his followers, we could quote passages to show that even among the Greeks themselves there were some who utterly discredited the oracles which were recognized and admired throughout the whole of Greece. But let it be granted that the responses delivered by the Pythian and the other oracles were not utterances of false men who pretended to a divine inspiration; and let us see if, after all, we cannot convince any sincere inquirers that there is no need to attribute these oracular responses to any divinities, but that, on the other hand, they may be traced to wicked demons —to spirits which are at enmity with the human race, and which in this way wish to hinder the soul from rising upwards, from following the path of virtue, and from returning to God in sincere piety. It is said of the Pythian priestess, whose oracle seems to have been the most celebrated, that when she sat down at the mouth of the Castalian cave, the prophetic spirit of Apollo entered her private parts; and when she was filled with it, she gave utterance to responses which are regarded as divine truths. Judge by this whether the spirit does not show its profane and impure nature, by choosing to enter the soul of the prophetess not through the more becoming medium of the bodily pores which are both open and invisible, but by means of what no modest man would ever see or speak of. And this occurs not once or twice, which would be more permissible, but as often as she was believed to receive inspiration from Apollo. Moreover, it is not the part of a divine spirit to drive the prophetess into such a state of ecstasy and madness that she loses control of herself. For he who is under the influence of the Divine Spirit ought to be the first to receive the beneficial effects; and these ought not to be first enjoyed by the persons who consult the oracle about the concerns of natural or civil life, or for purposes of temporal gain or interest; and, moreover, that should be the time of clearest perception, when a person is in close intercourse with the Deity.
>
> Accordingly we can show from an examination of the sacred Scriptures, that the Jewish prophets, who were enlightened as far as was necessary for their prophetic work by the spirit of God, were the first to enjoy the benefit of the inspiration; and by the contact—if I may say so—of the Holy Spirit they became clearer in mind, and their souls were filled with a brighter light, and the body no longer served as a hindrance to a virtuous life; for to

that which we call " the lust of the flesh " it was deadened. For
we are persuaded that the Divine Spirit " mortifies the deeds of the
body," and destroys that enmity against God which the carnal
passions serve to excite. If, then, the Pythian priestess is beside
herself when she prophesies, what spirit must that be which fills
her mind and clouds her judgment with darkness, unless it be of
the same order with those demons which many Christians cast out
of persons possessed with them ? And this, we may observe, they
do without the use of any curious acts of magic, or incantations,
but merely by prayer and simple adjurations which the plainest
person can use. Because for the most part it is unlettered persons
who perform this work; thus making manifest the grace which is
in the word of Christ, and the despicable weakness of demons, which,
in order to be overcome and driven out of the bodies and souls of
men, do not require the power and wisdom of those who are mighty
in argument, and most learned in matters of faith.[1]

As regards the classification of Apollo amongst the demons,
the Christians as a rule no longer made any distinction
between the states of inspiration of the Pythoness and those
of the possessed in the New Testament sense. Justin Martyr
classes both together amongst the evidence for the survival
of individual consciousness after death:

> . . . Let these persuade you that even after death souls are
> in a state of sensation; and those who are seized and cast about
> by the spirits of the dead, whom all call demoniacs or madmen;
> and what you repute as oracles, both of Amphilochus, Dodona,
> Pytho, and as many other such as exist.[2]

It is not surprising that St. Augustine shared the general
Christian conception.[3]

The attitude of the Pythian oracle towards Christianity
and Christ himself is not uninteresting. In Augustine's work,
De Civitate Dei, we find on the occasion of a polemic by the
author against Porphyry the text of an oracle which had been
vouchsafed to a man in answer to the question of how he
might recall his wife from Christianity.

> You will probably find it easier to write lasting characters on
> the water, or lightly fly like a bird through the air, than to restore
> right feeling in your impious wife once she has polluted herself.
> Let her remain as she pleases in her foolish deception, and sing
> false laments to her dead God, who was condemned by right-
> minded judges and punished ignominiously by a violent death.[4]

---

[1] Origen, *Contra Celsum*, bk. vii, chaps. iii-iv (Ante-Nicene Christian
Library, Writings of Origen, trans. Crombie, vol. ii.).
[2] Justin Martyr, *Apologia*, cap. xviii (Ante-Nicene Christian Library,
The Writings of Justin Martyr and Athenagoras, trans. M. Dods,
London, 1857.
[3] St. Augustine, *De Civitate Dei*, xix, 23, 2 sq. (Works of Aurelius
Augustine, ed. Dods, Edinburgh, 1888, p. 334).
[4] *Ibid.*, xix, 23 (p. 335).

But Porphyry says with reference to other oracles:

> For the gods have declared that Christ was very pious, and has become immortal, and that they cherish his memory: that the Christians, however, are polluted, contaminated, and involved. And many other such things . . . do the gods say against the Christians. . . . But to some who asked Hecate whether Christ were a God, she replied. . . . The soul you refer to is that of a man foremost in piety: they worship it because they mistake the truth."[1]

Belief in the demoniacal character of the Pythoness' inspirations has also found defenders in later centuries, amongst the number being Petrarch.[2] We even find similar ideas in recent Catholic literature, for example in F. X. Knabenhauer[3] and Stützle,[4] whom we have often quoted. These authors cannot escape the impression that true prophecies were given at Delphi, and profess themselves unable to explain it otherwise than by the influence of diabolic powers.

In this connection it should be noted that we have a very detailed poetic description of the Pythoness dating from the early days of the Roman Empire. It is to be found in Lucan's *Pharsalia*,[5] where he relates how the seeress was forced against her will by the General Appius to give an oracle. The text of this description,[6] which is naturally of no historic value, shows obvious traces of the fact that the author had in mind a similar description by another poet, that which Virgil in the fourth book of the Æneid gives of the Sibyl of Cumæ and with which we shall become acquainted later. Lucan's picture is yet rougher. True it admits that abnormal phenomena accompanied the enthusiasm of the seeress, but the " mighty hole " in the Adyton of the temple of which the poet speaks is pure imagination. There is, moreover, a grave contradiction: the oracles of the Pythoness are at first represented according to tradition as confused words, whereas the one which occurs later in the poem is in perfectly consecutive speech.

Beside the Pythoness there are other seeresses of whom

[1] *Ibid.*, xix, 23 (p. 335).
[2] Körting, *Petrarcas Leben und Werke*, Leipzig, 1878, p. 613, quoted by Friedländer, *loc. cit.*
[3] F. X. Knabenhauer, *Orakel und Prophetie*, Passau, 1881.
[4] Stützle, *loc. cit.* (cf. p. 311, note 2).
[5] Lucan, *Pharsalia*, v, 85-213.
[6] Cf. the eminent commentary *Adnotationes super Lucanum*, ed. Joannes Endt, Lipsiæ (Teubner), 1909, pp. 162 sq.

we unfortunately know still less. These are the Sibyls. What remains of the sibylline oracles is really mere literary fabrication in which several authors have had a share. The Greek forgeries passed through Jewish hands and suffered yet further modification in the process. A great number of Sibyls are mentioned, first one, then more and more up to a dozen. To what extent the beliefs surrounding them are merely imaginary is indicated by the fact that their alleged age is reckoned by centuries.

Did Sibyls ever really exist? We must admit that they did. Such figures are not created by the imagination; wherever they appear they have a foundation in reality, even when it can no longer be associated with individual cases.

The literature concerning the Sibyls is very rich,[1] but unfortunately the psychological content of these works is slight and has not repaid the time and labour which I have expended in perusing them. Similarly there is not much to be gleaned from the descriptions of antiquity, which are, moreover, all of a poetic nature and thus of merely secondary value.

The close relationship existing between the Sibyls and the Pythoness is already attested by the title of " Sibyl " which Heraclitus confers on the seeress of Delphi. According to Bergk the word Σίβυλλα derives from σοφός in Æolian dialect σύφος, in old Latin sibus, persibus. The Sibyl of Samos is called Φοιτώ, which Bergk regards as a noun signifying a raving or inspired woman.[2]

The later conception of these Sibyls is again reflected in Virgil's description of the Sibyl of Cumæ who was questioned by Æneas,[3] and side by side with this poetic narrative stand the *Oracula sibyllina* themselves. From them we gather the surprising fact that it is not as a rule the god who speaks by the mouth of the seeress. Already in Virgil the Sibyl says quite simply what will happen in the future. In the *Oracula* also no divine " ego " speaks through her mouth; she proclaims herself inspired but without losing her own identity.

---

[1] For guidance see J. Geffcken, *Aus der Werdezeit des Christentums* (Natur und Geisteswelt, vol. liv), Leipzig, 1904, ii, 2. E. Maas, *De Sibyllarum indicibus*, Dissertation, Greifenwald, 1879. C. Alexandre, *Excursus ad Sibyllina*, Paris, 1857.

[2] Bergk, *loc. cit.*, i, pp. 342 sq.

[3] Virgil, *Æneid*, vi.

Here is the opening of the first book of the *Oracula*:

> Beginning with the earliest race of men
> Even to the latest, I will prophesy
> Of all things past, and present, and to come
> In the world through the wickedness of men.
> And first, God bids me utter how the world
> Came into being.[1]

It appears from several other passages that the form in which the Sibyl, when not possessed, professes to have received her inspiration should be regarded as at least partly auditive.

The second book begins:

> Now when my song of wisdom God restrained
> Much I implored, and in my heart again
> He put the charming voice of words divine.
> Trembling at every form I follow these,
> For what I speak I do not comprehend,
> But God commands each thing to be declared.[2]

Also in the third book:

> And then a message from the mighty God
> Pressed on my heart, and bade me prophesy
> On all the earth, and in the minds of kings
> These things deposit which are yet to be.[3]

The following words show how inspiration was felt as a constraint:

> Now, when my soul had ceased from hallowed song,
> And I prayed the great Sire to be released,
> Again a message of Almighty God
> Rose in my heart, and he commanded me
> To prophesy o'er all the earth and place
> In royal minds the things which are to be.[4]

Similarly in another passage of the same book:

> Now when my soul had ceased from hallowed song,
> Again a message of Almighty God
> Rose in my heart, and He commanded me
> To utter prophecies upon the earth.[5]

In another place she says that she will be called mad: αὐτὰρ μεμανήοτι θυμῷ and the true seeress of the oracle: πάντες φημίξουσι μάντιν χρησμῳδὸν.[6]

---

[1] *The Sibylline Oracles*, trans. M. S. Terry, New York, 1890, book i, ll. 1-6, cf. iii, 808-828.
[2] *Ibid.*, bk. ii, ll. 1-5. [3] *Ibid.*, bk. iii, ll. 190-193.
[4] *Ibid.*, bk. iii, ll. 346-50. [5] *Ibid.*, bk. iii, ll. 580-584.
[6] *Ibid.*, bk. ix (xi), ll. 396-399.

More than once she complains of the heavy burden which inspiration lays upon her.

The third book begins:

> Thou blessed One, loud Thunderer of the heavens,
> Who holdest in their place the cherubins,
> I pray thee give me now a little rest,
> Since I have uttered what is all so true.
> For weary has my heart within me grown.
> Why should my heart be quivering now again,
> And my soul, lashed as with a whip, be forced
> To utter forth its oracle to all ?
> Yet once more I will speak aloud all things
> Which God impels me to proclaim to men.[1]

Also the tenth (twelfth) book ends:

> And now, King of the world, of every realm
> The monarch, pure, immortal, for thou hast
> Into my heart set the ambrosial strain,
> Cease thou the word, for I am not aware
> Of what I say; for all things thou to me
> Dost ever speak. But give me a brief rest,
> And place thou in my heart a charming song.
> For weary has my heart within me grown
> Of words divine, foretelling royal power.[2]

It is obvious that these expressions reflect genuine experiences of inspiration, if not on the part of the author himself, on that of some other person. From the psychological standpoint it is comprehensible that in a civilization like that of antiquity where poetic creation was held, at least in part, to be veritably inspired by the divine powers, such experiences of involuntary inspiration must have been much more frequent than to-day, simply by reason of the autosuggestive influence of the belief.

The states described in the *Oracula Sibyllina* cannot, on the other hand, be regarded as true possession. We have never admitted this except when a second personal consciousness has manifested itself either in place of or side by side with the first. A case where the " I " who speaks professes to be a god would be slightly indicative of this, as shown by the glossolalia;[3] but it is not necessarily so, for the glossolalia may appear in simple inspiration. In the absence of any more detailed description we cannot form an opinion; the two introductory verses are inadequate for the purpose.

---

[1] *Ibid.*, bk. iii, ll. 1-10.   [2] *Ibid.*, bk. x, ll. 362-370.
[3] Cf. my *Einfuhrung in die Religionspsychologie*, Berlin, 1917, ch. v.

Only once, so far as I know, does the god apparently speak directly through the Sibyl in the *Oracula Sibyllina*, and this one case concerns a copy of the above-quoted Delphic oracle vouchsafed to Crœsus.

In the eighth book there is—brusquely interpolated—a passage in the " I " style:

> All these things to my mind did God reveal,
> And all that has been spoken by my mouth
> Will He fulfil.   The number of the sands,
> And measured spaces of the sea I know:
> I know the secret places of the earth
> And Gloomy Tartarus, and men who are
> And who shall be hereafter, and the dead.
> I know the numbers of the stars and trees
> And all the species of the quadrupeds,
> And swimming things, and birds that fly aloft
> For I myself the forms and minds of men
> Have fashioned, and right reason have bestowed,
> And taught them knowledge.   I who see and hear
> Formed eyes and ears; . . .
>
> *   *   *   *   *
>
> For I alone am God, and other God
> There is not.[1]

The fact that with the exception of this passage the god never speaks directly by the mouth of the Sibyl in the *Oracula Sibyllina* seems to me to indicate with irresistible cogency that in the later days of antiquity it was no longer known by experience how these seeresses had really spoken in former times, for the substitution of the personal ego by that of a god was surely its most characteristic feature.   The phenomena described in the *Oracula* are states of inspiration of a milder nature similar to those manifested in highly civilized times; unlike true possession they do not show any transformation of the personality.   Under the influence of general progress this latter must have disappeared gradually; Virgil himself clearly never saw an authentic Sibyl.

It should be noted that Cicero classes two seers, the Bœotian Bakis and Epimenides of Crete, with the Sibyl.[2]

The third phenomenon which claims our attention is the cult of Dionysos.   Here too the information is scanty, although slightly more abundant than in the subject already dealt with.

---

[1] *Sibylline Oracles* (Terry), viii, ll. 448 sq.
[2] Cicero, *De divinatione*, i, 18.

The following passage from Erwin Rohde may serve to describe the Thracian cult:

> The ceremony took place on mountain heights at dead of night, by the flickering light of torches. Loud music resounded; the clashing of brazen cymbals, the deep thunder of great hand-tympani and in the intervals the " sounds luring to madness " of the deep-toned flutes whose soul was first awakened by the Phrygian Auletes. Excited by this wild music the crowd of revellers dances with piercing cries. We hear nothing of any song; the fury of the dance leaves no breath for it. For this is not the measured dance-step with which Homer's Greeks swung rhythmically forward in the Pæan, but in a frenzied, whirling, and violent round the ecstatic crowd hastens upwards over the mountain-sides. It is mostly women who turn to the point of exhaustion in this giddy dance. Strangely clothed: they wear " basseren," long flowing garments made, it seems, from fox-skins sewn together; over these roebuck skins, and horns upon their heads. Their hair flies wild, their hands grasp snakes, sacred to Sabazios, they brandish daggers or thyrsi with hidden lance-heads under the ivy. So they rage until every emotion is excited to the highest pitch and in the " holy madness " they fling themselves upon the animals destined for sacrifice, seize and dismember the assembled booty and with their teeth tear the bloody flesh which they swallow raw.[1]

Unhappily we have no first-hand evidence concerning the cult. It is not surprising that the participants were almost exclusively women; nevertheless there has come down to us at least one poem in which there appear male as well as female participants in the Dionysiac cult: it is the *Bacchæ* of Euripides. Having passed the latter years of his life in Thrace the poet had the opportunity of observing the Thracian cult very closely. The meaning of the play is much debated, as it is not free from difficulties and these persist even in the most recent interpretation by Norwood.

We are inclined to imagine the Dionysiac cult as a kind of Cologne or Munich carnival, a wild abandonment to the senses. It is indubitable that such an effect was not seldom produced, the excesses committed at Rome, and against which the Senate was obliged to take strong action in 186 B.C.,[2] being of this kind. But on the other hand it would be entirely erroneous to regard the cult of Dionysos as a whole in this light; this is specifically contradicted by Euripides' play, in which we find no indication of any tendency to excess. It is true that one of the characters in the play, Pentheus, king of Thebes, believes in something of the kind; he fears

[1] E. Rohde, *Psyche*, 2nd edit., vol. ii, Tübingen, 1898, pp. 9 sq.
[2] Livy, xxxix, 8 sq.

sexual excesses. But the partisans of the cult, as well as a disinterested eye-witness, formally deny the accusation and are to all appearances profoundly convinced to the contrary. A shepherd relates to the king:

> Thine herds of pasturing kine were even now
> Scaling the steep hillside, what time the sun
> First darted forth his rays to warm the earth,
> When lo. I see three Bacchant women-bands. . . .
> All sleeping lay, with bodies restful-strown;
> Some backward leaned on leafy sprays of pine,
> Some, with oak-leaves for pillows, on the ground
> Flung careless; modestly, not, as thou say'st,
> Drunken with wine, and the sighing of flutes
> Hunting desire through woodland shades alone.[1]

And also the son of Tiresias, himself seized by the intoxication of the dance, explains to the king:

> Dionysus upon women will not thrust
> Chastity: in true womanhood inborn
> Dwells temperance touching all things evermore.
> This must thou heed: for in his Bacchic rites
> The virtuous-hearted shall not be undone.[2]

Since Euripides the sceptic would not have depicted the Dionysiac cult which he had learned to know in Thrace as moral had he found it grossly licentious, we are also obliged to admit that the frenzied movements of the Mænads and the few male participants were really filled with *earnest religious feeling*. This assumption is supported by numerous other passages in the *Bacchæ*.

The question which principally concerns us is to know whether the Dionysiac intoxication should be considered as a form of possession. The word possession, κάτοχος, ἔνθεος, etc., served to designate it and moreover Erwin Rohde speaks of " a transient derangement of the psychic balance, a state in which the conscious mind is dominated, of ' possession ' by outside forces (as it is described to us)."[3]

But the problem is not solved by the mere use of the word " possession "; we should like more substantial proofs in order to decide up to what point the states are identical with those described in the first part of this work. A presumption in favour of identity is the fact, apparent from the statements

[1] Arthur S. Way, *Euripides in English Verse*, vol. iii, p. 400, ll. 677-689.
[2] *Ibid.*, vol. iii, p. 381, ll. 313-318.
[3] Rohde, *loc. cit.*, p. 4. For the words κάτοχος, ἔνθεος, etc., see p. 11, note 1, and pp. 18 sq. *notes*, of this work.

22

collected by Rohde, that the consciousness was filled with the presence of the god; it was therefore as a direct result of the whole excitement into which the worshippers worked themselves up that contact with the god was established.

> The sense of this violently provoked intensification of feeling was religious. It was only by such tension and extension of his being that man seemed able to enter into relation and contact with creatures of a higher order, with the god and his spirit-legions. The god was present but unseen amidst his inspired worshippers or else was very near and the din of the festival served to bring the hoverer right to the spot.[1]

But the main question is not yet answered. Was there simply a " consciousness of presence " of Dionysos, or was he felt within the worshippers, as vividly real as was the demon to the possessed ?

From Euripides we gather only the former, probably enhanced by hallucinatory phenomena.

O trance of rapture, when, reeling aside
   From the Bacchanal rout o'er the mountains flying
One sinks to the earth, and the fawn's flecked hide
   Covers him lying.
With its sacred vesture, wherein he hath chased
The goat to the death for its blood—for the taste
   Of the feast raw-reeking, when over the hills
Of Phrygia, of Lydia, the wild feet haste
   And the Clamour-king leads, and our hearts he thrills
      " Evoe !" crying !

Flowing with milk is the ground, and with wine is it flowing, and flowing
   Nectar of bees; and a smoke as of incense of Araby soars;
And the Bacchanal, lifting the flame of the brand of the fire, ruddy-
      glowing,
   Waveth it wide, and with shouts, from the point of the wand as it
      pours
Challengeth revellers straying, on-racing, on-chasing, and throwing
   Loose to the breezes his curls, while clear through the chorus that
      roars
         Cleaveth his shout, " On, Bacchanal-rout,
On, Bacchanal maidens, ye glory of Tmolus the hill gold-welling,
Blend the acclaim of your chant with the timbrels thunder-knelling,
         Glad-pealing the glad God's praises out
   With Phrygian cries and the voice of singing. . . ."[2]

These verses clearly show that the god was regarded as present, or was even felt and his voice heard. How is this to be explained ?

There remain only two possibilities: either the excitement

---

[1] Rohde, *loc. cit.*, vol. ii, p. 11 sq. Cf. also p. 14, in the notes on original documents.
[2] S. Way, *loc. cit.*, p. 374, ll. 136-158.

of those taking part in the worship was so great that it ended in illusion and hallucination, even perhaps of a collective nature; or else, and this is a hypothesis which does not appear hitherto to have been considered, the god was personified by someone. Any participant, no matter who, played his part, somewhat as King Carnival is represented by a living man. In that case the personage styled " Dionysos " in Euripides would not be the god himself in the strict sense but the god-actor (who when intoxicated identified himself more or less with the god). That would probably resolve many difficulties in the play and foremost amongst these the fact that this personage alternately does and does not seem to be Dionysos himself and to proclaim himself as such. The probable historical connection of Carnival with the Dionysiac cult (in a debased form) and the historical identity of Prince Carnival with Dionysos render the truth of the conjecture extremely probable. Its proof in particular cases must be left to Philology.

Let us now consider whether the god also entered into the souls of the Mænads and their possible male companions. The most important circumstance in favour of such a theory is the name of the participants: they are called σάβοι, σάβαι σαβάζιοι, βάκχοι, βάκχαι, that is to say they bear, as, moreover, in the cult of Cybele also, the name of the god Sabazios or Bacchus.[1]

Such identification always indicates a psychic transformation. If the worshippers had not been changed into Dionysos the transference to them of the god's name would be inexplicable.

This identification at least proves that transformation of the personality originally existed, although it may have disappeared at a higher stage of civilization. In support of this hypothesis we must moreover quote the similarity of conduct between Dionysos and his worshippers. " Like the wild god himself they fell upon the sacrificial beast to devour it raw." " The horns which they wore recall the horned bull-god himself."[2]

Sometimes even the crude idea that the torn and devoured beast was the god peeped through,[3] a conception in which

---

[1] Cf. Rohde, *loc. cit.*, p. 14, note 4.
[2] *Ibid.*, vol. ii, pp. 14 sq.   [3] *Ibid.*, vol. ii, p. 15, note 1.

union with the god is realized in the most naïf manner and one which might also give rise to the genesis of possession. In other cases the Mænads play the part of nymphs, Pans, Silenus and Satyrs or other beings accompanying the god— such as the μαινάδες originally were themselves.[1]

To these must be added other data of a positive nature, although partially derived from somewhat later times. Tiresias also speaks in the *Bacchæ* of a visitation of the god:

> . . . in his fulness when he floods our frame
> He makes his maddened votaries tell the future.[2]

In the scholia of Euripides' *Hippolytus*, 144, we read:

> Those men are called " filled with god " whose reason has been taken away by an apparition and who are possessed by the god who gave the vision and behave according to his will.[3]

Neither does Rohde doubt that the Bacchantes themselves were under the illusion of living in a strange personality.[4] In support of this opinion he adds:

> The terrors of the night, the music, especially of those Phrygian flutes to whose sounds the Greeks attributed the power of rendering the hearer " full of the god," the whirling dance: all these could really create in certain predisposed natures a state of visionary excitement in which the inspired saw as existing independently of themselves all that they thought and imagined.[5]

In this connection we should observe that visions and possession are not in any way identical. These two phenomena may co-exist, but they are quite distinct and it is not permissible to argue the presence of the one from a demonstration of the other.

Visions are always easier to prove. No doubt is possible as to their reality amongst the Bacchantes.

> " It is only during possession that the Bacchantes draw milk and honey from the streams," says Plato, " and not when they are themselves."[6]

> " Flowing with milk is the ground, and with wine it is flowing, and flowing
> Nectar of bees; and a smoke as of incense of Araby soars,"

says Euripides.[7]

[1] *Ibid.*, vol. ii, p. 14, note 3.
[2] Euripides, *loc. cit.*, p. 380, ll. 300-301.
[3] Quoted by Rohde, *loc. cit.*, vol. ii, p. 20, note 1.
[4] *Ibid.*, vol. ii, p. 16.   [5] *Ibid.*, vol. ii, p. 16.
[6] Plato, *Ion*, 534 A.   [7] Euripides, *loc. cit.*, p. 90.

And later:

> One (Bacchante) grasped her thyrsus-staff, and smote the rock,
> And forth upleapt a fountain's showering spray:
> One in earth's bosom planted her reed-wand,
> And up therethrough the god a wine-fount sent;
> And whoso fain would drink white-foaming draughts
> Scarred with their finger-tips the breast of earth,
> And milk gushed forth unstinted: dripped the while
> Sweet streams of honey from their ivy-staves.[1]

Lucian relates also:

> The Bacchic dance to which they are addicted in Ionia and
> Pontus, has, although satyric in nature, gained such a hold upon
> the people of those countries that at the appointed time they forget
> everything else and for days together behold Titans, Corybantes,
> Satyrs and herdsmen.[2]

The sources are unhappily too scanty to afford us exact knowledge of whether the phenomena of possession and the visions appeared in the same persons, or the first more particularly in some and the second in others. Co-existence of the two kinds of phenomena would have its parallel, for example, in the case of Sœur Jeanne des Anges and Eschenmayer's C. St. case. As already stated, I have not lingered over the phenomena of vision amongst possessed persons because they are of no importance to the analysis of true possession and I shall here confine myself to remarking that in the cases quoted (which are only a few amongst many), visions were very frequent.

The most recent English commentary on the *Bacchæ* (by G. Norwood) advocates the theory that the personage appearing under the name of Dionysos is not at all the god himself (which interpretation entails certain difficulties although the new theory immediately gives rise to further ones). If this is so the identification of god and man would be accomplished in the play itself.[3]

It cannot be exactly determined up to what point these states were somnambulistic or lucid. According to Rohde we should believe that they were generally somnambulistic in character. "The ἔνθεος," says he, "is entirely in the god's power. The god speaks and acts in him. His own conscious-

---

[1] *Ibid.*, p. 401, ll. 705-710.
[2] Lucian, *De Saltat*, 79, quoted by Farnell, *loc. cit.*, vol. v, p. 207.
[3] G. Norwood, *The Riddle of the Bacchæ, the Last Stage of Euripides' Religious Views*, Manchester, 1908.

ness has entirely left the ἔνθεος "[1] Rohde bases his theory on one single passage of Plato and Philo.[2] In Plato's *Meno* we read: οὗτοι ἐνθουσιῶντες (meaning οἱ χρησμῳδοί τε καὶ θεομάντεις) λέγουσιν μὲν ἀληθῆ καὶ πολλά, ἴσασι δὲ οὐδὲν ὧν λέγουσιν, *i.c.*, "the god-possessed men speak much truth, but know nothing of what they say."

The interpretation of these last words in the sense of a loss of personal consciousness is, however, untenable. It is clear from the comparison which Plato makes in this place between the god-possessed and creative politicians that he is not thinking of a loss of personal consciousness; he simply means that what they say under inspiration exceeds their normal spiritual capacity.

The second quotation to which Rohde refers is from Philo. The latter says, speaking of divinely inspired prophets:

> For in general the prophet announces nothing personal, rather he merely lends his voice to him who prompts him with all that he says; when he is inspired he becomes unconscious; thought vanishes away and leaves the fortress of the soul; but the divine spirit has entered there and taken up its abode; and this latter makes all the vocal organs resound, so that the man gives clear expression to what the spirit gives him to say.[3]

For the sake of completeness, let us give another quotation from the same source, to which Rohde makes no reference and which runs:

> Moses has said: . . . But there shall suddenly appear a prophet sent from God and he shall prophesy without saying anything of himself—for he who is really inspired and filled with God cannot comprehend with his intelligence what he says; he only repeats what is suggested to him, as if another prompted him; for the prophets are those who speak on God's behalf, who use their organs to reveal his will.[4]

These two messages are designed to testify to a suspension of consciousness and consequently to the somnambulistic nature of the possession. Unfortunately, however, they offer no immediate demonstration of the somnambulistic character of Dionysiac intoxication, relating as they do to prophets and diviners. Nothing but the fact that the ancients were generally accustomed to associate these

[1] E. Rohde, *Psyche*, 2nd edit., Tübingen, 1898, vol. ii, p. 20, note 1.
[2] Plato, *The Meno*, 99c.
[3] Philo, *De special. legibus*, iv, 343 M., ed. Cohn and Wendland, vol. v, p. 219.
[4] Philo, *loc. cit.*, p. 222 M., ed. Cohn and Wendland, vol. v, p. 16.

states authorizes us to generalize from the one to the other, and even this does not fully compensate for the lack of direct evidence.

In the first place, it cannot be said how great a number of those participating in the Dionysiac intoxication-cult fell into a state of true possession; but neither do we know how numerous these participants were. The only thing ascertainable is that the number of adherents was greater than that of the possessed. Εἰσὶ γὰρ δή, ὥς φασιν οἱ περὶ τὰς τελετάς, ναρθηκοφόροι μὲν πολλοί, βάκχοι δέ τε παῦροι.[1]

We will supplement by a quotation from Jamblich's work on the Mysteries.

> There are, therefore, many species of divine possession, and divine inspiration is multifariously excited; thence, also, the signs of it are many and different. For either the gods are different, by whom we are inspired, and thus produce a different inspiration, or the mode of enthusiasms being various, produces a different afflatus. For either divinity possesses us or we give ourselves up wholly to divinity, or we have a common energy with him. And sometimes, indeed, we participate of the last power of divinity, sometimes of his middle, and sometimes of his first power. Sometimes, also, there is a participation only, at other times, communion likewise, and sometimes a union of these divine inspirations. Again, either the soul alone enjoys the inspiration, or the soul receives it in conjunction with the body, or it is also participated by the common animal.
>
> From these things, therefore, the signs of those that are inspired are multiform. For the inspiration is indicated by the motions of the [whole] body, and of certain parts of it, by the perfect rest of the body, by harmonious orders and dances, and by elegant sounds, or the contraries of these. Either the body, likewise, is seen to be elevated, or increased in bulk, or to be borne along sublimely in the air, or the contraries of these are seen to take place about it. An equability also, of voice, according to magnitude, or a great variety of voice after intervals of silence, may be observed. And again, sometimes the sounds have a musical intension and remission, and sometimes they are strained and relaxed after a different manner.[2]
>
> But it is necessary to investigate the causes of divine mania. And these are the illuminations proceeding from the gods, the spirits imparted by them, and the all-perfect domination of divinity, which comprehends indeed everything in us, but exterminates entirely our own proper consciousness and motion. This divine possession, also, emits words which are not understood by those that utter them; for they pronounce them, as it is said, with an insane mouth, and are wholly subservient, and entirely yield themselves to the energy of the predominating God.[3]

---

[1] Plato, *Phædo*, 69 c.
[2] Jamblichus, *De Mysteriis*, Sect. iii, ch. v, pp. 123-24. English trans. by Th. Taylor, London, 1895.
[3] *Ibid.*, iii, 8, pp. 128-29.

Unfortunately this description is so meagre as to be in itself incapable of detailed interpretation. It will be one of the future tasks of a deeper research into Neo-Platonism to arrive at a complete understanding of the passage.

Jamblich, moreover, considers it the general view of his contemporaries that " many, through enthusiasm and divine inspiration, predict future events, and that they are then in so wakeful a state, as even to energize according to sense, and yet they are not conscious of the state they are in, or at least, not so much as they were before."[1]

These words, like the preceding ones, are not sufficiently clear to permit of a considered judgement as to whether a true somnambulistic state is meant or merely a marked distraction of the attention.

Very closely related to Dionysiac possession is the so-called Corybantism[2] manifested at the festivals of the Phrygian divinities. But the possessing spirits in this case were not Dionysos or his companions, nymphs, satyrs, etc., but Rhea Cybele or her companions, the so-called Corybantes.

> " They rage possessed by Rhea and the Corybantes, that is to say, they rage like the Corybantes possessed by the demon. As soon as the divine attribute has taken possession of them they rush in, cry aloud, dance and foretell the future, raging and god-driven," relates the Phrygian Arrian.[3]

Graillot's new work on the worship of Cybele gives no psychological explanation of any importance.[4] The phenomena reported are those best known as characteristic of possession in Greece. They are not the only ones; it has also been possible to establish a series of less important cases.

> There are few places but have oracles set up, where priests and priestesses, in a mad ravishment, announce what Apollo inspires them to say. The prototype of these oracles is that of Delphi.[5]

The prophetess of Apollo Deiradiotes at Argos is alleged to have become possessed by drinking the blood of the sacri-

[1] *Ibid.*, iii, 4, p. 121.
[2] Rohde, *loc. cit.*, pp. 47 sq.
[3] Arrian in Eustathius, *ad Dionysium Periegetem*, 809, quoted by Rohde, *loc. cit.*, vol. ii, p. 48. Cf. the *Dionysius Periegetes* of G. Bernhardy, Leipzig, 1828.
[4] G. Graillot, *Le Culte de Cybèle*, Paris, 1912.
[5] Rohde, *loc. cit.*, vol. ii, p. 60; G. F. Schoemann, *Griechische Altertümer*, 4th edit. rev. Lipsius, Berlin, 1902, vol. ii, p. 330.

fices: κάτοχος ἐκ τοῦ θεοῦ γίγνεται, as was the priestess of the Earth at Ægira in Achaia.[1]

Pausanius, moreover, says of the priest of the oracle at Amphikleia in Phocis: χρᾷ ἐκ τοῦ θεοῦ κάτοχος.[2]

At the oracle of Claros, near Colophon in Asia Minor, the priest, descended from a certain local family, went to a cavern, drank of a running stream and gave in verse his reply to the question put, although he was often an uneducated man.[3] Similarly it is said of the priestess of the Didymaic oracle near Miletus, that she had drunk of an ecstasy-inducing spring; there is also mention of inhaling vapour arising from the spring.[4]

In the cases of blood-drinking the autosuggestive nature of the ecstasy is indubitable. Where the water of certain springs is drunk doubt might exist, particularly when the inhalation of vapour is mentioned, but it is nevertheless very noteworthy that springs producing this effect are no longer known to-day.

E. von Lasaulx has collected in a special work[5] all the documents on the oracle of Dodona, where exactly as at Delphi priests prophesied in a state of psychic excitement. These include a very important piece of information, nowhere to be found in the literature concerning the Pythoness, namely that those states were somnambulistic in character, the priestesses preserving no memory of them. The rhetor Aristides, who lived under Hadrian, attests that the priestesses " do not know, before being seized by the spirits, what they are going to say, any more than after having recovered their natural senses they remember what they have said, so that everyone knows what they say except themselves."[6]

---

[1] On the priestess of Apollo at Argos, cf. Pausanius, ii, 24, 1, quoted by Rohde, loc. cit., p. 58, note 1. On the prophetess of Achaia cf. Pliny, Natural History, xxviii, 147, quoted by J. G. Frazer, The Magic Art, London, 1911, vol. i, p. 383. Frazer also gives other cases from various civilizations of prophetic possession induced by drinking blood.

[2] Pausanius, loc. cit., x, 33, 11; quoted by Rohde, loc. cit., vol. ii, p. 59, note 2.

[3] Rohde, loc. cit., p. 331.

[4] Ibid., p. 328.

[5] E. von Lasaulx, Das pelasgische Orakel des Zeus zu Dodona, Würzburg, 1840, p. 14.

[6] Aristides, Opera, ii, 13, quoted by Lasaulx, loc. cit., p. 14.

Jamblich says almost the same thing of the priestess of Apollo at the Oracle of Colophon:

> But this divine illumination is constantly present, and uses the prophetess as an instrument; she neither being any longer mistress of herself, nor capable of attending to what she says, nor perceiving where she is. Hence, after prediction, she is scarcely able to recover herself.[1]

It has been possible to establish identification between priests and divinities in a few cases, always in connection with phenomena of possession. Thus Farnell remarks:

> The priestess of Artemis Laphria at Patrai appears to have embodied the goddess on a solemn occasion; the priestesses of the brides of the Dioscuri are called Leukippides, the youthful ministrants of the bull-god Poseidon are themselves " bulls " at Ephesos, the girls who dance in honour of the bear-goddess at Brauron are themselves " bears." But these examples are rare exceptions.[2]

It should also be noted that the Greeks themselves gave a wider extension to the term " possession." They understood by it all the phenomena of inspiration, particularly of the poetic kind. In the beginning it must surely have been understood in the literal sense when the poet invoked the Muse at the opening of his work: ἄνδρα μοι ἔννεπε μοῦσα—μῆνιν ἄειδε, θεά—*Musa, mihi causas memora.* Perhaps already the words may have been used from tradition, and therefore symbolically, by Homer as they certainly were by Virgil; they were nevertheless originally meant in good earnest. What meaning had they when literally used ? Were they simple prayers to a divinity as a Christian poet prays God to grant him grace ? The text itself contradicts this view, since it says that it is the Muse and not the poet who must sing, an expression only explicable if the poet was convinced that he did not create, but that another, the Muse, did so in his place. It is very remarkable that the epics of other peoples contain nothing analogous. Such a conception, existent to an enhanced degree amongst the Greeks and entirely peculiar to that nation, can only be explained by admitting that the voluntary activity of the creative artist was unconnected with his work and that his most perfect productions were obtained as a gift. This manner of envisaging himself in his work shows once more the enormous creative force of the Greek.

---

[1] Jamblichus, *loc. cit.*, iii, ch. 11, p. 142.
[2] L. R. Farnell, *The Cults of the Greek States*, vol. v, Oxford, 1909, p. 150.

Plato makes Socrates say to Ion:

> . . . the Muse communicates through those whom she has first inspired. . . .
>
> . . . For the authors of those great poems which we admire, do not attain to excellence through the rules of any art, but they utter their beautiful melodies of verse in a state of inspiration, and, as it were, *possessed* by a spirit not their own. Thus the composers of lyrical poetry create those admired songs of theirs in a state of divine insanity, like the Corybantes, who lose all control over their reason in the enthusiasm of the sacred dance; and, during this supernatural possession, are excited to the rhythm and harmony which they communicate to men. Like the Bacchantes, who, when possessed by the god, draw honey and milk from the rivers, in which, when they come to their senses, they find nothing but simple water. For the souls of the poets, as poets tell us, have this peculiar ministration in the world. They tell us that their souls, flying like bees from flower to flower, and wandering over the gardens and the meadows, and the honey-flowing fountains of the Muses, return to us laden with the sweetness of melody; and arrayed as they are in the plumes of rapid imagination, they speak truth. For a poet is indeed a thing ethereally light, winged and sacred, nor can he compose anything worth calling poetry until he becomes inspired, and, as it were, mad, or whilst any reason remains to him. For whilst a man retains any portion of the thing called reason, he is utterly incompetent to produce poetry or to vaticinate. Thus, those who declaim various and beautiful poetry upon any subject, as for instance upon Homer, are not enabled to do so by art or study, but every rhapsodist or poet, whether dithyrambic, encomiastic, choral, epic, or iambic, is excellent in proportion to the extent of his participation in the divine influence, and the degree in which the Muse itself has descended on him. In other respects, poets may be sufficiently ignorant and incapable. For they do not compose according to any art which they have acquired, but from the impulse of the divinity within them; for did they know any rules of criticism, according to which they could compose beautiful verses upon one subject, they would be able to exert the same faculty with respect to all or any other. The God seems purposely to have deprived all poets, prophets and soothsayers of every particle of reason and understanding, the better to adapt them to their employment as his ministers and interpreters; and that we, their auditors, may acknowledge that those who write so beautifully are possessed, and address us, inspired by the God. . . ."[1]

This theory of Plato's once more attains full literal acceptation in the philosophy of the Restoration, at the end of classical antiquity. The Emperor Julian[2] is imbued with the idea that the poet is filled with the godhead, and he discriminates, as did Plato, between mental derangement

---

[1] Plato, *Ion*, trans. Shelley (Everyman edit., *Five Dialogues of Plato*, pp. 6-7).

[2] Julian the Apostate, *Orat.*, iv, Loeb Library. This quotation as well as the following are taken from Georg Mau, *Die Religionsphilosophie Kaiser Julians*, Leipzig, 1907, p. 55.

and inspiration.   He calls the seers ἐνθουσιῶντες πρὸς τὴν ἀλήθειαν[1] and similarly Homer θεόληπτος.[2]

It is very interesting to note that the word ἐνθουσιασμός in itself already means possession, not merely enthusiasm in our sense of the word—a mere state of psychic excitement without further significance. In this connection the particulars given in Guida's Lexicon are very instructive. It reads: ἐνθουσιᾷ = ὑπὸ ἐνθέου κατέχεται πνεύματος (not a completely clear definition— we should expect to find ἔνθεος as designating one possessed by a god, but as corollary to πνεῦμα it seems strange).

ἐνθουσιαζόμενοι = ἐφορμῶντες ἤ ἐλλαμπόμενοι
ἐνθουσιασμός =ὅταν ἡ ψυχὴ ὅλη ἐλλάμπηται ὑπὸ τοῦ θεοῦ.

The existence of prophets who vaticinate in an abnormal state of excitement can also be demonstrated in Egypt. A case is even known in which a prophet fell dead in the midst of an access of prophetic frenzy.[3]   But so far as I am aware it cannot be shown that real states of possession occurred; the expression τὸ θῖον (θεῖον) πάσχειν is inadequate for this purpose.

(ii.) In the Present

We still encounter artificial possession amongst the higher civilizations of to-day, principally in Asia, and more especially in India and China.

In India it is not really found amongst the educated classes, but is by no means unknown amongst followers of the Hindu religion. In this connection I may quote from a document which the missionary, Herr Fröhlich, has been kind enough to send me at my request as supplementing his work on the popular religion of the Tamils:[4]

> I have not myself observed any cases of possession amongst the Hindus, but have heard of them times without number.   They always concerned women or priests of the " village gods."
> The manifestations in question amongst Hindu women of every caste are, according to all that I remember to have heard of them, entirely similar (except for the discourses) to those of Christian women (already described on p. 218). The priests, on the other hand,

---

[1] *Ibid.*, 136 b.   [2] *Ibid.*, *Orat.*, iv, 140 c.
[3] R. Reitzenstein, *Ein Stück hellenistischer Kleinliteratur* (Ges. der Wissensch.), Göttingen, 1904, pp. 314 sq.
[4] H. Fröhlich, *Tamulische Volksreligion*, Leipzig, 1915.

are as it were the official mediums through whom the village gods speak, make known their will, and reply to questions. One of these priests, who later became a Christian, related when questioned that he had always felt that " something came over him," and after his conversion was still persuaded that in the states referred to " a devil " had taken possession of him. The worshippers of the village gods (particularly Kali, Mari, and Murugen) believe that through their priests they are in direct communication with their gods—through these very utterances of the priest when in a state of possession. They sometimes point a frank contrast with the Christians: " Your God never talks to you, but we have a god who converses with us."

As regards manifestations by the priests or others of the god's adorers during these states I have only observed a staggering and reeling gait like that of a drunken man when they went towards the temple of their god or goddess. What then occurred in the temple itself and how they comported themselves outwardly when delivering the oracle, I have not been able to observe. The tenor of the " divine sayings " may be typified by the following examples: " Last year you brought us no offerings, therefore I have made your child sick; vow to offer me a hen and the child shall grow well " (reply to a question in a case of sickness). " I shall take many more from this village " (oracle of Kali on the outbreak of a cholera epidemic). " I am Mari; here will I live, build me a temple here." " Have we no music, no flowers, no lemons ?" (oracle on the occasion of a festival when nothing in the way of music, etc., had been provided). " Bring the child to my temple, then it will be cured."

This account depicts for us the primitive form of the oracle, such as may once have formed the basis of the Hellenic one. The most characteristic feature is the complete lack of moral superiority on the part of the divinity; it is only the egotism of the Hindu peasant which speaks through the visiting gods, who generally demand offerings before they will give their help. It should be observed that even at this early stage the impression is produced of a strange objectivity intruding upon the consciousness, and those who believe that this takes place in the higher stages of inspiration will hardly be able to deny it here. It is naturally an assumption extraordinarily fertile in consequences to admit that there is not only a divine and transcendental power able to enter the human consciousness, but also lesser powers—it brings us perilously near to belief in the devil. It is also noteworthy that according to these declarations of the priests there is, at least in general, no somnambulistic possession, otherwise they would not remember these states at all.

In Southern India and Ceylon possession is found particularly in the so-called devil-dances. These are religious dances which by their whole character recall the dervish-dances of Islam. Emil Schmidt writes in the account of his travels:

> If the altars of the higher demons are poor enough, those of the inferior spirits, the Bey-kovils or temples of the devil, are still more so. They often consist of a roof of leaves resting on four bamboo-stems, or are even uncovered; a red painted stone or a tree-stump, a pyramid of earth flattened at the top and painted with red and white bands, then constitutes the whole place of worship. There are no special priests; the chief of the village or family or any other person who fills the vocation, be he man or woman, accomplishes the sacrifices and ceremonies pleasing to the spirits. These ceremonies are of the same kind as for the superior demons; it is rare that the blood of a cock is not shed. But there are certain particularly efficacious ecstatic states, the devil-dances, which bear the strongest resemblance to the shamanistic dances of Northern Asia. Bishop Caldwell has given a suggestive description of them.
>
> Fantastically dressed, amidst the din of rattles, drums and flutes, the conjuror of spirits begins his dance. ". . . the music is at first comparatively slow, and the dancer seems impassive and sullen; and either he stands still or moves about in gloomy silence. Gradually, as the music becomes quicker and louder, his excitement begins to rise. Sometimes to help him to work himself up into a frenzy he uses medicated draughts; cuts and lacerates his flesh till the blood flows; lashes himself with a huge whip; presses a burning torch to his breast; drinks the blood which flows from his own wounds; or drinks the blood of the sacrifice, putting the throat of the decapitated goat to his mouth. Then, as if he had acquired new life, he begins to brandish his staff of bells, and dance with a quick, but wild, unsteady step. Suddenly the *afflatus* descends. There is no mistaking that glare, or those frantic leaps. He snorts, he stares, he gyrates. The demon has now taken bodily possession of him; and though he retains the power of utterance and of motion, both are under the demon's control, and his separate consciousness is in abeyance. The bystanders signalize the event by raising a long shout attended with a peculiar vibratory noise.
>
> "The devil-dancer is now worshipped as a present deity; and every bystander consults him respecting his disease, his wants, the welfare of his absent relations, and the offerings which are to be made for the accomplishment of his wishes.
>
> "As the devil-dancer acts to admiration the part of a maniac, it requires some experience to enable a person to interpret his dubious or unmeaning replies, his muttered voices and uncouth gestures; but the wishes of the parties who consult him, help them greatly to interpret his meaning."[1]

As regards Eastern Asia we are indebted to Bastian for several accounts. This indefatigable researcher whose im-

[1] E. Schmidt, *Ceylon*, Berlin, p. 296, from R. Caldwell, *A Comparative Grammar of the Dravidian or South-Indian Family of Languages*, London, 1856, p. 522. Another work by Caldwell, *On Demonolatry*, published in the " Journal of the Anthropological Society of Bombay," vol. i, has remained inaccessible to me, but a quotation, perfectly compatible with the above, is given by J. G. Frazer, *The Magic Art*, London, 1911, vol. i, p. 382. Numerous photographs of devil-dancers and their appurtenances in W. L. Hildburgh, *Notes on Sinhalese Magic* in the Journal of the Anthropological Institute, xxxviii, 1908.

portance to scholarship is still underrated owing to the
mediocre and confused literary style of his publications, (he is
not merely important as collector and organizer of the Berlin
Ethnographical Museum), recognized the great importance of
states of possession and understood their psychological nature.
His accounts, which relate to Siam, Burmah and China, are
for the most part all too short.[1]

Declarations made by Indian spirit-dancers themselves to
the missionaries are not without interest, showing as they do
the violently compulsive character of these states and how
even converted natives are once more suddenly seized by
them against their will.

> The spirit-dancer (amongst the Arayer) is gripped not so much by
> the arak which he has drunk during the dance as by an external
> influence (on the entry into him of the Pisachi) or so the converts
> explained their state and the pricks which are felt by those passing
> the holy places, and also afterwards, in hands and feet. A native
> leaning towards conversion gave to Mr. Painter the missionary
> the figures which are worn, the dress hung with bells, the belt
> adorned with pictures, etc. (without consenting to take any money
> for them), but nevertheless as on his return he passed the shrine
> which he had theretofore regarded as sacred he was seized with a
> sudden fit which caused him to leap high into the air and then
> drove him to flee into the jungle (in order to be reconciled with the
> offended Pisachi).
>
> A converted Bhuta-dancer admitted, moreover, to the missionary
> Herr Götze (in Mangalora) that the Brahman communicated in
> advance what was to be said, so that at the instant when the
> Bhuta seized him all these things might come vividly into his
> memory (and control him).[2]

In a Burmese town a native spoke to Bastian of the
" witches (*Dzon*) who wandered about at night spitting fire
from their mouths, and put something into people's food so
that they fell ill. In a town where a witch dwelt her example
was often epidemic; in his quarter almost every week women
or girls danced in the street. A *Mo-Zea* (doctor or medicine-
man) was then sent for who caused her head to be hidden in
a tamein (woman's robe) and beat her soundly with a stick.
The patient, however, felt nothing of the trouncing but only
the demon (*Nat*) within her."[3]

[1] Bastian, *Die Völker des östlichen Asiens*, vol. iii, Jena, 1867,
pp. 274 sq. Short description of choreographic possession, amongst
the Molukka, vol. i, pp. 2 sq. Further details on possession, *ibid.*,
pp. 11 sq. Case of a Burman Pythoness diagnosing maladies, vol. ii,
p. 110.

[2] A. Bastian, *Ideale Welten*, vol. i, Reisen auf der Vorder-Indischen
Halbinsel im Jahre 1890, Berlin, 1892, p. 81.

[3] Bastian, *Die Völker des östlichen Asiens*, i, p. 103.

Another Burman related that the exorcist showed the possessed a stick and threatened her with it.

> The witch who is within her then grows anxious and adores her master with joined hands. She must tell everything exactly and in minute detail: what she is called, where she lives, who are her relations or friends, etc. On further examination she generally admits that she has caused this misfortune through hatred or vengeance. The exorcist could then slay the witch by his magic *mantras*, but the patients' families generally beg him not to do so, for they dread the sinful consequences which might drag them down into hell. When gifts are added to these prayers the doctor allows himself to be moved and merely administers to the witch as a reminder a sound correction with his stick for so long as she remains in the patient's body. Then he commands her to go and return no more. Generally the witchmaster (from considerations of good-fellowship) persuades the relatives not to molest the witch further when she has had her punishment.

These narratives are the more interesting since we find in them a possessing spirit of the feminine, not masculine, sex. Such cases are extremely rare. It seems, moreover, that at least in the case referred to in one of these accounts, the possessing spirit is regarded as that of a living person, since it is stated that in the street where a witch lives choreographic possession not seldom occurs. In this connection the case related on p. 27 where a girl was possessed by the spirit of a hunter's boy should be borne in mind.

Bastian's work also gives cases of possession in Siam.[1] It may be multiple in character. There are cases in which the possessing spirits are demons,[2] in some they are the souls of ancestors,[3] in yet others certain crocodile spirits[4] which make their way into men. The criterion of the last-named form of possession is insensibility to pain and alleged invulnerability.[5] It must, however, be remarked that in Siam, just as in the Germany of Kerner's time,[6] possession is first " diagnosed " from purely physical signs and true psychic possession subsequently brought on by exorcism.[7] Possession takes the following course:

> When the Chao or demon lord is invited to enter into the possessed (Xön Chao) the chorus of bystanders sings: " King and god (Phra Ongk) we invoke thee. We adjure thee to descend, dweller in heaven (Thevada), and to reveal thyself in all thy might. Come down into his body, come to abide in the Khon Song (the person of

---

[1] *Ibid.*, vol. iii, pp. 274 sq.   [2] *Ibid.*, p. 280.
[3] *Ibid.*, p. 280.   [4] *Ibid.*, p. 263.
[5] *Ibid.*, p. 263.   [6] Cf. *supra*, p. 96.
[7] *Ibid.*, p. 300.

majesty).[1] Richly adorned, in pomp and splendour stands the vessel waiting to be taken by thee. The Khon Song makes for thee a worthy dwelling, gleaming in beauty like the angels. Look within thyself, thou royally endowed, enter into him and abide there. We adore thee, we pray to thee from the dust. We desire to receive from thee thy revelation, the unveiling of thy celestial home.

When the Chao is obliged by the conjurations to descend into the body of the Khon Song[2] the latter remains invulnerable so long as he is there and cannot be touched by any kind of weapon. Through this evidence is manifested the marvellous power (Sakrith) of the demon. Chinese familiar with these arts give displays in which they seat themselves with impunity on lances and swords.

It is rather by way of diversion that possession by Meh Suh (the Mother of Colours) is sought and the people amuse themselves in this way on festival nights by moonlight, especially at the new year. The company places someone blindfolded and with stopped ears in the middle and intones incantations. This does not generally last long before the Mother of Colours manifests her presence by twitching in one or other of the person's limbs. Soon the possessed moans with increasing agitation, and dances more and more furiously until at length he rolls on the ground, exhausted and out of breath. It is then possible to question the spirit and know whence he comes. The various demon-temples are enunciated until the possessed makes an affirmative sign, when the right name has been found. A hymn is sung to the " Lady radiant with Colours " inviting her to descend.[3]

When the Chao enters into a person (Chao Khao) the latter flings himself to the ground in the most violent convulsions and foaming at the mouth, because he must struggle with a great lord of potent strength. Nevertheless it is possible in such an event to snatch hints, precious because emanating from the Beyond, as to suitable medicines.[1]

There is also possession by other male spirits similarly evoked by the artifice of drums and noise in order to obtain information about an illness or ascertain the whereabouts of a wandering son.[5]

In Siam possession is frankly provoked as a dramatic spectacle, or at least was so in the middle of the nineteenth century when Bastian travelled in that country.

At the Lakhon Phi (theatre of the demons) a person, man or woman, is requisitioned, who becomes possessed by the Chaon Phi (chief of the demons) and by the Thepharak (the guardian angel)

---

[1] Bastian adds the following note: The Khon Song puts on the god's clothing, as the Californian Indians dressed as Tobet when they danced for Tshinigtshinish.

[2] When no suitable mediator can be found, the divine force is conjured to descend into the sanctuary which only the priests (Karen) dare approach.

[3] *Ibid.*, pp. 282 sq.   [4] *Ibid.*, pp. 294 sq.   [5] *Ibid.*, pp. 286 sq.

who, when invoked, enters into him. The other onlookers beat the drum or clap the hands.[1]

This possession by a *phi* (another sort of spirit) is rather a jovial farce to entertain the onlookers by the marvellous leaps of the dancer. A poor devil of this kind has hardly the strength to bring his opponent to his knees, unless the latter is paralyzed by dislocation of the hips.[2]

Here is a long extract from a native Siamese work published in English, *Siamese Customs*, which Bastian, as unhappily so often occurs with him, has reproduced without particulars as to place and year of publication:

The Siamese, the inhabitants of towns as well as the dwellers in mountains and forests, hold the opinion that there exist male and female Chao (a Lao word, meaning a noble lord and entering as Phra-Chao in the name of God; with a slight modification it is used for the pronoun of the second person in the familiar style). Phi, the word for demon, means also a corpse; the Siamese of Ligor call them shuet (ancestors or ancestral spirits). During life they have been great men and lords, and after death they are deified. There are some persons who understand the art of possession, and they suppose that they may invite them to enter their bodies if they observe certain rules. Those who hold to this opinion are of the low classes of people, ignorant and stupid, and therefore not able to distinguish between false and true. If one of their relatives has fallen sick, if property has been lost, or if some other misfortune has come upon them, they go to an old witch, well versed in sorcery, and beg from her to invite the deified lord or a demon to take up his temporary abode in her body, so that they may be able to put questions to him. Then the necessary preparations are made to celebrate the spirit dance. They build a shed of wood, and put a round roof, like a haystack, on it, which is sometimes overlaid with straw, sometimes with reed grass, sometimes with cloth. In this shed are placed the different articles for offerings, as eatables of all kinds, arrack, rice, ducks, fowls, curried fish, and chiefly a pig's head, which is never wanting. Fruits are added, as soft cocoanuts, bananas, sugar-cane, ripe oranges, and whatever other kind they can get, according to the season. If the preparations are finished, they beat the drum and play the flute, to invite the demon to come down to the dance. The sorceress then takes a bath, and having rubbed herself with scented curcuma-flour, dresses out in a red waistcloth, and a silken jacket, of the dark shining colour of the xomphu fruit (sambossa). Then the music increases; they blow the flute, they strike the drum, they beat the clappers and sing the verses of incantation for the demon to keep himself in readiness. When the deified lord or the demon has entered the body of the magician, the person possessed begins to tremble, and her body shakes all over, she shuts her eyes and laughs out loud; she yawns and belches; she has her clothes (which were tied up after the manner of working people) float down (as worn by nobles), and puts flowers behind the ears. At that time the old woman assumes the manners and behaviour of a great personage conducting herself as far superior to all the rest of the people around her.[3]

---

[1] *Ibid.*, p. 286.   [2] *Ibid.*, p. 295.
[3] A. Bastian, *Zur Kenntnis Hawaii's*, Berlin, 1883, pp. 58 sq., note.

The relatives and bystanders do homage, and sometimes she threatens to take vengeance on their children for the slight respect they have paid to the noble lord who is in her, etc. As may be seen, there is nothing new in principle in the Siamese narrative.

Possession is of more importance in the Chinese world than in India. The spiritualist doctrine which in Europe and North America exercises no influence outside a very restricted sphere, there reigns supreme; amongst civilized countries China is that *par excellence* of belief in spirits. Of J. J. M. de Groot's great work[1] in six volumes on Chinese religion, exactly half is devoted to belief in spirits and ghosts, and this book creates a really alarming impression of the point to which a country of such high achievement in the realm of art and perhaps in that of politico-economics is dominated in the religious domain by ideas identical with those of primitive peoples.[2]

This reign of spiritualism in China is very ancient. It does not arise from subsequent reaction against the negations of a period of enlightenment, as at the end of classical antiquity and again in present-day Europe. Given the excessively conservative character of Chinese civilization we are much more likely to discover it in an immediate genetic connection with general Asiatic Shamanism. The priesthood of the Wu, which is still to-day the repository of possession, is originally no other than the Chinese branch of Asiatic Shamanism, a fact still clearly recognizable at the present time.[3]

The old primitive religio-metaphysical conceptions, as also the autosuggestive states of consciousness, have remained quite unchanged for thousands of years, not as cultural foundations—as such they have lived on throughout the ages in all countries including Europe up to the present day—but as the general outlook, widely disseminated and essentially undisputed. It is noteworthy that in some quarters there has been a well-defined tendency towards Confucianism which professes an enlightened and sceptical rationalism as

[1] De Groot, *The Religious Systems of China, its Ancient Forms, etc.*, 6 vols., Leyden, 1892-1910.
[2] De Groot designates them under the name of " animism." This word should be taken in the sense of belief in spirits, not, as is usual in Germany, in the sense of the attribution of a soul to everything.
[3] *Ibid.*, vol. vi, p. 1190.

regards the Wu-priesthood, so that it has been subject to severe persecutions.

From the year 118 B.C. we have an account by a Chinese princess of the possession of a Wu-priest,[1] from the year A.D. 25, another of the entry of a prince into a Wu-priest;[2] and so the attestations continue throughout the various periods.

Amongst these old stories there is one which is of particular interest to us Europeans. It comes from the celebrated Italian Marco Polo, who visited China at the end of the thirteenth century. His testimony runs:

> And let me tell you that in all those three provinces that I have been speaking of, to wit Carajan, Vochan, and Yachi, there is never a leech. But when any one is ill they send for the Devil-conjurors who are the keepers of their idols. When these are come the sick man tells what ails him, and then the conjurors incontinently begin playing on their instruments and singing and dancing; and the conjurors dance to such a pitch that at last one of them will fall to the ground lifeless, like a dead man. And then the devil entereth into his body. And when his comrades see him in this plight they begin to put questions to him about the sick man's ailment. And he will reply: " Such and such a spirit hath been meddling with the man, for that he hath angered the spirit and done it some despite." Then they say: " We pray thee to pardon him, and to take of his blood or of his goods what thou wilt in consideration of thus restoring him to health." And when they have so prayed, the malignant spirit that is in the body of the prostrate man will (mayhap) answer: " The sick man hath also done great despite to such another spirit, and that one is so ill-disposed that it will not pardon him on any account;"—this at least is the answer they get if the patient be like to die. But if he is to get better the answer will be that they are to bring two sheep, or may be three; and to brew ten or twelve jars of drink, very costly and abundantly spiced. Moreover it will be announced that the sheep must be all black-faced or of some other particular colour as it may happen; and then all those things are to be offered in sacrifice to such and such a spirit whose name is given. And they are to bring so many conjurors and so many ladies, and the business is to be done with a great singing of lauds, and with many lights and store of good perfumes. That is the sort of answer they get if the patient is to get well. And then the kinsfolk of the sick man go and procure all that has been commanded, and do as has been bidden, and the conjuror who has uttered all that gets on his legs again.
>
> So they fetch the sheep of the colour prescribed, and slaughter them, and sprinkle the blood over such places as have been enjoined, in honour and propitiation of the spirit. And the conjurors come, and the ladies, in the number that was ordered, and when all are assembled and everything is ready, they begin to dance and sing and play in honour of the spirit. And they take flesh-broth, and drink, and lign-aloes, and a great number of lights, and go

---

[1] *Ibid.*, pp. 1201 sq.   [2] *Ibid.*, p. 1209.

about hither and thither, scattering the broth and the drink and the meat also. And when they have done this for a while, again shall one of the conjurors fall flat and wallow there foaming at the mouth, and then the others will ask if he has yet pardoned the sick man ? And sometimes he shall answer yes ! and sometimes he shall answer no ! And if the answer be *no*, they shall be told that something or other has to be done all over again, and then he shall be pardoned; so this they do. And when all that the spirit has commanded has been done with great ceremony, then it will be announced that the man is pardoned and shall be speedily cured. So when they at length receive such a reply, they announce that it is all made up with the spirit, and that he is propitiated, and they fall to eating with great joy and mirth, and he who has been lying lifeless on the ground gets up and takes his share. So when they have all eaten and drunken, every man departs home. And presently the sick man gets sound and well.[1]

We see that the connection with primitive Shamanism is here established in the clearest possible manner. The case is not even one of relationship, but of veritable identity; it is " Chinese Shamandom," as may still be recognized to-day from the manner in which possession is provoked by music. In times of epidemic there are also processions with frenzied dances in which the priests wound themselves in the Turkish manner with sabres and balls stuck with points.

A Chinese author writes:

" Among men the dead speak " through living persons whom they throw into a trance and the " wu, thrumming their black chords, call down souls of the dead," which then speak through the mouths of the wu.[2]

In consequence of their accesses of possession in which the spirits even of princely personages entered into them, the influence of the Wu-priests was very considerable; from the purely political point of view it extended to the emperor. Once more we are involuntarily reminded of the position of the shamans amongst primitive peoples.

The capacity of the wu-ist priesthood to see spirits, and to have intercourse with them and understand them, naturally raised its members to the rank of soothsayers through whom gods and ancestors manifested their will and desires, and their decisions about human fate.[3]

As always, the documents are for the most part so laconic that in spite of their fairly large number it is not possible to

---

[1] J. Witle, *Das Buch des Marco Polo als Quelle für die Religions-geschichte*, Berlin, 1916. Quotation from Marco Polo is from Yule's trans., London, 1871, vol. ii, pp. 53 sq.

[2] De Groot, *loc. cit.*, p. 1211.   [3] *Ibid.*, p. 1217.

form the desired exact idea of the states of the Wu-priests. They are, moreover, in China often mingled with accounts of parapsychic phenomena as to the credibility of which no well-founded judgement can yet be given.

Possession by spirits is demonstrable in the case of men as well as women in the period round about 500 B.C.[1]

Exactly as in the Shamanism of the Asiatic primitives we find in Chinese Wu-Shamanism an inadequate distinction between states of possession and visions, as well as alleged prophecies, second sight, etc. From the material collected by de Groot we may conclude in favour of the reality of possession, but the discrimination of these other states, so important from the psychological point of view, is not achieved, so that we have no general survey. I do not know whether the sources permitted of such discrimination.

A specially interesting feature is that certain aspects of Wu-possession recall what we know of the Greek oracles, particularly the Pythoness, in many ways.

Amongst the Wu-priests there is a certain body of elect on whom devolves the duty of procuring ecstasy by macerations, these priests being susceptible in the highest degree to abnormal states.

They are called *sin tông—i.e.,* " godly youths," or " youths who have shen or divinity in themselves," or " youths who belong to a god." More popularly they are known as *ki tông,* " divining youth," or *tâng ki,* " youthful diviners," even simply *tâng tsi,* or " youths." They are, in fact, in the main young persons, and I have never seen one of advanced age. My Chinese informants probably spoke the truth when they asserted, that the eight characters which constitute their horoscope or fate, are light, so that their constitution is so frail that they are bound to die young. We may then admit that they must be a nervous, impressionable, hysterical kind of people, physically and mentally weak, and therefore easily stirred to ecstasy by their self-conviction that gods descend into them; but such strain on their nerves cannot be borne for many years, the less so because such possession requires self-mutilation entailing considerable loss of blood.

Most of these dancing dervishes come from the lower class. People of good standing seldom debase themselves to things which were spoken of in terms of contempt by the holy I-yin thirty-five centuries ago, however frequently they may have recourse to them for revelation of unknown things. It is generally asserted, that the capacity to be an animated medium for gods and spirits is no acquisition, but a gift which manifests itself spontaneously. It happens, indeed, especially at religious festivals, celebrated in temples with great concourse of people, that a young man suddenly

[1] *Ibid.*, pp. 1190 sq.

begins to hop, dance and waddle with wild or drowsy looks, and nervous gestures of arms and hands. Bystanders grasp his arms to sustain him, knowing that, while in this condition, his fall to the ground may cause sudden death. All onlookers at once realize the fact that one of the gods whose images stand in the temple or some other spirit, has " seized the youth," *liáh táng*, and the parish thus will henceforth rejoice in the possession of one more medium for its intercourse with the divine world. Some make obeisance to him, or even prostrate themselves in worship, and in a few moments the officiating *sai kong* is at hand, to devote all his attention to the interesting case. Uttering efficacious spells, and blowing his buffalo-horn with energy, he dispels all spectres which thwart the divine spirit maliciously, and stiffen the tongue of the youth in ecstasy. The latter now begins to moan; some incoherent talk follows, mingled with cries; but all this is oracular language which reveals unknown things, for in the meantime one or two bystanders have in reality brought the spirit into him, and thus made a seer of him, by busily burning small paper sheets, denoted by the significant name of *khai gán tsoá*, " paper for unsealing the eyes " or " eye-opening papers." These sheets are a very inferior kind of paper, yellow coloured, and are not even so large as a hand. By means of a matrix of wood, some ten or twelve men are printed on each in very slovenly fashion; some of these men have memorial tablets in their hands, and are deemed to be messengers in official costume; and the others are servants attending on them with banners and canopies. and wild horses and carriages which complete their equipment. The papers being burned, these men, horses and things are set free, and straightway depart to fetch the spirit, who but for such escort, suitable to its taste and dignity, would refuse to come.

An association of men, as a rule bearing his own tribe-name, is now quickly formed, anxious to attach themselves to the new found " godly youth," and attract to their pockets a part of the profits which his work, as prophet, seer, and exorcist will yield. Henceforth they are frequently seen in this temple to conjure the spirit into him and interpret the strange sounds he utters: and in the end it is they alone who, by dint of experience and exercise, can understand those inspired sounds and translate them into human language. First of all they try to discover in this way the name of the spirit; indeed, they want it for their spells whenever they have to call him 'down into the medium, and, moreover, they want to know before which image they have to do this. In this way it is almost always discovered that the spirit is that of an idol of inferior rank, seated or standing somewhere in a temple; for indeed, gods of a notable rank in the divine world and therefore, least of all those who occupy a place in the State Religion, will seldom deign to descend into a material, impure human body, save under exceptional circumstances. . . .

Many ki tông gods reside in images which stand on altars in dwelling houses, enjoying a good reputation among the people around for the many oracular hints which they give by the mouths of their mediums, hints whereby the sick are cured, and blessings of various kind obtained. . . .

When a consultation about a patient is to take place, one or more of his relatives repair to the altar of the ki tông god, light candles on it, and place on it a few dishes of food; and one of them having taken burning incense-sticks in his clasped hands, whispers to the idol the motives of their visit. The medium does not show as yet the slightest symptoms of possession, but is sitting at the altar-table on a stool or form, quietly chatting with his club-brethren,[1] while two of these on either side repeatedly utter an incantation in a chanting voice, in order to " invite or bid the spirit," meanwhile they burn incense and " eye-opening papers," dropping the ashes of the latter into a pot of water. The invocation is a formula which professedly was uttered once upon a time by the god himself by the mouth of his ki tông, with an additional promise to come whenever he might hear it.

The symptoms of the descent of the spirit into the medium shortly appear, that is to say, it effects the *koan tâng* or " communication with the medium." Drowsily staring, he shivers and yawns, resting his arms on the table, and his head on his arms, as if falling asleep; but as the incantation proceeds with increasing velocity and loudness with the accompaniment of one or more drums, and as the " eye-opening papers " are being burned in a quicker succession, he suddenly jumps up to frisk and skip about. Thus the spirit " sets the medium to hopping or dancing." Two club-brethren grasp him, and force him back upon the form; which is not always easy, and may require the full exertion of their muscles. His limbs shake vehemently; his arms knock on the table; his head and shoulders jerk nervously from side to side, and his staring eyes, half closed, seem to gaze straight into a hidden world. This is the proper moment for the consultant or the interpreter to put his questions. Incoherent shrill sounds are the answer; but the interpreter translates this divine language with the greatest fluency into the intelligible human tongue, while another brother writes these revelations down on paper. But the moment comes for the spirit to announce in the same way its intention to depart. This is a sign for a brother to beat a drum loudly; and for another to spurt over the medium a draught of the water in which the ashes of the " eye-opening papers " were dropped; and for a third to burn some gold paper money for the spirit, in order to reward it for its revelations, and to buy its forgiveness, should it have been involuntarily displeased or impolitely treated. And the medium jumps up, sinks into the arms of his brethren, or even to the ground, as if in a swoon; but he revives, rubs his eyes, gazes around, and behaves like a normal man. This moment marks the *tè tâng* of the spirit, its " retreat from the medium." It is asserted that the man thereupon has not the slightest notion or recollection of what has occurred to him.[2]

This information from the celebrated sinologist de Groot is particularly precious. It gives us a glimpse of the genesis of a civilization of oracular divinities, and this with such exactitude that no analogous evidence can be compared to it. The parallel with Delphi forces itself upon us, and we might even speak of identity; here as there we find a possessed medium through whom a god speaks incomprehensible words which are rendered into human speech by functionaries. If it is decided to regard as mere priestly trickery the person and

[1] Such a medium often becomes the centre of a kind of club.
[2] De Groot, *loc. cit.*, pp. 1268-75.

collaboration of the Pythoness, nevertheless genuinely possessed, the analogy is complete. It is probable that neither at Delphi nor in China was the performance purely fraudulent. Possession as described by de Groot naturally belongs to the somnambulistic type.

Just as the oracles of Delphi had an extraordinary influence on the political life of Greece, the declarations of the possessed in China have had the same effect, as is evidenced in the following account by von der Goltz:

When the Taoist and Buddhist priests act as mediums, it is assumed that their soul leaves the body in order to give place to a certain divinity. The medium sits down, his assistants arrange the altar, burn incense and invoke the desired deity. After some time one of them goes towards the medium and performs on him various movements which produce a kind of unconsciousness. This is the signal that the medium's soul has left his body and that the divinity has taken possession of the momentarily empty vessel. All that the medium says from this moment onwards is considered as coming directly from the divinity. Exhibitions are given in Canton (according to Dennys, *Folklore*, etc.), with hypnotized persons. The performer reads to the subject certain magic spells after which the state of somnambulism is produced. In this state the subject performs the most marvellous gymnastic feats, although he has not learnt them. According to the Chinese the body, which the soul has abandoned during the hypnotic sleep, is taken by the soul of a dead fencing-master. But this superstition is not confined to deceased heads of families, fencing-masters and divinities of the Taoist and Buddhist Pantheon. In the religious sect of the Shang-ti-hui, an association of worshippers of gods whose leaders became later the "kings" of the Taiping rebellion, it happened that when the sect had assembled for divine service one or other of the members had a fit, so that he fell down and his body was bathed in sweat. In this state of ecstasy he then uttered exhortations, reproaches and predictions. The phrases were often unintelligible, but generally rhythmical in arrangement. Yang-hsiu-ch'ing, later "King of the East," claimed that "Tien-fu," the heavenly father, used to descend from heaven to take possession of his body and speak by his mouth. Hsiao-chao-kuei, the "King of the West," proclaimed himself possessed by Jesus Christ. . . .[1]

Beside the above-mentioned form of possession there is another similar one designated by the name of "Spirit-hopping."

Hardly to be distinguished from the performances of the Shamans is also the T'iao-shân, literally spirit-hopping, as it is described by Liao-chai-chi-i. Here is a translation of the relevant description. In the Tsi country (*i.e.*, Shantung) it is customary for the women of a family when someone is ill to call in an old witch who acts as medium. She beats a tambourine stretched upon an iron

[1] Von der Goltz, *Zauberei und Hexenkünste in China* ("Ges. für Natur- und Völkerkunde Ostasiens," vol. vi, 1893-97, p. 21).

frame and executes dances which are called "T'iao-shân," spirit-jumps. At Pekin this pernicious custom is far more freely observed, and young women of good family often meet together to execute these dances. On a table in the reception-room of the house offerings of wine and meat are laid out, and the room is brightly lighted with large tapers. The medium who executes the dance tucks up her clothes, bends one leg and with the other executes the *shan-yang* dance. Two of the assembled women and girls support her, one on either side. The dancer mutters without intermission unintelligible words which seem to be now song and now rhythm. The words are not consecutive, but are subject to a certain rhythm. Meanwhile drums resound with a deafening din which contributes still further to make the dancer's words incomprehensible. Finally the latter's head droops and she begins to squint. She can no longer stand upright and would fall were it not for the help of her supporters. Suddenly she stretches her neck and leaps a foot into the air with joy. At this signal all the women present cry: "The ancestors have come to eat the offerings." Then the lights are put out and complete darkness reigns. The company hold their breath and dare not speak, and would not, moreover, be heard because of the noise of drumming. Suddenly the dancer calls by name the father, mother, husband or wife (*i.e.*, one of the deceased heads of the family). As it is customary to refrain out of respect from naming any of the elders, this is the sign that the spirit of one of them has entered into the medium. The tapers are relighted and the curious begin to put their questions concerning the future or other matters which are of interest to them. They see as soon as the lights are put on again that the food and drink have disappeared from the table (whether these have been eaten by the medium or her assistants or someone else is not stated in the text). It is seen from the dancer's face whether the spirit which has just manifested itself is well or badly disposed. To each question an answer is given. . . .[1]

The Manchu women believe firmly in these spirit-apparitions and seek as soon as they are in any doubt to procure a decision in this way.

Often mediums armed with a long lance seem to be riding a horse or tiger and execute wild dances on the wooden plank which represents the sofa in Chinese houses. This is called the t'iao-hu-shen (tiger-spirit-hopping). During the dance the tiger or horse utters terrifying cries. . . .

Should a man dare to look on secretly during the *séance*, the lance pierces the window, snatches his headgear from him and carries it off into the room where all the assembled women members of the family jerk round one after another in an apparently indefatigable goose-step.

According to some Chinese to whom Liao-chai's text was submitted and who were consulted in the matter, spirit-hopping is still performed in the same way in modern Pekin. This dance enjoys great favour amongst the women of the imperial palace and must be executed at least once a year in the dwellings of the princes and notables of the imperial court.[2]

Mrs. Howard Taylor, with whose accounts of spontaneous possession in China we have already dealt, also had experience of possession in mediums from which it emerges that, as

[1] See Appendix.	[2] *Ibid.*, pp. 17-19.

in India, the possession of Chinese mediums has a strongly marked character of compulsion, and is, moreover, extremely exhausting to them. Just as it is said that the Batak mediums of Sumatra when affected by particularly violent states die young, we find in Mrs. Howard Taylor a case of death attributable to possession. European doctors residing in China would earn our gratitude by investigating more narrowly such cases where the organism breaks down under the influence of compulsive states. Nor must we forget Father Tranquille of Loudon who also died under possession.[1] Mrs. Taylor writes of the cultivation of possession:

> Specially in North China is this (the practice of spiritualism) common, where Taoist and Buddhist priests alike obtain great influence and financial profit from communications, real or pretended, with the unseen world. . . . Men and women who in western lands would be described as spirit-mediums abound. There is scarcely a village in the Shan-si plain without one. Some calamity befalls a family—illness or disaster. Send for the medium at once. She comes, and is respectfully welcomed. Incense is offered before the idols, for the medium always plays into the hands of the priests. She sits down, usually in the seat of honour in the guest-house, and soon relapses into a curious trance. This is done by yielding the whole being, absolutely, to the familiar spirit. The medium just waits, like an empty vessel, for the advent of the influence desired. Suddenly:
> "Shen-lai-liao, shen-lai-liao!" The spirit has come!
> The medium is now possessed, filled, transported. She speaks in a new voice, with great authority, and declares what the trouble is and how it may be remedied. More paper money and incense are burned, and more prostrations made before the idols; while gradually, with horrible contortions, she comes out of the trance again.[2]
> A striking feature in these cases is the apparent inability of the mediums to shake off the control of the terrible power to which they have yielded. Unsought, and contrary to their own desire, the overmastering influence comes back, no matter how they may struggle against it. One case of the kind occurred near P'ing Yang about this time, and is recorded by the missionary who witnessed it.
> A well-known medium, who for many years had made his living by the practice, finding his health and nervous system greatly impaired, decided to give it up. Though only sixty years of age, he was so worn and haggard that he looked at least twenty years older. The struggle was long and terrible. In spite of all his efforts, the old tyranny reasserted itself again and again, until deliverance seemed impossible. He was about to give up in despair, when providentially he came into contact with some P'ing Yang Christians. Just how much he understood and received of the Gospel is not known, but through prayer and a measure of faith in Christ he obtained considerable relief.

---

[1] *Vide supra*, pp. 117 sq.
[2] The above is an exact description of one scene of this sort witnessed by the writer in the women's apartments of a house in North China.

But a night came when he was returning from the city by himself, and had to pass a sacred tree in a lonely spot, believed to be the dwelling-place of demons. As he drew near, an overwhelming impulse came upon him to fall down and worship as in former times. Desperately he resisted, but the inward urging was too strong. He stopped, fell on his knees, and bowed his forehead repeatedly to the ground. Immediately the old possession came back in redoubled force, and the misery he suffered was appalling.

Those about him sent for the Christians, and later on for the missionary, from whose memory the despairing look in those poor, hunted eyes will never be effaced. He was nearing the end then, for the physical and the mental anguish of his condition were more than the shattered powers could withstand. But prayer again prevailed. The distressed soul turned to Christ for deliverance, and shortly afterwards, in peace that was not of this world, he died.[1]

According to Bastian there is a verbal distinction between possession by evil spirits and possession by the nymphs (soothsaying), both in Chinese and Japanese.[2]

In many cases the possessing spirits amongst the Chinese are animal in character. This is what von der Goltz says:

In Tientsin there exists a popular belief in the superhuman qualities of the five families of animals. The professional mediums (*k'an-hsiang*, incense-burners) make their living by them. In Suchuang near Tientsin lives an old woman named Chêng. At the beginning of this month she suddenly fell ill and asserted that she was possessed by a member of the five animal families. The spirit of the possessed began to speak and said that his name was Lin (Lin is the word for a willow-tree, but in this case means serpent) a native of the lower Yangtse valley. The son of the possessed woman then invited an "incense-seer" named Yên to come into the house. When Yên came the snake cried out: "It is very good that Master Yên is here, I have been waiting for him for a long time. We are five in all of the Lin family, come from the valley of the Yangtse, five have for the moment gone elsewhere and will return at the end of four or five days, then we will go southwards together." Thereupon Yên replied: "But this is a woman and the mother of a family; how can you dare to enter into her?" The snake replied: "Can you then find me another abode ?" "We have here a very fine temple to the god of war, you can live there for the time being until you leave with your relatives." "The god of war is a true god, how should I dare to do that ?" "That does not matter, I will give you an incense-taper with which you can enter the temple in all security." Then the snake left the woman Chêng who immediately became well again.

Through the building of the imperial pleasure-palaces near Wan-shou-shan (west of Pekin) a great number of snakes have, according to the inhabitants of the capital, been deprived of their dwelling-places; nothing remains for these animals except to seek a new habitation in man, and the inhabitants drive a roaring trade in consequence.[3]

---

[1] Mrs. Howard Taylor, *Pastor Hsi*, pp. 160-162.
[2] A. Bastian, *Die Völker des östlichen Asien*, vol. iii, p. 287, note.
[3] Von der Goltz, *loc. cit.*, p. 24. Extract from an article published in a Chinese newspaper at Pekin.

From eastern Asia we now turn to European civilization together with its derivative in North America. Here too we still find " artificial possession " at the present day, or, more exactly, we rediscover it, for in the period of " Enlightenment " it had all but disappeared. But since the middle nineteenth century it has once more attained to a much enhanced measure of consideration and practice; it finds no place in orthodox culture, but under the surface there is a pretty strong current which results in the rendering of a sort of cult to these states. This is spiritualism. Unlike belief in the devil and in possession as professed by the Catholic Church, this is not a belief founded on centuries of authority, but on relatively new convictions. Spiritualism originated towards the middle of the nineteenth century in America and from thence passed to Europe where it has become more or less widely disseminated in all countries.

There is a remarkable contrast between the various civilized nations. The classical conception of the universe which does not recognize free spirits in the world, has won its most comprehensive victory in Germany, where in consequence of the riot of speculation in the Romantic period the conditions were most favourable to victory. This has not, however, been complete.

Du Prel has become the most scientific thinker of the proclaimed spiritualists. Amongst others we should mention C. Z. Zoellner, the founder of astrophysics, as well as the philosopher Fechner, who was manifestly and completely convinced of the possibility of intercourse with the spirits of the dead, although he considered it a derangement of the normal relations between the present and the Beyond. Amongst psychologists Messer now seems desirous of leaving open the possibility of such communication,[1] which would entail the concession of a partial return to the earlier doctrine of possession.

Anglo-Saxon civilization has shown itself much more inclined to the revival of the mediæval conception of life. William James, the most important psychologist and philosopher that America has yet produced, may be considered as a partisan of spiritualism, although as might be expected from a person of his scientific eminence he gave a wide berth to

[1] A. Messer, *Psychologie*, Stuttgart, 1914, p. 367.

dogmatism.[1]   In England physicists of the importance of
Crookes and Lodge have adhered to spiritualism entirely on
the ground of the peculiar states of possession seen in certain
mediums, but yet more characteristic of the Anglo-Saxon
countries than these single names is the vast spread of the
spiritualist movement.   It is still more surprising that the
land which gave birth to the new physiological materialism
and indeed to the European movement of enlightenment,
France herself, should have proved increasingly accessible
to these ideas.[2]

A whole complex of abnormal phenomena, some authentic,
some contested, some counterfeit, forms the basis on which the
new belief in spirits is built.   The works of its partisans deal
with a varied collection of manifestations such as telepathy,
spirit-rapping, luminous apparitions, trances, automatic
writing, inspiration, mediumistic drawings, telekinesia,
materialization and yet others.   In various periods and circles
now one and now another phenomenon prevails and is, so to
speak, in fashion.   Only one group interests us here: certain
states of trance which are nearly related to possession.   It is
difficult to say how frequent in point of numbers these states
may be; this depends, as we have said, on fashion, for possession is susceptible in a high degree of psychological cultivation.

The mediumistic trances which we are about to study are
nothing more nor less than the substitution of another personality for the normal.   These are not states of tumultuous
excitement such as were presented by the energumens, but the
essential factor, the transformation of the personality,...is
reproduced in them.   By these states of trance the modern
world joins hands with that of primitive religion; spiritualism
and the Bataks alike believe in the possibility of intercourse
with deified ancestors.   It is a definitely religious movement,
its followers receiving the mediums' manifestations with
astonished awe and admiration; they are filled with intense

---

[1] William James never professed the spiritualist faith.   He did not
go beyond recognizing the parapsychic facts and rather pronounced in
favour of a "cosmic consciousness" as the source of supernormal
knowledge.   Cf. my edition of the works of W. James, *Études et réflexions
d'un psychiste*, Paris, 1925 (R. Sudre).

[2] Amongst the lower and uneducated classes, but spiritualism has
not penetrated amongst the aristocracy of intellect and no eminent
scientist has made overt profession of it (R. Sudre).

fervour and deep inward conviction, on account of their belief in a future life and the possibility of intercourse with those who have " passed over."[1] For this reason the movement renders it possible for investigators to study on living subjects manifestations of the religious life which would otherwise belong to the past, or rather it might so permit if spiritualist circles were less prejudiced against scientific research and conversely if psychologists showed a greater interest in this mine of remarkable psychological phenomena.

A few examples will serve to evidence the nature of spiritualist possession. The cases which have been thoroughly studied are much richer in psychic material than the mass of those which occur daily in spiritualistic séances when someone present—more often than not a woman—falls into a somnambulistic state and " a spirit " then speaks through her.

A particularly well observed and highly complex case is that of Hélène Smith, pseudonym of a Genevese medium whom Flournoy subjected to a thorough study. She manifested a whole series of states of spiritualistic possession—i.e., states in which the organism was alleged to be occupied by strange spirits. Spiritualists often speak of " incarnations." Now it was the spirit of Marie Antoinette, now that of a celebrated eighteenth-century magician Cagliostro, now those of alleged Martians. We have already reproduced the account which Flournoy gives of the incarnation of Cagliostro (p. 18).

Jung has described another case, not, however, of the same rich complexity, concerning a girl:

> In her somnambulistic conversations she copied with extreme skill deceased relations and friends with all their peculiarities, so that she made a lasting impression on impartial observers. She also, for instance, copied persons known to her by description only, and this in so striking a manner that those who witnessed it could not deny her at the least a very remarkable dramatic talent. Gradually to mere words were added gestures which finally led to " attitudes passionnelles " and even dramatic scenes. She assumed attitudes of prayer and ecstasy in which she spoke with shining eyes and a really seductive diction, ardent and passionate. She then used only literary German which, in marked contrast to her uncertain and confused bearing in the waking state, she spoke with the utmost confidence and mastery. Her movements were quite free, full of gracious dignity and reflected her changing moods in the most admirable way.[2]

[1] The works of Hans Freimark contain a good critical survey of the spiritualist world.
[2] C. G. Jung, *Zur Psychologie und Pathologie sogenannter okkulter Phänomene*, Leipzig, 1902, p. 24.

No fundamentally new phenomenon appears in these descriptions, they are somnambulistic imitations either of historical personages or else of pure phantasies. In my *Phänomenologie des Ich* I have already examined in detail the psychological genesis of these states, and shall therefore not return to them here. I can only give in a general way examples of the form assumed by possession in modern spiritualism.

In some—although rare—cases, there occur states of possession in which the individual preserves his understanding and does not fall into somnambulism.

Hélène Smith also had such states. Here is a particularly well described example in which we see the recrudescence of the primitive idea that possession is caused by a strange spirit possessed of a sort of etheric body penetrating spatially into the body of the possessed.

> . . . There are also cases of conscious fusion, in which Hélène undergoes and experiences a coalescence between her cœnesthesia and that of Leopold (Cagliostro). It is a state of consciousness *sui generis*, of which no adequate description is possible, and which can only be imagined by analogy with those curious states, exceptional in the normal waking life but less rare in dreams, when we feel ourselves change and become another person.
>
> Hélène has more than once told me that she has had the impression of becoming and of momentarily being Leopold. This happens to her during the night or particularly on waking in the morning; she first has a fugitive vision of her cavalier, and then he seems to pass gradually into her, she feels him as it were invade and penetrate her whole organic substance as if he became herself or she him. It is, in short, a spontaneous incarnation without loss of consciousness or memory, and she would certainly give no other description of her cœnesthesic impressions if at the end of the séances where she has personified Cagliostro with taut muscles, thickened neck, bust drawn up, etc., she preserved the memory of what she had felt during that metamorphosis. These hybrid states in which the consciousness and powers of reflection of the normal self persist while the second personality takes possession of the organism are of extreme interest to the psychologist. Unfortunately, either because they are generally blotted out or because the mediums who remember them cannot or will not give an account of them, we rarely obtain detailed descriptions—apart from analogous observations gleaned from the insane.[1]

In the case described by Jung these semi-somnambulistic and lucid states of possession show the following traits: the girl begins by assuming a character totally different from her

[1] Th. Flournoy, *Des Indes à la planète Mars*, Paris-Geneva, 1900, p. 117.

ordinary one, and which is then fully developed in somnambulism. She—

> . . . finds herself for some time before and after the fits of som-
> nambulism proper in a state predominantly characterized by what
> must be described as " absent-mindedness." The patient only
> shares in the conversation with half an ear, replies in a preoccupied
> manner, and is often subject to all sorts of hallucinations; her
> bearing is dignified, her glance ecstatic and extremely brilliant.
> Closer observation shows a profound change in her whole character;
> she is grave, reserved; when she speaks it is always of serious
> matters; in this state she can express herself forcefully and with
> penetration, so that one is almost reduced to wondering if this
> is really a little girl of fifteen and a half years; one has the im-
> pression of dealing with a mature woman possessed at the least
> of outstanding dramatic talent. The patient's gravity and earnest-
> ness are entirely due to the fact that she is, according to her own
> statement, on the borders of this world and the next and is as
> closely in touch with the spirits of the dead as with living men. In
> effect her conversation is divided between replies to objectively
> real questions and to hallucinations.[1]

The semi-somnambulistic possession in a case related by
Freimark is both striking and instructive. It concerns a
young sculptor who for a long period served as a medium for
incarnations. In this state he was subject to semi-somnambulism in which visiting spirits seemed to take possession of
his body. One of these spirits, an alleged Circassian named
Tia, so charmed a friend of the sculptor that he fell in love
with her in him, and the sculptor remained in a state of trance
for half a day at a time in order to please his friend. Amongst
the spirits which seemed to manifest themselves were others
whose characters were a source of unpleasantness. The case
was obviously one of semi-somnambulism or, as we have said
above, of lucid possession.

> The drawback was that amongst the growing number of spirits
> who communicated through me there were some definitely anti-
> pathetic. These brought on all sorts of terrible fits: I abused and
> struck my friend and threatened him with a knife, all against my
> will. Tears came to my eyes when I had to behave in this way,
> but nevertheless an extraneous force compelled me.

The unhappy state of these relations led the sculptor's
friend one day to ask him whether he would change personalities with Tia. Obviously a most remarkable request! But
not so much more remarkable than when Félida, Azam's celebrated patient who suffered from alternation of personality, felt
at times when something caused her unhappiness in her normal

[1] Jung, *loc. cit.*, p. 63.

state, a longing for her second personality, in which, as she was aware, she forgot all that she had lived and suffered in the first. It must be added that Tia herself, that is, the sculptor in his somnambulistic Tia-states, had expressed this desire. We are familiar with this kind of psychic " osmosis " between somnambulistic and normal states of personality from other cases such as that related by Lemaître.[1] But let us allow the sculptor to speak for himself:

> Thanks to all these episodes the nervous irritation of both my friend and myself was steadily intensified. Thus I was not surprised when one day he asked me to exchange with Tia. She had, it was said, made this proposal (the sculptor was evidently in a complete state of somnambulism when he incarnated Tia, so that he remembered nothing of these occasions). She wanted to enter into me, and during that time my soul and spirit would take up their abode in an intermediate sphere. Absurd as this proposal seems to me after a lapse of years, although I have become a spiritualist, I found it at that time and under the pressure of these strange experiences, perfectly natural. Nevertheless for a long time I refused. The growing tension between my friend and myself finally induced me, for love of him—I loved him dearly—to fall in with this proposal. The exchange of souls, if it may be so expressed, took place. I fell into a deep sleep, and when I awoke I was Tia: or else Tia was myself; I do not know how to explain the thing. I was completely different in every way. All my thoughts and sensations were transformed. I only lived, or properly speaking, Tia only lived, in my friend. My name must no longer be pronounced in his presence, and Tia executed this faithfully. Was I therefore Tia ? For I could hardly have been capable of such a self-repudiation. Externally I of course remained the same person and passed as such; only the expression of my face must have changed.
>
> Extraneous events, the fact that he was summoned to P. whither Tia or I, I or Tia, could not accompany him, put an end to this affair. He left for P.; Tia was still within me. A fortnight after his departure she went to the heath at D., where she sat down upon the grass; she or I had a feeling that everything was whirling round, it seemed to her that part of herself was being torn away. Then she lost consciousness, and when I came to myself again I found that I was once more myself. The spiritualist haunting—for so at that moment the years through which I had lived appeared to me—ceased from that time onwards. Tia (that is, the sculptor in somnambulistic or intermediate, semi-somnambulistic states such as often occurred in Hélène Smith's case) did no more than write from time to time through me a letter to my friend, who had an intense longing for her. To write these letters I always fell into a trance, as formerly when I wrote during the séances.[2]

This confession is like the narrative, done into present-day speech, of the ecclesiastic Surin which we studied in

[1] Cf. pp. 70 sq.
[2] H. Freimark, *Okkultismus und Sexualität*, Leipzig (no date), p. 376.

detail.[1] The essential expressions are repeated almost word for word. Neither person rightly knows whether he should use " I " or the name of the spirit which seems to have taken possession of him. The reader will also recall the words of the Tonga Islander to Mariner.[2]

Accounts cited up to the present contain nothing beyond the ordinary run of well-known psychological phenomena. But these are not all; the most important mediums present, simultaneously with states of possession, extremely singular parapsychic phenomena. They can, for example, in this state read the minds of those around them and penetrate not only their actual state of consciousness but also and especially their most recent memories. They are able to give an account of past experiences on the part of persons whom they have never known. What is more, they can often reveal particulars concerning absent persons and their past when given objects which have belonged to them. It is as if they read in these objects the history of their owners, or as if the objects were surrounded by an " aura " of past which they are able to decipher. We cannot, of course, enter here into the psychology of mediums and of parapsychic phenomena in general; a single example will serve to elucidate the preceding statements. It is borrowed from the most famous, the most minutely and lengthily studied of the mediums of this kind, Mrs. Piper, an American.

In her earlier period she was possessed in her trances by an alleged spirit of the name of Phinuit. Possession was somnambulistic. Richet thus describes it according to Sage:

> In order to fall into a trance she must hold someone's hand. She holds it silently for some minutes in semi-obscurity. After a certain time—from five to fifteen minutes—she is subject to slight convulsive movements which augment in intensity and finally result in a slight epileptoid fit. On coming out of this fit she falls, with a sort of rattling in the throat, into a state of torpor which does not last more than one or two minutes; then she suddenly comes out of the torpor with a cry. The voice has changed; it is no longer Mrs. Piper but another personality, Doctor Phinuit, who has a strong masculine voice and speaks a mixture of French, American, and negro dialect.[3]

In this state Mrs. Piper makes the most remarkable revelations concerning the name, personal relationships and past

---

[1] Cf. pp. 50 sq.   [2] Cf. pp. 278 sq.
[3] M. Sage, *Mme. Piper et la Société anglo-américaine pour les recherches psychiques*, Paris, 1922.

of the entirely unknown persons who are brought to her. W. James, who also studied her, was convinced from the time of the first séance that the medium had supernormal faculties, a conviction which was only strengthened by the subsequent investigations. From that time onwards it may be said that Mrs. Piper has remained constantly under scientific control and has always given the same results. The alleged spirits change and are innumerable, but the abnormal knowledge manifested in the trances remains constant. On awakening from the trance Mrs. Piper knows nothing of what has taken place in that state. She learns it from the reports when she looks through them.

By way of illustration, here is an extract from the report of a séance which Oliver Lodge held with Mrs. Piper and in which she had two different incarnations (Phinuit, Mr. E.). Notes were taken by his brother, Albert Lodge.

Sitting No. 47. Evening of Christmas Day, 1889, 6.20 p.m. Present O. J. L. and A. L. (taking notes).

" Captain, do you know that as I came I met the medium going out, and she's crying. What is that ?"

O. L.: " Well, the fact is she's separated from her children for a few days, and she is feeling rather low about it."

" How are you, Alfred ? I've your Mother's influence strong. (Pause.) By George ! that's your Aunt Anne's ring (feeling ring I had put on my hand just before sitting), given over to you. And Olly dear, that's one of the last things I ever gave you. It was one of the last things I said to you in the body, when I gave it you for Mary. I said: ' For her, through you.' " (This is precisely accurate. The ring was her most valuable trinket, and it was given in the way here stated long before her death.)

O. L.: " Yes, I remember perfectly."

" I tell you I know it. I shall never forget it. Keep it in memory of me, for I am not dead. Each spirit is not so dim (?) that it cannot recollect its belongings in the body. They attract us if there has been anything special about them. I tell you, my boy, I can see it just as plain as if I were in the body. It was the last thing I gave you, for her, through you, always in remembrance of me. (Further conversation and advice, ending.) Convince yourself, and let others do the same. We are all liable to make mistakes; but you can see for yourself. Here's a gentleman wants to speak to you."

" Lodge, how are you ? I tell you I'm living, not dead. That's me. You know me, don't you ?"

O. L.: " Yes. Delighted to see you again."

" Don't give it up, Lodge. Cling to it. It's the best thing you have. It's coarse in the beginning, but it can be ground down fine. You'll know best and correct (?). It can only come through a trance. You have to put her in a trance. You've got to do it that way to make yourself known."

O. L.: " Is it bad for the medium ?"

" It's the only way, Lodge. In one sense it's bad, but in another it's good. It is her work. If I take possession of the medium's body and she goes out, then I can use her organism to tell the world important truths. There is an infinite power above us. Lodge, believe it fully. Infinite over all; most marvellous. One can tell a medium, she's like a ball of light. You look as dark and material as possible, but we find two or three lights shining. It's like a series of rooms with candles at one end. Must use analogy to express it. When you need a light you use it, when you have finished you put it out. They are like transparent windows to see through. Lodge, it's a puzzle. It's a puzzle to us here in a way, though we understand it better than you. I work at it hard, I do. I'd give anything I possess to find out. I don't care for material things now, our interest is much greater. I'm studying hard how to communicate; it's not easy. But it is only a matter of short time before I shall be able to tell the world all sorts of things through one medium or another. (And so on for some time.) Lodge, keep up your courage, there is a quantity to hope for yet. Hold it up for a time. Don't be in a hurry. Get facts; no matter what they call you, go on investigating. Test to fullest. Assure yourself, then publish. It will be all right in the end—no question about it. It's true."

O. L.: " You have seen my Uncle Jerry, haven't you ?"

" Yes, I met him a little while ago—a very clever man—had an interesting talk with him."

O. L.: " What sort of person is this Dr. Phinuit ?"

" Dr. Phinuit is a peculiar type of man. He goes about continually, and is thrown in with everybody. He is eccentric and quaint, but good-hearted. I wouldn't do the things he does for anything. He lowers himself sometimes—it's a great pity. He has very curious ideas about things and people; he receives a great deal about people from themselves (?). And he gets expressions and phrases that one doesn't care for, vulgar phrases he picks up by meeting uncanny people through the medium. These things tickle him, and he goes about repeating them. He has to interview a great number of people, and has no easy berth of it. A high type of man couldn't do the work he does. But he is a good-hearted old fellow. Good-bye, Lodge. Here's the Doctor coming."

O. L.: " Good-bye, E. Glad to have had a chat with you." (Doctor's voice reappears.) " This (ring) belongs to your Aunt. Your Uncle Jerry tells me to ask. . . . By the way, do you know Mr. E's been here—did you hear him ?"

O. L.: " Yes, I've had a long talk with him."

" Wants you to ask Uncle Bob about his cane. He whittled it out himself. It has a crooked handle with ivory on the top. Bob has it, and has initials cut in it. (There is a stick, but description inaccurate.). . ."[1]

This report gives a clear idea of the nature of the Piper case, the séance-records of which fill whole volumes. In essentials it recalls numerous others which we have already met; the somnambulistic personalities pretend to be spirits who have entered into the medium and who have intercourse

[1] *Proceedings of the Society for Psychical Research*, vol. vi, p. 5 15.

with other spirits. There is nevertheless this difference, that Mrs. Piper in a state of trance possesses knowledge which she could not normally have acquired (with which are mingled errors, as the report shows). An enquiry lasting over several years, during which time her whole life was under unremitting observation by detectives, puts this matter beyond doubt, without, however, rendering possible any firm decision as to the nature of her parapsychic functions.[1] Naturally these supernormal phenomena have largely contributed to make the Piper case serve as a basis for the development of spiritualist doctrine in Anglo-American literature.

These examples may suffice to illustrate the forms of possession which appear in modern spiritualism. Exhaustive treatment is here absolutely out of the question and just as impossible as a complete survey of all the cases of demoniacal possession in Christian civilization. Modern spiritualist literature gives them in very large numbers.[2]

There are, moreover, other and more frequent phenomena often designated in spiritualist circles by the name of " possession " or " invasion by a strange spirit." Amongst these is *automatic writing*, in which the medium's hand seems to write in an entirely mechanical manner, without his participation or previous knowledge, communications apparently corresponding to an individuality other than his own.

In the realm of speech there is an analogous phenomenon: *automatic speech* or *glossolalia*, in which the mouth speaks without the subject willing or even knowing what it says; he learns it only while speaking, from the sound of his own words.* This state is also sometimes designated as possession, as, for example, by W. James.[3]

Even visions, real or alleged, and prophecies made in a kind of autohypnotic state have been subject to this description. We cannot here deal with these subjects, but let us at least

---

[1] In my works *Grundbegriffe der Parapsychologie*, Pfüllingen, 1921, and *Der Okkultismus im modernen Weltbild*, Dresden, 1921, I have tried to explain these phenomena, without recourse to spiritualist doctrine. Cf. also René Sudre, *Introduction à la Métapsychique humaine*, Paris, 1926.

[2] The starting-point of this literature is the complete works of Allan Kardec, particularly the *Livre des médiums*, which has in a certain sense become classic.

[3] W. James, *Psychology*, London, 1892, p. 212.

observe that such an extension of terminology has occurred more particularly in English literature. A case in point of an author stretching the term " possession " to cover one province after another is furnished by Andrew Lang, owing to the fact that he starts from a definition of possession which, together with changes of personality, embraces also parapsychic phenomena.

> They (the possessed) speak in voices not their own, they act in a manner alien to their natural character, they are said to utter prophecies, and to display knowledge which they could not have normally acquired, and, in fact, do not consciously possess, in their normal condition.[1]

Such summary definitions are rarely to the purpose. They make things accidentally juxtaposed (whose inner connection meanwhile escapes us) into an entity and then ticket this with a specific name. If phenomena forming only a part of this whole are subsequently encountered in real life, the authors generally apply to the part the name appropriate only to the whole, a proceeding which gives rise to intolerable confusion, since the same designation is used alternately for the whole complex and for mere partial conditions.

It is otherwise with the admission of automatic writing and glossolalia into the realm of phenomena described as possession, inasmuch as here the lay observer will doubtless gain the impression that a second soul has entered into the subject. These states have not been dealt with in the present work, in spite of the fact that they centre round demoniacal possession as known to us from the New Testament. But their relationship to it is only limited, and an examination of states in which the " existing " second personality appears to be entirely unknown, would have grossly exceeded the compass of this work. They must therefore be held over for separate treatment.[2]

[1] Andrew Lang, *The Making of Religion*, 2nd edit., London, 1900, ch. vii, p. 129.
[2] Those interested in such questions may consult the works of Pierre Janet, Binet, and Morton Prince.

CONCLUSION

THE foregoing documents have placed beyond doubt the wide distribution of the phenomena of possession over the habitable globe. However much they may differ in detail, at bottom they are all identical. Their importance from the point of view of the history of religion is profound but rigidly circumscribed: they are mainly responsible for inspiring and maintaining belief in the existence of demons and the survival of the souls of the dead, as well as a certain intercourse between these latter and the living world. They are not alone in this—in primitive states of civilization dreams must be added—but they are the most important and active factor.

The dominant conception of the present time is that no psychic life supervenes except in the presence of a material vehicle and that no spirit, either pure or possessed only of an etheric body, exists in this world. Now this idea, which has become one of the most firmly established constituents of our present-day outlook on life, is completely new as measured by the standard of history. It is another of the fruits of the " Age of Enlightenment," the importance of which has been so profoundly underestimated and which contains the roots of nearly every fundamental conception of our scientific thought. It may be said without exaggeration that the whole of the preceding centuries theoretically regarded the air as filled with demons, peopled with spirits of all sorts. The extent to which possession contributed to produce that belief is abundantly demonstrated by the fact that at the present time belief in a spirit-world resuscitates wherever kindred states are manifested; observers without a thorough preliminary knowledge of psychology are absolutely convinced that they are in the presence of a " spirit." Once produced, this belief must in turn have reacted very strongly on possession and produced it with great frequency.

It is not easy to exaggerate the importance of this belief in spirits.

Side by side with its function of exciting and maintaining

amongst mankind a belief in the existence of spirits and demons, possession has yet another significance, religious in character and intimately bound up with the first. Together with conspiousness of the presence of spirits it produces an impression of horror, of something sinister, and in general all the sentiments of *tremendum* of which Rudolf Otto has given an excellent analysis, demonstrating also their importance in primitive religion.[1]

By the artificial provocation of possession primitive man has, moreover, to a certain degree had it in his power to procure voluntarily at a set time the conscious presence of the metaphysical, and the desire to enjoy that consciousness of the divine presence offers a strong incentive to cultivate states of possession, quite apart from the need to ask advice and guidance from the spirits.[2]

The French missionary Junod has particularly stressed this effect of possession in the book mentioned earlier in this work.

> I will even go further and say that at the present time the practice of exorcism amongst the Ba-Ronga is of all their customs the act imbued with the highest religious significance. By devoting themselves with such intensity of passion to these dark ceremonies they are surely seeking to procure that vague emotion awakened in the human soul by contact with the supernatural. They strive to establish intercourse with the Beyond in which they firmly believe. They are not concerned with driving out spirits as were those who expelled demons in the middle ages and in apostolic times, but with getting into touch with them, knowing their name, their history, and ensuring by expiation, by blood, that these mysterious beings will no longer torture the sick by bodily afflictions, but will speak them gently and rather become their protectors.* The man on whose behalf the *gobela's* practices have been successful will become the friend of the gods. He will acquire a special influence over them and will practise daily intercourse with the spirits.[3]

Unfortunately the information given in this quotation from Junod, an author generally both detailed and accurate,

[1] Rudolf Otto, *Das Heilige*, Breslau, 1917.
[2] In many cases it is probable that, exactly as in modern spiritualism, the imperious desire for direct communication with departed ancestors and other relatives also plays a part, particularly if we remember the extraordinary extent to which memory of the dead is cultivated in ancestor-worship amongst many peoples with whom the deceased are not excluded by death from the general communion of the living.
[3] Junod, *Les Bâ-Ronga*, Neuchâtel, 1898, p. 450.

is so meagre that nothing much can be deduced from it with any degree of certainty. Nevertheless we must be meant to conclude from the expression " speak him gently " that there is no question of true possession by the " protecting spirits," but of acoustic or " psychic " hallucinations. They would be analogous to the often-quoted cases of C. St. and the Maid of Orlach, who as well as being demoniacally possessed were also attended by beneficent and protecting spirits. These facts are of precisely the same order as true Shamanism.

The spirits alleged to speak by the mouth of the possessed often afford to primitive peoples the means of obtaining revelations concerning the Beyond, as is particularly evidenced by the statements of the Batak natives. At bottom the whole mythology of these peoples seems traceable to this source, a fact of which too little has hitherto been made, but which is nevertheless worthy of closer study in view of its real general importance. It would, perhaps, have facilitated the solution of certain riddles still to-day unanswered; for it is indubitable that Wundt's theory of the origin of myths offers an explanation only so far as the mythological significance of soothsaying is concerned, and affords no enlightenment on the subject of primitive conceptions of those further worlds beyond mortal ken. Such myths can only grow up in psychic states differing from waking consciousness. It is not, of course, necessary that these should be states of possession; the dreams of normal sleep are sufficient, as are also visions such as those of the shamans. But possession must also be taken into account, at least amongst many peoples.

The extraordinary importance accruing to the phenomena of possession amongst primitive races has hitherto been insufficiently appreciated by ethnology. One single ethnologist, Adolf Bastian, whose numerous works have not attracted the attention they deserved owing to their abstruse literary form, was fully alive to it. In his works we meet possession at every turn, and their unsupported testimony would be adequate to demonstrate its significance in the savage world.

Possession begins to disappear amongst civilized races as soon as belief in spirits loses its power. From the moment they cease to entertain seriously the possibility of being possessed, the necessary autosuggestion is lacking. In modern Europe this point of time was marked by the advent of the Age of Enlightenment. Not all its rationalistic exaggerations can prevent the unprejudiced from seeing in that drastic intellectual criticism, to-day somewhat dull and prosaic in its narrowness, a great turning-point in the conception of the world, inasmuch as at this stage European thought achieved complete liberation from the older theological system or at least made definite and final preparations to do so.

Catholic polemics against the modern scientific system show by giving it the name of " rationalism "[1] a truer sense of the relationship between modern cosmologies and the Age of Enlightenment than is often found amongst the advocates of these systems themselves.

Since the Age of Enlightenment the conception of a spiritual life bound up with the organism, or eventually, if the animation of all matter is accepted, with matter in general, has acquired a more real authority.

As regards the extra-European world, manifestations of possession are everywhere in regression amongst primitive peoples in places where the Christian missions have struck deep root. Not because these missions operate in the direction of rationalism and combat the possibility of possession—although the Protestant missionaries are for the most part Christian positivists—but they inspire the natives with trust in God and free them from the fear of demons and their attacks on the souls of the living. It would, however, be going too far to say that conversion to Christianity causes the complete disappearance of possession. It must also be admitted that the phenomena of possession amongst primitive races are not in all cases on the decline. Junod reports the exact contrary of the Ba-Ronga; under the influence of the Portuguese Colonial authorities the inhuman excesses of primitive sorcery and magic have died down, but in their place " another superstition was growing up and acquiring an extraordinary spread and potency; that is, the belief that the spirits of the dead can enter into a living man and cause sickness or even death."[2]

In the civilization of Eastern Asia, on the other hand, the philosophy of enlightenment, modern European monism, is

[1] Cf., for example, O. Willmann, *Geschichte des Idealismus*.
[2] Junod, *loc. cit.*, p. 440.

engendering a fever of proselytism which, in the opinion of the missionaries, is compromising their work and gravely endangering it.   I have no doubt that as a result the phenomena of possession are there regressive, although I can offer no evidence in support of such a statement.

APPENDIX ON PARAPSYCHOLOGY

THE Piper case, through which the existence of parapsychic phenomena is established with complete certainty, permits us to affirm that these phenomena are not infrequent in possession. Accounts even exist of parapsychic physical facts. We have hitherto encountered such facts several times, although I have had doubts of their possibility.

It is particularly common to find gifts of prophecy and clairvoyance or telepathy attributed to the possessed. They are alleged to see the future or, for example, to reveal where hidden objects are placed.

Codrington gives several examples of this.[1] But he has not verified the cases, so that nothing more can be said about them. In no single case is it indicated whether the possessed disclose the hiding-place at the first question or whether they go around seeking it for a time with those who have hidden the object, which naturally could and would be of material (unconscious) assistance to them.

The most noteworthy source of further information is the documents concerning the Bataks collected by Warneck.

Livingstone has given a fairly detailed description of a case of possession amongst the Zulus.[2]

Similar gifts are also attributed to the Asiatic Shamans. Fraud has often been discovered amongst them, but in one case a traveller has declared that the shaman was able to give concerning the plans for his journey and other matters information which could only come from supernormal faculties.[3]

As amongst primitive peoples, these facts have also been observed amongst civilized ones, and even the existence of supernormal physical phenomena is alleged.

In this connection we should refer to the aforementioned narrative by Flavius Josephus of a successful exorcism, in the

[1] Cf. above, pp. 281 sq.
[2] Livingstone, *Missionary Travels*, p. 86, quoted by Andrew Lang, *The Making of Religion*, 2nd edit., London, 1900, p. 135.
[3] Unfortunately I forgot to note this case at the time and cannot now trace it.

381

course of which a vessel of water was telekinetically over-thrown (p. 170).

In an analogous case in present-day Polish Jewry (pp. 207 sq.), it is reported that during an exorcism a hole was made in a window to the accompaniment of a loud report.

How widespread was belief in the reality of supernormal intellectual phenomena accompanying possession in the early centuries, is clearly demonstrated by the fact that even to-day Catholic dogma does not recognize possession (in the true sense of domination by a strange spirit), except where a priest establishes such supernormal phenomena with a view to exorcism.[1]

Quite recently a doctor has reported cases of clairvoyant faculties amongst the possessed in Russia.

Numerous physical and mental[2] parapsychic phenomena are also reported from China. For example, in the quotation from von der Goltz, p. 362, the following passage occurs where an omission is indicated by dots:

> If a question is put in a sceptical tone the spirit notices it at once; then the medium leaps upon the doubter crying: " Impudent mocker, I will pull your trousers off !" If the person spoken to then looks down at her feet she sees that she is naked and that her trousers are on a tree in the courtyard."[3]

It is evident that accounts of parapsychic phenomena in possession are quite common. What are we to think of them ? The number of parapsychic phenomena scientifically estab-lished up to the present time is extraordinarily restricted. Is possession really a state in which such manifestations are often produced, or are we simply dealing with inaccurate accounts due to excitement or to the lack of critical sense in those participating ? In default of the necessary groundwork, no well-founded and convincing answer can be given in either sense. Nothing is easier than to produce arguments in support of one or the other hypothesis, but we cannot be satisfied with mere assumptions. The whole question is, in fact, obscured by a cloud of assumptions which are continually

[1] The *Rituale Romanum* of to-day still gives as criterion of possession (x, 1): Ignota (antea) lingua loqui pluribus verbis vel loquentem in-telligere; distantia et occulta patefacere. Cf. Cornelius Krieg, *Wissen-schaft der Seelenleitung*, vol. i, Freiburg, 1904, p. 180.

[2] Naum Kotik, *Die Emanation der psychischen Energie*, Wiesbaden, 1918, p. 13.

[3] Von der Goltz, *loc. cit.*, p. 18.

adduced, instead of facts which might serve as a hand-hold. We have therefore no choice except provisionally to suspend judgement.

In the first place, we shall show great reserve as regards information emanating from primitive societies. The majority of the reports come immediately from the natives, and while this does not necessarily mean that they are fallacious, the lack of critical faculty of the narrators is greater than in the case of Europeans, and we should be very sceptical even when these latter affirm the existence of the supernormal. We cannot, however, but be struck by the fact that it is always these same states which give rise to stories of analogous parapsychic phenomena, and the task of studying such problems in primitive societies is therefore ineluctable. Given the freedom with which states analogous to possession occur amongst many primitive peoples and the alleged frequency of accompanying parapsychic phenomena, it is possible that they offer to students of parapsychology a rich field of investigation. If it be true that these phenomena are intimately bound up with disturbances of the personality and manifested chiefly by unstable and easily dissociable persons, they must necessarily be of very frequent occurrence amongst primitives. In any case the problem is of an importance to warrant serious handling.

From the historical point of view the question of the reality of parapsychic phenomena in possession is one most urgently requiring solution, in the first place as regards the Pythoness. I have already referred to the awkward predicament in which we find ourselves on the subject of the Delphic oracle; either the whole of Greece allowed itself to be fooled for centuries by a crowd of priests, even if well-intentioned, or else there was an uneducated local peasant-woman, chosen in accordance with no one knows what principles by the priests of Delphi, who fell in the Adyton of the temple into a quite peculiar parapsychic state, and gave, with a regularity even more singular, counsel and information of a supernormal character.

Du Prel has collected and studied in a not uninteresting work the early evidence concerning the psychic manifestations of the Pythoness. According to him these remarkable women not only foretold the future many times but also on occasion gave the reply before the visitant had formulated his question, which means that they also read the minds of others. (This is, however, in contradiction to the other tradition according to which the Pythoness did not give her replies direct but communicated through the priests attached to the temple.) Knowledge of events occurring in distant places has also been attributed to the Pythoness.[1]

Belief in these statements has been subject to extraordinary fluctuations. The oracle of Delphi has had the same fate as many others; in the rationalistic period everything was held to be trickery on the part of the priests, whereas previously there had been general belief in malign and demoniacal spirits. In the romantic period there was a reaction; for many philologists of the German romantic movement the Greek world was transfigured, not only from the æsthetic and political point of view, but from the parapsychic also. It was then believed that Hellenism had possessed peculiar spiritual gifts to a higher degree than the other epochs of human history. Niebuhr questioned whether men were not nearer to nature in these primitive times, a very clumsy way of formulating the question. Wachsmuth considered the ecstatic states as beyond dubiety, at least in the early period of the Delphic oracle. K. Fr. Hermann was unwilling to admit either fraud or demoniacal influences.[2]

Lasaulx similarly believes in the reality of prophecy, and this not only in connection with the oracle of Delphi but also the other Greek oracles. According to him we must admit " ecstatic states analogous to magnetism ";[3] he alleges that the human soul has an " innate power " of knowing the future which sometimes bursts forth.[4]

Strauss' works show a partial recognition of parapsychic manifestations in possession, which may safely be regarded as a result of the impression made upon him by Justinus Kerner and the " clairvoyante " of Prevorst. But we have already seen that he was not influenced by demonology. This is how Strauss construes the story of how the demons

---

[1] Cf. du Prel, *Die Mystik der alten Griechen*, Leipzig, 1888.
[2] For quotations from these authors cf. Stützle, *Das griechische Orakelwesen* . . ., Ellwangen, 1891.
[3] E. von Lasaulx, *Das pelasgische Orakel des Zeus zu Dodona*, Würzburg, 1840, p. 14.
[4] *Ibid.*, p. 4.

recognized Jesus as the Messiah, which he regards as a true one:

> That demoniacs like somnambulists establish during their attacks contact with those present and are thus capable of entering into their inner life and sharing in their sensations, feelings and thoughts, has been not infrequently observed, and it might well be, after Jesus had spoken from the full consciousness of his Messianic character, that the demoniac perceived it through magnetic *rapport*.[1]

Philologists and historians have not, moreover, been alone in this opinion; it was fully shared by philosophers such as Fichte, Schelling, Baader, Hegel and the other romantics.

In the following generation we meet it again in speculative theism, that strong and still underestimated current in the German philosophy of about the middle nineteenth century.

Whereas this period is remembered as the epoch of materialism—although the word is used to describe only the popular philosophy which invaded certain regions of the natural sciences—technical philosophy followed a different course. It was theistic and spiritualist, showing, moreover, great interest in the facts which through an all-too-hasty interpretation were made the foundation of the spiritualist movement.

Fichte's son, Immanuel Hermann, was particularly prominent in this respect; he illustrates a return to the conviction that the Delphic oracle was no fraud but veritable divination. When Cicero states that in his day the oracle and all things of a like nature had lost their power and gift of prophecy, Fichte does not conclude that the men of that period had become educated to a degree where they could no longer be so lightly deceived as before; he believes, on the contrary, that it was rationalism and the domination of the intelligence which caused the powers of divination to decline. " Before the more conscious reflection which characterized later antiquity the inner power of spiritual divination declined in a like measure to men's belief in it."[2]

[1] D. E. Strauss, *Das Leben Jesu*, 3rd edit., Tübingen, 1889, vol. ii, p. 30.
[2] I. H. Fichte, *Zur Seelenfrage, eine philosophische Konfession*, Leipzig, 1859, p. 280. For the author's general outlook, his work *Der neuere Spiritualismus, sein Wert und seine Täuschungen*, Leipzig, 1878

A work fully accepting the veracity of the Delphic oracle and which, once widely read, has fallen into unmerited oblivion, is Chr. C. J. Bunsen's treatise on religious philosophy, *Gott in der Geschichte*, etc.[1] In connection with the Pythoness and the other Sibyls he speaks of a " state of clairvoyance " which has often been proved. By this unusual expression he means the vision of the future (vol. ii, pp. 276 sq.).

It is hardly necessary to emphasize that the spiritualism of the period, whose principal exponent in Germany was M. Perty, pronounced in favour of the reality of Delphic prophecy.[2]

Professor Friedrich Fischer of Bâle arrived at a theory of possession very closely resembling my own.[3]

The generation of speculative theism is for the time being completely forgotten. This was already so when about 1880 similar parapsychic views were once more advanced and a rather more favourable attitude towards the Greek oracles manifested itself in literature, although still outside the confines of the narrow technical branch.

Du Prel was the first, in his *Die Mystik der alten Griechen* (Leipzig, 1888), to try to interpret certain obscure aspects of the life of antiquity: the temple-sleep, the oracles and mysteries and the *dæmon* of Socrates, by saying that they were the early counterparts of modern spiritualism, all the essential root-phenomena of which he found, as he believed, in antiquity. There follows naturally a return to belief in the divinations of the Pythoness.

> It would be unscientific to deny the gift of divination to the oracles, simply because it is contrary to the current habit of thought, while to admit that a people which had reached a level of civilization since unequalled allowed itself to be duped by its priests during a period of three thousand years, would be not only historically but also psychologically false.[4]

Although a spiritualist, du Prel does not, as might have been expected, reach conclusions in accordance with the traditional doctrine of possession, but sees in the Pythoness a

---

[1] Chr. C. J. Bunsen, *Gott in der Geschichte oder der Fortschritt des Glaubens an eine sittliche Weltordnung*, Leipzig, 1857-58.
[2] Max. Perty, *Die sichtbare und die unsichtbare Welt*, Leipzig, 1880, p. 124.
[3] Fr. Fischer, *Der somnambulismus*, vol. iii, Bâle, 1839, pp. 367-412.
[4] C. du Prel, *loc. cit.*, p. 87.

somnambulist who in the dream-state transcended by her knowledge the limits of time and space. He therefore agrees with Plutarch who already repudiated the theory of possession and believed that there were awakened in the Pythoness special faculties peculiar to the human soul.[1] It would be ridiculous to admit that " Apollo enters into the body of the soothsayers, speaks through them, and uses as instruments their mouths and voices." He nevertheless concedes that Apollo imparted to their souls the impulse necessary to the exercise of their supernormal faculties.

Later philologists and historians such as Jakob Burckhardt assume towards accounts of prophecy a positivist and completely sceptical attitude.[2]

Beloch finds a simple solution of the problem by asseverating that the alleged supernormal oracles were never uttered. According to him there was no question whatever—

> . . . of revealing the future to the questioner, a thing which would very soon have discredited the oracles, but rather of formulating prescriptions for practical use, particularly directions for the conduct of religious ceremonials designed to win divine favour or expiate past guilt.[3]

By way of refutation Nägelsbach showed as early as 1837 that there still remained a substantial number of cases in which the oracles contained no instructions but either a divination of the future such as could not be foreseen by the persons concerned, or else information about past facts which they were not in a position to know. This does not prevent him from explaining these facts in a normal psychic manner, although on the other hand he feels obliged to recognize the existence of the πνεῦμα ἐνθουσιαστικόν of the Pythoness and its influence on the rendering of oracles.[4]

The philologist Bergk is the most important exception to the scepticism of contemporary historians.

> Many a prophetic utterance has been fulfilled in a surprising manner, not only the predictions which were restricted to general terms, as for example the Delphic oracle foretelling that Sparta would perish by her love of lucre,[5] but also where the eventuality

---

[1] For fuller details cf. ibid., pp. 41 and 64.
[2] J. Burckhardt, Griechische Kulturgeschichte, 3rd edit., vol. ii, chap. iv.
[3] J. Beloch, Griechische Geschichte, vol. i, Leipzig, 1893, p. 243.
[4] K. F. Nägelsbach, Die nachhomerische Theologie des griechischen Volksglaubens, Nuremberg, 1857, p. 186.
[5] Thucydides, v, 26.

was specifically fore-ordained. Thucydides relates[1] that at the beginning of the Peloponnesian war the duration of hostilities was predicted by the oracles as three times nine years. It does not matter that these were not Delphic oracles. Delphi similarly predicted to the Spartans from the beginning of the war its happy issue if vigorously pursued and promised them divine assistance. The credibility of all the early oracles which are of the greatest interest to us has been subjected to a general attack without adequate reasons.[2]

Doehler in his monograph on the Greek oracles also arrives at this conclusion:

> With the exception of a small number of cases in which the Pythoness seems to have been ill-inspired, the oracles which have come down to us justify the reputation for wisdom of the prophetic sanctuaries and particularly that of Delphi.[3]

The author of the most recent research into the nature of the oracles, A. W. Persson, is of the same opinion:

> However sceptical one may be on the subject of the oracles, it must be admitted that the priests of Delphi too often had extremely good information at their command."[4]

The question of the reality of parapsychic phenomena in the Pythoness is complicated by the fact that we are not dealing with one person but that, as is alleged, several women produced these phenomena at the same time. This is, in its assumption, a completely unique situation. We cannot help wondering—supposing that the information is true—how women possessing the gift could always be found in the neighbourhood of Delphi and how the priests set about discovering them. Are we to suppose that the Greeks were not only, from the standpoint of general civilization, the most richly endowed people known to us, but that they also possessed special parapsychic faculties ? Even so we should be obliged to grant that predisposed persons were so plentiful in ancient Greece as to render it always possible for the priests of Delphi to find one or several Pythonesses with a capacity for supernormal practices amongst the women of the countryside. If the probability of such a wealth of supernormal temperaments in Greece could be established from documentary

---

[1] *Ibid.*, i, 118 and ii, 54; cf. Plutarch, *de Pyth. or.*, 19.
[2] Bergk, *Griechische Literaturgeschichte*, i, Berlin, 1872, p. 331.
[3] E. Doehler, *Die Orakel*, Berlin, 1872, p. 15.
[4] A. W. Persson, *Vorstudien zu einer Geschichte der attischen Sakralgesetzgebung*, i, en Lunds Universitet, N.F. avd., i, vol. xiv, No. 22, p. 72.

evidence, the spiritual picture of the Hellenes would be enriched by a new and most interesting trait. For it does not seem plausible that there existed at Delphi an emanation from the earth which released parapsychic faculties in everyone, but rather that the priests must have had to seek out gifted persons.

The acceptance as real of parapsychic phenomena does not, of course, signify any return to the old doctrine of possession.

There is a sort of intermediate position between belief in real possession by spirits and the complete rejection of early accounts of the inspiration of the Pythoness. It is possible to hold the latter as genuine without attributing it to the entrance of a strange soul into her soul or body.

Unhappily our knowledge of parapsychic states is up to the present so restricted that we are quite unable to contemplate bringing psychologico-historical criticism to bear on these documents with a view to discriminating between the false and the true. We must defer an answer to these questions until we know more of parapsychic phenomena, their frequency and conditions of origin. The purely negative reply which so greatly facilitated for rationalism the historical criticism of all these accounts is frankly no longer possible to-day.

INDEX

Milton Keynes UK
Ingram Content Group UK Ltd.
UKHW041327180823
427104UK00001B/98